10/98

McFarland Classics

1997

Dark Romance

Sexuality in the Horror Film

by

David J. Hogan

McFarland & Company, Inc., Publishers

Jefferson, North Carolina

Front cover: Carroll Borland as the eerie wraith Luna and Bela Lugosi as Count Mora in *Mark of the Vampire* (MGM, 1935).
Back cover: The doomed *King Kong* (RKO, 1933) regards his golden-haired prize (Fay Wray).

The present work is a reprint of the library bound edition of Dark Romance: Sexuality in the Horror Film, *first published in 1986.* **McFarland Classics** *is an imprint of McFarland & Company, Inc., Publishers, Jefferson, North Carolina, who also published the original edition.*

British Library Cataloguing-in-Publication data are available

Library of Congress Cataloguing-in-Publication Data

Hogan, David J., 1953–
  Dark romance.

  Filmography: p. 291
  Bibliography: p. 311
  Includes index.
  1. Horror films—History and criticism.   2. Sex in moving-pictures.
  I. Title.
  PN1995.9.H6H59   1997   791.43'09'0916   86-161

ISBN 0-7864-0474-4 (paperback : 50# alkaline paper) ∞

Manufactured in the United States of America

McFarland & Company, Inc., Publishers
  Box 611, Jefferson, North Carolina 28640

To my three favorite ladies,
whose love, encouragement, and support
helped me to succeed as a writer—
My mother, Nancy,
My dear friend Margie,
And my beloved wife, Kim.

Table of Contents

Acknowledgments

Another World Comics & Books
Book Castle
Eddie Brandt's Saturday Matinee
Collectors Book Store
Dr. Pauline Degenfelder
Larry Edmunds Bookshop
Don Glut
The Hollywood Book & Poster Co.
Ed Lerner
Jim Maher
Dr. Harold Medford
Steve Rubin
Bob Skotak
Gregory Walcott
Bill Warren

Preface

Sexuality and the horror film?

Let me assure the reader at the outset of my awareness of the specious nature of a certain amount of film criticism. Occasionally, the learned examination of auteurs, genre, metaphor, structuralism, and suchlike gets out of hand. I had a conversation not long ago at a major film school with a graduate student who very earnestly filled me in on the religious significance of dance as expressed in Hollywood musicals. As he prattled on about the deep symbolism he had found in choreography that had surely been meant to be nothing more than inventively eye-pleasing, I wondered how he honestly felt about film. Did he have a passionate love, or had his self-conscious, almost apologetic approach served only to cut him off from cinema's joy and urgency?

At the other extreme we have tabloid and television "critics" who cater to lazy moviegoers with critical judgments limited to "It was great" or "It was lousy." Some of these reviewers *really* give everybody's brain cells a vacation by assigning films a number on a 1–10 scale. Ennui and intellectual laziness win the day. Experimentation is rebuffed, style is ignored, and we come away with no knowledge except the names of the stars and a rough notion of the plot. Insights? Not likely.

Undeniably, a film critic or historian treads dangerous ground when he attempts to move beyond simple reportage of fact. Yet he is, within limits, obligated to do this. Film is priceless archeology, as valuable as any museum's treasures in that it informs us of what we are. Film, particularly popular film, is *us*, and so the critic/historian must try to relate cinema to human and cultural experience — to place it in a sociological context. Now: we know that sociology has become a dirty word. The discipline has been cluttered with a lot of meaningless jargon and pseudo-intellectual cant. I have tried mightily to avoid such pitfalls. My concern here is as much with human experience as with film, and what is more vibrant than that?

Vibrancy is what has drawn me repeatedly to the horror genre. Besides being the most purely entertaining of all movie genres, the horror film warrants serious study because it is also the most vivid and unrestrained. If motion pictures in general reflect our dreams and fears, then the horror film liberates the dreams and beats back those fears. At the core of the genre is our acute awareness of human mortality. The realization that we, as individuals, will one day cease to exist is a sobering one. Dealt with in a realistic film context, it is often too much to comfortably bear. But the horror film, with its reassuring guise of fantasy, makes such uneasy speculation possible, and even liberating. It is not merely monsters and aliens that we watch stamping across the screen, but our own fears, presented in forms that we can begin to deal with. Frankenstein's Monster is much more than a soulless, artificially-created beast—he is our collective fear of the unknown, the unknown we call death.

These are obvious insights, and yet not so obvious as to have allowed the horror film to enjoy the sort of critical attention it has deserved. A lot of film critics have allowed the child inside them to go away. Their minds and emotions have become earthbound and literal, and the antipathy they hold for the genre seems to border on flat-out hatred. We like to tell ourselves that we live in an ordered, logical world, but the horror film (with its irrational monsters, demented scientists, and often motivationless terrors) exposes the fallacy. Since horror films are acted out on the dark playground of the subconscious, they are often at their best when as illogical as our unfettered minds. A wildly improbable film like Don Coscarelli's *Phantasm* (1979) is very much like a dream. It provocatively bends the rules of the real world as it rushes to meet horror after horror. One must *voluntarily* bend those rules in order to enjoy and appreciate movie horror. And with enjoyment comes an understanding of the value.

Which leads us to the sexual aspect of horror cinema. Because the genre is predicated upon an awareness of the inevitability of death, its exploration of sexuality has been unavoidable. Sexual behavior and its ultimate purpose, children, are quite clearly the antithesis of death. If one is to examine death, then, one must examine sex.

The mechanics of sexuality are wonderfully ordered. As sexual machines, we have been beautifully designed. And yet, there are many among us whose sexual lives have not been as beautifully realized. Why not? We share similar equipment and urges, but are very independent in our uses of them. A shared consciousness gives each of us a general idea of appropriate sexual conduct, but our free will may cause us to behave in a way that leads to conflict. That sexual behavior is cued by the expectations of society is both the beauty and the sadness of the gift. As sexual beings, we possess an explosive talent, and innate genius. It is no secret that great talent can be frustrating. And genius can be frightening.

Since Thomas Edison's *The Kiss* in 1896, cinema has expressed a keen interest in sex. If the subject has been handled clumsily by individual films, it is excusable. We can glean a lot from a broader study. Film affords us a remarkable opportunity to trace the evolution of our mores and manners. Clara Bow is unmistakably a product of the breezy 1920s. Jane Fonda may today be embarrassed by some of the suggestive films she made in the 1960s, yet she could not logically have achieved her present persona without them. The cynical detachment of Clint Eastwood is a pole apart from the jaunty, self-assured quality of Cary Grant. The persona of each actor is a product of its time. Eastwood, if he embraces a woman on screen at all, will never embrace her in the same manner as Grant. Popular film is inextricably bound up with contemporary culture and point of view. We shape and determine what we will see next on the theater screen. The horror film, as the most basic and primal of all movie genres, has always been in a unique position as ideal chronicler of contemporary mores. No holds barred: the censor has seldom blinked at the blatantly erotic carryings-on in vampire films, for instance, but would have worn out his scissors had similar things been presented in a mainstream picture. If cinematic horror has suffered the most critical abuse, it has also enjoyed the most freedom. It keenly tells us what we are about. This book attempts to cover the full range and history of the genre, from the silent era to modern 70mm and Dolby stereo.* It is hoped that the book will not simply inform and entertain, but provoke thought. The horror film's two great preoccupations—death and death's perplexing cousin, sex—are topics which intrigue, amuse, and worry us above all others. This is the double-edged lure of movie horror. This is the Dark Romance.

I have included science-fiction/horror hybrids, like Not of This Earth *(1957) and* Demon Seed *(1977).*

Someone once defined horror
for me as the relationship
between sex and death—*Diane Arbus*.

I
Keeping It in the Family

In 1931 actor Edward Van Sloan stepped from behind a curtain onto a stage and addressed movie audiences thusly:

> How do you do? Mr. Carl Laemmle feels it would be a little unkind to present this picture without just a word of friendly warning. We are about to unfold the story of Frankenstein, a man of science, who sought to create a man after his own image, without reckoning upon God. It is one of the strangest tales ever told. It deals with the two great mysteries of creation: life and death. I think it will thrill you. It may shock you. It might even *horrify* you. So if any of you feel that you do not care to subject your nerves to such a strain, now is your chance to — well, we've *warned* you!

So begins *Frankenstein*, the James Whale adaptation of Mary Shelley's 1818 science-horror novel, *Frankenstein or: the Modern Prometheus*. To say that the Frankenstein story has entered folklore is to understate. Mary Shelley's exploration of science gone awry is a popular theme of literature and thought. The phrase "He created a Frankenstein" has become part of the common lexicon. The image of Frankenstein's Monster (as created by makeup artist Jack Pierce and actor Boris Karloff in 1931) has become one of the world's most familiar, adorning everything from billboards to children's lunchboxes. Synopsized, *Frankenstein* is a story of bungled science, but on a deeper, more meaningful level it is about failed paternity, and the deadly rivalry that can exist between father and son.

Because of the biology which creates us, we are closer to no one than to our parents and our children. The sexual tensions that arise from parent-child relationships are often subtle, but no less pointed than those that exist between, for instance, a woman and an unwanted suitor. The most inattentive freshman psychology student can enumerate the pitfalls that may await members of a family: the jealousy, the rivalry, the competition, the development of an Electra or Little Oeddy. Because power has traditionally been held by men, horror films that deal with family tensions have tended to focus upon perverse father-son relationships. This point of view has made for some provocative films, but hasn't been much of an endorsement of the male sex's skill at parenting. The father-son horror films are based on an unfortunate cultural assumption: that fathers are neither as loving nor as wise with their children as mothers. The driving ambition that has been a prized virtue of the male sex has been used by filmmakers as a springboard for all sorts of unhappy relationships experienced by men who become fathers for the wrong reasons or by unseemly methods. In a way, the films that make use of the Frankenstein theme are much-needed refutations of the male sexual arrogance that has dominated human societies for tens of centuries. Dr. Frankenstein, well-meaning though he may be, embodies the arrogance of men who would create the world in their own image, heedless of morality and consequence.

Frankenstein was filmed as early as 1910 (by the Edison Company), but the most vivid early example of Shelley's theme was Paul Wegener's *The Golem* (1920). As stated by Jewish legend, the Golem is an enormous man of clay who will defend the Jewish community if called upon to do so by a rabbi who knows the magic word. In Wegener's version (his second; a 1917 adaptation covered much of the same ground) Rabbi Löw (Albert Steinrück) consults the spirit Astaroth when the Emperor of Prague decrees that all Jews be driven from the city. Löw fashions the Golem (Wegener) from clay, and inscribes the word AEMAET on a scroll, which he places inside the Golem's chest and seals with a Star of David. The Emperor is properly cowed and revokes his decree, but Löw has not reckoned with the text of the book of magic: "Astaroth will take back his creature. Then the dead clay will scorn its Master and destroy him and all living things." The Golem runs amok at the Emperor's palace and later strides off with Löw's innocent daughter (Lydia Salmonova) after killing her lover (Lothar Müthel). The clay man is beyond Löw's power; in one chilling sequence, the Golem fixes Löw with a decidedly malevolent sneer. Finally, the monster confronts a group of children playing in a sunny courtyard. The children run off in fright, leaving a single little girl (Greta Schröder), who stands her ground and offers the Golem an apple. The monster picks up the child and does not prevent her from thoughtlessly plucking the Star of David from his chest. The Golem lets the little girl slip from his grasp, then teeters and falls. Rabbi Löw's destructive offspring — designed to protect the family of Jews — has been brought under control by one of that family's weakest members.

Though the Golem story has been filmed numerous times and as recently as 1966 (*It!*), the legend was quickly superseded by the saga of Dr. Frankenstein. Boris Karloff's justly famous performance in the 1931 version has overshadowed the picture's other merits, notably Colin Clive's splendidly twitchy performance as Henry Frankenstein, the neurotic, obsessed scientist who creates a living man from stolen body parts. Clive was a Briton who rose from repertory drama and musical comedy to international acclaim when he took the role of Stanhope in the 1929 London stage production of *Journey's End*. Clive, bisexual and married to a lesbian, brought to the role of Frankenstein the sort of feverish intensity that reflects the character's ambivalence about his achievement. Frankenstein shows off the still-unmoving body of his creation to staid Dr. Waldman (Edward Van Sloan) and gloats like a new father, but is

"The dead clay will scorn its Master and destroy him and all living things." Ernst Deutsch (left), Paul Wegener and Albert Steinrück in *The Golem* (1920).

not blind to the fact that he is neglecting his fiancée, Elizabeth (Mae Clarke). By the time Frankenstein comes to his senses and agrees to be wed, the Monster is roaming around the village. A little girl (Marilyn Harris) who quietly tosses daisies into a lake is unfrightened when the Monster appears, and invites him to join her game. When the daisies are used up, the Monster blithely throws the little girl into the water, hoping that she will float as prettily as the flowers. Later, a villager (Michael Mark) despondently carries his daughter's soaking corpse through the streets. Frankenstein's perverse brand of fatherhood has led to the destruction of another man's child.

Frankenstein's own father (Frederick Kerr) is a titled curmudgeon who

The heedless father (Colin Clive) confronts the malevolent son (Boris Karloff) in *Frankenstein* (1931).

gives no evidence of ever having understood his son. When a visitor describes Henry as "such a fine young man, the image of his father," the elder Frankenstein retorts, "Heaven forbid!" Henry's only significant family ties, then, are to his soulless creation, and to Fritz (Dwight Frye), the demented, toadying hunchback who becomes Frankenstein's surrogate wife. It seems as though Henry will never wed in the traditional sense, for on his wedding day the Monster breaks into Elizabeth's boudoir and terrifies the woman into unconsciousness. The conflict comes to a head in a bloody confrontation of father and "son" inside a burning mill. When the Monster snarls at his creator it isn't just the snarl of inarticulateness, but a sound of fury at being put on the Earth. He recognizes Frankenstein as the man who gave him not life, but a parody of it. The Monster determines that his "father" must pay, and tosses Frankenstein over the side of the mill moments before the structure collapses. The Monster is trapped by flaming wreckage and presumably perishes.

The sexual dread of *Frankenstein* is unfortunately diminished by a cheery, needless epilogue which reveals that the doctor has survived his fall and has wed Elizabeth. Contemporary audiences, though, have forgotten this scene. Karloff's alternately sensitive and violent portrayal is the element which remains most vividly in our conscious minds, while our subconscious continues to react to Henry Frankenstein's urgently misspent sexuality. Vengeful sons have stalked fathers in other films, but seldom with the brute potency evident in this, one of the highest achievements of the horror genre.

As is well known, *Frankenstein* was a tremendous box office success, and, along with *Dracula* (1931), established Universal as Hollywood's preeminent purveyor of horror. James Whale returned to direct *Bride of Frankenstein* (1935), a precocious example of the sort of black comedy that would not become fashionable until the sixties. Frankenstein (Clive) has apparently learned nothing from his ordeal (if he had, there would have been no sequel), and rather willingly allows himself to be coerced by the dotty Dr. Praetorius (Ernest Thesiger) into creating a mate for the Monster, who has been discovered alive in a cavern below the wreckage of the mill. The Monster is ecstatic at the prospect of a companion, but is sorely disappointed when his mate (Elsa Lanchester) recoils from his touches, hissing in outrage. In one of cinema's great deus ex machina climaxes, the Monster grabs a convenient switch and blows himself, his mate, and Praetorius "to atoms."

Lanchester's female Monster is nearly as familiar an image as Karloff's. With her Nefertiti hairdo electrified with platinum waves, and her skittish, bird-like demeanor, she's the ultimate in soured blind dates. Though the film brims with mordant humor (Praetorius is a particularly vivid eccentric), we can empathize with Karloff's Monster, who time and again comes agonizingly close to establishing familial relationships, only to have them snatched away. In the film's most famous segment, the Monster stumbles into the isolated cabin of a blind hermit (O.P. Heggie) who gratefully and gracefully accepts his visitor as a "friend." The Monster learns not just the joys of wine, food, and cigars, but companionship, trust, and music. The father-son tableau is touching, but is abruptly destroyed when a pair of hunters happens by and hysterically informs the hermit that his guest "is the fiend that's been murdering half the countryside!"

The Monster seems doomed to a lonely, miserable life as a misunderstood outcast. The grim parallel with the life of Christ is not accidental; much of the film's cleverness lies in Whale's impudent religious symbolism. The hermit, for instance, kneels before a crucifix to thank God for the arrival of someone who will deliver him from loneliness. After being routed from the hermit's cottage, the Monster stumbles through a cemetery, where he angrily topples the statue of a bishop. And when finally captured, the Monster is trussed — arms outstretched — to a pole, where he must endure the jeers and stares of the villagers. The climactic Adam and Eve parallel is obvious. In essence, the Monster has been thoroughly betrayed and abandoned by his creator. Unlike Christ, however, the misunderstood Monster has no hope of reward or redemption.

The Monster's hatred for his creator carries over to the second sequel,

Rowland Lee's *Son of Frankenstein* (1939). This time the focus is on Henry Frankenstein's son Wolf (Basil Rathbone), who discovers that the miraculously *un*atomized Monster (Karloff, for the final time) is being tended to by a broken-necked shepherd named Ygor (Bela Lugosi, in one of his finest performances). Wolf wishes to restore his father's creation to full potency and utilize it in research. This idea is fine with Ygor, who feels that Wolf is *obligated* to resurrect the Monster. Ygor reminds Wolf, "Your father made him, and Heinrich [sic] Frankenstein was *your* father, too!" Ygor's line of reasoning is clear: Wolf and the Monster are brothers. On a more symbolic level, Ygor is a brother, too, since he looks after the Monster's welfare with all the concern of an older (if devious) sibling.

Once revived, the Monster has his usual difficulties with socialization. Ygor is manipulating him into committing murder, and the villagers once again rise in revolt. The Monster is further enraged after learning that Wolf has shot and killed Ygor. In retaliation, the Monster kidnaps Wolf's son (Donnie Dunagan), intending to throw him into a boiling sulphur pit that bubbles below the castle. As in the earlier films, the climax of *Son of Frankenstein* hinges upon the antagonisms and perils of fathers and sons. At the last moment, the Monster relents and gently sets the child upon the floor. Wolf seizes the moment and swings on a chain, knocking the Monster into the pit.

Son of Frankenstein is the last of the genuinely thoughtful Universal Frankenstein films. Subsequent sequels are entertaining and often clever, but it is obvious that Universal was keeping the series alive strictly for money's sake. The subtlety of the films declined; psychological ramifications lessened and the pictures became little more than enjoyable spook shows. Ygor (Lugosi) inexplicably returns in *Ghost of Frankenstein* (1942) and continues his dominance of the seemingly indestructible Monster (Lon Chaney, Jr.). The most interesting scene takes place in a courtroom where the Monster is on trial for past crimes. Brought before the accused is Ludwig Frankenstein (Sir Cedric Hardwicke), still another of Henry's offspring. Ludwig rightfully denies any knowledge of the Monster, whereupon the beast become enraged and tears himself free of the chains that bind him. It would seem that the Monster's abandonment will continue indefinitely, but the crafty Ygor contrives to have his own brain implanted into the Monster's head. Ludwig performs the operation, believing that the brain he is working with belonged to someone other than Ygor. The operation seems to be a success — spiritual brothers Ygor and the Monster become a single entity. But Ludwig is not exempt from the curse of his father, for he is beaten to death by the Monster shortly after the operation. The Monster does not escape retribution, either, for Ygor discovers that, because of mismatched blood, his monstrous body is blind. "What good is a brain without eyes?" Ygor wails. He blunders into Ludwig's electrical equipment and sets the castle and himself ablaze.

Roy William Neill's *Frankenstein Meets the Wolf Man* (1943) is notable primarily for Bela Lugosi's unjustly maligned portrayal of the Monster.

Though Bela, at 61, was too old for the role, his casting is nevertheless apt, since it is Ygor's brain that supposedly directs the blind monster. Beyond this, the film is an enjoyable but very childish stomp 'n' smash show, as the two great Universal monsters come together for a climactic battle. The remaining films in the series — *House of Frankenstein* (1945), *House of Dracula* (1945), and the delightful *Abbott and Costello Meet Frankenstein* (1948; see Chapter VI) — do not explore the father-son theme. Mary Shelley's novel fell out of favor as movie source material until the latter half of the fifties, when it inspired a few low-budget, teen-oriented versions. While *I Was a Teenage Frankenstein* (1957) and *Frankenstein's Daughter* (1959) have their share of cheap thrills, the Frankenstein Monster later became an object of simple-minded ridicule in sex-comedies like *The House on Bare Mountain* (1962) and *Kiss Me Quick* (1963). American filmmakers had lost interest in the traditional approach to the Frankenstein story; it was left to Britain's Hammer Studios to revive the tale's classical — and familial — aspects. Indeed, as expressed in more than a half-dozen films, Hammer's interpretation of the Frankenstein legend became a sanguine, impossibly convoluted soap opera.

Hammer was a small production company that got into horror when the market for its low-brow comedies and traditional adventures began to dry up in the middle fifties. Producers Anthony Hinds and Michael Carreras enjoyed success with a pair of science-fiction thrillers — *The Quatermass Experiment* aka *The Creeping Unknown* (1955) and *X the Unknown* (1956) — then gambled with *Curse of Frankenstein* (1957), a sensational but intelligent retelling of the original story. The film's worldwide box office success was gratifying to Hammer, especially since Mary Shelley's book had been in the public domain, free for the taking. In addition to color and the attendant grue, the times afforded Hammer and director Terence Fisher a far more buxom and earthy heroine (Hazel Court) than was available to Universal in 1931. Beyond these innovations, though, *Curse of Frankenstein* does little to expand upon the father-son theme. The only twist is that Frankenstein (Peter Cushing) is accused of his creation's crimes, his assertions to the contrary not corroborated by his assistant (Robert Urquhart). Frankenstein, like any parent of an unruly child, discovers that he is culpable for his child's misdeeds.

Curse of Frankenstein was a major career step for a gaunt, towering actor named Christopher Lee, who found sudden fame the following year when he portrayed Dracula in Hammer's *Horror of Dracula*. As Frankenstein's Monster, Lee was obscured beneath a waxily unimaginative makeup designed by Phil Leakey, who was restrained by copyright from duplicating the classic image Jack Pierce had created for Universal.

Terence Fisher's *The Revenge of Frankenstein* (1958) continued Hammer's commitment to glossy production values but left no doubt that, henceforth, the focus of the studio's Frankenstein films would be the doctor, and not his creation. The series has no emotional or psychological continuity because the Monster is new and different in each film. In other words,

Hammer was blind to the special strength of the best films of the Universal series, which utilized the Monster as an empathetic character and not simply as a mechanical device designed to provoke essentially meaningless mayhem. In *Revenge* and subsequent films, Dr. Frankenstein (Peter Cushing in all) inevitably commits the same blunders, usually brain transplants which backfire. By the time of *The Horror of Frankenstein* in 1970, the Hammer Monster had become a bald muscleman (David Prowse) possessed of all the personality of a piece of thrift shop furniture.

Hammer's final Frankenstein film was Terence Fisher's *Frankenstein and the Monster from Hell* (1973) which, though plodding and excessively gruesome, at least offers a novel variation on Shelley's father-son theme. Dr. Frankenstein, now in charge of an insane asylum (appropriate after all these years), cannot resist transforming an injured patient into a mute, furry hulk (David Prowse). Given the good doctor's track record, you'd think he would have learned about going one step too far, but he takes it anyway by trying to mate his creation with a comely female patient (Madeline Smith). Will Frankenstein become a grandfather? Alas, 'tis not to be, for the enraged inmates tear the inarticulate Monster to pieces.

As the seventies wore on, the Frankenstein legend found its fullest expression in parody. Mel Brooks' *Young Frankenstein* (1974) offers Peter Boyle's zipper-headed interpretation of the Monster; his relationship with Dr. Frankenstein (Gene Wilder) is more confused than hostile. Family virtues win out at the conclusion, in which the (now urbane) Monster retires to a life of leisure and giddy sex with his frazzle-haired bride (Madeline Kahn). A less traditional sexual point of view was offered by director Jim Sharman and writer-actor Richard O'Brien when they adapted their parodistic musical-comedy, *The Rocky Horror Show*, to film as *The Rocky Horror Picture Show* (1975). Though overdone and self-congratulatory in moments, the picture is generally lively, clever, and entertaining. It has suffered from its popularity as a cult film: in theaters across America and England on Fridays and Saturdays at midnight fans dress as their favorite characters, mouth dialogue and song lyrics, and in general intrude themselves into the film. This adolescent adoration has not only drawn attention to itself and obscured the film's merits, but has undoubtedly diminished the pleasure of curious patrons who might otherwise have surprised themselves and enjoyed the film hugely. For all its glitter and sass, *Rocky Horror* is very easy to like.

Dr. Frank N. Furter (Tim Curry) is a crazily uninhibited "transvestite from Transsexual, Transylvania" who conducts weird experiments in an isolated (American) castle. Furter—in his black mesh stockings, corset, and heels—is theatrical to the *n*th degree, a giggly boy's idea of naughty sexuality. He creates a "monster" named Rocky (Peter Hinwood), a musclebound pin-up boy with blond locks and a well-filled G-string. In an amusing if obvious twist, *Furter* is the real monster, a sex-crazed hedonist who frightens the timid Rocky and causes him to run away—"Daddy's" sexuality is too much for Rocky to

The scientific imagination spurred onward: Leila Hyams, Richard Arlen and Kathleen Burke as Lota in *Island of Lost Souls* (1933).

deal with. A square couple named Brad and Janet Majors (Barry Bostwick and Susan Sarandon) happens upon Furter's castle and becomes caught up in his mad pursuit of sensual pleasure. Furter seduces the husband and wife in turn (releasing undreamt-of passion in Janet) but continues to lust after Rocky. The latter third of the film is excessively frenetic and disjointed, and unwisely expands the limits of its satire by introducing a needless science-fiction element. Still, *The Rocky Horror Picture Show* amuses movie buffs (the climax, for instance, involves a huge replica of the RKO Radio tower), aficionados of bouncy rock 'n' roll, and people who think that energetically vulgar song-and-dance numbers about bisexuality are the height of sophistication. Although the seriousness of Mary Shelley's theme seems to have been superseded by irreverent jokiness, the very fact that the story survives at all is evidence of its particular strength and truth.

In addition to direct and semidirect adaptations of Shelley's novel, the story has inspired dozens of thinly disguised variations, many of which draw from literary works that were themselves derived from Shelley's book. Earle C. Kenton's *Island of Lost Souls* (1933), for example, is an adaptation of H.G. Wells' 1896 novel *The Island of Dr. Moreau*. As filmed, the story is a particularly unpleasant Frankenstein variant, remarkable for its oppressive ambience and unrelieved sadism. Charles Laughton played Moreau, a plump, primly bearded genius whose fussy manner and ice cream suit suggest a eunuch, or a malevolent child. Moreau has isolated himself to a nameless island in the South Seas, where he performs hideous surgical experiments which transform animals into quasi-men: "manimals." A shipwrecked traveler named Edward Parker (Richard Arlen) finds himself an unwelcome guest, surrounded by Moreau's peculiar servants and laborers; one "man" resembles a dog, another a pig. Moreau introduces Parker to Lota (Kathleen Burke), a dark, feline beauty who exudes a raw sexuality. As well she should, for she is another of Moreau's creations, the most advanced yet produced. The scientist observes Parker and Lota sitting together and whispers to an assistant, "How that scene spurs the scientific imagination onward! I wonder how nearly perfect a woman Lota *is*. It is possible that I may find out with Parker."

Parker is drawn to Lota ("You're a strange child," he murmurs), but recoils when he sees the girl's panther-like nails. Moreau, who had earlier asked Parker if he knows "what it is to feel like God," explodes in fury when Lota's secret is revealed: "It's the stubborn beast flesh, creeping back!" he cries. "I may as well quit. Day by day it creeps back." Moreau is not simply a merciless god, but also an incompetent one. When he murders one of Parker's would-be rescuers (Paul Hurst) he thoughtlessly breaks the manimals' prime directive: "not to shed blood." The manimals, who embody all the brute maleness that Moreau does not possess, descend upon him in a fury and drag him into his laboratory, which Moreau has significantly dubbed The House of Pain. There, his creations vivisect him with his own instruments.

Island of Lost Souls is a dark and claustrophobic film experience. Director

Kenton's images are dim and crisscrossed with ominous shadows. The viewer becomes apprehensive almost from the first frame. There is no musical score, so although the tension is not underscored, neither is it relieved. The atmosphere of the island is heavy and foreboding. Vegetation is obscene in its lushness and fertility. Humidity hangs like a curtain. It is in this unforgiving milieu that Moreau, the loveless father, passes his undesirable traits on to his children, and ultimately suffers for it. The manimals are merely extensions of Moreau's own unchecked cruelty. A 1977 remake, *The Island of Dr. Moreau*, stars Burt Lancaster as the doctor, and features Richard Basehart as the leader of the manimals. Despite attractive production values and effective action direction by Don Taylor, the film hasn't nearly the sense of pregnant menace as its inspiration. Vivid color cinematography and clear views of the manimals' faces diminish much of the impact. The matter of Moreau's fatherhood becomes blatant and strictly physical — the psychological ramifications are missing.

A more successful variant on Wells' story is *Terror Is a Man*, a modest, seldom-seen thriller that was directed by Gerry DeLeon in 1959. Shot in the Philippines, the film is set on mythical Blood Island, where an obsessed scientist named Girard (Francis Lederer) experiments to turn a panther into a quasi-man. Like *Island of Lost Souls, Terror is a Man* was shot in black-and-white, and achieves a similarly constricting atmosphere. The beast (Flory Carlos) is violent, but also a figure of pity: it is established that the creature is in constant, unendurable pain as a result of Girard's surgery. Many shots focus upon the panther-man's bandaged face and moving, tormented eyes. After the beast finally rebels and abducts Girard's beautiful wife (Greta Thyssen, a former Miss Denmark), he is chased to a cliff edge. He releases the woman unharmed, but hurls his creator over the cliff and into the surf below. On the beach, a native boy puts the wounded beast into a boat and pushes him out to sea. This strangely satisfying conclusion recalls the ending of Shelley's *Frankenstein*, in which the Monster drifts off on an Arctic ice floe. The injured son has triumphed.

More typical of father-son horror films is the ultimate punishment of both son and father. In *Man-Made Monster* (1941) Lon Chaney, Jr., played Dan, a likeable fellow who becomes resistant to electricity after being involved in a freak bus accident. He goes to work for a carnival as Dynamo Dan the Electrical Man, where he is discovered by Dr. Rigas (Lionel Atwill). Rigas dreams of conquering the world with an army of electrically charged supermen. He supercharges Dan, who undergoes an unpleasant personality change. In his bulky rubber suit and with outstretched arms and staring eyes, Dan is very much a descendant of Frankenstein's Monster. He kills Rigas and abducts the scientist's daughter (Anne Nagel). Later, the electric chair only increases Dan's power, and he does not perish until tearing his insulated suit on barbed wire.

Fifteen years later Chaney took revenge upon another imprudent father figure as *The Indestructible Man* (1956). Chaney played The Butcher, a vicious killer who is executed in the electric chair, but brought back to life by a well-meaning but reckless scientist (Robert Shayne). The Butcher's first official act upon returning to life is to strangle the man who gave it to him. The remainder of the film is an orgy of strangulation and back-breaking as The Butcher stalks San Francisco in search of the former confederates who had squealed on him. The carnage does not end until The Butcher is accidentally electrocuted on a power station dynamo.

Fatherhood by science continued to stagger on: in *The Colossus of New York* (1958) scientist Otto Kruger transplants the brain of his dead son into the mechanical body of a supremely powerful robot, only to be hypnotized by his creation and stand by as the robot jealously murders its brother, Kruger's other son. Joseph Sargent's intelligent *Colossus: The Forbin Project* (1970) concerns a highly-sophisticated computer that is created in the hopes of being a boon to man. But Colossus is more clever than its creators realize, and eventually fathers a family of its own: a global, linked system of computer brains that will subjugate mankind to its will. *Demon Seed* (1977; discussed more fully in Chapter IV) is similar, as super-computer Proteus rapes a captive woman and fathers a half-human, half-mechanical son. Intention: to cheat mortality.

Perhaps the most fiendish and unholy instance of unnatural fatherhood is found in Franklin Schaffner's improbable but highly entertaining *The Boys from Brazil* (1978), which is about the culmination of a Nazi plot to clone Hitler and raise youthful versions of Der Führer in various cities around the world decades after the end of the war. The scheme, masterminded by Dr. Josef Mengele (Gregory Peck), is uncovered by Nazi-hunter Ezra Lieberman (Laurence Olivier), but not without cost: in an isolated American farmhouse Lieberman is savaged and nearly killed by Dobermans commanded by one of the boy Hitlers (Jeremy Black). Mengele arrives, confident that the boy—*his* creation, after all—will listen to him and give the dogs the command to finish off Lieberman. But Mengele has forgotten Hitler's perverse turn of mind. At the last moment, the boy commands the dogs to kill the Nazi doctor. Lieberman is saved, and with Mengele dead, the mad scheme will come to naught.

Relatively few father-son horror films deal with fathers and their true, biological sons. A particularly outlandish one that does is *Night of the Blood Beast* (1959), in which astronaut Michael Emmett, lone survivor of an expedition to another planet, returns to Earth with an alien life form gestating in his abdomen. His offspring is a lumbering, warty horror that is decidedly lacking in the social graces. Predictably, both father and son are eventually destroyed. This sort of male distaste for the mechanics of childbirth is also apparent in *The Creeping Unknown* (1955) and *Alien* (1979). In each film, a man becomes unwilling host to an alien life form; indeed, in the former film the child gradually absorbs its father's entire body. The chest-burster sequence in Ridley Scott's *Alien* has become perverse movie folklore: the rude violation

Unorthodox fatherhood: Peter Dyneley and uninvited offspring in *The Manster* (1959).

of the man's body, the blood, and his screams say a lot about the way in which we view pregnancy and childbirth.

Similarly, *The Manster* (1959) is an American gangster (Peter Dyneley) in Japan who runs afoul of a demented scientist, and wakes up one morning to find an eye blinking in his shoulder. Soon, the eye becomes a hideous head, then a bestial body. The "manster" finally splits free of its father and kills him.

Curse of the Werewolf (1961; see Chapter II) and its unofficial remake, *The Beast Within* (1982) focus upon young men who were conceived in rape, and who have inherited their fathers' bestial tendencies. In the science-fictional milieu we have George Lucas' *Star Wars* trilogy; in the series' third film, *Return of the Jedi* (1983), forthright young hero Luke Skywalker (Mark Hamill) learns that his father is the Nazi-like villain Darth Vader (David Prowse; voice by James Earl Jones). Does Luke have an undreamt-of evil side to his nature? Given the splashy, kinetic nature of Lucas' vision, the audience hardly has time to care.

The *Star Wars* films are innocuous, essentially thoughtless bubblegum. The father-son relationship is not explored in much depth, nor, I suppose, should it have been. Because the series was lavishly produced and attractively cast, critics accepted its limitations. In 1960, reviewers were far less kind to Michael Powell's *Peeping Tom*, a thoughtful, deceptively sensitive story of a young man who has been psychologically destroyed by his father, and rendered incapable of receiving what he desires most: love. It is a horror film in the truest sense of the term. Earlier Powell movies (often in collaboration with screenwriter Emeric Pressburger) explore obsessions with art and love, so *Peeping Tom* is not as unexpected a film as some Powell-watchers have felt.

Powell began in the industry as a screenwriter in 1930 and became one of the most important and prolific writer-directors of post-war British cinema. His best films (*The Red Shoes* [1948] is one) are colorful, lively, and ambitious, and burn with an awareness of the joys and pains of life.

In *Peeping Tom* the protagonist is Mark Lewis (Karl Boehm), a quiet, almost soulful young recluse who works as a focus puller at a movie studio. The studio specializes in banal comedies and romances; one of Mark's co-workers, Vivian (Moira Shearer), hopes to be a musical star. Mark supplements his income by taking pornographic photographs, which are sold under-the-counter at a neighborhood newsagent's. But Mark has an obsessive avocation: murder with a voyeuristic twist. He stalks young, pretty women with his movie camera, stabs them with a blade that is mounted on his camera's tripod, and films their death agonies. The horrible psychosexual implications of Mark's crimes are doubled because his camera is framed with a curved mirror which allows the terrified victims to observe their own deaths.

Never once in *Peeping Tom* is Mark presented as anything but a sympathetic character. We accept him as such. Powell accomplished this remarkable feat with bone-chilling sequences of Mark quietly viewing silent film footage of himself as a child that had been shot by his late father. We learn that Mark's father had been a behavioral psychologist, keenly interested in the fear mechanism. One film shows the young Mark squirming in his bed as he is blinded by the camera light, then shrieking in terror when his father drops a lizard on the bed covers. In another sequence the young Mark wrinkles his nose in distaste as he observes a young couple kissing. Only once is the boy captured in the frame with his father, in footage shot (as Mark explains to a visitor) by his young stepmother, whom he bitterly refers to as his "surrogate female." The presence of the stepmother, then, was an additional block in Mark's psychological development; the boy's relationship with his father was clinical and perverse, but at least it was *exclusive*. The stepmother — simultaneously a mother figure and an object of allure — destroyed that exclusivity, and distorted the boy's perception of young, attractive women. The end result of all this psychological battering is that the adult Mark is an anguished killer whose life revolves around *looking*. He is incapable of physical or emotional connection — his crippling disability limits him to the role of observer.

A touching and well-played subplot concerns Mark's relationship with Helen (Anna Massey), a plain, sweet girl who lives in Mark's apartment building. (Mark owns the building, but confines himself to two small rooms, and rarely collects rent from his tenants.) Helen views the world through innocent eyes: she has just sold a children's book and thinks it would be grand if Mark's camera were to capture the fanciful images she visualizes as ideal illustration. Mark is excited at the thought of such a magical opportunity, but realizes that he is only fooling himself. He has already murdered his friend Vivian while pretending to film her screen test, and knows that he will

Mark (Karl Boehm) unreels the cause of his madness for Helen (Anna Massey) in Michael Powell's *Peeping Tom* (1960).

probably do the same to Helen if he allows himself to become involved with her. Mark's camera—with its phallic blade and dreadful mirror-eye—will never photograph joy. Helen is innocent enough to be oblivious to the hints of mental disturbance that radiate from Mark, but her blind mother (Maxine Audley) picks up the vibrations like sonar. The irony of the woman's blindness is as elegant as it is obvious. Free of the need to *look*, she sees Mark more clearly than anyone. She is the strong, caring parent Mark never had, and urges him to find help.

Mark murders again—this time one of the hardboiled girls who poses for the pornographic pictures. A police detective who has become suspicious of Mark discovers the body. As the police close in, Helen enters Mark's flat and discovers the film of Vivian's murder. Mark arrives and demonstrates his method of murder by setting up his movie camera and rigging trip wires that will click the shutters of still cameras. When the police clatter up the stairs, flashbulbs pop and the movie camera whirs as Mark resolutely runs to his tripod blade and impales himself through the throat. With this final act, Mark both honors his father and frees himself from his father's influence.

British trade critics gave *Peeping Tom* lukewarm approval, but mainstream reviewers savaged it. According to Powell's vision, we are all voyeurs of some sort. A scene in which a middle-aged businessman enters the newsagent's and euphemistically asks for "views" illustrates the insipid tastelessness of hypocritical people who secretly cherish pornography. More damning (and disturbing) is Powell's juxtaposition of popular cinema with Mark's perverse murder movies. Mark works in an industry that counts on public voyeurism for its survival. The very fact that we are in a darkened theater or living room watching *Peeping Tom* becomes an indictment. Whenever Mark approaches a victim, we view the scene through the eye of Mark's camera. We *become* Mark. It is not simply this matter of shared guilt that unenlightened critics objected to, but the fact that Mark is a sympathetic protagonist. When he has a date with Helen he allows the girl to persuade him to leave his camera at home. The evening goes well, and we are pleased that our murderer — our protagonist — is able to free himself from the pernicious influence of his father, if only for a few hours. As is required of a tragic hero, Mark struggles but — in the end — cannot escape his destiny. *Peeping Tom* is a poisonous celebration of Father's Day, and is cinema's bleakest look at paternity.

Father-*daughter* horror films have been few, and are usually predicated on the simple, unenticing novelty of the monster being female instead of male. The most amusing example may be Terence Fisher's *Frankenstein Created Woman* (1967), made at a time when Hammer felt itself running out of ideas. Baron Frankenstein (Peter Cushing) discovers that the human soul can be transplanted from one body to another, and does just that when he gives a crippled girl the soul of her wrongfully executed lover. After the operation the cripple becomes a dishy blonde (Susan Denberg) who systematically murders the men who had conspired against her lover. Dr. Frankenstein is left without a daughter when his comely creation wearies of her mission and commits suicide.

In *Dracula's Daughter* (1936) Countess Marya Zaleska (Gloria Holden) arranges for shipment of her father's corpse to America so that she can burn it and escape the family curse. No luck: vampire's blood is the thickest sort of all. Marya cannot resist her heritage, and entices young women into vampirism (with lesbian overtones which are remarkably apparent for the period) before being destroyed by the redoubtable Dr. Van Helsing (Edward Van Sloan). The picture was Universal's first official sequel to *Dracula* (1931) but has been largely forgotten, not because it is a poor film but because director Lambert Hillyer substituted a sense of subtle menace for the extravagant evil that characterizes the Lugosi original. Though Gloria Holden is a dark, broody presence, *Dracula's Daughter* seems destined to remain an obscure footnote.

Sensation-seekers are invariably disappointed by *Daughter of Dr. Jekyll* (1957), in which the scientist's offspring (Gloria Talbott) is convinced that she is cursed, and responsible for a wave of murders that plagues a small town.

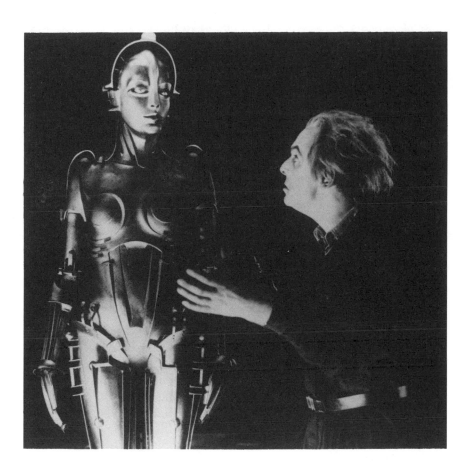

The wizard Rotwang (Rudolf Klein-Rogge) instructs his soulless offspring, the magnificent Robotrix, in Fritz Lang's *Metropolis* (1927).

The revelation that the real monster is the woman's avuncular guardian (Arthur Shields) is a brazen cheat. Boo, hiss. Other father-daughter films that are committed to similar silliness include an oddball trilogy released by Universal: *Captive Wild Woman* (1943), *Jungle Woman* (1944), and *Jungle Captive* (1945), each of which involves a scientist's attempt to.turn an orangutan into a woman. These bargain-basement Moreaus (played, respectively, by John Carradine, J. Carroll Naish, and Otto Kruger) inevitably bungle their experiments, so that Daddy's Little Girl is not only hirsute, but homicidal.

The finest father-daughter horror film is Fritz Lang's *Metropolis* (1926), the great social and political allegory of class antagonism. Though fanciful and heavily stylized, the film is as deeply concerned with revenge, mob rule, and personal responsibility as Lang's other great films: *Der müde Tod* (1921), *M* (1931), *The Testament of Dr. Mabuse* (1933), and *Fury* (1936), to name just a few. *Metropolis* — didactic but also a film of great heart and sensitivity — was written by Thea Von Harbou, Lang's wife, who later became an ardent Nazi and refused to leave Germany when her husband fled the country in 1933. Von Harbou's screenplay (which she translated into novel form after the film's release) is clearly the work of a political zealot of some sort. Jon Fredersen (Alfred Abel) is the Master Industrialist of Metropolis, a glorious futuristic city that seems to embody all of mankind's noblest dreams. Fredersen's idealistic son Freder (Gustav Frohlich) gradually unravels the truth of Metropolis, and learns that the city is dependent upon the forced labor of thousands of dispirited workers who toil in factories far below the city's surface. Freder falls in love with Maria (Brigitte Helm), a lovely young woman who is a leader of the workers' resistance.

When Fredersen discovers his son's affair and that the workers are planning to revolt, he consults the wizard Rotwang (Rudolf Klein-Rogge), a curiously medieval figure who lives in a dark cottage in a dim corner of the city. Rotwang introduces Fredersen to the Robotrix, a beautiful, gleaming robot that Rotwang has fashioned in the form of a woman. Fredersen is impressed, and asks Rotwang to transform the robot into the image of Maria, and to use the imposter to destroy the workers' revolt. Rotwang agrees, and later kidnaps Maria; in a laboratory scene that must surely have inspired James Whale when he directed *Frankenstein* five years later, Rotwang's electrical equipment captures Maria's essence and transfers it to the Robotrix. The mechanical Maria sows discontent among the workers, urging them to destroy the great underground machines. (Rather a harebrained scheme; surely Rotwang realizes that Fredersen would not wish to see the backbone of the city destroyed.) The true Maria escapes too late.

The workers riot. The robot Maria explodes the huge dynamo that powers the city, flooding the underground and drowning hundreds of the workers' children. At this, the rioters stop their revel and turn on the false Maria. The robot is seized, trussed to a pole, and set ablaze while Freder and the true Maria try separately to escape the destruction. Rotwang spies the woman and seizes her a second time, intending to kill her and cover his deception. He struggles with Freder on a narrow rooftop and falls to his death. When Fredersen approaches, Maria speaks metaphorically of the ruined city: "There can be no understanding between the hand and the brain unless the heart acts as mediator." As Freder and Maria embrace, Fredersen clasps hands with one of the underground workers.

Metropolis is a film of archetypes. Fredersen is the epitome of the steely and heartless bourgeois who exploits the proletariat. His son Freder is the late-blooming idealist, while Rotwang is the obsessed father figure who becomes an evil manipulator. And Maria/Robotrix represents the opposite poles of womanhood. As Maria, she is noble, loyal, and well-intentioned. But the mechanical Maria is the wanton, uncontrollable daughter, a primal female force that has been unleashed by a cruel and foolish father. When Rotwang instructs his creation to arouse the workers, the robot slowly—almost obscenely—winks one dark eye, as if in awareness of her special power, and her debt to the man who gave it to her. Later, a distressed Freder dreams that Maria—*his* Maria—performs a carnal dance before a crowd of lustful businessmen. The political aspect of *Metropolis* now seems naive, but two elements—the visual spectacle and the sexual undercurrent—remain undiminished. Von Harbou's script is distressingly ambivalent about parenting; hundreds of children die so that Fredersen can realize how badly he has misunderstood his own son and his fellow man, while Rotwang—though not directly destroyed by his creation—becomes a victim of the unrest that his offspring fomented.

Horror films that have women as their central characters are a relatively new phenomenon, and seem to have developed parallel with the growth of the women's movement in the United States and Europe. As women became increasingly vocal about social inequities, filmmakers reasoned that audiences would be receptive to horror films that focused on women caught in situations more overtly sexual than any the genre had explored in the past. Unfortunately (but not too surprisingly), nearly all of these films are obvious and childish. Most explore strained or unnatural motherhood, which is fine except that the explorations, characteristically, are strictly physical.

Unlike father-son horror films—which are typically heavy with psychological ramifications—the impact of most of the matriarchal horror films comes from simple physical repulsion at what the woman has given birth to, or what her child has become. In other words, the films acknowledge that women have wombs, but not that they have brains or very much subtlety of emotion. Not unexpectedly, the pacesetting films that defined the matriarchal horror subgenre have more intelligence and depth than other examples. Roman Polanski's *Rosemary's Baby* (1968; see Chapter III) concerns itself less with motherhood than with the role of women in contemporary society. Still, the picture prompted filmmakers to think about the dramatic and commercial possibilities of stories about victimized mommies.

Far and away the most notable of the mother-child horror films is William Friedkin's *The Exorcist* (1973). This slick adaptation of William Peter Blatty's novel has become so celebrated that an objective discussion is difficult. To this day, audiences react with equal measures of dismay and horror when 12-year-old Regan MacNeil (Linda Blair) speaks in the Devil's throaty voice, vomits directly into the face of a priest, and gleefully masturbates with a crucifix. Regan's mother (Ellen Burstyn) is helpless to deal with the child's possession; this powerlessness is especially disturbing because the early portion of the film establishes that mother and daughter share a warm and spontaneous relationship. The Devil's personality is far from warm, however, and Mrs. MacNeil eventually turns to an unhappy priest, Father Karras (Jason Miller), who recruits aged Father Merrin (Max von Sydow) to perform an exorcism. After a lot of screaming and thrashing, and a coronary that fells Merrin,

Karras taunts the demon into leaving the body of the girl and entering his own. This accomplished, Karras leaps through a window to his death.

Audiences predisposed to the idea of a true Devil and the reality of demonic possession react strongly to the studied tone and general air of self-importance that surround *The Exorcist*. Further, the film's catalogue of miserable parent-child relationships provides a believable and distressing context for the supernatural mayhem. One subplot revolves around Karras' guilt over the lonely death of his invalid mother. At one point, the possessed girl speaks to Karras in the voice of his mother, and begs for an explanation of why he "abandoned" her. Another plot element involves Regan's father, who is estranged from his wife and living in Europe, unable (or unwilling) to help. *The Exorcist* is predicated upon relationships that have been shattered, truncated, squandered, or otherwise altered. Friedkin handled this aspect of the film intelligently—if not fully rounded, his protagonists at least seem to be real people with everyday problems. This sense of verisimilitude contributes greatly to the film's undeniable impact.

Ultimately, however, *The Exorcist* is a shamelessly manipulative piece of work that arouses audiences with bludgeoning shock rather than true horror. Scenes of little Regan vomiting or bouncing on her bed crying, "Fuck me! Fuck me!" to the gathered priests and physicians may outrage our sensibilities, but fall short of achieving true horror. Dick Smith's unrestrained makeup effects—such as the child turning her head completely around—are cleverly executed, but only underscore the film's lack of real substance. Well directed and convincingly acted, *The Exorcist* is also blatant and crude. It hasn't nearly the finesse of, say, *The Bad Seed* (1956), Mervyn LeRoy's adaptation of the Maxwell Anderson play about a little girl (Patty McCormack) who inherits her mother's dormant evil. Before the child is finally struck down by a lightning bolt (the only power that seems able to stop her), she drowns a playmate and burns a stupid handyman (Henry Jones) to death in the cellar.

The Bad Seed is truly horrific because nearly everyone believes that the little girl is an absolute angel—only the mother (Nancy Kelly) knows the truth. In *The Exorcist*, the truth is relentlessly obvious. But whatever the artistic merit of Friedkin's film, its astonishing box office success galvanized dozens of moviemakers, worldwide.* Theater screens were quickly overrun with hysterical women whose bellies swelled with monsters, or whose children started murdering the neighbors. Most of these films are predicated upon some aspect of demonology, and nearly all express a cultural ambivalence about pregnancy, a phenomenon that simultaneously enchants and dismays many of us. Children, too, are viewed in these films with mixed feelings: the filmmakers realized that tradition tells parents to treasure their offspring as

---

John Boorman's Exorcist II: The Heretic *(1977) was an unexpected critical and commercial disaster. A good cast and plenty of action could not save it; audiences actually laughed out loud.*

expressions of love, but that the emotional and financial burdens of parenting inevitably color parental response. The matriarchal horror films inspired by *The Exorcist* exploit this ambivalence and turn it into outright disgust.

Richard Donner's *The Omen* (1976) has been the most commercially successful of the *Exorcist* spinoffs. It is a slickly attractive piece of filmmaking, well-shot and bolstered by a splendid cast. David Seltzer's screenplay concerns the Antichrist, raised by American diplomat Robert Thorn (Gregory Peck) and his attractive wife (Lee Remick). The child, Damien (Harvey Stephens) seems normal enough until his fifth birthday, when people involved in his life begin to die. His young nanny cheerfully hangs herself from a dormer in full view of a lawn party, a priest who has a clue to Damien's origin is caught in a violent thunderstorm and impaled by an iron rod that is torn from a church tower, and a photographer (David Warner) is decapitated by a pane of glass that slips from the bed of a truck. Damien's presence in a wild animal park agitates a troop of baboons to a frenzy, and dogs go wild in his defense. The child eventually knocks his mother from a stepladder and allows her to fall over a stairwell to the floor below. In the hospital, Mrs. Thorn is visited by Damien's *new* nanny (Billie Whitelaw), and is thrown through a window to her death. The startlement of these visual set pieces pales beside the revelation that Mrs. Thorn's real child died shortly after birth, and that her boneheaded husband accepted a substitute baby from a mysterious priest. So it is that the Antichrist becomes the son of wealthy, privileged, and influential parents. When Thorn discovers that the skull of his real child had been purposely crushed, he resolves to destroy Damien. After a bloody fight with the demonic nanny, Thorn prepares to kill the boy in a church, but is gunned down by police just as he squeezes the trigger of his revolver. Damien survives.

The sequel, *Damien: Omen II* (1978) follows the Antichrist's (Jonathan Scott-Taylor) journey through a bloody adolescence as the adopted son of William Holden and Lee Grant. The film did not earn anything near the $60 million that had been raked in by its predecessor, but nevertheless led to a second sequel, *The Final Conflict* (1981), in which the adult Damien (Sam Neill) becomes U.S. Ambassador to England.

To say that the *Omen* trilogy is illogical and contrived is to offer a mild reproach, indeed. People who have no truck with the darker mythology of Christianity may be mystified by the films' popularity, while those viewers predisposed to a belief in such things will feel richly rewarded, perhaps even vindicated. Like *The Exorcist, The Omen* and its sequels look at children whose evil places them completely beyond the control of their parents. The films may have been embraced in some quarters because they are an abrogation of parental responsibility—Damien is the problem child with whom we don't wish to deal. We're powerless because of an insidious outside force.

Foreign malevolence came to dominate children in a succession of mostly inferior films. *The Devil Within Her* (1975) features Joan Collins as the perplexed mother of an infant that (somehow) is able to shove adults into fish

Violation of the form we prize: Susan Strasberg pregnant with *The Manitou* (1978).

ponds and bludgeon them with hammers. Director Peter Sasdy was un-doubtedly inspired by the success of Larry Cohen's *It's Alive!* (1974), another improbable tale of a homicidal baby. A 1978 sequel, *It Lives Again*, brought Cohen's diaper-clad killer back for a second go-round. While *Rosemary's Baby* and *The Exorcist* are obvious reference points for these films, they draw more directly from Ray Bradbury's short story "The Small Assassin," a chilling ex-ploration of paranoia as it is expressed by a new mother who is irrationally con-vinced that her infant son is trying to kill her. The story succeeds because we never know for certain if the woman is correct. She has reacted to her own body with morbidity, and views her baby as an intruder, an enemy. By the time the mother dies in an accidental (was it?) fall, her paranoia has infected her husband. He confides his fears to the doctor who brought the baby into the world. After the husband dies mysteriously, the doctor is convinced. At the story's end, he confronts the infant with a scalpel.

Bradbury realized that the suspension of disbelief is a fragile thing; still, we can accept the outlandish premise of "The Small Assassin" because the story is purposely circumspect, relying on suggestion instead of blunt direct-ness. The inherent unreality of the written word convinces us that the woman's claim *could* be true. An attractive 1952 adaptation by writer Al Feldstein and artist George Evans for the fabled *Shock SuspenStories* EC horror comic book falters simply because it visualizes Bradbury's prose with something other than the mind's eye. The suspension of disbelief has been compromised. This, of course, is the failing of films like *The Devil Within Her* and *It's Alive!*. The premise is fine, but the visualization makes that premise seem ridiculous. The films unwisely *show* us a horror that is essentially psychological.

Most exploitation filmmakers had sense enough to steer clear of killer babies, and concentrated instead of more reasonable horrors. *Demon Witch Child* (1976), *The Redeemer, Son of Satan* (1977), *The Child* (1977), and *The Godsend* (1979) concern malevolent older children who astonish their parents by demonstrating supernatural power, and a flair for murder. The acceptance of such films seems to be symptomatic of the ongoing human struggle for explanations and scapegoats. The movies link life's mysteries with the supernatural, and parental misery with the Devil.

William Girdler's *The Manitou* (1978) is the most entertaining of this silly lot, involving a young beauty (Susan Strasberg) whose pregnancy manifests itself as a tumorous lump on the back of her neck. The dwarf-like horror that she gives birth to is revealed to be the reincarnation of the spirit of Misquamacus, a vengeful American Indian sorcerer. Only Indian exorcist John Singing Rock (Michael Ansara) can save the day. Other than the presence of respected performers like Strasberg, Ansara, Tony Curtis, Ann Sothern, Burgess Meredith, and Stella Stevens, the most disturbing aspect of *The Manitou* is its undeniable loathing of female biology, or rather, its reflection of a loathing held by many. *The Manitou* is just the movie for people who refer to pregnancy as "being in the family way," and for those hilarious souls who relish jokes about menstruation. Strasberg's condition is an insidious, disfiguring disease that is a violation of the sleek female form we prize so dearly.

The aforementioned chest-burster of *Alien* is cinema's rudest such violation; it is shamelessly aped at the conclusion of Barbara Peeters' amusing *Humanoids from the Deep* (1980; see Chapter V), in which a young lady who has been raped by an oversexed sea monster gives violent birth to a mewling *thing* which erupts through the mother's abdominal wall. Blatant, gratuitous shocks of this sort provoke a quick scream from the audience, but are invariably forgotten by the time said audience hits the parking lot. It is the subtle horrors that stay with us, perhaps not on a conscious level, but certainly in our twilight mind, where they will niggle and disturb. This is the effect and great success of Wolf Rilla's *Village of the Damned* (1960), perhaps the finest of all British horror films, and certainly the best of the matriarchal subgenre.

Rilla, Stirling Silliphant, and George Barclay based their screenplay on John Wyndham's excellent 1957 novel *The Midwich Cuckoos*, which concerns an English village that is mysteriously stopped dead for a half day, its people quietly rendered unconscious, its women impregnated by a sinister alien life force intent on world domination. As filmed, the hybrid boys and girls who result from this cosmic rape are beautiful, cooly dispassionate blonds who exhibit terrifying mental powers when aroused. An annoying normal child is knocked to the ground by a blast of mental force, and a man who has thought of killing the children with a shotgun is mentally instructed to turn the weapon on himself. George Sanders and the patrician Barbara Shelley played one set of unhappy parents, and are the very models of British civility and quiet bravery. Their child (brilliantly played by 11-year-old Martin Stephens) dominates the household like an aggressive, influential visitor. The father (who is, of course, not the father at all) is mystified and fascinated.

As the truth of the children's origin becomes apparent, the town is dotted with little pockets of violence; in one shocking sequence, a man is mentally commanded to drive his car full tilt into a stone wall, where it explodes in a sickening gout of flame. Finally, Sanders resolves to destroy the children, and assembles them in a schoolhouse. Because the children can read minds, Sanders must struggle to block his thoughts. His son is perplexed by Sanders' mental image of a brick wall, which is shared with the audience via superimposition. The child senses the truth when the brick wall in Sanders' mind begins to literally crumble, revealing his plan. Before the boy can react, the bomb that is in his father's briefcase goes off, destroying the school and everyone in it.

Wolf Rilla had been a workmanlike director prior to *Village of the Damned*, and was known for a dull facility that was equally applicable to comedy or adventure. One of his earlier films, *The End of the Road* (1954), involves a retired engineer who is on the verge of being packed off to an old folks' home by his grown children. *Village of the Damned* is certainly a provocative extrapolation of a similar theme. This time, though, the motive of the children is not selfishness, but hatred. Scenes of Barbara Shelley attempting to be motherly with young Stephens—straightening his tie, combing his hair—are fascinating and repellent. The woman must surely sense that the child was not sired by her husband, but cannot bear to forego the tender niceties of motherhood. The boy, on the other hand, is supremely disinterested, his eyes and mind invariably fixed elsewhere as his mother fusses over him. The child spurns and silently mocks his parents at every opportunity.

The film is a collection of such sober disquiet. Particularly uneasy moments occur early on, when the town is under the alien influence: a woman sprawls behind her washtub as the water runs over, an iron steadily burns through a dress, and, most chillingly, a tractor with an unconscious driver putts round and round until stopping against a tree. Investigating soldiers encircle the village, and those who venture into the affected area must be dragged back with ropes. Later, a succession of perplexed and frightened women visit the village doctor, who must inform them that they are pregnant. A teenage girl bursts into tears, and a married woman whose husband has been away becomes hysterical.

Its science-fictional trappings aside, *Village of the Damned* is about rape, involuntary motherhood, and the misery caused by loveless, unloved children. On a broader level, though, it is concerned with the disintegration of the family, a danger which has become a hot topic since World War II. Other filmic examples abound: Jack Arnold's *The Space Children* (1958), for instance, concerns a group of youngsters who abandon their parents and

The victim (Barbara Shelley) of cosmic rape regards her alien child (Martin Stephens) in *Village of the Damned* (1960).

homes after their minds are controlled and fortified by an alien intelligence. The combined brain power of the children will be used to sabotage the project their parents are working on: the U.S. space program. Because *The Space Children* was released just one year after Russia launched Sputnik, its political overtones are at least as urgent as its familial ones. Antone Leader's semisequel to *Village of the Damned*, entitled *Children of the Damned* (1963), is also politicized, dealing with the discovery of a half-dozen exceptional children whose brilliance is turned to evil — not by space aliens, but by an unscrupulous political establishment.

The vulnerability of children and their dismay at the occasional helplessness of their parents has been a recurring motif in horror cinema. A viewer may remember the little monsters of *The Bad Seed* or *The Nanny* (1965) with special clarity, but with none of the poignancy reserved for young victims like the little girl (Sandy Descher) in the opening moments of Gordon Douglas' *Them!* (1954), who catatonically wanders the New Mexico desert (pathetically clutching a baby doll) after her parents have been devoured by giant ants. Later in the film, police and military authorities search for two little boys whose father was dismembered before their eyes as the group flew a model plane in the Los Angeles "River," the barely damp concrete reservoir that runs the length of the city. Hero James Whitmore eventually finds the kids cowering in a dark sewer tunnel, and rescues them at the cost of his own life. *Them!* proposes that children are the most valuable human resource: before the boys are discovered, a military official suggests that they should be sacrificed in order to insure the safety of the rest of the city. "Why don't you tell that to their mother?" demands FBI agent James Arness. "Yeah," adds Whitmore, "she's standing right over there." The official takes a look at the fraught woman and softly replies, "Yeah, I see what you mean."

William Cameron Menzies' *Invaders from Mars* (1953) is told entirely from a child's point of view, using subtly outsized, distorted sets and childlike logic to underscore the fright and helplessness of the little boy (Jimmy Hunt) who is awakened one night by a flying saucer, and can later do nothing as his playmates, neighbors, and even mother and father (Hillary Brooke and Leif Erickson) are taken over by evil Martians. In one horrifying scene, the boy's parents come to pick him up at the police station; everything seems normal and the boy is relieved until he notices a tiny pinprick in the back of his father's neck, the only physical giveaway of a Martian possession. At home, the boy is brutally slapped by his father after asking an innocent question. When it seems that the Martians have won, the boy abruptly awakens, realizing that all that has happened has been a dream. But when a flying saucer lands outside his window, the events begin again—this time for real.

A similar sort of childlike paranoia is at the core of Don Siegel's *Invasion of the Body Snatchers* (1956), set in the cozy town of Santa Mira, where children hysterically insist that their parents are *not* their parents. As will be discussed more fully in Chapter III, this is not paranoia at all, but awful truth. Tobe Hooper's *Poltergeist* (1982) also exploits the dark fears of childhood: an angelic little girl (Heather O'Rourke) is abducted from her bed by howling phantasms, and cries to her parents from an invisible fourth dimension. Her young brother (Oliver Robins) keeps a wary eye on his grinning, stuffed clown, and is surprised one night by a gnarled tree that crashes through his bedroom window to drag him outside. On a more fanciful level, five hundred youngsters kidnapped by cruel Dr. Terwilliker (Hans Conreid) are forced to play at the keyboard of his giant piano in the Dr. Seuss–inspired *The Five Thousand Fingers of Dr. T*, directed by Roy Rowland in 1953. As in *Invaders from Mars*, the tormented child protagonist (Tommy Rettig) is suffering from a bad dream. The same gambit was clumsily utilized by writer-director Phil Tucker in *Robot Monster* (1953), in which a little boy (Gregory Moffett) dreams that Earth has been razed by bubble-blowing, extraterrestrial gorillas. The boy's adult protector (George Nader) is tossed off a cliff, and—in a scene that must surely strike home to every misogynistic little boy who sees it—the killer gorilla slowly strangles the young dreamer's bothersome sister.

Don Coscarelli's wildly inventive *Phantasm* (1979) is about dreams, a sinister mortuary, killer dwarves from the fourth dimension, and a supernatural undertaker (Angus Scrimm). At the center of this maelstrom is a

14-year-old boy (Michael Baldwin) whose greatest fear is not the mortuary and its attendant horrors, but that his older brother (Bill Thornbury)—who has cared for him since the death of their parents—will abandon him.

That a child will cling fiercely to a brother or sister is well demonstrated by Robert Mulligan's *The Other* (1972), in which an idyllic rural setting in the 1920s is turned upside down by Niles and Holland (Chris and Martin Udvarnoky), towheaded young twins whose mischief escalates into murder. The horrible revelation is that Holland—the particularly impish brother—no longer exists, having died some time before, but returned as a demonic presence to take control of his brother. When a baby disappears, Niles is in a panic: "Holland," he demands, "where is the baby?" The infant is dead, of course, and Niles is the killer. Grandmother Uta Hagen tries to force Niles to admit his crime and delusion, and finally attempts to destroy the child in a burning barn. But Niles escapes while Grandma fries. The brothers will remain inseparable.

Adult siblings are the focus of *The Possession of Joel Delaney* (1972), another thriller about demonic visitation. Delaney (Perry King) is dominated by the spirit of a vengeful Puerto Rican who uses his host to abuse wealthy Anglos, and otherwise even up the socioeconomic score. This jackhammer approach to social issues is a bit much, but the conclusion—in which the evil spirit moves from the dead body of Delaney to Delaney's sister (Shirley MacLaine)—is good, nasty fun.

Particularly violent adult sibling rivalry informs Robert Aldrich's *Whatever Happened to Baby Jane?* (1962), the story of onetime child star Baby Jane (Bette Davis), who sadistically looks after her sister Blanche (Joan Crawford), a former movie queen who is now a cripple. Jane has never forgotten that Blanche's career eclipsed her own, and delights in malicious pranks like serving Blanche a rat for supper, and denying her access to the telephone. Blanche's victimization eventually grows so severe that Jane commits murder in order to hide it. *Baby Jane* legitimized Hollywood Grand Guignol and brought work to a number of aging leading ladies who were not averse to a little scenery-chewing. Besides Davis and Crawford, actresses the caliber of Olivia de Havilland, Agnes Moorehead, Shelley Winters, Tallulah Bankhead, and Mary Astor starred in campy thrillers that aped the *Baby Jane* formula. *Hush, Hush Sweet Charlotte* (1965), *Die, Die My Darling!* (1965), and *Who Slew Auntie Roo?* (1971) are just a few of the cloyingly titled melodramas that detail oddball families done in by propinquity and bad genes.

Baby Jane's brand of sibling rivalry was considered shocking in its day, but standards loosened so greatly in subsequent years that, by 1977, nobody blinked when the evil little girl (Paula Sheppard) of *Communion* aka *Alice, Sweet Alice* stuffed her younger sister (Brooke Shields) into a box and set it afire. In fact, Brookeophobes cheered. Less easy to take is the scene in which the child smashes her father in the mouth with a brick, then shoves him through a window to his death. Deeper violations of the integrity of the

The life of the father (Donald Sutherland) is effectively ended by the death of his daughter in Nicolas Roeg's *Don't Look Now* (1973). Julie Christie looks on.

nuclear family are offered by Paul Schrader's *Cat People* (1982), which suggests not only that antagonistic brother and sister Malcolm McDowell and Nastassia (now Nastassja) Kinski are actually shape-shifting panthers, but that the logical thing for them to do is mate. Marriage — and morality — have become superfluous.

Of all familial bonds, the one between husband and wife may be the simplest to corrupt. *I Married a Monster from Outer Space* (1958; see Chapter IV) is almost self-explanatory, while the unhappy husband (Peter Wyngarde) of *Burn, Witch, Burn* (1961) is shocked to discover that his wife (Janet Blair) has been possessed by the spirit of a witch, and is trying to kill him. Wyngarde escapes death only because his wife is conveniently crushed beneath a heavy piece of masonry fashioned in the shape of an eagle.

In Gary Sherman's surreal *Dead and Buried* (1981), small-town sheriff James Farentino investigates a rash of bloody murders at great risk to his own life and sanity. In a scene calculated to throw the viewer for a real loop, Farentino watches grainy, monochrome film footage of a bulky man who busily copulates with a barely-glimpsed woman. As the man in the film climaxes, the woman plunges a knife deep into his back. The corpse tumbles from the bed, and as the woman straightens and gives the camera an evil smirk, the sheriff sees that the lustful killer is his wife (Melody Anderson). The sheriff eventually learns that the entire town is populated with corpses (his wife included) who have been animated by the local mortician (Jack Albertson), one of those malevolently talented characters who usually exist only in fever dreams and moldering EC comic books. The final revelation is that the sheriff, too, is one of the walking dead.

Dead and Buried makes its points about the fragility of the family unit with gross good humor, but the theme is so heavy that it has inspired a number of films that confuse callow sociology with social relevance, and ponderousness with entertainment. George Lucas' *THX-1138* (1971)—a feature-length version of a prize-winning short the director made while a student at USC—is a passionless, antiseptic look at a passionless, antiseptic future society where individual identity is squashed and sex is forbidden. People have numbers instead of names, and women look the same as men: pale, bald, and uniformed. The citizenry is strictly controlled by a totalitarian state that has assumed the roles of Mother and Father. The birthrate is closely monitored, and is achieved with artificial insemination. The film comes to life when THX (Robert Duvall) escapes the authorities after being arrested for making his wife pregnant. Inevitably, though, we wonder just where he will escape *to*. Similarly, the persecuted father (Oliver Reed) of *ZPG* (Zero Population Growth; 1972) flees with his wife (Geraldine Chaplin) and baby in a rubber raft that hardly seems up to the task of removing the family from a society where the smog is as thick as cheese, and births have been prohibited for thirty years.

Richard Fleischer's *Soylent Green* (1973) is a fairly well-reasoned dystopian story which proposes that the family tradition has gotten so out of hand by 2022 that the population of New York City is 21 million. Food rioters are scooped up in the streets and alleys by bulldozers, and suicide is encouraged as a way to ease the population load. Entire families make their homes in stairwells and abandoned automobiles. A bleak view, to be sure, and made bleaker when a police detective (Charlton Heston) discovers that the country's staple food, Soylent Green, is synthesized from human corpses. There is a certain beautiful symmetry here, but neither Heston nor the audience cares to appreciate it.

Doomsayers who bemoan the death of the family are not simply premature, they are naive. As long as we retain the tiniest smidgen of racial memory, the family will remain the dominant structural force of human existence. It is the emotional equivalent of a warm fire: we huddle around it for strength and security. That the family is changing and will continue to change there is no doubt, but it will not be abandoned as a necessary aspect of human life. If the family brings pain and frustration, it also brings joy, serenity, and satisfaction. Horror cinema will continue to concern itself with the mismanagement and destruction of the family unit, even as the filmmakers acknowledge the family's power and vital importance. Nicolas Roeg's brilliant *Don't Look Now* (1973) is a particularly lucid example. Architect John Baxter (Donald Sutherland) is psychologically destroyed by the accidental drowning of his daughter. Because the family unit has been shattered, the father's life is effectively ended. The wound cannot be repaired. Baxter's work takes him and his wife (Julie Christie) to Venice—not the Venice of gilt and eternal romance, but a dank, disintegrating place where death hangs in the air. Indeed, during Baxter's visit the city is being terrorized by a mad killer. The architect presses on with his work (he is restoring a church), but has odd visions of his wife in mourning. He cannot shake the feeling that he is about to become privy to a profound revelation. When the figure of his little girl darts around the perimeter of one of the city's slimy canals, Baxter follows. He joyously spins the child around, only to discover that the tiny figure is not a child at all but a hideous, aged dwarf who grips a long knife. Baxter is killed, his premonition fulfilled.

Roeg's fragmented, kaleidoscopic visual style expresses pure emotion. We view the disquieting city through Baxter's obsessed eyes, and realize that his finest, most meaningful creation has been his daughter, and that without her he is no longer whole. He has nowhere to go—all paths must lead to the violent act that will end his physical life as surely as his daughter's death ended his emotional life. The joy must be counterbalanced with pain, because that's the price of being in a family way.

II
Just the Two of Us:
The Horror of Duality

In the opening moments of Rouben Mamoulian's *Dr. Jekyll and Mr. Hyde* (1932), Jekyll (Fredric March) addresses a group of physicians and medical students. The soul of man, Jekyll says, is composed of two selves. One of these selves "strives for nobility," while the other, the bad self, "seeks an expression of impulses that bind (man) to some dim animal relation with the earth. These two carry on an eternal struggle in the nature of man...." Dr. Jekyll is a humanitarian who unselfishly ministers to the indigent. Yet there is another aspect to Jekyll, a violent, hedonistic personality capable of lustful assault and murder. The chemicals which liberate this evil self—Mr. Hyde— are only a device; Hyde has existed all along, needing only the proper set of circumstances in order to roam freely.

Robert Louis Stevenson's short novel *The Strange Case of Dr. Jekyll and Mr. Hyde* was published in 1886. The story was instantly popular, and has become a worldwide favorite. The phrase "Jekyll and Hyde personality" has entered the language of psychiatry. Although the novel's surprise has been diminished by continued exposure and interpretation, Stevenson's notion of the silent war that rages inside each of us is still startling. The Victorian England which birthed the novel—an England that valued moral propriety above all else—was especially shocked and intrigued. Hyde is an open defiance of all that was held dear by the Victorian ruling class. But the public at large loved the tale because Stevenson articulated an inescapable truth.

There have been sixteen direct film adaptations of *Dr. Jekyll and Mr. Hyde* since 1908. Variations like *Dr. Pyckle and Mr. Pride* (1925; starring Stan Laurel) and *Dr. Black and Mr. Hyde* (1976) number in the dozens. The story has inspired animated cartoons and even a 1973 musical version starring Kirk Douglas. Mamoulian's 1932 version is not only the finest of the more literal adaptations, but also the most pointed in its sexual implications. Mamoulian had been a stage designer and director before coming to Hollywood in the late twenties. He had an intuitive feel for the visual. *Dr. Jekyll and Mr. Hyde* impressed audiences with its clever and innovative use of subjective camera and voice-over. Diagonal wipes were employed to compress time, or to suggest that two scenes were occurring simultaneously. Because Stevenson's narrative is relatively simple, Mamoulian interpreted the story with a minimum of dialogue. It is images, primarily, that reveal Jekyll's great sexual longing for the prostitute Ivy (Miriam Hopkins). After Jekyll examines bruises Ivy has sustained in an altercation with another man, the girl coyly suggests that Jekyll turn his back so that she may undress. In a moment she is sitting in her bed, barely covered and obviously naked. One bare leg is provocatively thrust from beneath the covers. Jekyll sits next to her and they kiss. The couple is interrupted by Jekyll's friend, but the scene's sexual electricity is not diminished. This was highly-charged stuff, not simply because of the contrast between Jekyll's attraction to Ivy and his relationship with his fiancée, Muriel (Rose Hobart). Muriel and her father (a retired general) represent the cream of Victorian society. They exist a pole apart from the humble, ingenuous Ivy. Jekyll is eager to be married but Muriel's father insists that the couple wait eight months. Though frustrated, Jekyll keeps the flame going by mouthing romantic platitudes that are very nearly a parody of Victorian romanticism. His approach to formal courtship is stilted and coy: he tells Muriel, "I love you gaily, happily, high-hearted!" All of Jekyll's sexual energy has been channeled into sappy platitudes.

After Jekyll drinks his chemical formula, the first words uttered by his alter-ego Hyde are, "Free! Free at last!" Wally Westmore's Oscar-winning makeup turned Fredric March into more than an ugly brute—Hyde is the face of depravity itself. Fueled by lust, Hyde visits Ivy and becomes her tormentor. In a pathetic irony, the girl goes to Jekyll for help, but Hyde finds out (of course) and flings Ivy's words back at her the next time they meet. Eventually, Hyde assumes control of Jekyll and strangles Ivy in a monstrous fit of pique. "I'll give you a lover now!" Hyde sneers. "His name is Death!" Shortly thereafter, Hyde is cornered in Jekyll's lab and shot to death by police.

Frankenstein (1931), *Dracula* (1931), and Mamoulian's *Jekyll and Hyde* form the sturdy triumvirate that signaled the blossoming of the horror genre in the sound era. Fredric March—at the time an attractive matinee idol—was thought by some to have been inappropriately cast, but the genteel, almost foppish quality he brought to Jekyll is in splendid contrast with the libidinous menace of Hyde.

Stevenson's novel barely alludes to Hyde's sexual nature—this aspect of the story is one that has been developed primarily by filmmakers. The 1920 version which starred a wildly leering John Barrymore was the first to offer a sexual rationale for Hyde's behavior; exotic Nita Naldi was cast as the prostitute. In 1941 MGM wished to give the story the glossy Hollywood treatment, but realized that the 1932 version would dwarf any other. With despicable cleverness, MGM purchased the rights to Mamoulian's version from Paramount and "buried" the film, reasoning that if it were not available for screening, no one would make unfriendly comparisons. MGM gave the title roles to Spencer Tracy, who chose to suggest the transformations and Hyde's personality solely through gesture and facial expression. Tracy wore virtually no makeup, so his conception is more psychological than physical. In keeping

The horror of duality: Fredric March as *Dr. Jekyll and Mr. Hyde* (1932).

with this, director Victor Fleming and designer Peter Ballbusch devised some peculiar dream sequences that are filled with heavyhanded Freudian imagery. The women in Jekyll's life are dealt with symbolically: Ivy wallows in mud, while visions of Beatrix (the fiancée) are accompanied by white flowers. The most interesting aspect of this version of the story is the casting of the female leads. Originally, Ingrid Bergman was to play the fiancée, while sultry Lana Turner was set for the role of Ivy. Bergman, though, wanted it the other way around, and was able to steal the picture when MGM gave in. Her fresh good looks bring irony and poignance to the plight of the young prostitute. An inexperienced Lana Turner — then being groomed for stardom — could not do much with her uninteresting role, while Spencer Tracy was done in by the script, which tried too hard to be cerebral. Tracy's Hyde seems more grossly eccentric than evil.

Britain's Hammer Studios combined sex with horror in the late fifties and found great box office success. The studio had tried a comic adaptation of the Jekyll/Hyde story in 1959 with *The Ugly Duckling*, in which comic actor Bernard Bresslaw turns himself into Teddy Hyde, a jewel thief and dance hall lothario. The film's broad humor doomed it to the British provinces, but Hammer gave the story some nasty sensationalism in 1960 with *The Two Faces of Dr. Jekyll*. Paul Massie played Jekyll as a quiet, bearded researcher who loves children and loathes his unfaithful wife (Dawn Addams). Jekyll's experiments create Hyde, a handsome, clean-shaven sexual sadist who rapes Mrs. Jekyll and lets her fall to her death through a skylight. Hyde kills his wife's lover, and takes as his own paramour a snake-dancer who works in a local burlesque hall. She, too, is killed by Hyde, who disposes of the threat of Jekyll by murdering an innocent man and setting the body afire in Jekyll's lab. Hyde has arranged to be declared Jekyll's heir, and his scheme seems to have worked until he is abruptly transformed back to the gentle doctor.

The Two Faces of Dr. Jekyll is a remarkable film, not because it is intrinsically artful, but for the way in which director Terence Fisher and writer Wolf Mankowitz carried the story's sexual possibilities to the outer limits. The rape of the woman by her husband's alter-ego is matched by the outrageous snake symbolism provided by Hyde's mistress. Fisher's delight with the dirt is evident. The film is little known in the United States, where it was ambiguously titled *House of Fright*. Another seldom-seen version of the story, *I, Monster*, arrived in 1971 from Amicus. Christopher Lee starred as kindly Dr. Marlowe, whose obsession with Freud causes him to become the regressive and oversexed Mr. Blake. One noteworthy aspect of this rather muddled film is Blake's appearance, which grows more hideous with each transformation.

American variations on the theme were generally innocuous. Louis Hayward played *Son of Dr. Jekyll* with tepid results in 1951, while Gloria Talbott dreamt of pursuing victims across the countryside in her nightgown in *Daughter of Dr. Jekyll* (1957). Jerry Lewis contributed *The Nutty Professor* in 1964. As a writer/director/actor whose persona seems to shift between Self-Conscious Artist and Drooling Goon, Lewis was well-suited to interpret Stevenson's story of split personality. *The Nutty Professor* is Lewis' funniest film, and the most successful at sustaining a central idea. Professor Kelp is the familiar Lewis idiot: bespectacled, buck-toothed, totally inept. When Kelp isn't blowing up his chemistry classes he experiments with a formula that he hopes will cure his timidity. He is not motivated by scientific curiosity or altruism, but by the shame of being bullied in front of Stella (Stella Stevens), a pretty student for whom he has an adolescent crush. Kelp's raison d'être, then, is purely sexual. His formula is a success—of sorts. Kelp takes a swig and becomes Buddy Love, a supremely egotistical swinger who wows 'em at the college hangout. Lewis lacked the voice and looks needed to make the

The nerd who would be king: Jerry Lewis as *The Nutty Professor* (1964).

transformation thoroughly believable, but he certainly cultivated a disagreeable manner. Buddy sits in at the piano and melts hearts with an upbeat rendition of "That Old Black Magic," then puts the moves on Stella. When a beefy college boy objects, Buddy feigns terror, then handily beats the kid into insensibility.

Though repulsed by Buddy's arrogance, Stella cannot help being attracted by his swaggering sexuality. "Plant one right here," Love instructs, pointing to his lips. "It's the cure for all that ails you." Some contemporary critics were offended by the Love persona, feeling that Lewis was using it to dig at his ex-partner, Dean Martin. But Buddy—with his slicked hair, loud Italian suits, and assured but none-too-competent singing—seems uncomfortably like Lewis himself. The character is suggestive of the wild self-indulgence that precipitated Lewis' decline in the late sixties, when he became unwilling to allow anyone but himself to direct his vehicles. His comic inventiveness is often brilliant, but as a filmmaker he has been excessively eclectic, borrowing heavily from Stan Laurel and Harry Langdon. The sentimentality of Chaplin, in particular, seems to have influenced Lewis; films like *Cinderfella* are awash in treacle. *The Nutty Professor* avoids this. Lewis' sight gags (particularly some in a gymnasium) are wonderful, and Kelp's sexual backwardness is cleverly explained with flashbacks which show Kelp's father (played with a splendid snivel by Howard Morris) being bullied by Mrs. Kelp. The bespectacled baby Kelp (Lewis on his knees) watches from his playpen. But decency triumphs. Stella professes her devotion to Kelp after Buddy Love regresses in the middle of a dance. The film concludes with a feeble and awkward homily, as Kelp advises, "You might as well like yourself. Just think about all the time you're going to have to spend with yourself." Despite the flatness of the fadeout, the film is both funny and thoughtful. The irony of Buddy Love's name is made clear; Lewis saw to it that, *this* time, anyway, the humble *do* inherit. The shame is that Lewis could not bring himself to believe his own lesson.

The Nutty Professor will probably stand as the ultimate comic interpretation of Jekyll and Hyde. Its inventiveness has not been surpassed. The sexual slant of other films has been more blatant, as in *Dr. Sexual and Mr. Hyde*, a hardcore sex-comedy which arrived in 1972. It was followed a year later by something called *The Adult Version of Jekyll and Hide*. In 1982 television comic Mark Blankfield starred in *Jekyll and Hyde — Together Again*, in which lame jokes about drug use replaced sexual innuendo. Apparently, suggestive humor for the eighties will come from the pharmacy, not the bedroom.

The Jekyll/Hyde story has indirectly inspired a number of films that have provocatively blended horror and sex. In the sixties director Robert Aldrich released a number of pictures that popularized Grand Guignol, and shaped Hollywood myths into stylishly decadent burlesques. *Whatever Happened to Baby Jane?* (1962) is the best-known, but *The Legend of Lylah Clare* (1968) is the most grotesque. Peter Finch played a washed-up film director whose chance for a comeback is a biopic of his ex-wife Lylah Clare, a German actress whose wanton bisexuality and taste for high living led to her accidental death. The director is amazed when he meets Elsa (Kim Novak), a young actress who is the image of Lylah. Elsa is cast in the role and gradually assumes the dead actress' personality and voice. Her relationship with the director grows more brutal and pernicious as Lylah's influence becomes stronger. During the shooting of the biography's final scene, Elsa falls from a trapeze and breaks her neck. Her last words are in Lylah's voice.

The Legend of Lylah Clare is the sort of film you love in spite of yourself. Overlong at 130 minutes, it is tacky, vulgar, and full of improbable circumstance: Lylah's odyssey to stardom began in a brothel; her death occurred on her wedding day, and was caused by a fall from a staircase during a struggle with a female lover. Her reincarnation, Elsa, inspires a number of sexual advances — lesbian and otherwise — from people who had known the actress. Lylah *consumes* Elsa, and finally assumes control of her body. Kim Novak's blankness of demeanor perfectly expressed Elsa's suggestibility. An uncredited actress provided Lylah's throaty Germanic voice, and though the effect is hard to swallow at first, the film's campy tone makes the device seem appropriate. In this gaudy movie, anything is possible.

Kim Novak possessed by the violently hedonistic spirit of a dead actress, in *The Legend of Lylah Clare* (1968).

What hurts the film is its imprecise point of view. Obviously, it is a Jekyll and Hyde story of sorts. Elsa assumes Lylah's nasty demeanor with great relish, telling the director, "Get your ass out there and tell them Lylah's coming!" But we learn next to nothing about Elsa. Has she truly been possessed, or is she only expressing a facet of her own personality? Probably a little of both, but the insufficient clues prevent us from being sure. Further clouding matters is the film's sledgehammer satire, aimed at Hollywood and the filmmaking community. The picture ends on a bizarre freezeframe, as mastiffs in a dog food commercial go wild with hunger. Whack! we get the message: Elsa and Lylah have both been victimized and ruined by a rapacious Hollywood that let them think they were in control of their own lives. Okay, but we still don't know what it was in Lylah and Elsa's personalities that allowed them to be taken advantage of. Like *The Nutty Professor, The Legend of Lylah Clare* is a film with clear links to real life. As the last of the wholly manufactured star images, Kim Novak was almost totally the creation of one man, Columbia chief Harry Cohn, who saw her potential in the early fifties when she was still Marilyn Novak. After the name change (Cohn originally wanted to call her

Kit Marlowe), Novak was less an actress than a deliberately manipulated product. Though her undeniable talent was seldom properly showcased, her films made big money for years. Early in *Lylah Clare*, Peter Finch refers to Elsa as "a piece of meat," a comment which echoes Harry Cohn's opinion of his creation. But the real Novak is a survivor; she wisely took the money and ran. Unlike Elsa, she was not destroyed by trying to maintain a dual persona.

Lylah Clare was followed by other beauteous female Hydes. In *Play Misty for Me* (1971) a mellow FM disc jockey (Clint Eastwood) is pestered with phone calls from a woman who seductively demands to hear Errol Garner's "Misty." The DJ is intrigued and makes the mistake of giving his caller mild encouragement. Jessica Walter played the Garner fan as a model of sweetness — for a while. As she insinuates herself into the DJ's life, her other side shows itself. Her demands become frequent and strident. She accosts Eastwood in person, and follows him home. When rebuffed, she slips over the edge and kidnaps the DJ's girlfriend (Donna Mills). An investigating police detective (John Larch) is stabbed to death with a butcher knife, and Eastwood — pursued through a dark beach house — is badly slashed. He seems defenseless against the fury of his admirer's illness until he tags the woman with a tremendous punch to the face which sends her out a window and to her death.

Play Misty for Me is an almost perfect thriller, made with craft and a lack of pretension by first-time director Eastwood. The role reversal is convincing because of Jessica Walter's beautifully considered performance; the fan is intimidating because she's so *reasonable*. The DJ has come into her home through the radio, warmly and with affection. The woman feels as though she knows him. Surely there can be no doubt as to romance. It is the tender art of the schizophrenic, this magical transformation of the impossible into the oh-so-logical.

Sexual longing, some films suggest, can turn women into terrifying juggernauts. The premise was amusingly twisted in 1972 when Hammer Studios — ever on the lookout for titillating variations on established themes — released *Dr. Jekyll and Sister Hyde*. Jekyll (Ralph Bates) is a quiet researcher who discovers that life can be prolonged with a serum derived from female hormones. A fly Jekyll has experimented on lives to a ripe old age, but also becomes female. Predictably, Jekyll samples the serum and turns into Hyde, a knife-happy woman (Martine Beswick) who murders other ladies in order to make more serum. The film's premise lent itself to a certain amount of jokiness; director Roy Ward Baker had fun with a scene in which Jekyll forgets himself and makes a pass at a man who had expressed an interest in Ms. Hyde. The facial configurations of Ralph Bates and Martine Beswick were quite similar so, in a physical sense, the film is convincing. Beswick, a beautiful actress in the Barbara Steele mold, was both seductive and maniacally bloodthirsty. Clever too, for Hyde sees to it that her murders are blamed on Jack the Ripper, another notable schizophrenic from the Victorian era.

The Ripper terrorized London's East End in the autumn of 1888, killing at least five prostitutes and dissecting four of them with surgical precision. Mocking notes and poetry were sent to the police after two or three of the killings; one package contained a victim's kidney. Jack, whoever he may have been, was not an unintelligent man. Some authorities theorize that, because Jack was able to get close to prostitutes, he was a gentleman of means. One audacious source (Frank Spiering: *Prince Jack*, 1978) claims that the Ripper was Albert Victor, homosexual grandson of Queen Victoria. In any case, Jack loathed women, and gave special care to the mutilation of the sexual organs of some of his victims. He almost certainly walked the daylit streets unsuspected. It is both fitting and ironic that Stevenson published *Dr. Jekyll and Mr. Hyde* just two years before Jack's reign of terror. By the time Marie Belloc-Lowndes published her novel *The Lodger* in 1913, the Ripper had become a perverse figure of folklore. Films like Paul Leni's expressionist *Three Wax Men* (1924) utilized Jack in grotesque dream sequences. Two plays by Frank Wedekind—*Erdgeist* ("Death Spirit") and *Der Buchse der Pandora*—inspired three films in which the heroine is joltingly murdered at the climax by Jack: *Erdgeist* (1923), G.W. Pabst's *Pandora's Box* (1929; starring the stunning and unforgettable Louise Brooks), and *Lulu* (1962). Of these, Pabst's masterpiece is the most provocative, as it depicts its amoral, murdered heroine as a martyr to her own unfettered hedonism.

Belloc-Lowndes' *The Lodger*, which supposes that a quiet young man who takes a room in a boarding house is the mad killer, was adapted first in 1926 by Alfred Hitchcock, and again in 1932. Both of the films were set in modern times, and revolved around an innocent man (Ivor Novello, in each) who is mistaken for the Ripper. It was not until the 1944 Hollywood version that Jack's milieu was properly Victorian. Director John Brahm abandoned the business of mistaken identity and found a brilliantly understated Jack in Laird Cregar, a bulky young American character actor who began specializing in middle-aged villains while still in his early twenties. *The Lodger* catapulted him to stardom, but he died the year the film was released, at age 27. Cregar's conception of the Ripper was influenced by modern psychology; director Brahm focused heavily upon the actor's face—particularly his dark eyes—and captured the terror of schizophrenia when the lodger's features shift oddly from tranquility to pain. The Ripper's savagery and bulk suggest animalism, a quality that is emphasized by repeated shots of the killer lurking behind windows or crisscrossed in shadow, as though caged. His victims are not prostitutes but actresses. Barré Lyndon's script allowed that Jack is motivated by a desire to avenge the death of his brother, who was driven to suicide by a lady of the theatre.

Cregar's next film, *Hangover Square* (1945), is similar in its depiction of a dual personality. Cregar was cast as a brilliant pianist whose schizoid nature is released by loud noises. His victims, mostly female, meet messy ends. In one memorable sequence, the pianist disposes of a body in the middle of the street by placing it atop a huge celebratory bonfire that has been set for Guy

Laird Cregar's definitive Jack the Ripper in *The Lodger* (1944); the landlady is Sara Allgood.

Fawkes' Day. The film's climax is no less audacious, as the mad pianist pounds out his final concerto amid the smoke and rubble of a burning house.

Cregar's conception of sexual madness may have been definitive, but filmmakers hardly turned their backs on the Ripper. Jack escapes from a mental institution and rents from a crippled widow in *Room to Let* (1950), and turned up in the person of Jack Palance in 1953's *Man in the Attic*. The 1966 *A Study in Terror* is a clever pastiche, in which the Ripper is pitted against the skill of Sherlock Holmes. The unambiguously titled *Jack the Ripper* (1960) is an uncredited adaptation of *The Lodger*; this time, Jack (Ewen Solon) is a surgeon who murders prostitutes because one had driven his son to suicide. Apparently, the working girls just couldn't win, no matter *who* they fooled around with.

Nicholas Meyer's imaginative and romantic *Time After Time* (1979) is the most notable recent incarnation of Jack. In it, H.G. Wells (Malcolm

The thoroughly deadly Ripper (David Warner) threatens Mary Steenburgen in Nicholas Meyer's *Time After Time* (1979).

McDowell) demonstrates his fabulous time machine to a friend, Dr. John Stevenson (David Warner). Soon afterward, constables stop at Wells' home inquiring about a murdered prostitute. Bloodied gloves are found in Stevenson's bag: he is Jack the Ripper. He escapes in the time machine and—after a homing device returns the machine to 1888—Wells sets out after him. The remainder of the film is colorfully played out in 1979 San Francisco. Writer/director Meyer offered some amusing variations on the expected time-travel gags (Wells' puzzlement over jets, hot pants, and McDonald's french fries), and created a charming romance between the inventor and Amy, a quirky young bank officer played with dark-eyed ingenuousness by Mary Steenburgen. Stevenson exchanges currency at Amy's bank, then kidnaps her after discovering her relationship with Wells. The Ripper has already savaged a number of San Francisco women—Amy's innocent friend among them—and is on the verge of killing Amy, too, when the girl wrenches from his grasp. Wells yanks a vital component from the machine and exiles Stevenson to timelessness.

    Time After Time is one of the few genuinely romantic American films of the late seventies. It is an indictment of violence and cynicism, and a celebration of love. Wells—dry and faintly ascetic—is at first taken aback by Amy's forwardness, but falls for her honesty and sweetness. She is charmed by his "little boy lost" quality. Stevenson becomes the disruptive element: devious and thoroughly deadly. His misspent sexual passion seems all the more pernicious because it is directed at Amy, a person we come to know and like. Her benign purposefulness makes her the antithesis of the Ripper. Wells, by nature and circumstance, must abhor his former friend. The film boils down to a struggle of philosophies: visceral action vs. gentle comtemplativeness. Stevenson gives 1979 a cursory examination and decides that it mirrors his personality perfectly. In a scene that is only slightly overstated, the killer flips through a television's channel selector, reveling in images of war, pro football, and violent rock music. He sneers at Wells' piety by crowing, "I *belong* here." To be sure, Stevenson adapts, at least superficially. He sports swinger's threads and learns how to maneuver in the city's gaudy nightlife. But he never really *connects* with anyone; he's doomed to be a free-floater, and that is what makes him vulnerable. Unlike Wells, he does not have the special strength of love.

The violent hedonism of Hyde and the Ripper has been reflected in another significant figure: Dorian Gray. Oscar Wilde's novel *The Picture of Dorian Gray* was published in 1891. The title character is a wealthy London dilettante who accepts a portrait from a friend. Aloud, Gray wishes that his life of pleasure could continue indefinitely, his portrait aging instead of he. The wish is granted and Gray embarks upon a spree of lust and cruelty. His callousness drives a lover and a close friend to suicide, and enmeshes him in blackmail. He grows no older, but his portrait shows the ravages of his activities, becoming an image of decay and horror. Gray finally goes over the deep end, stabbing the painter of the portrait, then stabbing the picture with the same knife. Instantly, Gray's sins catch up with him. His beautiful facade ages and falls to ruin, while the portrait becomes a thing of youthful attractiveness.

Albert Lewin wrote and directed a splendidly-mounted adaptation in 1945. Though the novel had inspired moviemakers as early as 1910, Lewin's version was the most literal, and the first to make use of Technicolor (reserved for glimpses of the horrid portrait). Hurd Hatfield played Gray with fine arrogance, while Angela Lansbury made an impressive screen debut as an innocent chorus girl who is victimized by Gray.

An R-rated Italian version of the story called *The Secret Life of Dorian Gray* arrived in 1971, costarring Helmut Berger and porn princess Marie Lijedahl. As if to atone for offering frequent glimpses of naked women, the filmmakers turned Gray into a late-blooming moralist who commits suicide after realizing the depths of his depravity. Some of us were not convinced by this change of heart.

In the sound era, variations on Wilde's theme have been inspired more by Barré Lyndon's play *The Man in Half Moon Street* than by Wilde's novel.

The play concerns a debaucher named Georges Bonner who maintains his youth with periodic glandular implants. Problems arise because the glands must come from living people. Nils Asther starred in a literal Hollywood adaptation in 1944, while Anton Diffring was featured in a 1959 British version called *The Man Who Could Cheat Death*. In both films, the cheating was strictly short-lived. Diffring was very lively as Bonner, romancing the daughter (Hazel Court) of a prominent surgeon, then kidnapping the girl when her father refuses to commit murder in order to obtain the glands. The surgeon (Christopher Lee) is forced to capitulate, but only pretends to perform the operation. Bonner withers and dies mere moments after releasing his captive.

The Hydes, Rippers, and Grays act more or less from free will, but what about the tormented werewolves? These miserable souls, once stricken, are doomed to walk as normal men by day, and stalk as beasts beneath the full moon of night. Furry, snarling, and nearly always male, they are masculinity carried to an outrageous extreme. *Werewolf of London* (1935) was one of the earliest Hollywood films about werewolfdom; as such, it is ponderous and self-important. Wilfrid Glendon (Henry Hull) is attacked by a strange beast in the mountains of Tibet. Upon his return to London, Glendon is transformed by the light of the full moon into a werewolf. He murders a woman on the foggy streets, and nearly kills his own wife (Valerie Hobson) before being cut down by police. Probably the most interesting aspect of *Werewolf of London* is its development of werewolfism as an expression of sexual jealousy; the monster's attack on his wife comes after he sees her strolling with a childhood sweetheart. Henry Hull's makeup, designed by Jack Pierce to be light and easily applied since the actor would not tolerate long sessions in the makeup chair, is also noteworthy. With its belligerent fangs and dramatic widow's peak, the design is one of Pierce's finest.

The definitive werewolf film is *The Wolf Man* (1941), upon which Universal lavished a great deal of care. The studio hoped that the film's star, Lon Chaney, Jr., would develop into as hot a property as his father. The younger Chaney did not, but *The Wolf Man* enjoyed box office success and entered the national consciousness. Not surprisingly, the film's sexual content is muted. Director George Waggner and writer Curt Siodmak took pains to establish that Larry Talbot's (Chaney) attacks on women are not motivated by lust, but by the irresistible fury which is a symptom of lycanthropy. Talbot does not enjoy his impolite affliction, nor does he revel in his evil. In fact, he is not evil at all. Wise old gypsy woman Maria Ouspenskaya sums it up well: "The way you walk is thorny through no fault of your own." Talbot is a victim. His death at the hands of his father (Claude Rains) is not punishment, but blessed liberation. Although *Werewolf of London* had flirted with the idea of a werewolf as a sympathetic character, the point of view was not fully articulated until *The Wolf Man*. Chaney professed love for the character, calling it his "baby." More significantly, Larry Talbot is pop culture's fuzziest tragic hero.

The brilliant makeup that Jack Pierce created for *The Wolf Man* was an image that Universal and Hollywood were loath to abandon. Larry Talbot was resurrected for four more films, while other studios ground out variations of their own. By the time Universal featured the Wolf Man in *Abbott and Costello Meet Frankenstein* in 1948, the public had finally tired of boo-hooing for Talbot and his hirsute counterparts. Werewolfism went into remission. The fifties brought "space age" spinoffs like *The Neanderthal Man* (1953) and *Monster on the Campus* (1958), curious combinations of lycanthropy and the Jekyll/Hyde story. By the early sixties, the werewolf film seemed nearly extinct. Examples were few but notable. Hammer's *Curse of the Werewolf* (1961) starred Oliver Reed as Leon, a werewolf born of a deaf-mute serving girl who had been brutally raped by an insane, animalistic beggar. The baby Leon causes holy water to boil at his christening, and, as a little boy, attacks sheep in the fields. When a wolf is shot by villagers, Leon writhes in sympathetic anguish. His affliction is discovered by his stepfather, who hopes that a loving home life will cure the boy. Leon grows into manhood without further incident, but reverts one evening in the sordid atmosphere of a brothel. He slaughters a friend and a young woman. His only solace is his pretty fiancée (Catherine Feller), but Leon must flee from her when he feels the change coming on again. Trapped on a rooftop by villagers, Leon pleads with his stepfather to shoot him with the silver bullet Leon knows he carries. His stepfather unhappily obliges.

Curse of the Werewolf offered the first sexy wolf man. Roy Ashton's marvelous makeup design covered Oliver Reed's face and hunky torso with silky blond fur. It's a bet that young ladies in the audience wanted to hug him as much as run away from him. The film is also the first to forcibly link werewolfism with aberrant sexuality. Given the circumstances of Leon's conception, he seems doomed from the start. Small wonder that his savagery is awakened by the ambience of a brothel.

The Spanish weightlifter-cum-actor Paul Naschy dabbled with sexy werewolves in the seventies, but not until Joe Dante's *The Howling* and John Landis' *An American Werewolf in London* (both 1981) did lycanthropes become downright erotic. In the former film, werewolfism is studied at a retreat called The Colony, where lycanthropes are counseled in ways of expressing themselves that are more genteel than chewing on humans. Unfortunately, some of the patients prefer the old ways: "Screw all this 'channel your energy' crap!" shouts old werewolf John Carradine; "I want to bite somebody!" Dante and screenwriters John Sayles and Terence H. Winkless were careful to preserve familiar genre elements like foggy nights, eerie hoots and howls, and plenty of moonlight. The film is littered with wolfish in-jokes: Alan Ginsberg's *Howl* lies on a desk, a psychiatrist is named Dr. Waggner (after the director of *The Wolf Man*), and droning television sets show Disney wolf cartoons and clips of Lon Chaney, Jr.

The wit in *The Howling* is clever enough but awfully unfocused. The gags don't really lead anywhere. One element that does work beautifully is Dante's exploration of the sex habits of the werewolf set. Dark-eyed Elisabeth Brooks played a particularly sultry lycanthrope; a moonlit mating sequence in which she and a lover undergo the transformation while coupling on a beach is at once horrid and starkly erotic. Rob Bottin's startling makeup effects are accompanied by all manner of orgasmic gasps, groans, and snarls. In essence, Dante's love for the genre did not inhibit his vision. *The Howling* is a new and thoroughly fresh interpretation of familiar elements.

John Landis' *An American Werewolf in London* arrived the same year as *The Howling*. While the films are superficially similar, *American Werewolf* is more subversive because it purposely *explodes* the genre conventions that *The Howling* merely stretches. David Naughton played an American student named David who is tramping across England with a friend, Jack. On a foggy moor, the two are attacked by a snarling beast which seriously injures David and kills his friend. While in the hospital David falls for a pretty nurse (Jenny Agutter), but is plagued with guilt and hideous dreams. He imagines, among other things, that he stalks naked through the forest, hunting small game and eating it raw. In a particularly inventive touch, the spectre of his mangled friend Jack pops up to advise him that the creature that attacked them was a werewolf, and that David will become one at the next full moon.

Griffin Dunne played Jack with a self-deprecating wit that is a clever approach to problems of exposition. Not only did Landis utilize a corpse to set up the film's premise, he also turned said corpse into a viable and amusing character. Still, with his ravaged face hanging from his skull in shreds, Jack is a bit difficult for David — and the audience — to deal with. By his third visit he has decomposed so badly that he is barely more than a bright-eyed mummy.

David's romance with the nurse develops with disarming wit and a fair amount of eroticism. The couple caress in the shower after David has been discharged from the hospital, and enjoy each other's company in bed. But David still dreams, this time of the girl being slaughtered by monsters. As is probably apparent, the film's tone varies wildly, almost uncomfortably. Light, ad-lib banter in some scenes gives way to hideous violence in others. The picture puts us on a seesaw and keeps us there. Creedence Clearwater Revival's bouncy "Bad Moon Rising" throbs from the soundtrack moments before David turns into a wolf for the first time. Rick Baker's Oscar-winning special makeup effects and Naughton's lusty shrieking make for the most convincing transformation yet seen. For the first time, moviegoers saw the sheer physical torment in the change of man into beast. Muscles grind, joints pop, and bone and cartilage crack. Fangs, claws, and a snout are grown. David becomes a snarling, muscled quadruped (another nice break with tradition), and stalks off to slaughter innocent people. Though David has no memory of his activities, he feels marvelously alive the following morning. He can hardly wait to carry his new girlfriend to bed. Killing, then, is established as a sexual turn-on, an aphrodisiac of the most primal sort. Like the previous screen

The agony before the ecstasy: David Naughton becomes *An American Werewolf in London* (1981).

werewolves, David has our sympathy (we know that he will die because Jack tells him that he must), but there is an aura of youthful revelry that removes much of the sting. According to Landis, werewolfism is a curse not because it is intrinsically evil, but because the physical pleasures it provides are short-lived and come at the expense of other people. When Jack tells David that a werewolf can be killed only by someone who loves him, the film seems to be setting us up for an ironic but appropriate conclusion. But Landis inexplicably settled for an anticlimactic ending in which David (in wolf form) is gunned down by police after an apocalyptic rampage amid the traffic and neon of Piccadilly Circus. The girl is qualified only to sob over his body. *An American Werewolf in London* is as schizophrenic as its protagonist. Some critics objected to the film's sass (in one scene David is visited by the mangled bodies of his dead victims, who cheerily suggest ways in which he might commit suicide), but audiences appreciated its energy and irreverence. Part homage, part spoof, it shrewdly cushions the shocks with laughter.

Less traditional variations on the theme of dual personality can get pretty perverse. In *Dr. X* (1932) Preston Foster played Professor Wells, a handsome but one-armed researcher whose experiments with "synthetic flesh" allow him to create a new arm useful for strangling women and eating portions of their brains. The murders occur only when Wells is driven mad by the power of the full moon. In the fashion of the day, the film is full of red herrings, latent schizos who are likely suspects. One of the scientists at Wells' lab is fascinated with the effects of the moon, while two others are former shipwreck victims who resorted to cannibalism in order to survive. Wells cannot resist when Dr. Xavier (Lionel Atwill) uses his daughter (Fay Wray) as bait in an attempt to trap the murderer. Stealing to his laboratory, Wells withdraws his synthetic arm from behind a secret panel, charges it with electricity, and fits it to his stump with all the glee of an impotent man trying out a new sex organ. The innocent girl is nearly killed, but is rescued by a reporter who throws a kerosene lamp at Wells, ending his double life.

One of Peter Lorre's most powerful roles was the surgeon Gogol in Karl Freund's *Mad Love*. This 1935 adaptation of Maurice Renard's novel *The Hands of Orlac* revolves around a concert pianist (Colin Clive) who has lost his hands in a terrible train accident. Orlac's musical career seems ruined until he is treated by the brilliant Gogol, who sews to Orlac's wrists the healthy hands of an executed killer. The film proceeds to detail the psychological deterioration of surgeon *and* patient: Gogol becomes obsessed with Orlac's wife (Frances Drake), while Orlac is gradually possessed by the spirit of the dead murderer. Gogol displays a replica of Mrs. Orlac in his home and hopes that, like Pygmalion's Galatea, the statue will come to life. He perceives the obstacle posed by Orlac, and contrives to drive him mad. In the film's most chilling sequence, the pianist is visited by a disguised Gogol, whose round face is obscured by dark glasses and an oversized hat. Gogol claims to be the unwilling donor of Orlac's new hands, and lifts a pair of gleaming glass and metal claws to make his point. Orlac counters that the visit is an impossibility, that the donor was executed, his head cut off. Gogol drops his cloak to reveal a hideous leather brace around his neck and upper chest. "It *was*," he says, "but Dr. Gogol sewed it back on." When Gogol is visited later by Orlac's wife, he believes she is the statue come to life. The woman resists his advances, and Gogol is killed by Orlac, who uses his murderer's hands to perfectly throw a knife.

Orlac's new hands raise some very provocative psychosexual considerations. The pianist's plight is a sort of castration, and the surgical solution seems terribly dubious. We are not surprised that Orlac's keyboard technique has suffered, but we are compelled to wonder, for instance, about his *lovemaking* technique. Are murderers less skilled at foreplay than other men? Perhaps. Orlac is undeniably a miserable fellow. Like Gogol, he is directed by an insiduous force he cannot control. The love triangle he is enmeshed in does not involve three personalities, but five.

Mad Love was Peter Lorre's first American film. He had caused an international sensation four years earlier in Fritz Lang's brilliant *M*, in which he played a moon-faced pervert who kills children after seducing them with sweets. Lorre's skill at suggesting dual personality ("I can't help myself!" he screams in *M*. "I haven't any control over this evil thing that's inside me — the fire, the voices, the torment!") made him the ideal choice to play the demented Gogol. Pudgy and owl-eyed, his head shaved bald, Lorre brought a faintly repellent androgynous quality to the role. Gogol seems caught in a sexual trap. His brilliance as a surgeon has done nothing to enrich his personal life. In reinforcement of his schizophrenia, he speaks to his mirror image and laments, "I, a poor peasant, have conquered science. Why can't I conquer love?" Gogol's desires have driven him mad. It is to the credit of director Karl Freund that *Mad Love* does not become a distateful burlesque. Freund's experience as a top cinematographer helped him maintain the film's peculiar tone without lapse. Though eccentric, *Mad Love* is also laudably consistent. Because it so stylishly suggests that evil desires and unfulfilled sexuality can be expressed in deadly splits of personality, the film remains one of the most singular creations of the sound era.

A similar story was tricked up with nudity and gore in Oliver Stone's *The Hand* (1981), which cast Michael Caine as a comic strip cartoonist whose drawing hand is severed in a freak auto accident. The hand cannot be relocated. Stone's script milks the castration metaphor dry: the cartoonist's strip (which revolves around a macho barbarian) is taken over by another artist, his marriage crumbles, and he takes a passive teaching job at a second-rate junior college. His affair with an unambitious coed is something less than scintillating. When people close to the cartoonist are murdered, he is convinced that the culprit is his disembodied — but still living — hand. One dark evening, the hand has the temerity to attack its former owner; the scenes of Michael Caine strangling himself stretch the limits of credibility, so Stone was quick to suggest that the cartoonist is the killer, and that the hand exists only in his mind. Sounds reasonable, and after therapy the cartoonist seems willing to believe it, too. But in the picture's final scene, the hand creeps from nowhere and strangles a smug female psychiatrist while the cartoonist watches from across the room. Hallucination? Reality? Does anybody still care?

Horror buffs are still ecstatic about Louis Friedlander's *The Raven* (1935), a sublime teaming of Bela Lugosi and Boris Karloff. Lugosi played Dr.

Vollin, a plastic surgeon with equal lusts for the works of Poe and a lovely young patient (Irene Ware) who has been slightly injured in a car crash. When the woman's father rudely informs Vollin that his daughter is engaged, the surgeon reveals his madness. He is not a selfless benefactor, but a sexual psychotic whose isolated home bristles with Poe-like torture devices, including a razor-sharp pendulum and crushing walls. Vollin disfigures an escaped convict named Bateman (Karloff) and extorts a promise of assistance in his pursuit of the girl. Bateman agrees but has a change of heart when the girl's father is about to be sliced by the pendulum. At this, Vollin loses all control, mortally wounding the convict and trapping the girl and her fiancée in the crushing room. Vollin's psyche is as twisted a thing as Bateman's face; he will gladly destroy the girl if he cannot possess her. But the dying Bateman intervenes, freeing the captives and crushing Vollin between the moving walls.

The Raven features Bela Lugosi at the height of his powers. Sleek, cultured, and thoroughly elegant, his Dr. Vollin may be the screen's sexiest schizo. The film was a big hit in America, but raised some eyebrows in England, where American horror films were banned altogether in 1937. Dr. Vollin's excesses aside, the disturbed protagonists of other films are often engaged in professions that, if not ordinary, certainly seem benign. *The Great Gabbo* (1930) was Erich von Stroheim (in his first talkie), a ventriloquist who forms an unhealthy attachment to his dummy. He destroys the little wooden man when it seems on the verge of destroying *him*, only to realize that his life without the dummy is empty and loveless. The obsessed ventriloquist quickly became a stock figure of the horror cinema. Michael Redgrave's performance in one segment of the splendid anthology film *Dead of Night* (1946) is the most celebrated example, but the most sexual was provided by Anthony Hopkins in Richard Attenborough's *Magic* (1978).

Hopkins played Corky, a successful ventriloquist who rekindles a romance with a now-married woman (Ann-Margret). Corky is unhappy about his adultery, and his guilt is exacerbated by the lewd goading of his dummy, Fats. Corky's deterioration worsens to the point of the dummy becoming the dominant personality. Possessed, the ventriloquist severely beats his manager (Burgess Meredith) and stabs the cuckolded husband. At the conclusion, Corky no longer exists — Fats has conquered all. As can be gleaned from this quick summation, *Magic*'s narrative is pretty familiar stuff. Whatever effectiveness the film has is due to its relentlessly nasty tone, and a sweatily convincing performance by Hopkins. Only one nagging question remains: precisely what does little wooden Fats plan to do with voluptuous Ann-Margret? If we're lucky, we'll never find out.

In Irvin Kershner's glossy and soulless *Eyes of Laura Mars* (1978), Faye Dunaway is Laura, a celebrated fashion photographer who is tormented with visions of brutal murders that bear uncanny resemblance to her kinky photo sessions. Clues suggest that Laura may be responsible without being aware of it. Kershner and writer John Carpenter (whose original script, reportedly, was greatly altered) took full advantage of the freedom of an R-rating, littering the screen with trashily exploitative views of underclothed, mascaraed models in their death throes. The unhappy photographer falls in love with an earthy police detective (Tommy Lee Jones) who, surprise! turns out to be the crazed killer. Laura may be a low-grade talent, but at least she's not a Jekyll/Hyde. The cop's motivation remains unclear but, what the heck, he slobbers *real* good.

Eyes of Laura Mars is effective only in isolated moments. Its soft-core approach to sexuality may have been devastatingly trendy, but only heightened the film's hypocritical point of view. We are supposed to be shocked by the murders, yet there is a pernicious suggestion that the exhibitionistic victims "deserve it." Their naked corpses are displayed for no reason but our satisfaction and amusement. Further, we are asked to empathize with the miserable photographer, even as we are (a) titillated, or (b) shocked (take your pick) by her brand of porno-chic. The film's approach is so brainlessly callous and confused that we don't know whether to scream or cheer when the schizo detective reveals himself. Is his repressed side truly villainous, or is society going to benefit if he disposes of Ms. Mars? Clearly, the filmmakers themselves did not care, and neither did audiences: *Eyes of Laura Mars* died a quick death at the box office. Mr. Hyde would have approved.

Laura Mars was the product of a studio system that had looked with envy at the commercial success of low-grade thrillers made on the cheap outside the Hollywood mainstream. A quasi-underground had been offering drive-in and urban audiences blood 'n' guts and naked girlies for years. Since the early sixties, sensationalism and visceral terror had meant fat profits. In the mid-seventies, horror fiction spawned a superstar author named Stephen King, whose novel *The Shining* became a best seller in 1977. The book had gore, sex, and arresting central characters. Warner Brothers smacked its lips, bought the rights, and set out to create a "legitimate" hybrid of pulp horror, Hollywood high-gloss, and art. *This* time a terror film was going to be sure-fire because Stanley Kubrick—who had made his name with acclaimed pictures like *2001: A Space Odyssey, Dr. Strangelove,* and *A Clockwork Orange*—would write and direct. It seemed that art and commerce would be served in equal measure.

The story of Jack Torrance—a schizophrenic teacher who assumes caretaker's duties at an isolated hotel and is driven mad by the hotel's evil spirits—brings Jekyll and Hyde into the modern world. King's novel brims with squirming horror and clever set pieces, but its primary strength is the beautifully constructed tensions within the relationships of the central characters: the alcoholic Torrance; his wife Wendy; their young son Danny; and a sympathetic outsider, Halloran, the Negro cook who perceives Danny's precognitive powers, his "shining." The family is tense and worn out because of Jack's failed jobs, frustrated writing career, and history of alcoholic violence. The caretaker's job is Jack's last-ditch attempt to salvage himself. But

Jack Nicholson and Shelley Duvall in Stanley Kubrick's stylish but overblown *The Shining* (1980).

the Overlook Hotel has murder in its past, and is the last place Torrance should be. Though he struggles mightly to resist the hotel's encouragement of the depraved side of his personality, he finally succumbs and nearly murders his wife and child. The Overlook's victory is hollow, however, for the boiler that Torrance should have been tending reaches its limits and explodes, destroying the Overlook.

The Shining (1980) was among the most eagerly awaited films of the last twenty years. Before it was released, a number of critics complained of its "pulp novel" origins, the implication being that no horror novel can be any good but, don't worry, Stanley Kubrick can fix anything. This blindness to the book's powerful virtues was apparently shared by Kubrick, who chose to ignore King's boiler metaphor, and a lot of other elements which could have made Nicholson's Torrance a believable and sympathetic character. Worse, Kubrick allowed Nicholson to overact shamelessly: Torrance capers, chuckles, pouts, and simpers. Attempts at domestic horror ("Honey, I'm home!" Jack cheerfully exclaims as he smashes through a door with an axe) are undercut by overuse, and become sick parodies of *I Love Lucy*. This isn't horror, it's a baggy-pants burlesque of it. Audiences laughed out loud. Torrance's descent into madness—a slow slide in the novel—becomes an inexplicable headlong dash in the film. There is no time for us to relate to Jack as a real person before he is off and drooling.

The film's greatest success is its development of sexual tension. Big-eyed Shelley Duvall brought a skittish, painfully vulnerable quality to Wendy, who becomes a classic victim. We realize through common sense and implication that her sex life with Jack is nil. He blames her for his failures. In Jack's eyes, Wendy is no longer a wife or playmate or supporter but an adversary, a living reminder of his misery. She knows his secrets, and Jack's insanity will not allow him to share his secrets with anyone. The answer, to Jack, is obvious: Wendy must be destroyed.

The duality of Danny (Danny Lloyd) is developed with similar success. The boy's precognitive powers are embodied in a separate personality, an invisible friend named Tony who periodically takes control of the boy and "tells" him of the horrors to come. The disquietude in this instance of duality is not linked with evil, but with the boy's youth. Not only is he unable to act upon the things Tony has shown him, he can't even *absorb* them. His most hideous vision—a naked old lady submerged in a bathtub—is a profound emotional and sexual affront. The boy understands that danger is posed by the hotel and his father, but can do nothing about it.

Visually, *The Shining* is masterfully realized. Certain sequences are brilliant: the nubile goddess who rises naked from her bath to embrace Torrance, only to turn into a decayed crone in his grasp; low-level Steadicam shots of the boy pedaling his trike through the hotel, the wheels silent on carpet, then suddenly noisy on hardwood; and Wendy's discovery of her husband's attempts at writing, page after page of the idiot epigram "All work and no play makes Jack a dull boy." These are brilliant moments from a brilliant auteur, and one can only wish that Kubrick had come to grips with his protagonist with as much assurance. A banal revelation at the conclusion of the film suggests that Kubrick did not find horror a congenial genre; certainly, he seems to have been unaware of the vital importance of a protagonist with whom the audience can identify. The failure of *The Shining* is painfully frustrating. The Overlook, unfortunately, has been the victim of mismanagement.

What is perhaps the most potent dual personality horror film ever made may not, at first glance, seem to be a horror film at all. Admittedly, Martin Scorsese's *Taxi Driver* (1976) is set in a familiar urban environment. It is not a costume film, nor does it have a werewolf or a mad scientist. But by the time cabbie Travis Bickle (Robert DeNiro) storms a tenement building, slaughters every man inside, and rescues a preteen prostitute—all because his original plan to assassinate a Presidential candidate has been thwarted—there is no doubt that, yes, *Taxi Driver* is a horror film. The picture arrived with relatively little fanfare, but quickly generated an astonishing level of controversy. Critics hailed its artistry, while groups representing parents and churches assailed its

Robert DeNiro in Martin Scorsese's *Taxi Driver* (1976).

queasy ambience and sickening violence. Like sex and death, *Taxi Driver* became a topic about which no one could be neutral.

Travis Bickle is a rootless, disaffected young man who pilots a cab through the grime of New York City. His life is an emotional vacuum, his city a place of brutalizing dehumanization. He must clean his cab's back seat of semen and blood every night. One passenger (Scorsese himself, in a marvelously edgy performance) asks him, "Do you know what a .44 magnum will do to a woman's pussy?" In a delicatessen, Travis dispassionately shoots a young holdup man, then steps aside as the owner finishes the job with a tire iron. His daily journal (shared with us via voice-over) is a chronicle of frustration, ennui, and mounting range. Because he cannot sleep, Travis spends his days watching grainy, ugly sex movies in 42nd Street porno houses. He becomes attracted to Betsy (Cybill Shepherd), a cool, blonde political campaign worker, but takes her to one of his porno palaces on their first date. The woman stalks from the theater in a fury, and Travis soon shifts his attentions to a 12-year-old hooker named Iris. Jodie Foster played Iris with a calculated insouciance that conveys a heartbreaking vulnerability. She is funny, tough, and forever lost.

Travis wants Iris to get away from the ugliness: "Go home and date boys," he suggests, but how *can* she, this 12-year-old who specializes in masturbating her clients? But Travis looks at Iris and sees his own lost innocence. He resolves to make a statement; his journal becomes a tract of frightening megalomania. Now we know: beneath Travis' cool exterior lurks a hopeless psychotic. Bristling with guns at a political rally, he comes close to carrying out an assassination before being chased off by the Secret Service. On impulse, he storms the tenement out of which Iris and her handlers operate. Travis is wounded in a ferocious exchange of gunfire, but manages to maim and kill three or four men. As Iris sobs in the background, Travis tries to kill himself, but cannot. His guns are empty. In a chilling coda, Iris' father (in halting voice-over) tells Travis of his gratitude at the return of his daughter. As we listen, Scorsese's camera slowly pans over the walls of Travis' apartment, upon which have been tacked numerous newspaper clippings. One describes Travis as the "Cab Driver Hero."

The irony implicit in Paul Schrader's powerful and insightful screenplay was lost on many people. Scorsese was accused of glorifying violence, when in fact he was condemning its glorification. The film's tawdry sexuality was roundly criticized, even as Scorsese lamented the death of romance. Travis Bickle is a split personality, all right: he represents the schizophrenia of our nation. He feels victimized by a society which applauds violent solutions to complex problems. Without the capacity to give or receive love, his emotional and sexual frustrations fester. He retreats inside himself. Real life isn't real anymore — Travis becomes motivated by fantasy. Iris is in no sense evil, but neither is she the wayward little princess Travis would like her to be. When she has breakfast with him she says, "You're funny." If she only knew how much at odds his glibness and quirky sense of humor are with the deadened monotone that recites the journal. Travis brims with passion, lust, and tenderness, but the world has made him forget how to properly express such feelings. So he fantasizes and plans. In the celebrated "You talkin' to me?" scene he blusters and struts, threatening his mirror image. Neither the real Travis nor the one in the mirror is quite human. The shriveled Hyde-thing within him has flexed and grown until Travis is *brand new*: a Humbert Humbert imbued with deadly force, a mythic hero who is not fully born until the moment of bloody confrontation.

The carnage in the tenement is perhaps the most explicit and awful violence ever filmed, an excruciatingly prolonged descent into pure nightmare. All the demons that live inside of Travis erupt in this climactic sequence. The horror is heightened by a peculiar sense of ritual, as Travis shoots first, the enemy shoots back, Travis takes another turn, and on and on. The duel becomes an insane interpretation of the methodical destruction perpetrated by Laurel and Hardy in *Big Business*: each side taking proper turns and being terribly patient, but annihilating one another, nonetheless. That Travis' attempt at suicide fails is proper. There is no call for his death. His act of violence, in purging him, inspires sexual metaphor: Travis has shot his wad. Though his demons will likely return, Travis has made his statement. He fits in at last. New York applauds him. He hasn't been merely victimized by his city, he's been absorbed — ingested. Travis is Mr. Hyde and Dorian Gray and the Ripper rolled into one, and he's walking right next to you, grinning.

Are you grinning back?

III

Dangerous Curves:
The Perils of Sexuality

When quickie producer Sam Katzman put together a ratty compilation of scenes from old Bela Lugosi movies in 1956, he unknowingly created an epitaph, not only for Lugosi (who would die later that year), but for the sleek, elegant sexual allure Lugosi had personified in the twenties and thirties. Katzman's film was called *Lock Up Your Daughters*, an embarrassingly blatant title for the assembled works of a horror star who had once enjoyed bags full of mail from adoring female fans. Lugosi was guilty of the lothario's only unpardonable sin: he grew old.

Bela Lugosi was a movie star, but he was also just a man. Like many of us — particularly many women — he was largely defined by his sexuality. He had flourished in a world that (in retrospect, at least) was a simpler, more innocent place than atomic-age 1956. His talent alone was not up to the task of carrying him into a graceful dotage. Like the aging cover girl who can no longer find work, like the secretary who is propositioned by her boss, and like the teenagers who stumble into premature marriage, Lugosi was victimized by his own sexuality.

Horror films made prior to World War II reflect sexual anxiety, but seldom with the disturbing ambivalence of much of the postwar product. The war was a disquieting lapse in the smooth, assured continuity of Western, and particularly American, culture. The six years of struggle and the final horror that exploded over Japan were too much to comfortably absorb. The good guys had won, but at what cost? Into what sort of new world had our politics and technology led us?

The movies came forward to exploit our fears. Sexuality, a staple element of the horror genre from day one, began to be reflected in increasingly disturbing ways. Horror movies began to tell us that there is a price to be paid for being a sexual creature in a dangerous, unfathomable world. The victimization of men and women was presented with new vigor. A generation's anxiety was reflected by a parade of monstrous females, and venal or careless men who abused women or were duped by a pretty face. The new approach was epitomized by a frightened girl being gnawed on by a giant bug, or by the deadliness of a scarred harridan whose self-appointed mission was to destroy men. Some men, determined not to be victimized, struck the first blow. In

Horrors of the Black Museum (1959), for instance, madman Michael Gough sends a pair of binoculars to a blonde lovely, whose eyes are put out when spring-loaded needles jump from the eyepieces. Horror cinema was selling paranoia, fifties-style. Joe McCarthy told us that our neighbor could be "one of them," while the movies showed us that terror can come in unexpected guises, and at unexpected moments.

The change was not without precedent. In Victor Halperin's *White Zombie* (1932), for example, a wicked Haitian voodoo priest named Legendre (Bela Lugosi) utilizes black magic so that a confederate can steal the innocent fiancée of another man. Madeline (Madge Bellamy) is mesmerized from afar during her wedding ceremony, and later falls dead. Legendre resurrects her as a blankly staring zombie. When the unscrupulous would-be lover Beaumont (Robert Frazer) expresses dismay at Madeline's condition, Legendre chuckles and captures Beaumont's image in wax, an act which reduces the man to babbling insensibility. Legendre seems invincible, but is eventually carried over to a precipice when Beaumont summons a last bit of will. Madeline revives and is reunited with her new husband.

White Zombie is a richly visual film that explores the consequences of sexual greed with a minimum of dialogue. Images like a poisoned rose that has been placed in the bride's bouquet, and Madeline herself standing dull and speechless in her wedding raiment, are at once horrible and poetic. Legendre's evil — unlike Beaumont's — is not sexually motivated. The voodoo priest brings death and misery for no reason except that he *enjoys* doing so.

Lugosi unexpectedly played a sympathetic (if violently inclined) hero in Edgar Ulmer's *The Black Cat* (1934), the first of the actor's momentous teamings with Boris Karloff. Lugosi appears as Dr. Verdegast, a cultured but driven man who lives only to avenge himself on Hjalmar Poelzig (Karloff), the perverse wartime traitor who built a fortune on the misery of Verdegast and countless others. A chance bus accident brings Verdegast and other travelers to Poelzig's intimidating Art Deco mansion. The two adversaries circle each other warily, but Verdegast explodes after learning that Poelzig had been married to his own former wife, whose dead body Poelzig has enshrined in a glass coffin. Worse, Poelzig's current wife is Verdegast's daughter! When Poelzig abducts an innocent young traveler (Jacqueline Wells) with the intention of sacrificing her to the Devil in an ornate Black Mass, Verdegast intervenes. He gleefully *skins* Poelzig alive, is mistakenly shot by the girl's lover, and finally blows up the house.

Lugosi's Verdegast seems restrained when contrasted with Karloff's conception of Poelzig, whose widow's peak, flaring eyebrows, black robes, and darkened lips identify him as a corrupt degenerate. The women in his life do not live for long. *The Black Cat* is perhaps the most outré horror film of its period. Ulmer's fondness for quasi-expressionism and heightened melodrama turn the film into a perversely clever comic strip.

Somewhat less bizarre sexual villainy is on view in Edward Sutherland's

Murders in the Zoo (1933), in which demented husband Lionel Atwill contrives to eliminate his wife's lovers by feeding them to wild animals. The lips of one unhappy victim are sewn together so that he cannot cry out. Another man is nibbled by a poisonous mamba. The wife (Kathleen Burke) receives her comeuppance when her husband shoves her into a crocodile pool. Though undeniably amusing (Atwill is splendidly nasty), *Murders in the Zoo* is hardly a thoughtful look at the perils of sexuality. Artistry was left to director Tod Browning, whose *Freaks* — though the object of a storm of controversy when it opened in 1932 — is a deceptively gentle story of love, loyalty, and bonding. It is also the prewar era's most chilling look at the abuses of sexuality. Browning had directed milestone films like *The Unholy Three* (1925) and *Dracula* (1931), demonstrating a flair for the grotesque that had been honed by experience as a circus performer. Visually, a number of his films (notably *Mark of the Vampire*, 1935) seem a bit stale today, but Browning's skill with setting and nuance of character has maintained his critical reputation.

The sideshow oddities of *Freaks* were the real thing: dwarves, pinheads, a legless boy, even pretty Siamese twins. To Browning's credit, his approach to these brave performers is never exploitative. He presented them as full human beings capable of as much warmth and dignity as anyone else. The grotesques of the story are a beautiful but heartless high-wire artist called Cleopatra (Olga Baclanova) and her physically impressive but dim consort, Hercules the Strongman (Henry Victor). They conspire to steal the fortune of midget Hans (Harry Earles), who is infatuated with the normal-sized Cleopatra. The woman encourages Hans' interest, accepts his pathetically tongue-tied proposal of marriage, then slowly poisons him. As Hans grows weaker, we see the way in which normal sexuality becomes monstrous and unconscionable when directed with malice towards another. Baclanova, a Russian dancer who made too few Hollywood films, is remarkable as Cleopatra; she is perhaps the most repellent beauty in cinema history. Because Hans looks like a little boy, Cleopatra's transparent advances seem all the more gross. Yet Browning made it clear that tiny Hans *is* a man, with a man's desires and vulnerability. Cleopatra's most profound crime is her refusal to acknowledge this.

The community of freaks is bound by loyalty; this is something else to which Cleopatra and Hercules remain oblivious. Hans' friends are aware of what the conspirators are up to, and their revenge is more heartening than horrifying. It has been conjectured by various writers that the strongman is emasculated at the climax of *Freaks*. The continuity of the sequence in existing prints is choppy, but such retribution does make for a good, if obvious, irony. More imaginative is the fate the freaks reserve for Cleopatra, who is stripped of all the obvious aspects of her sexuality and somehow transformed into an eyerolling chicken woman. The beautiful face has been cruelly scarred, the silky voice replaced with an improbable squawk. Her breasts have vanished in an expanse of feathered chest. Most hideously, her legs, the beautiful long

Harry Earles and Olga Baclanova in a publicity still from Tod Browning's *Freaks* (1932).

legs that excited Hans' desires and gave Cleopatra dominance over him, are gone all together.

Freaks caused MGM considerable embarrassment. Some prints carry an apologetic printed prologue. The picture was briefly issued as *Nature's Mistakes*, but was later pulled from release completely. It remained largely unseen until prints reappeared in the 1960s. Undeniably grotesque, the film can today be seen as a valuable examination of love's power to combat misspent sexuality. Tod Browning died in obscurity in 1962; one hopes that he would be pleased that his most deeply felt film continues to move, excite, and horrify.

The disturbing new slants to the battle between the sexes that began to be explored in the war years and after are epitomized by *The Cat People*, the moody 1942 classic by producer Val Lewton, writer De Witt Bodeen, and director Jacques Tourneur. Irena (Simone Simon) is a dark, seductively feline beauty who lives in dread of her eerie Balkan heritage. She cannot consummate her marriage because of her obsession with cats. When her husband (Kent Smith) becomes involved with another woman (Jane Randolph), Irena apparently reverts to a bestial state and unsuccessfully tries to kill her competition. Randolph's peril in a darkened indoor swimming pool is subtly frightening; the room is visited with peculiar noises and odd, jigging shadows. We do not clearly see Irena or the panther she believes she can become, but know that *something* pads around the perimeter of the pool, looking for a chance to strike. Later, Irena savages the psychiatrist (Tom Conway), who has stupidly tried to cure her "delusion" with lovemaking. Irena is wounded by her victim and dies with the big cats in a zoo.

The extent of Irena's power is suggested but never blatantly shown. If Lewton had had his way, no cat would have been seen at all, but RKO executives insisted upon a shadowy glimpse of a panther that glides through a room. Still, *The Cat People* is a gem of understatement. Irena—tormented not only by her peculiar talent but by an implied fear of sex—is among the more intriguingly ambivalent figures of the horror genre.

Francis L. Lyon's *Cult of the Cobra* (1955) is superficially similar to *The Cat People*, but more blatant. At the close of World War II, five G.I.'s unwittingly defile an Asian temple. The shape-shifting snake goddess who has been offended follows the soldiers to America and destroys them. The irony is that the victims go to their deaths almost willingly, for the vengeful goddess can assume the form of a beautiful woman. As played by Howard Hughes discovery Faith Domergue, the goddess' human form is every boy's masturbatory wish-dream: lush of figure and wet of mouth, with sultry dark eyes and a sibilant way with consonants. Her dresses and gowns are stunning. She sexually entices her victims, maintaining her human form until the lovemaking becomes so intense that the men cannot stop. At the last possible moment the disguise slips; awkward jump-cutting and shadow choreography suggest the transformation of woman to snake. The men fall out of windows or simply die of fright. Hey, kids, how's *that* for the realities of lovemaking?

Journey to the 7th Planet borrows from Ray Bradbury's short story "Mars is Heaven!" In this variation, astronauts exploring a strange planet discover idyllic villages and beautiful women. The men lower their guard, and realize almost too late that the plant is controlled by an evil intelligence that can create tangible images of the astronaut's fondest memories and desires. The women are worse than simply the tools of an alien intellect—they are the *projections* of that intellect and do not exist at all.

The disquieting juxtaposition of sex and death in Julian Roffman's *The Mask* (1961).

Likewise, the shapely temptresses of *The Mask* (1961) exist only in the hallucinations of madmen. The film was directed by a talented Canadian named Julian Roffman, and is a provocative piece of prepsychedelia. Its plot concerns an ornate Aztec mask that causes the wearer to hallucinate and commit murder. Roffman shot the hallucinatory sequences in 3-D, and the sight of thrusting skulls, daggers, and scantily-clad women is startling and bizarre. The film's equating of sex with death is handled with enough outré originality to be keenly disturbing. Roffman slipped into anonymity quickly, but *The Mask*, retitled *The Eyes of Hell*, continued to enjoy bookings in drive-ins and second-run houses as recently as 1977.

A fascinating subgenre that arose in the early fifties could be called the "cinema of lost women." A string of shoddy thrillers made primarily by independent producers celebrated the physical attributes and fiendish intellects of women who existed in societies bereft of men. *Queen of Outer Space* appeared in 1958, and concerns a Venusian (Zsa Zsa Gabor, truth!) who helps an expedition of Earthmen overthrow the planet's scarred, man-hating queen. When the stalwart spacemen are not menaced by giant spiders, they must contend with Venusian women, who look more like usherettes than extraterrestrials. (If the ladies loathe men, why do they wear heavy eye makeup, miniskirts, and spiked heels?) The masked queen (Laurie Mitchell) has vowed to destroy all men (and the planet Earth, while she's at it) because a man ruined her beauty. She has built something called the Beta Disintegrator, which looks like a huge cardboard box painted with polka dots. The weapon is precisely a smug male screenwriter's idea of the sort that would be created by a gaggle of insipid women. But even the most militant feminist, the film tells us, will abandon her principles if the nearest available male is sufficiently handsome. The queen comes on to hero Eric Fleming, but he will have none of it, and unmasks her before blowing up the Beta Disintegrator. The Venusian women die as virgins, Earth is saved, and Zsa Zsa Gabor returns to Earth to face the protracted horrors of *The Merv Griffin Show*.

Queen of Outer Space was based on "Queen of the Universe," a satirical 1952 story by Ben Hecht about incompetent extraterrestrial women who cannot manage the affairs of their planet. The film's director, Edward Bernds, had apprenticed at Columbia as director of some of the more energetic Three Stooges two-reelers, and also directed a number of Bowery Boys comedies. Out of such peculiar genius are our sexual attitudes shaped and reflected.

Fittingly, one supposes, the most entertaining films of this subgenre are a pair of two-reel shorts directed by Jules White that starred The Three Stooges. In *Space Ship Sappy* (1957) the boys travel to the planet Sunev with crazy scientist Benny Rubin and his sumptuously upholstered daughter (Doreen Woodbury). Sunev is not a particularly hospitable place, inhabited as it is by beautiful but deadly Amazons. "They will love you to death!" cries out Rubin to the captive Stooges. "What a way to go!" gushes Stooge Joe Besser. The Amazons do not know how to kiss (they bite) and don't say much except, "I yi-yi! Be bop!" They finally lash the boys to stakes and prepare to assault them with clip-on vampire fangs and nails, but are scared off in the knick of time by stock footage of an iguana blown up to dinosaur size.

In *Outer Space Jitters* (1957) the boys travel to Zunev (imagination did not exactly run riot at Columbia's two-reel department), where they meet leggy, electric-charged girls who eat bolts and battery acid. The girls' kisses are, um, shocking: corn in Larry Fine's pocket is popped, and the Cornish hen that Besser has been inexplicably carrying with him is instantly cooked. The boys escape the girls' clutches when their attention is diverted by the gold ingots and jewels that litter the planet. These shorts, cheerful and sufficiently hip not to take themselves seriously in any sense, are an amusing and inoffensive commentary on the ongoing war between men and women. As two-reelers, they came and went without the notice of critics or film scholars, but at least their benign silliness remains accessible on television.

A significant aspect of many of the "lost women" films is the presence of the lone female who inevitably defies what is presented as the inherent nature of the others, and rescues the men who have disturbed the Sapphic splendor. Zsa Zsa and her counterparts in pictures like *Cat Women of the*

Moon (1953) and *Abbott and Costello Go to Mars* (1952; featuring the characterless Miss Universe contestants) are clearly the exceptions to the man-hating rule. Most of the women in these films are sexy fiends who will go to absurdly illogical lengths to entrap and destroy any man careless enough to blunder into their territory. In *Mesa of Lost Women* (1953) Tarantula Girl Tandra Quinn (an obvious descendent of Kathleen Burke's Panther Girl in 1933's *Island of Lost Souls*) performs a graceless dance for hero Allan Nixon, and turns into a spider; to hell with survival of the species, men were not born to be daddies, but dessert.*

As entertaining as the "lost women" films may be, there is something disquieting about their insistence upon the adversary aspect of man-woman relationships, and the crass way in which they reinforce stereotypes. The scanty costumes and inept schemes of planetary conquest turn women into fatuous, sexual jokes. The men they encounter are usually barrel-chested hunks who think with their biceps and make wisecracks about the ladies' bustlines. Separatist and misogynistic, the "lost women" films foster nothing but puerility and prejudice.

An implied natural ferocity in women is at the forefront of *The She-Creature* (1956) and *Voodoo Woman* (1957). Marla English stars in both as a woman who is hypnotically regressed to an earlier, more primitive level of existence. Costume maker Paul Blaisdell designed the monsters to look like armor-plated gargoyles, complete with long hair and knobby breasts. The veneer of civilization, the films suggest, is thin indeed. Very little separates modern woman from the beast that lives within. To their credit, *The She-Creature* and *Voodoo Woman* give their female leads some motivation for their primitive rage, in that each is manipulated by an unscrupulous, self-serving man. Still, one wonders how a female writer and director might have approached similar material.

In Herbert L. Strock's *Blood of Dracula* (1957) the evil manipulator is female. Sandra Harrison plays a sullen teenager who is packed off by her emotionless father to a remote boarding school, where she becomes an unwitting pawn of a scheming science instructor (Louise Lewis). The older woman despises men, and uses an amulet from the Carpathian Mountains to transform her student into a slavering vampire. A few victims fall before Harrison turns upon her tormentor.

It is surely no accident that the evil teacher in *Blood of Dracula* is an instructor of science. After Hiroshima, few people clung to the image of scientists as eccentric, comically absent-minded fellows in white coats. Science was

A hilariously wicked extrapolation of the man vs. woman theme is "How to Succeed ... at Murder," a 1965 episode of the splendid British television series, The Avengers. High-ranking business executives are being strangled and blown up by their militant secretaries, whose motto is, "Ruination to All Men!" It is ultimately revealed that the feminine voice that has guided them belongs to a man who has manipulated his followers to achieve his own ends.

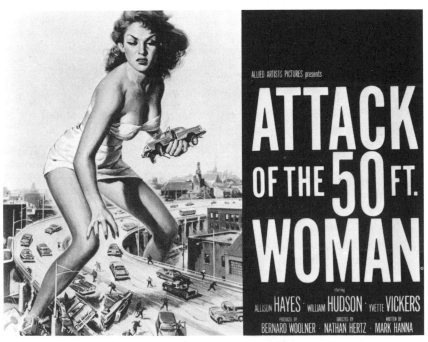

Top: Welcome to the Female Planet—original publicity for *Queen of Outer Space* (1958). Bottom: Horror kitsch—original poster art from *Attack of the 50-Foot Woman* (1958), featuring the indomitable Allison Hayes.

suddenly no laughing matter. The future no longer looked quite as rosy as it once had. *The Terror From the Year 5000* (1958) was stage actress Salome Jens (in her film debut), who travels backward in time from the radioactive year 5000 to the 20th century in search of virile men to revivify the faltering human race. She disguises herself as a nurse (an amusing switch on the "angel of mercy" concept of nursing) and murders people who block her mission. In order to hypnotize her victims, the Terror cleverly waggles her shimmering fingernails. One supposes that the men in the audience at least appreciated the fact that their macho talents will still be in demand in the year 5000.

Czech actress Florence Marly played the *Queen of Blood* in 1966. Like the Terror, the Queen is an accomplished mesmerist who turns her sultry, greenish gaze on the male members of a space crew in order to drink their blood. Though the vampire is eventually destroyed, the film's conclusion reveals her plant-like offspring quietly growing in a corner of the ship.

The ready gullibility of the Queen's victims suggests that we best like our ladies sleek and beautiful. Millions of dollars have been squandered by unhappy women on fad diets, pore-clogging cosmetics, dubious exercise regimens, and silly clothing. A lot of time and effort is put toward achieving society's idea of the ideal woman. Ironically, the movies often demonstrate that it is the beautiful women who are the least trustworthy and most dangerous. In 1958 came *The Astounding She-Monster* (Shirley Kilpatrick), an extraterrestrial whose mission of goodwill is misinterpreted by the backwoods people whose territory she invades. Dressed in a silver lamé body suit and high heels, Kilpatrick looks more like a fugitive burlesque queen than an emissary from the stars. Director Ronnie Ashcroft shot through gauze and in slight double exposure to suggest the creature's deadly radiation. The message is clear, boys: look, but don't touch.

When actress Allison Hayes launched the *Attack of the 50-Foot Woman* in 1958, she became the most kitschy of untouchable love objects. Wealthy but ignored by her dilettante husband (William Hudson), Hayes wanders into the desert and encounters a giant, bald alien whose touch induces startling growth. When she reaches the height of 50' (courtesy of appallingly bad matte work) she assumes the role of moral arbitor, electrocuting her faithless husband and pulping his dye-job girlfriend (Yvette Vickers). *Attack of the 50-Foot Woman* is amusing junk, enlivened by Allison Hayes' enthusiastic performance as the dumped-on wife. An intensely sexual, coldly beautiful B-movie regular whose life was cut short by cancer in 1977, Hayes appeared in a number of horror thrillers in the fifties and early sixties. In *The Disembodied* (1957) she is an icily attractive voodoo queen, and in *The Undead* (1957) she is Satan's sexy girl Friday. Her most pointed role came in George Blair's distasteful 1960 thriller, *The Hypnotic Eye*, in which she appears as the beautiful assistant to a hypnotist (Jacques Bergerac) whose specialty is inducing women to mutilate themselves when they act on his posthypnotic suggestions. Blair's directorial style is blunt and flatfooted. The screen is filled with tasteless closeups of women washing their faces with acid and setting their hair afire at kitchen stoves. One victim is visited by police after she has thrust her face into the whirling blades of a fan. The mesmerized heroine (Merry Anders) is rescued moments before stepping into a scalding shower. Hayes later screams her defiance at police from a swinging theater catwalk: "What else could I do with a face like mine?" she screeches, ripping off a mask to reveal the scarred features beneath. Her beauty had been lost years ago in an accident, and she has used the weak-willed hypnotist to destroy the beauty in others. *The Hypnotic Eye* is an exploitative exercise that makes its point in spite of itself: beauty is worth killing for.

Similarly, *The Leech Woman* (Coleen Gray; 1960) is a duplicitous beauty who steals the youth from others in order to maintain her own. Her male counterpart is *The 4-D Man* (1959), a scientist (Robert Lansing) whose experiments in the fourth dimension have accelerated his aging, and made him a carrier. At one point, he unwittingly ages his blonde pickup with a single kiss.

The high premium we place on beauty has been reflected in a succession of horror films, many from Italy and Spain, in which women are literally or figuratively masked. In some, like *The Awful Dr. Orloff* (1961) and *The Diabolical Dr. Z* (1966), the women are hideously disfigured, and barely exist as characters, functioning primarily as raisons d'être for the nasty activities of mad scientists and demented surgeons. The films become more absorbed with the unwilling donors of beautiful faces than with the miserable patients. Occasionally, subject matter of this sort is treated with sensitivity and a certain elegance of style, as in Georges Franju's *Eyes Without a Face* (aka *The Horror Chamber of Dr. Faustus*; 1959). Despite Franju's unflinching graphicism (a skin graft sequence is particularly harrowing), his unexpected sentiment and Eugen Schüfftan's vivid monochrome cinematography evoke a melancholy beauty. The disfigured heroine (Edith Scob) hides her scars beneath a sculptured white mask through which only her enormous, haunted eyes are visible. As she wanders along dim corridors, or pines for her fiancée, she resembles nothing so much as a miserable harlequin.

In other films, the masked or disguised woman is the perpetrator of mayhem. In John Moxey's stylish *Horror Hotel* (1960) handsome British character actress Patricia Jessell was cast as Elizabeth Selwyn, proprietor of a cozy inn near modern-day Salem, Massachusetts. She is also the reincarnation of a witch who was burned on the town square three hundred years previously. One special room of the inn is reserved for nubile young women who have been chosen as sacrifices for the Witches' Sabbath. In her role as innkeeper, Selwyn is low-key and solicitous. But when the clock makes ready to strike thirteen, she becomes a bloodthirsty, cloaked harridan who slices bosoms with skill and relish. Chief among her accomplices is a debonair college professor (Christopher Lee) who slyly suggests the inn as a lodging place for female students interested in researching the history of witchcraft. At the climax, a

The ultimate face of horror is one of maddening, perfect beauty: Alice Krige in *Ghost Story* (1981).

young man who has come to rescue his sister is stabbed in the back with a sacrificial dagger, but the coven is destroyed when its members are touched by the shadow of the cross. Elizabeth Selwyn is discovered slumped behind the inn's front desk, her face as charred as it was on that day three hundred years earlier.

The notion of attractive but monstrous figures who prey upon the sexuality of others may have found its fullest expression in John Irvin's *Ghost Story* (1981), a studied, sometimes painfully slow adaptation of the successful novel by Peter Straub. As a literary form, the horror novel has enjoyed a popular renaissance since the 1971 publication of William Peter Blatty's *The*

Exorcist. Many of the novels that have appeared since are inferior pulp, but a few notable authors have emerged. Chief among them is Stephen King; Straub, a greater if less explosive talent, follows closely in popularity. A onetime New England academic, Straub has expressed a consistent interest in the revenant: the vengeful and merciless female spirit who returns from beyond the grave to crush the men who tormented her in life. *Ghost Story* was published to widespread popularity and critical acclaim in 1980. It is an audacious blend of most of the significant elements of horror fiction that have characterized the genre in the last century, offering lycanthropy, vampirism, shape-shifting, and, of course, a ghost. The novel is unusual in that its four protagonists are elderly men, solid New England professionals who call themselves the Chowder Society. Their special fondness is relating spooky stories over brandy. When they are suddenly troubled by nightmares and, later, suicide, it gradually becomes clear that they are being victimized by the spirit of a young woman whom they had accidentally killed a half-century earlier. Implicit in the novel (less so in the film) is the Jacksonian notion that evil spirits exist only in response to the particular guilts and fears of the people they plague. In essence, the evil that tortures men comes from within; the ghost is merely an externalization. Because Straub leaves no doubt as to the sexual allure of the ghost, one Eva Galli, the guilt which troubles the Chowder Society is sexual in nature.

Ghost Story is a long and complex book. Screenwriter Lawrence D. Cohen, faced with the task of paring it down into a workable two-hour screenplay, had his hands full. Many characters and sequences were eliminated, but Straub's heavy sexual angle is intact. Director Irvin was apparently anxious to avoid the heavyhandedness that characterizes the genre and undercuts the effectiveness of many horror films; *Ghost Story*'s tone is intelligent and understated. Fred Astaire, John Houseman, Melvyn Douglas, and Douglas Fairbanks, Jr., old pros all, are splendid as the Chowder Society. The film comes to throbbing life with the first appearance of Alice Krige, a remarkable young South African actress who, as Eva Galli, embodies a singular brand of perverse sexuality. Titian-haired and blessed with a face and body out of Botticelli, she is every man's dream of a bed-partner; even her nostrils are exquisite. Krige's performance has a startling depth: Eva Galli is at once elusive, sexually enticing, and fiercely repellent. In a protracted flashback sequence that mounts steadily to an awful tension, Galli abandons her ladylike pose when the four young men, drunk, come to call. The woman responds to the visit's lecherous intent with bald attempts to seduce and humiliate each of the youths, going so far as to rather shockingly lick one of the men on the face. The youngsters react with a mixture of revulsion and panic, and Galli is accidentally knocked cold after being shoved against a wall. Taken for dead, she is bundled into her car and pushed into a lake, but revives just as the car sinks beneath the black water. The young men clearly see her panicked face through the car's rear window, but they are too shocked to even attempt a rescue. They live with the secret of the woman's death for the next fifty years.

Because Eva Galli dies in water, her reappearance in ghostly form is presaged with clever water imagery. Director Irvin made repeated visual references to swimming pools, leaking sinks, and bathtubs. Water comes to symbolize not life, but menace and death. Things are not what they seem. In order to affect her revenge, Galli cloaks herself in a variety of guises. She appears to one old man as a rotted corpse, to another as she looked in life, and to her last victim, most significantly, as a bride. Her face is barely visible beneath the bridal veil, as she lifts the lace we see a grinning death's head. But the final irony of *Ghost Story* is that the ultimate face of horror is one of maddening, perfect beauty. Sex is death, and beauty has become horror. Eva Galli has paid for her sexual sinning with her life, but the Chowder Society, because its members initiated the sinning, must pay even more dearly.

Ghost Story was only a moderate commercial success. The film's insistence upon harsh retribution for sexual misconduct may have intimidated audiences that expected thrills of a more traditional sort. We probably do not care to be reminded of our ambivalent attitude toward female beauty, or that every pleasure has its price. We fear and distrust the sexuality that we claim to revere and enjoy. Eva Galli pricks the conscience of us all.

Horror cinema has been accused of many absurd things. If it will not turn little Johnny into an axe murderer, detractors say, it will at least encourage him to strangle the cat. Some critics feel that the genre destroys imagination. Others claim that youthful addicts will suffer nightmares, or that the films subvert the moral tone of the nation. At times, horror buffs feel more put upon than insurance salesmen. Interestingly, most complaints against horror films focus upon the genre's tendency toward gleeful violence, but ignore a far more significant offense: the genre's trivialization of women. Filmic brutality can be affecting — even meaningful — if the brutalized ones are presented as three-dimensional beings. But when the women in horror films are not being depicted in hysterically negative ways (à la *Queen of Outer Space*), they are depicted as objects. Shapely, warm, and desirable objects, to be sure, but objects nonetheless. There is a chilling but hilarious moment in Stanley Kubrick's *Dr. Strangelove* (1964) in which Strangelove (Peter Sellers) describes to an assemblage of generals the way in which the human race can be perpetuated after nuclear war. A new society will flourish underground in refurbished mine shafts, he explains. There, men with practical skills and women who have been selected for their "physical attributes" will propagate. In order to ensure success, there will be ten women for each man. At this, General Buck Turgidson (George C. Scott) raises an eyebrow and licks his chops. Civilization may come to an end, but who cares as long as the aftermath is the ultimate male fantasy? Kubrick's darkly comic vision exposes the absurdity of middleaged wet dreams about sexuality and postnuclear survivability. We have entrusted our fates to junior grade Hugh Hefners who play with guns and bombs.

Curiously, postholocaust films had played themselves out as a subgenre at about the time real life concerns peaked. *Dr. Strangelove* and its deadpan counterpart *Fail-Safe* (1964) were the last significant fictional treatments. Subsequent offerings have tended more toward documentary, like Peter Watkins' numbing *The War Game* (1966), *The Atomic Cafe* (1982), and television's *The Day After* (1983).

The role of women in a postholocaust society (assuming there can *be* such a society) poses legitimate questions. Among the earliest and most intelligent films to approach the subject was *Five* (1951). As the title suggests, five people have survived an atomic war. One of them is a pregnant woman. Writer/director Arch Oboler had had wild success as creator of radio's "Lights Out" series in the forties, and brought to *Five* — his fourth film — a highly structured sense of drama. The dialogue is deliberate and at times excessive. The director displayed few gifts for movement, but did bring the enthusiasm and freshness of a creative artist who is excited about the didactic potential of the film medium. Framing is careful, almost classically correct. The visuals bring an earnestness to the subject matter that subsequent, more sensational films do not have. Actress Susan Douglas is attractive in a plain sort of way, and is turned by Oboler into an unassuming Everywoman. Three of the men are gentle and unremarkable; only the racist of the group (James Anderson) regards the woman as a prize. The woman's relationship with one man (William Phipps) is developed with beguiling naturalness. Oboler did not harp upon the special significance of the woman's pregnancy, but worked it into a grim undercurrent. After radiation sickness and violence have destroyed three of the group, the woman tells the only surviving man that she has lost the baby. But perhaps the two of them, she suggests, can start anew.

Five was shot entirely on location outside Los Angeles. Its naturalistic mountain setting is attractive without being overwhelming. The film is almost totally forgotten today, which is a shame, for its dignity and subtlety mark it as a deceptively artful accomplishment. Oboler's film career continued until the late 1960s, but faltered when he explored contrived, oddball humor and technical trickery like 3-D. The sensitivity of *Five* has proved to be a one-shot, not only of Oboler's canon but of Hollywood's as well.

The career of director Roger Corman will be discussed in detail in Chapter IX, but one of his films should be noted here: *The Day the World Ended* (1956) is the archetypal Hollywood postholocaust movie, and set much of the tone of its releasing company, American International Pictures (then called American Releasing Corporation). A ragged group of survivors straggles to an isolated mountain house after the Bomb has fallen. Corman and scripter Lou Rusoff offered an improbably diverse group, which includes a hoodlum (Touch — later Mike — Connors), his floozy girlfriend (Adele Jergens), even a crusty old prospector and burro. Richard Denning and pretty Lori Nelson fill the requisite hero/heroine roles. Menace is provided by a hideous atomic mutant who looks more Kentucky Fried than irradiated. When Adele Jergens falls from a cliff, the virginal Nelson is the only woman left alive. Oh, boy. We can almost hear the collective smacking of male lips. Denning and Connors stake claims, but the lumpy monster also seems interested. The creature abducts the girl, but is thwarted when caught in the cleansing rains. At the conclusion, the girl realizes that the monster's designs have not been lecherous at all, for he is her long-lost brother. At any rate, nature has disposed of the aberration, and Denning and the girl stride off into a sunrise as the screen proclaims, "The Beginning."

The Day the World Ended is good silly fun. It is the first of many science fiction films the prolific Corman would direct, and has energy and a naive charm. Paul Blaisdell's mesomorphic design for the monster is among the genre's most amusing images. Blonde and petite Lori Nelson was ideally cast as the atomic-age Eve. She functions more as a piece of property than as a real person, and gives the men something to fight about. Her happy fate is in sharp contrast with that suffered by the sluttish character played by Adele Jergens. In this after-the–Bomb world, Providence allows only the pure to survive. Cliff edges were expressly made for the sexually indiscreet.

When a glossy film from a major studio attempts to deal with postholocaust sexuality, the results can be insincere and plastic. In *The World, the Flesh, and the Devil* (1959) director Ranald MacDougall sets up an obvious sexual tension when Last Woman Inger Stevens meets Last Man Harry Belafonte. Mel Ferrer later adds a grim note of racism to the narrative, but the overall effect is undercut by the facile understanding the trio reaches at film's end. The casting of a black man opposite a WASP goddess like Stevens is a bit too manipulative to go unquestioned. Just a few years earlier, white Americans were stoning black schoolchildren in Arkansas. The year 1959 was not exactly one of enlightenment, and MacDougall's contrived "message" picture plays to our fears and prejudices even as it pretends to uplift us. The casting of light-skinned Belafonte, in particular, seems like a sop to easily outraged white sensibilities. The film's worst sin is its wishy-washiness; it cries for an actor with the strength of, say, Brock Peters in the Belafonte role. A poverty row item like *The Day the World Ended* may be trivial, but at least it accomplishes what it sets out to do, without pretension. An overblown white elephant like *The World, the Flesh, and the Devil* tries to say something meaningful, but is doomed by its fear of the very attitudes it hopes to condemn. In 1959, at least, the lissome Miss Stevens need not have worried about reflecting anything but the stodgiest of notions.

In sharp contrast, Ray Milland's *Panic in Year Zero* (1962) has all the grimness and blunt force anyone could hope for. It is the story of a middle-class family's fight for survival after nuclear war, and demonstrates to what lengths a man will go in order to protect his children, his women, and his honor. Milland starred as well as directed. As Harry, he is a picture of robust male determination, and takes firm charge of the family unit. Harry quickly discovers that good help is hard to find. Mom (Jean Hagen) is portrayed as an indecisive weakling, and the daughter (Mary Mitchel) is a chronic whiner. Milland's most ardent supporter is son Frankie Avalon; it seems no coincidence that the film unreels like an adolescent boy's power fantasy. Dad takes what he needs, sometimes at the point of a gun. Junior learns how to shoot, and learns to like it. After the daughter is raped by a trio of greasy perverts, father and son storm an isolated farmhouse and dispassionately gun down two of the men. A girl (Joan Freeman) who has been an unwilling concubine is rescued. When the son is later menaced by the surviving hood (Richard Bakalyan), Freeman grabs a rifle and kills the rapist. Because the girl has learned how to kill, she is the film's most worthy female.

Panic in Year Zero is unsettling because it may contain more truths than we would like to admit. The same spirit that motivates people to steal television sets during blackouts prompts Harry. Order has broken down, and authority is measured by a man's guts. Women, agreeable enough in civilization, are insipid baggage in the brave new world. When Harry shoots the rapists he is not avenging his daughter, but his own honor. His daughter, frankly, is a jerk. Harry cares about her not as a person, but only as a female object that is part of his sphere. It is the son who becomes Harry's aggressive counterpart. The mother repeatedly asks Harry to "make friends" with menacing people; it is all Harry can do to keep the family alive in light of such stupidity.

More than twenty years have passed since the release of *Panic in Year Zero*. If the film were to be remade today, it would probably reflect the new spirit of female independence. Dad would not be quite so brutally macho, and Mom would have a little savvy. Sis would still be raped, but would probably dispatch her attackers herself. Without smudging her lip gloss, naturally. One might suppose this is progress.

Betty Friedan is correct: women rarely excelled in serious endeavors because nothing was expected of them. Everything was groovy as long as they could cook, keep house, bear children. And stand the hell out of the way when the menfolk start throwing lead. In American film, women have been restricted to the level of children; the trailer for Kurt Neumann's *Rocketship X-M* (1950) heralds the adventures of "Four Men and a Girl!" Did star Lloyd Bridges bring his daughter along? Nope, the "girl" is 35-year-old Osa Massen. In *Unknown World* (1951) a team of scientists explores the center of the earth. The character played by Marilyn Nash is described in the voice-over narration as an "ardent feminist," but when it looks as though the expedition is going to be trapped 2500 feet underground, the woman suddenly questions the values that have guided her life: "I wondered if I could compete in a man's world ... I was afraid of life." With this, she clasps the hand of the itinerant playboy who has become her lover. She has seen the light. This woman will snag a man and be a success, in *spite* of her college degrees.

In 1956, screenwriter Cyril Hume looked to *The Tempest* for inspiration when he wrote *Forbidden Planet*, MGM's big-budget sf extravaganza of the fifties. Morbius (Walter Pidgeon) is a scientist who lives with his daughter on an outpost planet called Altair IV. Like Shakespeare's Miranda, Altaira (Anne Francis) has never seen a man other than her father, so she has no defense when an amorous Earthman decides to teach her the mechanics of kissing. The girl is beautiful, of course, but quite bubbleheaded. Ironic, since Morbius is characterized as a man of awesome intellect. Apparently one must not hope for too much to rub off on a "girl." Inevitably, there is something vaguely unwholesome about Altaira's relationship with her father. He cannot, it is revealed at the climax, control his id (which Hume represents as a bloodthirsty sort of Caliban), and one is compelled to wonder what else he has been unable to control.

Altaira is a character who says a lot about sexual attitudes. Lovely and pliable, she is intensely sexual without being aware of it. She is vain (demanding that servant Robby the Robot create a jewel-studded dress) and heedless of things that exist beyond her realm. She seems to have no redeeming qualities besides beauty and an uncertain chastity. Hero Leslie Nielsen spirits her away to Earth at the conclusion, and he is welcome to her. She is a colossal bore. But Altaira's shallowness is vindicated. Prince Charming shows up right on schedule. Altaira's sexual naïveté and low-watt brainpower have paid handsome dividends.

It is characteristic of the genre and of commercial cinema in general that female characters who embrace a lustier view of life are often punished for it. In the fifties, blonde Yvette Vickers (the July 1959 *Playboy* Playmate) was a starlet of unusual spunk and vivacity. In one year, 1958, her presence enlivened a pair of amusing B-horrors. In the aforementioned *Attack of the 50-Foot Woman* she is Honey, a good-time girl who hopes to marry her middle-aged boyfriend as soon as he disposes of his rich wife. Honey spends most of her time in a tacky roadhouse, and does not seem especially interested in her paramour unless he is discussing his wife's loot. In one sequence, Honey performs a suggestive dance to a sizzling rock 'n' roll number. No doubt: the lady is *hot*. Not surprisingly, she does not last until the final credits.

Vickers took a similar role in *Attack of the Giant Leeches*, though the significant differences are that it is *she* who is married, and that her boyfriend (Michael Emmett) has only good looks to recommend him. Vickers' reason for being is completely sexual. When her unfaithfulness is discovered, her cuckolded husband (Bruno VeSota) forces her and Emmett into a swamp at gunpoint. The hungry leeches of the title have a picnic; once again, nature has punished untoward sexual conduct.

The Bad Girl that Vickers typified is infinitely more interesting than the virtuous maidens who are allowed to live happily ever after. Commercial cinema, in essence, has vilified and punished the independent spirit when that spirit should have been celebrated. Because the audiences of the fifties (and beyond, no mistake) had problems believing that a woman can be both sexual and "good," an active sex life (implied or otherwise) was almost invariably equated with immorality. (One notable and delightful exception is Marilyn Monroe's 1955 part in Billy Wilder's *The Seven Year Itch*.)

It is a rare occasion when horror films offer independent, likeable women whose sexuality is a treasure. Actress Dana Wynter created such a woman for director Don Siegel in *Invasion of the Body Snatchers* (1956), a tight and intelligent thriller which involves the alien takeover of the people of a small California town. A woman claims her Uncle Ira is *not* Uncle Ira, and a little boy runs screaming from his mother. Eventually only Miles Bennell (Kevin McCarthy) and his elegant friend Becky (Wynter) are left. The takeovers occur when the human victims fall asleep, and Miles and Becky must struggle to stay awake after they have fled from a howling mob. In the dimness of the cave where they have taken refuge, the two are united not simply as man and woman, but as human beings. They share a supportive hug, but when Miles leaves to investigate a noise, we know what will happen. The man returns and must shake Becky awake: Siegel fills the screen with the woman's face as her eyes slowly open. The gaze is flat, unhuman. Miles screams. His friend has been taken over, and the loss is telling because we like Becky. She is beautiful and bright, witty and independent. She is, in short, *human*, and serves a legitimate dramatic function instead of a role as a characterless icon. The film's small town milieu contributes to Becky's innate appeal, for the intimacy of the setting suggests that she is someone we might have known.

Philip Kaufman's 1978 remake covers the same ground as Siegel's version, but has an added dimension of horror because it is set in the anonymity of a big city, San Francisco. Brooke Adams brings a husky-voiced charm to the character of the doomed woman, but the shock of her takeover is somewhat diminished by unnecessarily hideous special effects. Both versions of *Invasion of the Body Snatchers* are based on Jack Finney's novel, *The Body Snatchers*, written in 1954. The book is a clever fictionalization of the horrors of paranoia and McCarthyistic thought. Few horror films have reflected this sort of sociopolitical thought, but one that does with reasonable success is Michael Anderson's *1984* (1956), an adaptation of George Orwell's fabulous 1949 novel. Like the novel (and Michael Radford's stylishly bleak 1984 interpretation), Anderson's version is a stinging examination of a world in which behavior and even thought are strictly controlled. Sex has become illicit in the overpopulated, passionless society inhabited by Winston (Edmond O'Brien) and Julia (Jan Sterling). The couple pretends to follow the tenets of the No-Sex League, but Winston and Julia are secretly lovers. When their indiscretions are discovered, Winston turns against the woman in order to save himself. Both are "re-educated," and act like cordial strangers when they meet again. Because Winston has chosen to abandon Julia, he has thrown away a vital part of himself. He has been victimized by faceless bureaucrats who claim that love and sexuality run counter to the aims of the state. Worse, he has believed them.

When television refined the situation comedy in the early fifties it created an idiom which reduced the complex components of daily life to easily-recognized archetypes. Everything was suddenly in capital letters: Snoopy Wife, Grouchy Neighbor, Meddling Mother-in-Law. The sitcoms turned our lives into shorthand, and the awful part is that many of us believed it. The simplistic characters we saw on television seemed to ring true, but we wondered why *our* problems could not be resolved in 30 minutes. What were we doing wrong?

William Castle was a producer/director who really grasped the structure and appeal of the television sitcom. His trivial and entertaining sit-*horror* films of the late fifties translated many comedic archetypes to the theatrical horror genre. In a commercial sense, Castle (who died in 1977) was the ideal filmmaker because he gave us precisely what we expected to see. As a staff director at Columbia in the forties, Castle worked almost exclusively on amusing B-films, notably the popular Whistler mystery series that starred Richard Dix. Castle became a producer in the fifties, and successfully combined the breezy simplicity of situation comedy with the cheeky approach to mayhem that had been pioneered by American International Pictures. His first significant release as a producer/director was *House on Haunted Hill* in 1958. A witty screenplay by Robb White was interpreted by star Vincent Price, a self-confessed ham and Renaissance man who had been typed in horror films since 1953, when he starred in *House of Wax*. By 1958, Price was (happily) becoming something of a caricature. Like the folks who populated television's HaHa Land, Price could be summed up in caps: Suave Villain. His elegant bearing, pencil mustache, and rich voice made him instantly believable as a charming fiend.

Castle cleverly seized upon this built-in characterization and audience identification by casting Price as a bored rich man who offers a group of strangers $10,000 apiece if they can endure one night in his isolated mansion. The film is not exactly what one would call spontaneous, but it is obvious that everybody concerned had a ball making it. The director pulled out all the stops, and gave us a walking skeleton, an acid vat, a leering witch, and a head that bounces noisily down the stairs. Party favors for the paranoid guests are .45 automatics. The hero and heroine (Richard Long and Carolyn Craig) are as virtuous and as exciting as potato pancakes. Price nearly walks off with the film, but is matched by actress Carol Ohmart, who brings a satiny, sluttish indolence to her role as the Whorey Wife. The character never once registers as a real person, but only as a sexual icon, a bad girl who diddles with the family doctor and makes eyes at the hero. She wears negligees and slinky jumpsuits, in sharp contrast with the heroine, whose wardrobe is strictly high-necked. Ohmart, like the younger Yvette Vickers, is a hot item. She wants to murder Price, but he turns the tables and backs her into the basement acid vat: tootsie and negligee bubble away.

The big joke is that while society supposedly disdains women like the one played by Ohmart, movies like *House on Haunted Hill* throw them out to us like smarmy rewards for being bad little boys and girls. I wouldn't cross the street for the film's heroine, but for the femme fatale? You betcha. The appeal of Ohmart's character is firmly grounded in our sexual hypocrisy. Men may marry the heroine, but it is the villainess who fills their dreams.

Castle and Price followed *House on Haunted Hill* with *The Tingler* (1959), in which Price is a scientist who discovers that the human body's fear mechanism is triggered by an organism that attaches itself to the base of the spine. Unless the frightened person relieves the tension by screaming, the organism (named the "tingler") will grow and kill the victim. Such a discovery lends itself to certain malevolent uses. In a sequence obviously patterned after the climax of Henri-Georges Clouzet's *Les Diaboliques* (1955), the mute wife (Judith Evelyn) of a theater owner is frightened to death in her apartment. Her own death certificate confronts her in the medicine cabinet, and a black figure with a death's head quietly rocks in the living room. But the ultimate terror is found in the bathtub, which has been filled with blood. In original-release prints of *The Tingler*, the film shifts at this point from black-and-white to shocking color, as a human arm slowly rises from the viscous goo. The woman, unable to scream, collapses dead.

Castle was no Clouzet (who in *Les Diaboliques* frightened actress Vera Clouzet to death when the body of the woman's supposedly-dead husband rises fully-clothed from the bathtub), but *The Tingler* is more vile in its imagination than Clouzet's film. The murderer is revealed to be the woman's husband, played by cadaverously gaunt Philip Coolidge. In an odd touch, he and his wife operate a revival theater that shows nothing but silent films. The woman's world is utterly silent. She cannot hear or speak. Given the premise of the story, her vulnerability is almost pathetic. Castle envisoned the tingler as resembling a giant slug, so the fate of its victims seems more grotesque than affecting. Still, the death of the mute wife (who is a victim of biology in a double sense) is shocking.

Even when dealing with potentially explosive themes, Castle's films have an unfortunate glibness that tends to trivialize. *Strait-Jacket* (1964) stars Joan Crawford as a woman who has returned home after 20 years' confinement for axe-murdering her husband and his lover. Crawford, gaunt but still striking and energetic in middle age, projected a splendid nervous energy, and suggests perfectly the confusion of a person who has been away from the world for a long time. She moves in with her daughter (Diane Baker) and is suspected when (surprise!) axe-murders begin again. Robert Bloch's facile script points all the clues in Crawford's direction but the daughter, insane since witnessing the original murders as a child, is finally caught in the act.

Strait-Jacket merely toys with some pretty heavy psychology. After the fashion of the final sequence of Alfred Hitchcock's *Psycho* (1960), Castle ties everything up in a big psychoanalytical knot, as a doctor explains that transference of guilt has caused the daughter to wear her mother's clothing (plus a wig and rubber mask) and imitate her murderous behavior. The film's flashback sequences place the axe murders squarely in the world of tabloid headlines. The opening is a bizarre montage of shattering glass, shrieking women, and newsboys who scream, "Extra! Extra!" Everybody, Castle would have us believe, loves a juicy sex murder. Though shallow, *Strait-Jacket* at least admits the possibility of deadly sexual tension between mother and daughter. Children do not grow up in a vacuum. The film, intent upon simultaneously shocking and entertaining us, capitalizes on the fact. Crawford's character is basically sympathetic, and *Strait-Jacket* is one of the few thrillers that makes a woman's sexual rage seem justified.* Clearly, Crawford has been woefully mistreated. Her husband was no prize — we shed no tears for him.

Paradoxically (or perhaps not), Castle's best film as director is also his most derivative. The tremendous success in 1960 of Alfred Hitchcock's *Psycho* altered the course of the horror genre forever after, and inspired Castle to put together *Homicidal* (1961), a high-energy thriller that plays with themes outré even by today's standards. A young woman (Jean Arless) offers a hotel bellboy $2000 if he will marry her. He agrees, and at the conclusion of the ceremony the woman stabs the justice of the peace to death. She flees, and begins what appears to be a quiet life as wife of *another* man in a small California town. Her sister-in-law (Patricia Breslin) is discomfited by Arless, but cannot put her finger on what is wrong. In the course of an increasingly convoluted story, we learn that the murderess had been born female but forcibly raised as a male. "She" and a companion have recently returned from Denmark. "What happened there," a psychiatrist muses later, "we don't know." Of course, the film is hinting broadly at a sex-change operation, which was pretty hot copy in 1961. We never do learn for certain just what sex Arless' character is supposed to be or, for that matter, what sex Arless is in real life, for she also took the role of her own husband. Castle purposely kept audiences in the dark by giving Arless a split-screen curtain call, but revealed in his 1976 autobiography that his star's real name was Joan Marshall. The actress abandoned her androgynous nom de plume following *Homicidal*. Research has yielded only one more credit for her, a small role in *Tammy and the Doctor* (1963).

People who have tried to make sense of *Homicidal* come away feeling as though they've been trapped inside a kinky jigsaw puzzle. The killer is motivated by revenge and, as in other Castle films, the prospect of a meaty inheritance if the right people die. No attempt was made to explore Arless' psyche, and one can easily come away with a rather queasy feeling about transsexuals. Arless favors that most phallic of weapons, the butcher knife, and in one sequence watches with keen interest as a peddler sharpens one for

Disaster can result when a film uses this point of view as a springboard for cheapjack exploitation, as in Lamont Johnson's inept Lipstick *(1976).*

Jean Arless as the sexually ambiguous protagonist of William Castle's *Homicidal* (1961).

her. In a florist shop, she angrily destroys the tiny figures of bride and groom that adorn a wedding bouquet, but later gazes with fondness at a baby doll. Our sex and the behavior it prompts informs us of what we are more pointedly than any other part of our makeup. We recoil instinctively from people whose sexuality seems ambiguous or "wrong." *Homicidal* is predicated upon this fear. Because the film is nothing but an entertainment, it makes us laugh even as we squirm. There is a giddy, forbidden-fruit quality about its unusually graphic violence. Blood pumps through the fingers of the justice of the peace after the woman has stabbed him in the belly, and an old lady's head falls from her shoulders and drops to the floor after her body is nudged on a dark staircase. The extreme explicitness of approach forcibly links unorthodox sexuality with violence. In a psychosexual sense, *Homicidal* was perhaps the most distressing Hollywood film until William Friedkin's numbing and misunderstood *Cruising* (1980). Because *Homicidal* favors a small town milieu that would seem to be a cozy haven, it is an especially threatening experience. As in *Invasion of the Body Snatchers*, the beast lives among us, in disguise, smiling, plotting our overthrow.

Mia Farrow as the bearer of a demonic male conceit—*Rosemary's Baby* (1968).

By the late sixties the market for gimmicked horror films had died, and canny William Castle bought the screen rights to Ira Levin's bestselling novel, *Rosemary's Baby*. Castle wished to direct as well as produce, but acquiesced to the wishes of Paramount and handed the assignment to Roman Polanski. A good thing, too. Castle was a solid, professional filmmaker whose sensibilities did not include much besides dollar signs. One shudders to think how he would have, as director, trivialized or hoked up Levin's pointed views on the cultural and social impotency of women. *Rosemary's Baby*, simply, is about a woman whose ambitious husband arranges for her to bear the Devil's child. As has been discussed in Chapter I, the film's success helped inspire a flood of movies that deal with demonic children. Most of the imitators work flat-footedly, and offer simpleminded shocks instead of thoughtfulness. *Rosemary's Baby* is the notable exception. Mia Farrow, all angles and worry, was ideally cast as Rosemary. Her husband (John Cassavetes) has found a New York City apartment that seems full of mysteries: oddly walled-off closets, a pretty neighbor who inexplicably commits suicide, and a bevy of eccentrics next door who take an untoward interest in Rosemary's pregnancy. Rosemary begins to panic when she realizes that she is in some way being manipulated. The film becomes a case study of paranoia, as the woman imagines she is being followed and purposely misdirected. She is tormented by a harrowing rape dream, and cannot trust even her husband. Her fears are laughed off and trivialized by people who could help her if they were so inclined. She's a woman and she's pregnant. She can't be *expected* to make any sense. Nobody listens. By the time Rosemary gives birth she has been so thoroughly drained that we know she will willingly care for her child, the Antichrist.

Rosemary's Baby is a wicked parody of middle-class domesticity and sexual role-playing. The witches (played by such marvelous folk as Ruth Gordon, Sidney Blackmer, and Patsy Kelly) fuss over Rosemary like hens. They invite her to dinner. They bring goodies to her door. They are fiends who cluck and simper but, of course, it is not Rosemary they simper for. Rosemary has been victimized and objectified. Her sexuality has been turned against her in a hellish manner, and she ceases to exist as a person. She becomes a mere vessel, a bearer of a male conceit. Most chilling of all is the implied notion that she is merely fulfilling her destiny. She was built for such work. Rosemary's final descent into numb passivity is awful only because it has such basis in truth.

Another Ira Levin novel was adapted in 1975 by British director Bryan Forbes. *The Stepford Wives* is a slick but empty film that makes a half-hearted attempt to cover much of the same ground explored by *Rosemary's Baby*. Levin's novel is weak, and Forbes' translation is positively lame. In brief, men of an affluent American bedroom community are replacing their wives with androids. A photographer (Katharine Ross) senses something is wrong shortly after she and her husband take up residence. New friends suddenly act strangely, turning themselves into prettied slaves for their husbands. By the end of the film, Ross, too, has been replaced.

This is pretty flimsy stuff; the comic book writer Stan Lee cranked out the same story (with variations) a dozen times during the 1950s. Forbes' point that many men prefer their women docile and dumb may be well taken, but his execution is too clumsy and vapid to allow the film to be taken seriously as satire. Vast continents of thematic possibilities are left unexplored. How do these lipsticked robots raise the children of the women they have supplanted? Can the children sense a difference? Why is Ross' husband drawn so easily into the scheme? Has he felt threatened by her career? The film ignores these questions and, ultimately, accomplishes nothing but to raise the greatest question of all: what man would care to make physical love to a robot? Not this one. *The Stepford Wives* is pastoral and well-crafted, but hasn't the guts or savvy to be the devastating piece of ironic social comment it wants to be. It has all the depth of a well-drawn comic strip.

Hard as it may be to believe, occasional horror films explore tormented *male* sexuality. Most of these revolve around the male fear of diminished sexual capacity; *size* is the predominant element. With this in mind, *The Incredible Shrinking Man* (1957) may sound like a perverse joke, but is actually a quite sensitive film that is ambitious both thematically and technically. Grant Williams stars as Scott Carey, who is engulfed in an odd tingling mist while sunbathing on his boat. To his horror, he begins to shrink at the rate of one inch per week. As he loses stature (in a dual sense), his frustrations and anxieties grow. Ashamed to make love to his wife, the child-sized Carey begins a relationship with a pretty midget (April Kent, a full-size actress; her scenes were shot with oversized sets and props). Carey's spirits are buoyed by the relationship but, horribly, the second time they meet the woman is taller. The shrinking process continues, and Carey becomes a freak in his own home. His wife outfits a doll house for him (a toy of female children), and he is later knocked down the basement steps by the family cat. His wife assumes the cat has eaten him. Carey, lost, must fight the spider with whom he shares the cellar. Eventually, Carey grows *so* small that he is able to step through the mesh on a window screen and enter a new world. The shrinking process will continue but he knows that "to God, there is no zero."

Richard Matheson's uplifting screenplay is adapted from his 1956 novel, *The Shrinking Man*. The book is pointed in its examination of Carey's unhappy sexual predicament, and director Jack Arnold displayed a nice sensitivity to it. It is important to many men that their sexual relationships be on strictly male terms. Carey, accustomed to being in control, is embarrassed and diminished (in his eyes only) because he cannot effectively follow through on his erotic intentions. His wife (Randy Stuart) is willing to accept him as he is, but Carey will not let her. He can deal with being short — any man can — but his problem is unique because it strips him of his sexual identity and self-perceived essence as a man. To Carey, it is castration by degrees.

Jack Arnold directed a number of effective, often thoughtful genre films while under contract to Universal in the 1950s. His *The Creature from the Black Lagoon* (1954) and *Revenge of the Creature* (1955) are solidly crafted thrillers. *The Incredible Shrinking Man* is probably his finest film; beautifully constructed oversized sets and clever trick photography help make Scott Carey's preposterous situation seem utterly believable. The film is an unorthodox look at the way in which a man can be destroyed by his anxiety over the sexual role society tells him he must play.

In contrast to Jack Arnold we have writer/director/producer Bert I.

Gordon, a cheerful hack who has specialized in trivial trick films for more than thirty years. In 1958, apparently reasoning that if one tiny guy was good then a *bunch* of tiny guys would be great, Gordon unveiled *Attack of the Puppet People*. John Hoyt is featured as a crazed doll maker who shrinks actors John Agar, June Kenney, and others to teeny-weenyness. Hollywood had nearly exhausted this gimmick in previous (and more amusing) films like *Devil Doll* (1936) and *Dr. Cyclops* (1940). There is a grand moment in James Whale's *Bride of Frankenstein* (1935) when looney Dr. Praetorius (Ernest Thesiger) displays his collection of tiny homunculi: a shrunken ballerina, a soldier, et al. Bert Gordon took pains to see that *Attack of the Puppet People* had its share of women; at one point, the crazed doll maker expresses interest in having *more* dolls, if you get what we mean... Size is relative, and if the women are as tiny as the men, everything is dandy.

The aforementioned *Freaks* remains cinema's finest exploration of the "tiny man" motif. But one must not forget the converse — Bert I. Gordon didn't. His *The Amazing Colossal Man* (1957) is an overambitious film saved by some clever insights. Glenn Langan played an Army colonel who is unwittingly caught in the blast of the first plutonium bomb. Burned to a crisp, he is given up for dead until his tissues begin regenerating themselves at an amazing rate. Finally, he towers 70 feet into the air, a freak to his wife (Cathy Downs) and a puzzle for the authorities. Hairless and dressed only in a loincloth, he is the classic image of infantile helplessness transformed to one of potential menace. When he can no longer tolerate the stupid stares of scientists and soldiers he escapes his specially-built enclosure and strides into Las Vegas. As in most Gordon films the special effects are miserable, but an especially telling scene shows the giant cynically eyeing the huge prop over the Golden Slipper casino. His status as a total outcast is made clear with fine irony: there will be no woman to fill that shoe. Because Gordon threw away any pretense of thoughtfulness by indulging in a deus ex machina ending in which the giant is bazooka'd over Hoover Dam, *The Amazing Colossal Man* must be regarded as a provocative failure. It shows us that our sexual roles and behavior can be altered by events outside our control. The plutonium bomb, like the mysterious mist that shrinks Scott Carey, is pure circumstance. We may live nobly, but may one day be forced by an outside agent into a role with which we cannot cope.

Some men bring the horror upon themselves. In Don Siegel's horror gothic *The Beguiled* (1971) Clint Eastwood played McBurney, a Union soldier who is given shelter in an isolated Southern girls' school after being wounded and left behind enemy lines. McBurney, handsome and glib, arouses the desire of the school's headmistresses (Geraldine Page and Elizabeth Hartman), and that of various students. The soldier begins to play the women against each other, enjoying their attention and eventual sexual favors. But McBurney is too sly for his own good. One jealous lady shoves him down the stairs, and another amputates his leg on the pretext of saving his life. This

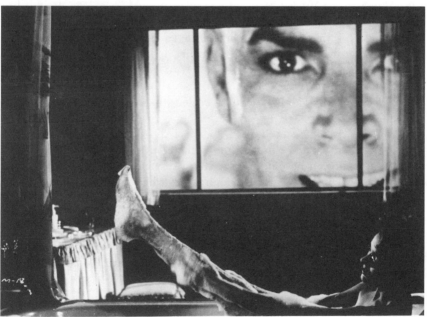

Top: The diminished male — Grant Williams as *The Incredible Shrinking Man* (1957).
Bottom: Too large to act on his desires, the irradiated protagonist (Glenn Langan) of
The Amazing Colossal Man (1957) must resort to peeping; the unsuspecting bather
is Jean Moorehead.

symbolic castration is the beginning of the end of the soldier's destructive sexuality. When he threatens to turn the women over to advancing Union troops, he signs his own death warrant. At a deceptively cheerful dinner, McBurney is served poisonous toadstools. The women bury him in the woods outside the school.

McBurney's downfall is precipitated by his overactive libido and an excess of guile. He does not care to inhibit his sexuality. Precisely the opposite sort of man is the focal character in *The Wicker Man* (1973), Robin Hardy's elegant interpretation of a deft screenplay by playwright Anthony Shaffer. Sergeant Howie (Edward Woodward) is a stiff, sexually repressed Scottish constable who travels to the island of Summerisle in search of a missing girl. He is greeted warmly by regal Lord Summerisle (Christopher Lee), but cannot find satisfactory answers to his questions. The islanders seem courteous but deliberately obtuse. Howie gradually realizes that the island is a hotbed of paganism, its people devoted to fertility rites and human sacrifice. He begins to fear for the missing girl, and engages Lord Summerisle in a battle of wits. After disguising himself and participating in a pagan parade, Howie discovers the girl in a cave. To his horror, he learns that the child was merely a lure, and that *he* is to be this season's sacrifice. His stolid Anglicanism avails him little as he is ceremoniously dressed in a linen gown and led along the rocky island coast to the Wicker Man, a huge, man-shaped straw icon designed to hold captive animals . . . and a man. Howie is placed inside the icon's chest, and shouts to Summerisle, "I believe in Jesus Christ and the life eternal!" Summerisle replies, "That is good, for believing as you do, we bestow upon you a rare gift these days: a martyr's death. You will sit with the Saints among the Elect." With this, the Wicker Man is set ablaze; Howie dies so that the gods will be appeased and grace Summerisle with a successful crop the following fall.

The Wicker Man is predicated upon a clash of philosophies. Unlike the villains in other, vaguely similar films (such as *Horror Hotel*), Lord Summerisle and his followers have nothing to hide. Their paganism is not concealed but openly celebrated. Their hedonism (as when the innkeeper's naked daughter — Britt Ekland — orgiastically bumps and writhes against the outer wall of Howie's room) is freely expressed. Schoolchildren are taught the glories of the penis and procreation, while adolescent maidens gather in naked fertility rites. The island's annual festival is not ugly but gloriously free-spirited, a riot of pastel costumes and happy faces. Harry Waxman's crisp cinematography captures the beauty of an island that seems to be truly blessed.

Howie refuses to accept any of it, not because he is a constable in search of a missing child, but because his inflexible religious beliefs have suppressed his sexuality and locked his mind into rigidity. His officer's uniform, deliberate manner of investigation, and humorless demeanor identify him as a man who has extinguished his own life energy. Howie has dedicated himself to the pursuit of rationalism and order. To his mind, Summerisle is as alien a place as Mars. To Lord Summerisle's way of thinking, Howie is precisely the man the island needs. The constable has lived his life in unknowning preparation for his death.

The distribution history of *The Wicker Man* has been nearly as unnerving as Sergeant Howie's predicament. The 102-minute film passed through the hands of several distributors in England, was butchered to 87 minutes, and dumped on the British marketplace. Warner Brothers eventually acquired the picture, test-marketed it in America in 1974, but did nothing further with it. The film later fell into more sympathetic hands but, to date, only the 87-minute version has had any significant theatrical release. (A 97-minute version aired on American cable TV in 1985.) *The Wicker Man* has become synonymous not only with the perils of sexuality, but of moviemaking.

Howie and McBurney contribute to their own downfalls, but some people — no matter what the circumstance or individual code of behavior — are doomed by some subtle flaw to a life of sexual turmoil and misery. This is the central idea of Shirley Jackson's 1959 novel, *The Haunting of Hill House*, a story of psychosexual terror which reached the screen as *The Haunting* in 1963. Directed by Robert Wise, the film is a deliberately paced look at the entwined lives of two mediums, Eleanor (Julie Harris) and Theodora (Claire Bloom).

While investigating a house that has been haunted since the accidental death of its mistress, the women have experiences which make apparent their peculiar sexual natures. Theodora is a lesbian who seems comfortable with her dominant personality. Eleanor, on the other hand, is an unhappy virgin: timid, hypersensitive, and vaguely unwholesome. The similarity of the names Eleanor and Theodora suggests that the women represent opposite sides of a single sexual persona. The repressed half, Eleanor, is immediately victimized by psychic phenomena which build from an eerie touch on her face to a thunderous blast of force that threatens to shake the house down. Nelson Gidding's script utilizes all the latest psychological jargon to explain that the fury has not come from a ghost, but from within Eleanor's neurotic mind. Her repressed desires and jealousies have manifested themselves psychically. As in *Ghost Story*, sexual conduct and identity lead to supernatural mayhem. The conclusion of *The Haunting*, in which Eleanor commits suicide on the spot where the house's original mistress died, is too pat to be absorbed comfortably — the problem is solved too neatly. But the film is noteworthy for its suggestion that a firm sexual identity, like Theodora's, is infinitely more desirable than one that is neurotic and half-formed. Eleanor has been destined from the start to be a victim. She was born to be at war with herself.

Repressed sexuality is explored also in Jack Clayton's *The Innocents* (1961), in which Deborah Kerr is a governess in charge of a child (Martin Stephens) who may be in the evil thrall of a deceased gardener. As in *The Haunting*, we have a woman whose repressed sexuality becomes the focus of supernatural activity. Unlike Robert Wise, Clayton chose an ambiguous

Julie Harris as the repressed virgin who attracts psychic phenomena in Robert Wise's
The Haunting **(1963).**

approach that does not attempt to spell out too clearly what is going on. Truman Capote's script has an obvious sensitivity for the delicate artfulness of the film's source material, Henry James' novella *The Turn of the Screw*. Evil here is of a deceptively subtle sort. As the governess, Kerr must tread a fine line between fantasy and reality. The character's neuroticism is made plain, but we never know for certain if the boy is truly possessed or if his behavior is merely exaggerated in her eyes. In a particularly startling sequence, the boy gives Kerr a very adult kiss on the mouth, a kiss that is at once carnal and childlike. The climax of *The Innocents* is a perverse variation on the Sleeping Beauty story, as Kerr symbolically liberates the boy from his presumed possession with a kiss after he has fainted. Do we see the hand of the dead gardener as the boy falls? Perhaps. There is about *The Innocents* a gentle quality that is expressed in elegiac cinematography by Freddie Francis, and the quiet underplaying of Deborah Kerr. The governess may have a problem with her sexual identity, but is able to work within it. Her adventure is self-liberating.*

Some prisons, though, cannot be escaped. The most profound horror may be the sort that happens next door, the banal terror that can creep into the most pedestrian of milieus. Sexual psychosis may not be as unusual as we think. In 1943 the Russian-born avant-garde filmmaker Maya Deren explored commonplace madness brilliantly in *Meshes of the Afternoon*, an unrelenting short film that places sexual insanity firmly in suburbia. Deren herself appears as a ravishingly beautiful young woman who suffers morbid hallucinations while alone in her home. A key mysteriously appears in her hand, then disappears. She lurches crazily down the stairs and confronts a male intruder. Outside, she follows another man along the sidewalk, but sees only his pants cuff as he repeatedly disappears around the corner ahead of her. She imagines herself being strangled by the man in her house, and later sees herself sitting dead in a chair, a key in her limp hand. The premonition is borne out when she commits suicide.

Although by no stretch of the imagination a "commercial" film, *Meshes of the Afternoon* is significant for the way in which it acts as a bridge between the Dadaist images of Luis Buñuel and Salvador Dalí's *Un Chien Andalou* (1928; famous for the eyeball that is slit by a razor) and a mainstream thriller like Roman Polanski's *Repulsion* (1965). So intense is the latter film's subject matter that it could not have been a mainstream project much earlier than 1965, and surely not before *Psycho* opened the door in 1960. Polanski cleverly cast against type when he chose beautiful Catherine Deneuve to play a London manicurist who is tortured by morbid sexual fantasies and hallucinations. What is remarkable is that Polanski refused to give us a firm grounding in the real world, as Hitchcock did in *Psycho; Repulsion* depicts psychological aberrance from the *inside* out. The central figure, Carol, is a victim of the everyday elements of life and sexuality. She shares a small apartment with her sister and the sister's married boyfriend, and must suffer the tensions of that relationship while enjoying none of the benefits. Left alone in the apartment during a long weekend, Carol's fragile psyche begins to crumble. She hears strange voices and imagines she sees intruders. Grabbing hands shoot from the walls. She has no support, no one to help her. Her mind, like a failing gyroscope, is hopelessly off-kilter. She murders her own boyfriend when he pays an innocent visit, and later slashes the landlord to death after the man has mistaken

Michael Winner's The Nightcomers *(1972) works from the same source material, but is a sort of "prequel" that makes the living gardener the focal point. As in most of Winner's films, the approach is blatant and unaffecting.*

her incoherence for a come-on. Carol is finally discovered by her sister lying mutely beneath a bed. The disintegration is complete.

Repulsion is a landmark film because it places sexual misery in an everyday context. Carol is victimized not simply by her sexual identity and loneliness, but by a cold, banal society which hasn't the means or inclination to treat its members with equanimity. Carol must deal with ugly, pushy women at her work. Louts whistle at her on the street, and she must listen to the sounds of her sister's lovemaking. When her situation becomes unbearable, she retreats within herself. Like a strand of a woven basket, she encounters the real world only at intervals. She is as disconnected as the cold iron she absently uses to smooth her clothes. The apartment building in which she lives is as anonymous and impersonal as every other aspect of her life. Polanski's suggestion that sexual psychosis can result from general social malaise is chillingly reasonable. The repulsion of the title, then, is not simply Carol's reaction to her own sexuality, but to her essence and the entire world. Because she exists, she is in peril. Only in the web of insanity does she achieve a deadened sort of peace.

Polanski himself twisted the psychology of *Repulsion* into a grotesque black comedy in *The Tenant* (1976), which concerns an unprepossessing but ordinary-seeming young Pole (Polanski) who rents a Paris flat that had belonged to a young woman who committed suicide by leaping from the apartment's window. Like *Repulsion*, *The Tenant* explores schizophrenia, the perils of solitude imposed by an acrimonious society, and, especially, paranoia. The tenant visits the shattered, dying woman in the hospital and becomes curiously enmeshed in her suffering. The woman does not speak, but the young man soon becomes convinced that her neighbors drove her to jump. When the woman dies, the tenant is gradually possessed by her spirit — or at least he *thinks* he is. He begins to smoke her brand of cigarette (humorously, it is Marlboro) and acquires her taste for morning hot chocolate. He discovers a tooth that had been wrapped in gauze and inserted in a wall of the apartment (the woman had given him a gap-toothed grimace from her hospital bed), and later awakens to a bloody pillow and one of his *own* teeth in the hole. He wears a dress that had been left behind in the apartment, and buys a wig, makeup, and high heeled shoes. He paints his nails and makes a seductive moue at his mirror image as he models stockings. His life and actions are soon beyond his control, and he imagines that his neighbors are goading him to suicide. He finally hurls himself from the window, not once but, sickeningly, twice. In the hospital, he looks as the woman had: a mummy-wrapped cripple who cannot speak. He is visited by *himself*, and screams the same scream the woman had uttered when he had come to see her at the beginning of his adventure.

The relentless circularity of *The Tenant* (which Polanski wrote with Gerard Brach) is underscored by the film's casting and photography. Actors were seemingly chosen for their grossness of feature. The concierge (Shelley

Winters) is a shuffling bloat, and the aged landlord (Melvyn Douglas) is living parchment. Subtly distorting camerawork emphasizes the noses, mouths, and wattles of other characters. The lips of leading lady Isabelle Adjani look like slabs of liver. A whining little boy is ugly to the point of deformity. Everybody's face is excessively ruddy — not the ruddiness of blood, but of bile. Social intercourse is characterized by insults and indifference. The tenant has slipped into a world of loathsome insanity.

But *The Tenant* does not have the flat objectivity of *Repulsion*. The young man is not dispassionately mad — he is *flamboyantly* mad, and the film ultimately becomes a gleefully perverse, highly theatrical mix of *Charley's Aunt, Rear Window,* and *The Snake Pit*. Eleven years and a lot of tragedy had crossed Polanski's life since *Repulsion*. This time, there is no peace in madness. The young man's sexual neuroticism becomes his ticket for a trip on a Möbius strip: unceasing, never ending, unfailingly horrific. There is no end in sight.

IV
Beauty and the Beast

Among the supreme achievements of world cinema is Jean Cocteau's 1946 masterpiece *La Belle et la Bête* (*Beauty and the Beast*). Cocteau based his simple screenplay upon a French fable, creating a film of surreal elegance and lyric beauty. Josette Day played Beauty, a 17th century girl of the middle class whose family has been made penniless by the failure of her father's business. Beauty's sisters—vain and cruelly self-centered—are oblivious. Because Beauty is unassuming, she spends her days scrubbing floors while her sisters flit about the town and pretend to be ladies of quality. When Beauty's father unthinkingly plucks a rose from the grounds of a mysterious estate, he is confronted by the Beast (Jean Marais), a glowering creature in velvet breeches who resembles a cross between a werewolf and a lion. The Beast demands that the theft of the rose be paid for with the life of the merchant or the life of one of his daughters. Resigning himself to death, the merchant returns home and tells his story. Beauty unselfishly steals off to the Beast's estate in her father's place. When she enters the Beast's castle her plain clothes are transformed into finery. The Beast is entranced with Beauty, and becomes her benign jailer, appearing each evening at seven to ask if she will marry him. She refuses, but gradually grows accustomed to the Beast's intimidating appearance. When her father lies dying, Beauty leaves the Beast's estate, promising to return in a week. The Beast gives her the key to a pavilion that holds all his riches, expressing his hope that the key will symbolize his trust and Beauty's agreement to return. At home, Beauty's sisters deceive her into revealing the secret of the key. Beauty's brother and a friend, Avenant (Jean Marais) conspire to kill the Beast and steal his riches. Beauty sees an image in her mirror of the lonely Beast dying of grief, and goes to him as her brother and Avenant enter the pavilion. Inside, a statue of Diana comes to life, fits an arrow to her bow, and kills Avenant. The Beast, now liberated from his curse by Beauty's love, assumes Avenant's body. He and Beauty leave the estate by magically ascending into the clouds.

With its celebration of the powers of love and its marvelous attention to detail, *La Belle et la Bête* is a truly magical fantasy. Candelabra that line the hallways of the Beast's castle are supported by human arms. Carved faces in mantelpieces observe Beauty as she paces. The Beast provides Beauty with magical transportation: a white horse named Magnificent One who will take Beauty anywhere at all, and a gauntlet that can instantly transport the wearer from one place to another. Only Beauty is worthy of such gifts. When the father asks his daughters what gifts *he* might give them, one of Beauty's sisters asks for a monkey, the other for a parrot. Beauty asks for a rose. A pearl necklace given to Beauty by the Beast turns to dirty rags when touched by the unworthy sisters, who are reflected in a magic mirror as a crone and an ape. And when Beauty later comforts her sick father, her tears turn to diamonds. Beauty is an archetype, the epitome of feminine loveliness and spirituality. Her physical beauty is considerable, but it is her beauty of the spirit that enables her to deal with the Beast's untamed appearance and gruff manner. Beauty is also able to come to grips with the Beast's powerful sexuality, maintaining her composure after realizing that she is being observed in her chambers, and allowing the Beast to lap water from her cupped hands. The latter scene is so highly charged with eroticism that one is left breathless. Beauty's most significant quality is a remarkable unselfishness. When she believes the Beast to be dying, she runs through the halls and gardens of his estate, crying, "Beast! My Beast! I'm the monster, Beast. You shall live, you shall live!"

The Beast has admirable qualities of his own, among them a willingness to make himself vulnerable by confessing to Beauty his love for her. All the accoutrements of his power—his gauntlet, horse, key—become Beauty's. His faith in her is not misplaced, and although his final transformation to human form hardly seems necessary, he proves himself a suitable mate. "Love can make a Beast of a man," he tells Beauty. "It can also make an ugly man handsome." The couple's love, we can infer, will be both carnal and spiritual. Each partner has liberated the other. *La Belle et la Bête* is an oddity, a one-shot in every sense of the term. Never duplicated and seldom imitated, the film stands alone. Cocteau's insistence upon portraying powerful sexuality as a gift rather than a threat is laudable and uncommon. The "beauty and the beast" theme is seminal in art and literature, and has been featured on movie screens since film's earliest days. *La Belle et la Bête* is its noblest, most positive interpretation. The film tells us that, when there is no malice, sexuality and the love of even an ugly man can bring joy.

It can also bring terror, a reaction that has been more common to the horror genre because it is easier to provoke in an audience. We all worry about our physical vulnerability. Sexuality, with its connotations of the bedroom, the dark, and nakedness, places us at our *most* vulnerable. When the demonic somnambulist Cesare (Conrad Veidt) creeps into Lil Dagover's bedchamber in *The Cabinet of Dr. Caligari* (1919), director Robert Wiene was exploiting a fear common to us all. Prone and sleeping, the woman is utterly helpless. She wakes to see the fiend hovering over her. Plucked from her bed, she is carried off into the expressionist labyrinth that Wiene used to symbolize the darkest torments of the human mind and soul. The terror we have for such things is not diminished in more realistic settings. In *The Cat and the Canary* (1928)—a seminal film of the "old dark house" subgenre—heroine Laura

LaPlante sleeps, unaware that the shadow of the mad killer has fallen across her bosom. The image is primal, and leaves no doubt that the single greatest icon of the horror film is the female body, undraped and in peril. Typically, the genre has not been concerned with liberation, but *domination*. Ladies, the sky is dark and the monsters are horny tonight. And they have long arms: in Archie Mayo's *Svengali* (1931) the title fiend (John Barrymore) reaches out with his mind to touch the sleeping Trilby (Marian Marsh). Svengali's face fills the screen, his eyes large and perfectly white. Then, in an audacious pullback shot, the camera leaves his house through the window, glides above the roof-tops of 19th century France (created in disconcerting miniature by Anton Grot), and enters Trilby's window. The woman is in her bed, and as Svengali's evil intent gathers force beside her, she wakes. Her bedroom—that most private sanctuary of all proper ladies—has been invaded by a monstrous presence.

Attractive women have been regarded for so long as the rightful property of worthy men that the thought of a "beast" putting designs on a lady is doubly repellent, sexually *and* culturally. For reasons both justified and unjustified, we fear unrestrained sexual expression. Unwanted pregnancies and the psychological scars of rape are obvious drawbacks. But in the horror film, the wanton sexuality of monsters is not primarily feared because of the damage it may do to the hapless woman involved, but because it is an affront to male sexuality. Sexuality is power, and those who possess power are loath to share it. Men have determined that women are property, like an automobile or a baseball mitt. And a man's private property should be left alone.

There is another, slightly deeper level at work in the psychology of the beauty and the beast film. It is no coincidence that virtually all of the outraged men and women in such films are white. The monsters—dark, furry, subhuman—are the antithesis of the Anglo-Saxon ideal. Their desires mock and defy what we accept as the proper order of things. Brutal and unreasoning, the beasts are barely fit to live, let alone possess fair-skinned maidens. The beasts' crime, then, is infringement upon the arrogant power of the Anglo male. In matters as primal as this, there is little room for tolerance.

The early years of the sound era spawned a thriving horror subgenre in which beautiful women were coveted by snarly apes. *King Kong* (1933) is of course the most celebrated example, but there were numerous antecedents. In 1927, *The Wizard* proposed that a scientist could transplant the head of a man onto the body of an ape. The resultant mayhem—unfortunately lost for many years—undoubtedly gave heroine Leila Hyams plenty of opportunity to do some lusty screaming (which is what she did in the 1933 *Island of Lost Souls* when chased around a dank jungle by Ouran, the man-ape).

Beauty (Josette Day) learns to accept the love of the Beast (Jean Marais) in Jean Cocteau's elegant fantasy *La Belle et la Bête* (1946). Note the candelabrum and the living face in the woodwork.

Two versions of *The Gorilla* (1927 and 1930) are horror comedies in which an ape causes consternation among the residents of a spooky house. Similar goings-on are explored in *Seven Footprints to Satan* (1929), the last of the important silent horror films. Abraham Merrit's original novel is a grim read, but screenwriter Richard Bee and director Benjamin Christensen interpreted it quite lightly, turning the central element of satanism into a hoax. Thelma Todd was cast as the fortitudinous heroine who is lusted after by a gorilla that prowls the secret passageways and back stairs of a creaky mansion. Todd, a breathtaking beauty and skilled comedienne, later became popular as a two-reel star before her untimely and mysterious death in 1935 at age 30. Her aplomb as she deals with the grabby gorilla is admirable.

These early "ape on the prowl" pictures are pretty tame, suggesting more than their makers dared show. The breakthrough film was *Ingagi* (1931), a low-budget thriller from an outfit that called itself Congo Pictures Ltd. Its plot followed a pattern that was to become typical: great white hunters on expedition in Africa hear rumors of giant gorillas, and of a tribe that worships them. The gorillas are discovered, and a virgin is sacrificed before the eyes of the astonished explorers. After the hunters kill one of the apes, a buxom native girl mourns as though the beast had been her lover. Director William Campbell shot bogus jungle scenes in wild and wooly California, structuring them around silent footage of an authentic African expedition. The mix isn't bad but does have its peculiarities, such as gamboling animals indigenous to North America, and suspiciously light-skinned natives. An attractive black girl abducted by the gorilla Ingagi played the scene topless, which raised the ire of censors in Ohio, where the film was banned. Business elsewhere was brisk. Ad lines like "Amazing Discoveries of Jungle Life!" and "The Scientific Marvel of the Age!" doubtless appealed to the intelligentsia, while those of us with baser instincts were lured with come-ons like "Giant Gorillas! Wild Women!" Ingagi was played by Charles Gemora, a diminutive Manilan costume maker who went on to play the Martian in *War of the Worlds* (1953), but who is best-remembered by cineastes for his portrayal of the Alpine ape who bothers Laurel and Hardy in *Swiss Miss* (1938). As Ingagi, Gemora may have foregone any hope of dialogue, but at least he got the girl.

Ingagi inspired imitators, though none quite bold enough to feature nudity. *Love Life of a Gorilla* (ca. 1937) *was* intriguingly titled, though, as was *Forbidden Adventure in Angkor* (1937). In each, dusky beauties are cuffed around by amorous monkeys. In *The Monster Walks* (1932) actress Vera Reynolds is menaced by Yogi, which is not a bear but another monkey. The film is of the "old dark house" variety, offering secret passageways, sinister servants, and greedy people who squabble over a meaty inheritance. After the villain (Mischa Auer) whips Yogi into a frenzy, the heroine seems doomed to

Werner Krauss (left), Conrad Veidt, and Lil Dagover in *The Cabinet of Dr. Caligari* (1919), Robert Wiene's nightmare of predatory sexuality.

a messy death. Hero Rex Lease appears at the last moment, and rescues the girl as the ape strangles Auer.

The Monster Walks was one of the first gorilla pictures to place a white woman in jeopardy. The gambit proved to be immensely popular, and inspired *Savage Girl* (1932), in which Rochelle Hudson scampers around the jungle in a leopardskin miniskirt and pretends to be the "white goddess" who is protected by an ape. Charles Gemora again played the monkey, jealously disposing of an evil German who has designs on his consort.

Robert Florey's *Murders in the Rue Morgue* (1932) starred a glowering Bela Lugosi as Dr. Mirakle, a sideshow shill who titillates audiences with his harebrained theories about evolution. His primary visual aid is an overgrown orangutan (Charles Gemora, of course) whom Mirakle wishes to mate with a human woman. Preliminary experiments in which unlucky streetwalkers are transfused with monkey blood (an obvious sexual metaphor) fail miserably, the victims shrieking in agony before dying. Mirakle cannot pull off his miracle, and only succeeds in attracting the attention of the police, who shoot him to death. At 60 minutes, the film is economical and frightening. Designer Charles Hall created faintly distorted, claustrophobic sets that suggest the unreal quality of nightmare. Robert Florey walked away from the project when Universal cut the budget from $130,000 to $90,000, but eventually returned, probably wishing later he had not, for the studio took the finished film to the editing room and made hash of it. Nonetheless, it is good, improbable fun. Its premise seemed to have carried movie monkeyshines as far as they could go, and could well have been the end of the ape/woman subgenre if not for the arrival in 1933 of *King Kong*.

Kong's plot has become so well-known that it scarcely needs to be reviewed here. Indeed, the film has entered folklore, regarded as not only a riveting adventure, but as a classic tale of doomed romance. Willis O'Brien's stop-motion animation is brilliantly good, and glows with an impeccable understanding of personality: Kong is more than flashy movement and a loud growl—he is an individual. His brow puckers, his eyes roll, his nostrils quiver. He is an adept fistfighter (his display of poise as he battles a Tyrannosaurus is marvelous), and a sympathetically inept suitor. When the biplanes topple him from the Empire State Building, we have not disposed of a monster but lost a friend. Explorer Carl Denham (Robert Armstrong) knows that Kong has died for love; he informs the gloating police, "'Twas *beauty* killed the beast."

The great pity that we feel for Kong arises from the fact that in spite of his strength and size, he is a victim. He is destroyed because his love for the blonde maiden (Fay Wray) is greater than his instinct for self-preservation. Many critics have written rather pompously about the way in which Kong's predicament parallels that of the American black. Obviously, the parallel has been drawn because Kong himself is black, and because he is wrenched from his home by people who would exploit him. The critics who hold this view overlook the fact that Kong has made the black natives of Skull Island his own

The doomed *King Kong* (1933) regards his golden-haired prize (Fay Wray).

slaves. Kong is just one link in a *chain* of oppression. The film's racial aspect, then, is not most telling in a political sense, but in a sexual one. In spite of our affection for Kong, we are uneasy. Fay Wray's Ann Darrow is the archetypal blonde goddess, so lovely and ephemeral as to be almost heart-breaking. She is precisely the sort of vision (so the myth goes) coveted by lusting black men. No matter that Kong is simply too *large* to consummate the relationship (here we dally with another racial/sexual myth), Ann is *it*. Not only our eyes tell us the relationship is wrong, but the Caucasian sen-timents that shaped the film, the same sentiments that continue to shape our involuntary reaction to it today. Kong's size may be the last thing we fear; it is his color and especially his undisciplined sexuality that disturb us most. He has broken the most primal of the white man's laws.

Although horror films have traditionally escaped much of the censorship that has plagued "mainstream" films, *King Kong* touched a nerve with the celebrated sequence in which Kong tenderly plucks the clothes from Ann Darrow's body, then sniffs the womanscent that lingers on his fingers. The scene is benign, utterly charming, and a masterpiece of special effects technique. Yet it was excised from prints almost from the film's initial release, and has only recently been restored to theatrical prints shown in revival theaters. Most television prints are still abridged. The sequence is not graphic or even especially titillating. It continues to be suppressed because of its implications. Kong's fingers probe uncomfortably close to territory that is forbidden.

In the lame 1976 remake directed by John Guillermin, the story's sexual aspect is turned into the focus of adolescent humor. When the object of Kong's affection (Jessica Lange) is hoisted aloft in an enormous paw, she does not scream but coyly asks, "What's your sign?" She is clearly a girl of infinite jest, if not of infinite intellect. Ditto for actress Joanna DeVarona, the token Anglo in Paul Leder's dreadful Korean-American *A*P*E* (1976). Lifted into the air by the Kong clone, DeVarona poutily advises, "Be gentle, big fella."

The commercial success of the original *Kong* was enormous. Directors Ernest Schoedsack and Merian C. Cooper, and Willis O'Brien rushed a sequel into production, and managed to release it the same year as its inspiration. Unfortunately, *Son of Kong* backpedalled; its animation sequences are few and relatively unambitious, its story unnecessarily cute. Baby Kong (nicknamed Nikko) is an asexual albino who seems more taken with hero Robert Armstrong than with heroine Helen Mack. The same production team released *Mighty Joe Young* in 1949, in which perky teenager Terry Moore is looked after by a 15-foot ape named Joe Young. Their relationship is strictly brother-and-sister, and although Joe — like Kong — is exploited by an ambitious promoter, he lives to see the eventual marriage of Moore and hero Ben Johnson.

The Kong films and *Mighty Joe Young* were financed and released by RKO. Smaller companies could not duplicate their budgets or technical expertise, so were forced to recycle less novel formats. White goddesses whose consorts are (normal-sized) apes continued to turn up in pictures like *The House of Mystery* (1934) and *Nabonga* (1944); the latter film starred 18-year-old Julie London as an unlikely jungle girl. Bela Lugosi was *The Ape Man* in 1943, a scientist whose experiments transform him into an ape-like humanoid who must murder women for their spinal fluid. The film's funniest scenes involve a supposedly real ape who puts the moves on spinsterish character actress Minerva Urecal. *White Pongo* (1945) is an impressive blond gorilla who abducts heroine Maris Wrixon, but the best come-on of all was offered by *Beast of Borneo* (1935), which billed itself as "The Weirdest Triangle Ever Filmed!"

Predictably, *Beast of Borneo* was just one of many such films that did not live up to its advertising. Audiences were pleasantly surprised by Stuart

Heisler's *The Monster and the Girl*, which was ground out by Paramount's B-picture unit in 1941. Ellen Drew played a young woman who is unwillingly sold into prostitution after a phony marriage with a hoodlum. The "groom's" boss (Paul Lukas) is responsible for framing Drew's older brother (Phillip Terry) on a murder charge. Tried and convicted, Terry is approached on Death Row by a slightly dotty scientist (George Zucco) who inquires if he might have Terry's brain after the execution. In a moment of contrived agreeability, the condemned man replies, "Help yourself!" Zucco proceeds to implant the brain into the body of a gorilla; the monkey becomes an improbable sort of avenging angel, disposing of Lukas and other bad guys, and liberating his captive sister. The gorilla is eventually shot dead by the police, but Drew acquires a decent boyfriend (Rod Cameron) who will presumably whisk her off to a life of *legalized* servitude.

The Monster and the Girl is interesting because it reflects two approaches to moviemaking that flourished in Hollywood during the thirties and forties. Independently made exploitation cheapies with titles like *Wages of Sin* and *Damaged Goods* teased audiences of the period while pretending to expose the evils of dope, prostitution, and other subjects usually given a wide berth by the major studios. *The Monster and the Girl* is an odd, amusingly successful combination of that sort of simpleminded exploitation and the more legitimate horror genre. By today's standards, though, the circumstances of Ellen Drew's servitude seem mild. Her captors dress well and even use proper English. But to audiences of the time, any sort of sexual misadventure was horrid and exciting. A pity that every wayward girl does not have as impressive a big brother...

In *Zamba the Gorilla* (1949) the title anthropoid befriends 8-year-old Beau Bridges, but abducts the tot's mother. More unusual is *Captive Wild Woman* (1943), in which scientist John Carradine turns a gorilla into a sultry woman (Acquanetta). The scientist's big mistake is neglecting to reckon with female temperament; whenever the quasi-woman becomes jealous, she reverts to her original state. In the battle of the sexes, a talent such as this might be called an unfair advantage. But audiences apparently approved, for Acquanetta returned in a 1944 sequel, *Jungle Woman*, while Vicki Lane took the role in *Jungle Captive* (1945).

Gorilla love stories lost favor in the late forties, but surfaced again in the early fifties when Hollywood was desperate to distract potential patrons from television. How could Uncle Miltie have hoped to compete with high class stuff like *Bride of the Gorilla* (1952), in which Barbara Payton is unhappy because her husband (Raymond Burr) is no longer the man she married? A young starlet named Anne Bancroft earned her money in *Gorilla at Large* (1954) when cast as a high wire artist who is kidnapped by a murderous ape. The monkey was probably enticed by Bancroft's fishnet stockings. *Bride and the Beast* came from the fevered typewriter of Edward D. Wood, Jr., in 1958, and detailed the plight of a lovely young woman (Charlotte Austin) who is turned on by gorillas. As might be expected, her marriage suffers, but she finds true happiness after realizing that she is the reincarnation of an ape. She reverts to her true form and scampers off in search of lasting romance.

Moviegoers who were searching for truthful insights into the human condition were probably unsatisfied by these monkey soap operas. Finally, the only avenue left to filmmakers was satire. Director John Landis poked fun at the inanities of the subgenre with *Schlock!* (1973) and *Kentucky Fried Movie* (1977). The star of the former film is Schlockthropus (played by Landis in an intentionally cheesy ape suit designed by makeup artist Rick Baker), a drooling quasi-ape with a taste for ice cream cones and Southern California bathing beauties. *Kentucky Fried Movie* is composed of satiric vignettes; one of them is a bitingly accurate spoof of local television newscasts in which a deadpan report of an escaped gorilla is followed by the ape (Rick Baker) bursting into the studio in front of a live camera, clubbing the anchorman, and ripping all the clothes from the attractive anchorlady. One hopes the gorilla at least had the sense to wait until sweeps week.

Not all filmmakers were as perceptive as John Landis about the limits of the ape subgenre. In 1980, producer/writer Pierre Brousseau presented *Tanya's Island*, a romantic fable directed by Alfred Sole. Model D.D. Winters (now known as Vanity) starred as Tanya, who has a row with her boyfriend and dreams of a hot romance with an ape on a tropic isle. Conceptually, the film is little different from those made in the thirties and forties, but the freedom of the eighties allowed lingering sequences of the unorthodox couple's lovemaking. Winters is very attractive and the ape costume designed by Rick Baker and built by Rob Bottin is absolutely stunning. Auburn fur and a fully-articulated face frame striking blue eyes. Mime Don McCleod played the ape with laudable attention to gesture and nuance. The film falls down in the script department, as do so many films of the genre. Sole, who had directed an excellent horror thriller called *Communion* (aka *Alice, Sweet Alice*) in 1977, could not induce the audience to suspend its disbelief. The scenes of the girl willingly trysting with the ape are as unconvincing as ... a girl willingly trysting with an ape. *Tanya's Island* came and went virtually unnoticed; apparently, even the most fervent thrillseekers demand a bit of believability.

What could be more believable than a 3000-year-old Egyptian seeking the 20th century reincarnation of his mate? Well, probably a lot of things, but audiences didn't quibble in 1932 when Boris Karloff played *The Mummy*, a priest named Im-Ho-Tep who had been buried alive for daring to love a princess. After being revived in present-day Egypt by an unwitting archeologist, Tep is free to resume his quest for the princess, whose spirit lives on in a darkly beautiful English girl (Zita Johann). Tep gains access to the museum which displays the artifacts from his tomb, and performs a rite that mesmerizes the girl, who is miles away. Entranced, she attempts to break into the museum but is restrained by a young archeologist. When the girl later meets Tep (who calls himself Ardath Bey), she succumbs to his power. Dressed in Egyptian raiment, she will be killed and mummified so that she can rise as Tep's mate. "Bear with me, my princess," Tep intones. "In a few moments we will share immortality." But the girl's will to live proves stronger than Tep's hold on her. She appeals to a nearby figure of Isis for help, and Tep is destroyed by a crackling blast of force that issues from the figure's ankh.

Karl Freund directed *The Mummy* with remarkable restraint. Karloff is seen in his mummy guise only briefly, most famously when an archeologist reads aloud the chant that restores Tep to life. In the sarcophagus behind the archeologist, the mummy's eyes slowly open, and Tep steps forward. The archeologist (well-played by Bramwell Fletcher) shrieks in terror. Later, he is asked of the mummy's whereabouts. "He went for a little walk," he titters. "You should have seen his face...." Freund reasoned that just a few glimpses of that face would be sufficient to establish Tep's monstrousness. Karloff, in his guise as Ardath Bey, looks like living parchment. One can almost feel the dryness of his skin and breath. Zita Johann's large liquid eyes and softness of flesh are in startling and repellent contrast to Tep's withered features. The relationship promises to be nothing but obscene.

The Mummy was Karloff's first major triumph after *Frankenstein*, and established him as cinema's successor to Lon Chaney, Sr. as Master of Horror. Universal busily promoted sequels to *Frankenstein* and *Dracula* throughout the thirties, but returned to the Mummy in 1940 when cowboy star Tom Tyler took the role in *The Mummy's Hand*. The film was successful and inspired three sequels, each starring Lon Chaney, Jr. The series is entertaining, but nowhere near the level of craftsmanship that had been established by Freund and Karloff. The Mummy (now called Kharis) functions mainly as a mute stooge of evil and/or uninformed modern-day Egyptians, played by such diverse actors as John Carradine, Turhan Bey, and George Zucco. The horror of the Chaney films is blatant and uninvolving; the actor's conception suggests none of the distasteful desire of Karloff's wrinkled but otherwise normal Ardath Bey. Chaney's Kharis is merely the bandaged and shuffling figure we have come to know through comic books and plastic model kits.

Chaney first took the role in *The Mummy's Tomb* (1942), which establishes that Kharis' prime directive is the guardianship of Princess Ananka, who appears only as a mummy on display in a small New England town. The beauty and the beast theme did not get rolling until *The Mummy's Ghost* in 1944. The setting is the same town seen in the previous film. A college student (Ramsay Ames) who is the reincarnation of Ananka attracts the lustful attention of Kharis' manipulator (Turhan Bey), who orders the mummy to kidnap the girl. Kharis does so, but kills his mentor after realizing that the girl is in peril. The mummy lifts the girl in his arms and strides (rather inexplicably) to a swamp, where the young lady (just as inexplicably) ages in an instant. The reincarnation of Ananka is an aged crone by the time she and Kharis sink in a bog of quicksand. Early scenes of Miss Ames in a slinky satin negligee are mildly enticing, but Kharis seems disinclined to take unfair

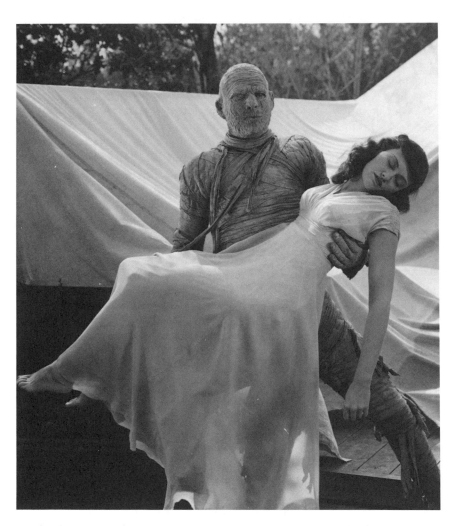

The implacable Kharis (Lon Chaney, Jr.) with the oft-reincarnated Princess Ananka (Virginia Christine) in *The Mummy's Curse* (1945).

advantage. His talent for lovemaking seems to be as highly developed as his skill at guardianship.

Kharis got a break in the final sequel, *The Mummy's Curse* (1945), when Ananka (Virginia Christine) rises from the bog after it is bulldozed. Her resurrection does not provoke nearly as many questions as an unexplained shift in locale from New England to Louisiana. Oh, well. Why let such trivialities stand in the way of romance? Kharis again stalks around town with his princess, putting her down only to commit an occasional strangulation murder. The mummy is finally destroyed by fire, and Ananka, unprotected once again, withers away a second time. Kharis is either very careless or just plain unlucky. Although Jack Pierce's makeup design for Chaney is splendid, the character itself has no personality or dramatic thrust. Chaney's Mummy is, in fact, the only horror movie character to have achieved icon status in spite of being very bland. Kharis has stuck in our consciousness probably because of his immobile white face and shambling gait. Of all the faces of sexual terror, the Mummy's may be the most fearsome because it is the most implacable.

Universal allowed Abbott and Costello to meet the Mummy before giving up on the character in the mid-fifties. Britain's Hammer Films released their own version, *The Mummy*, in 1959. Jimmy Sangster's script is very nearly a scene-for-scene reworking of the 1932 original. Despite some amusing sadism (notably a tongue-pulling sequence), a luscious leading lady (Yvonne Furneaux), and a good performance by Christopher Lee in the title role, Kharis seemed a creature of the past in more ways than one.

Undaunted, Hammer tried again in 1964 with *The Curse of the Mummy's Tomb*. Good use was made of color, but the film is excessively talky. The Mummy (Dickie Moore) is a barely-glimpsed, faceless automaton that halfheartedly abducts the heroine (Jeanne Roland) before being destroyed in a flooded sewer. *The Mummy's Shroud* arrived in 1967 to place chesty archeologist Maggie Kimberley in danger from the moldy fellow (Eddie Powell) she has resurrected. By this time, the concept was running out of steam, and Hammer knew it. So did audiences. Hammer's final attempt, *Blood from the Mummy's Tomb* (1971), was not strictly a mummy film at all, but a variation of the Jekyll and Hyde theme.* Based on Bram Stoker's novel *Jewel of the Seven Stars*, the film follows the misadventures of a magnificently endowed young woman (Valerie Leon) who is possessed by the evil spirit of an Egyptian princess whose tomb was defiled on the day the young victim was born.† Hammer knew where the money was, and allowed Kharis to be superseded by cleavage. The only mummy on view is the unmoving corpse of the princess.

The Mummy, particularly as characterized by Lon Chaney, Jr., is the most silent and unreasoning of the major horror figures. Like a steamroller with no operator, the Mummy triggers our fear but says nothing to our hearts or minds. His victims are doomed to the same sort of two-dimensionality. The trap is one that beauty and the beast films have fallen into with depressing regularity. It is the rare film, then, that can avoid the trap by creating believable characters and placing them in situations that arouse not simply our terror, but our pity as well. In the 1924 version of *The Hunchback of Notre*

It was, in fact, released in England on a double bill with Dr. Jekyll and Sister Hyde *(1972).*

†*The story was ineptly redone in 1980 as* The Awakening, *starring Charlton Heston and featuring Stephanie Zimbalist as the possessed girl.*

Dame, Esmeralda (Patsy Ruth Miller) is kind to the pathetic Quasimodo (Lon Chaney, Sr.), the misshapen bellringer who has loved her from afar. After the hunchback has been unfairly lashed to a wheel and whipped, he begs for water. Esmeralda—a gypsy girl who will gain nothing by drawing attention to herself—obliges, in a scene that is touching in its simple celebration of humanity. Maureen O'Hara, Gina Lollobrigida, and Lesley-Anne Down repeated the kindness in 1939, 1957, and 1982, respectively. Of course, Quasimodo is not a beast at all. The 70-pound hump and heavy facial makeup worn by Chaney in 1924 did not obscure the character's humanity, but heightened it. Quasimodo's romantic yearning creates pathos, not terror. We never doubt that his love for Esmeralda is innocently motivated.

Less innocent motives but ones nearly as piteous are at the heart of Rupert Julian's *The Phantom of the Opera* (1925). Lon Chaney, Sr., played Erik, a masked musician who haunts the catacombs beneath the Paris Opera House after being disfigured in a fire. He is in love with Christine (Mary Philbin), a young opera star who has benefited from his whispered (but unseen) tutelage. Erik finally kidnaps the girl and takes her to his dark catacomb. Thus the horror begins. Chaney's parents were deaf-mutes, so the actor grew up with an impeccable understanding of nonverbal communication. In a way, *The Phantom of the Opera* is the perfect silent film, for it allowed Chaney to exercise the full range of his pantomimic skills. Erik, masked until the picture's midpoint, moves with the grandiloquence of an impassioned genius. Christine is frightened by him but gradually develops an intrigued sort of respect. She resolves to see her abductor's face. The unmasking sequence is masterfully constructed: as Erik sits at his pipe organ, Christine creeps up behind, hesitates, then plucks the mask away. Erik stiffens, opening his gash of a mouth in rage ... or is it exultation? He turns and we see him subjectively, as Christine does, his face strangely out of focus at first, then sharpening as it moves towards us.

The sequence is a shocker, not simply because it exploits the hideous ugliness of Erik's skull-like face, but because it signals the sudden release of the Phantom's pent-up sexual energy. His ugliness is only external—the force that has driven him into exile and to kidnapping is not deformity, but *frustration*. By removing the mask, the girl has freed Erik, accomplishing what he could not do for himself. His manhood returned, he is able to draw upon his latent heroism when pursued by a mob of enraged Parisians at the film's climax. Erik is cornered but not defeated. He defies his tormentors by raising a clenched fist. Does he hold a weapon? The mob shrinks back. Erik unfolds his hand: it is empty. He is then killed by the mob, but the final jest, the final demonstration of power, has been his.

Though a tremendous moneymaker for Universal, *The Phantom of the Opera* was not without its problems. Chaney and director Rupert Julian did not get along well, and Chaney felt obliged to direct many scenes himself. The studio committed a great deal of money to the production and grew nervous when shooting wrapped, taking the picture out on "sneak previews" and fiddling with it in the editing room. Except for the presence of Chaney and some impressive sets, the film has not worn particularly well. Nevertheless, it is one of those rare love stories that successfully juggles horror, loathing, and pity. Its sexual energy could not have been greater if Chaney had played his role in the nude. Especially telling are sequences early in the film in which Erik hovers unseen above Christine and her lover. Omnipotent yet powerless, the Phantom is both judge and victim. A pair of fine actors—Claude Rains and Herbert Lom—were cast in 1943 and 1962 remakes, films which emphasized splashy set design and obvious makeup effects instead of insights into the title character. Chaney's Erik—a monument to sexual longing and rage—stands alone.

The sexual menace of a masked man became a popular and enduring horror film motif. Haunted house thrillers like *The Terror* (1928) and *The Bat Whispers* (1931) exploited it cleverly, but the greatest interpretation after Erik may be Lionel Atwill's Ivan Igor in *Mystery of the Wax Museum* (1933). Igor is a sculptor who is confined to a wheelchair after being trapped in a wax museum fire set by an unscrupulous business partner. Igor's sensitive sculptor's hands have been ruined, and he must rely upon inept assistants. But through the investigations of a crack newspaper reporter (Glenda Farrell) and the victimization of a young beauty (Fay Wray), it becomes apparent that Igor is a murderer who lusts after beautiful women so that he may coat them in wax and display them to an unwitting public.

In a climactic confrontation, Fay Wray strikes Igor's face, cracking its waxy surface to reveal the hideously burned flesh beneath. The moment is a classic one, happily preserved by film scholars who discovered a print of the movie in the late sixties, when it had been presumed lost forever. Director Michael Curtiz (whose early experience was abroad) brought a uniquely European tone to the film, but a major share of the credit for the film's success must go to set designer Anton Grot, who created spacious, almost vaulted rooms that bristle with odd angles and disconcerting shadows. There is a faintly expressionist flavor to Igor's milieu. Grot's design for a domed morgue (from which a body is stolen) is positively Gothic. Good use was made of two-strip Technicolor, a primitive process that was restricted to gradations of red and green. The green, in particular, is well-suited to the ghastly subject matter.

Glenda Farrell's snoopy, perpetually wisecracking reporter—a characterization typical of the period—wears thin, yet without some sort of comic relief the film could have become unbearably grim. Ivan Igor is among the screen's great monsters, not simply because he is disfigured, but because he has twisted his love of feminine beauty into a talent for abduction and murder. Lionel Atwill, who would later make a career out of playing crackpot scientists, brought a keen sense of irony to his role. The sculptor is courtly, even solicitous. He obviously appreciates beauty but, as a cripple, cannot act

upon that appreciation. Or so it seems. When he rises from his wheelchair to attack Fay Wray, the terror is of a particularly surprising and visceral sort: the bogeyman can walk!

Charlotte (Wray) is the image of Igor's Marie Antoinette, a cherished wax figure that was destroyed in the fire. When Igor sees Charlotte for the first time, it is in a subjective shot; for just a moment, the raiment of Antoinette is superimposed over Charlotte. The young woman has been marked. When Igor seizes Charlotte later, he advises, "You will always be beautiful! Think, my child, in a thousand years you will be as lovely as you are now!" Curtiz made a special point to establish Charlotte's loveliness, offering a scene of the girl provocatively raising her bare legs and pulling on her stockings. Shot before the advent of the restrictive Hays censorship code, the scene—like the earlier subjective shot of Charlotte as Marie Antoinette—turns the viewer into an accomplice. Curtiz utilized this psychological gambit again at the climax when Charlotte lies on a table in Igor's hidden lab preparatory to being showered by boiling wax. Ivory-skinned and obviously naked beneath a flimsy sheet, Charlotte is breathtakingly lovely. Igor's perception has become our own, and we can hardly blame him for his obsession.

Igor's sublimated sexuality and hidden lair are elements reminiscent of Erik and the Paris catacombs. Like the Phantom, Igor is a sympathetic monster, as much a victim as a perpetrator. Andre de Toth directed a disappointingly turgid remake called *House of Wax* in 1953. Vincent Price played the villain with some enthusiasm, but de Toth's direction is flat, his visual style unimaginative. The film was released at the peak of the 3-D craze of the fifties; de Toth seems to have been more absorbed with staging contrived dimensional effects (like a paddleball that is repeatedly bounced into the audience's lap) than with creating legitimate chills. As opposed to the present-day setting of *Mystery of the Wax Museum* (novel for a horror film of the early thirties), the action of *House of Wax* takes place in Victorian America. De Toth took full advantage of this only once, when the cloaked fiend pursues heroine Phyllis Kirk through the foggy, cobblestoned streets. Another sequence—in which Price's deaf-mute assistant (Charles Buchinsky, later Bronson) eyes Kirk in the otherwise deserted museum—is similarly foreboding. Phyllis Kirk did not possess the ethereal quality projected so aptly by Fay Wray in the earlier film, so the mad sculptor's obsession with her seems a bit mystifying. The climactic unmasking, though startling, hasn't nearly the sexual impact to be memorable. De Toth's style of moviemaking seems "modern" to audiences of the 1980s (the film did well in a 1982 reissue), so it is probably more appealing to a mass audience than its 1933 inspiration. Artistically, though, it is just a waxen replica.

A gallery of Phantoms and their women, from left: Lon Chaney and Mary Philbin (1925), Claude Rains and Suzanna Foster (1943), Herbert Lom and Heather Sears (1962).

One might expect a film entitled *The Face Behind the Mask* to be in the same horrific vein as *Mystery of the Wax Museum*. Surprisingly—and to its credit—this 1941 release directed by Robert Florey is a tender, touching love story, and among the best low-budget Hollywood films of the forties. Peter Lorre was Janos Szabo, a naive Hungarian immigrant who turns to crime after his face is hideously scarred in a tenement fire. He hides his ruined features beneath a taut rubber mask, and quickly rises to control a large criminal gang. Enter an attractive blind girl (Evelyn Keyes), whose innate sweetness brings out the best in Szabo. They fall in love but the girl is blown up by the gang when Szabo anounces his intentions to go straight. He avenges the girl's death by hiring a plane and stranding himself and his former associates in the desert.

Synopsized, the film's plot sounds like a bad revue sketch or something that might have starred Peter Sellers and Spike Milligan. Contemporary critics were not kind, and the film had a relatively unsuccessful first run. Remarkably, though, Florey avoided the sticky sentiment that could have very easily compromised the picture. The tone throughout is straightforward and unapologetic, with no false emphasis upon the "inner beauty" theme. Lorre's "mask" was his own face, covered with flat foundation powder and pulled unnaturally taut with adhesive strips. The design was appropriately eerie, but did not prohibit Lorre's facial mobility. Seldom was better use made of the actor's expressive eyes and soft-spoken quality. His scenes with Evelyn Keyes have a reflective tranquility that is rare in commercial cinema, low-budget or otherwise. Like Lorre, Keyes sidestepped the obvious aspects of her character. The fact that the girl is blind is never made a point of pity or saccharine sweetness.

Keyes is an appealing, talented actress who had the bad luck to hit Columbia at the same time as Rita Hayworth. Her career was never given proper attention by the studio, and remained relatively modest. Though Keyes shrugs off *The Face Behind the Mask* in her 1977 autobiography as "a Peter Lorre flick," Keyes seldom had the opportunity to give a more moving performance. Nor did Robert Florey direct a more unusual film. His skill with offbeat subject matter served him well, particularly in early scenes of Janos helplessly wandering the city in search of work, the streets dark, moody, and claustrophobic. The final image of Janos tied to the struts of his airplane while his enemies wait for him—and themselves—to die is powerful and ingenious. Above all, though, the film is a uniquely bittersweet romance. The face behind Janos' rubber mask may be scarred and disfigured, but it is also the face of love.

The Face Behind the Mask is an oddity in the beauty and the beast subgenre. The tender beasts have been rare; unpleasantness is the norm. Rouben Mamoulian's *Dr. Jekyll and Mr. Hyde* (1932) brought a grim psychological slant to the theme (see Chapter II) that inspired dozens of films. Until the fifties, the subgenre had at least a modicum of verisimilitude in that

Peter Lorre and Evelyn Keyes as unexpected lovers in Robert Florey's *The Face Behind the Mask* (1941).

the monsters were earthly things like gorillas and disfigured men. But after the A-bomb vaporized Hiroshima, commonplace horrors began not to seem horrifying anymore. Pulp science-fiction magazine covers of the late forties depicted busty space amazons in the grip of lascivious BEM's — Bug-Eyed Monsters. EC's legendary *Weird Science* and *Weird Fantasy* comic books of the early fifties proposed that Earth women might be impregnated by robots and hideous, pulpy Martians endowed with revolting and alarmingly dextrous tentacles.

In the early sixties, Bubbles Inc. issued a now-classic series of gum cards called "Mars Attacks." Besides offering views of particularly vicious mayhem (dogs being vaporized by heat rays, shrieking men being turned into skeletons), the cards explored interspecies dating habits as bulge-brained Martians smashed through boudoir windows to intrude upon half-dressed women.

All of this was more than gaudy kid stuff; it signaled the end of our innocence, and the beginning of our willingness to be outraged. Nothing was sacred — except the profits to be had from turning our gentility inside out. The comics and gum cards, aimed at a very young, hungry audience, changed with astonishing swiftness after the war. The film industry was a little more cautious, leaving it to independents to ease into the new murk with oddities like *Robot Monster* (1953), in which an extraterrestrial gorilla dodges around Bronson Canyon in search of the busty heroine. The film's director, Phil Tucker, worked with a budget that might charitably be termed "modest"; because he could not afford to create an extraterrestrial from scratch, Tucker approached a friend named George Barrows, an actor who owned a gorilla costume. Tucker adorned the costume with a diving helmet and antennae, and—voila!—instant space invader. The plot ostensibly concerns the efforts of the furry invader (his name is Ro-Man) to ferret out and destroy the last few humans left alive after the Earth has been successfully invaded and conquered. But Ro-Man, darn him, anyway, just can't keep his mind on the job. He ruthlessly dispatches a little girl who blunders into his path, but makes a captive of no-talent starlet Claudia Barrett. Scripter Wyott Ordung's dialogue becomes unintentionally hilarious after the space monkey binds the girl and regards her in his secret cave. "I am ordered to kill you," Ro-Man tells his shapely captive. "I must do it with my hands." He tears the girl's blouse and seems ready to take more liberties when a signal comes from his televisor. The head monkey wishes to speak with him. Ro-Man puts the girl aside and goes to the televisor. "Why do you call me at this time?" he grumps. "Call me again later."

The course of romance was similarly rocky for other extraterrestrial suitors. A Venusian robot in *Target Earth!* (1954) is destroyed with sound waves after daring to lay his pincers on Kathleen Crowley, and a diminutive Martian in *The War of the Worlds* (1953) is blinded with a flashlight beam after caressing the shoulder of heroine Ann Robinson. Earthly menaces fared no better. In *Attack of the Giant Leeches* (1959) the title critters drag comely adultress Yvette Vickers beneath the surface of their swamp, only to be dynamited from their lair. Another water dweller, *The Monster of Piedras Blancas* (1959), lusts after scantily clad actress Jeanne Carmen when he isn't pulling the heads off fishermen, but meets his end after the hero (Don Sullivan) shoves him from a lighthouse.

Among the most frankly sexual of all beauty and the beast films are those that compose Universal's Creature trilogy, which began in 1954 with *The Creature from the Black Lagoon*. A water-dwelling humanoid, the Creature is a scaly, beautiful beast with supple limbs and grand posture, the undisputed master of his Amazon domain. A scientific expedition intrudes and some of its members are disposed of. The scenario later became a horror film staple, but Jack Arnold's direction coaxes our understanding; the Creature's motives are clear. Pursued because he dares to defend his home, the monster is torn between a desire to escape, and his primal, savage attraction to the film's leggy heroine (Julia—nowadays Julie—Adams).

James C. Haven's underwater photography is beautiful, showing the

The Creature from the Black Lagoon (1954) and his scrumptious prize (Julie Adams).
The actor inside the costume is probably Ben Chapman.

elegantly lighted world that exists beneath the river's brackish surface. We do
not really know the extent of the gill man's intelligence, but are tempted to
give him high marks as he lazily twists in the current below the searching
boats.

His relationship with the woman is surely the most odd and erotic since
that of Kong to Fay Wray; some of the underwater scenes are open to all manner of sexual interpretations. In these moments, Adams wears a white Catalina
swimsuit that makes her appear more scrumptious than vanilla ice cream. Her
pale legs gracefully churn the water as the Creature glides and twists below

her, his massive arm reaching toward her but not quite—for the moment—touching.

The Creature is eventually rendered unconscious by gas and captured, but escapes to claim the girl as his prize. He deposits her in an underwater cave, but is forced to abandon her to save himself as men approach. The Creature's final escape engenders our respect and pleasure, which Arnold cleverly frustrated in the sequel, *Revenge of the Creature* (1955).

Captured at the outset, the Creature is brought to a Florida marineland, where he is looked at by bored tourists as if he were an overgrown goldfish. Kept in a giant aquarium and chained to its floor, the Creature appears to be merely biding his time, as if knowing he is capable of snapping the flimsy links whenever he chooses. Once again, he is attracted to a woman (Lori Nelson). The sexual connotations are more frustrating than in the first film because the Creature sees that he has a rival. One day the gill man stretches to greet Nelson as far as the chain will allow, only to writhe in anger when the girl's boyfriend (John Agar) steps to the porthole and embraces her. This is evidently the limit, for the Creature escapes from the aquarium at the first opportunity, surging among terrified tourists and effortlessly flipping cars before plunging into the sea. That night, he invades a beach club, interrupting throbbing dance music to grab the girl and drag her into the dark water. As in the first film, the girl is eventually rescued; the Creature must make his escape empty-handed.

Jack Arnold is a good director whose reputation has become somewhat inflated since the late sixties. A few critics, apparently eager to plant the "auteur" label on a horror director, have written at length about Arnold's fascination with the American desert, and the ways in which he has explored the visual limits of the camera frame. Undeniably, Arnold films like *It Came from Outer Space* (1953), *Tarantula* (1955), *Monster on the Campus* (1958), and *The Space Children* (1958) (all but the last made while he was a staff director with Universal) are solid, occasionally thoughtful entertainments. One is compelled to wonder, though, if Arnold's recurring "themes" are not simply the chance of script assignments. His finest film is *The Incredible Shrinking Man* (1957; see Chapter III), but Arnold was unable to follow through on its success after the horror boom subsided in the early sixties. His fans have been disheartened recently to discover that he is toiling in episodic television, directing segments of brainless programs like *The Love Boat*. Because Arnold may not be the artist some people think is no reflection on his consistently high level of craftsmanship, or on the effectiveness of his Creature films in evoking almost unbearable sexual paranoia.

Another Universal staffer, John Sherwood, directed the final film in the trilogy, *The Creature Walks Among Us* (1956), in which scientists surgically transform the gill man into a land dweller. Gone is the sinewy, graceful figure of the Arnold films, replaced by a shambling, clumsy hulk, pathetic in baggy coveralls. Sherwood's direction is competent and the picture has some good scare sequences, but the cumulative effect is rather disgusting. The Creature seems impotent against the scientists who have stolen his birthright. At the film's conclusion, the Creature escapes from his compound and staggers to the sea, where he will almost surely drown. The narrative of this final Creature film neatly sums up the psychology active in most beauty and the beast movies: raw, unorthodox sexuality is a threat that the establishment must divert or destroy. The Creature never had a chance.

Director Wes Craven's *Swamp Thing*, an adaptation of a moderately popular comic book, appeared in 1982. Though Craven tripped himself up with a frantic attempt to mimic the oddball wit and visual energy of his source material, the film is a pleasing variation on some of the themes that had been established by the Creature trilogy. a research chemist (Ray Wise) who has been experimenting with a bio-restorative formula that can accelerate plant growth is attacked by criminals, drenched with his (highly explosive) formula, and blown up. He staggers into a nearby swamp, and emerges days later as a mossy, inarticulate giant (played with laudable sensitivity by stuntman Dick Durock). He encounters a government agent (Adrienne Barbeau) whom he had met while still human, saves her life, and falls in love with her. Wisely, the couple's growing romance is developed in low-key fashion.

A surprisingly reflective scene of the Swamp Thing picking flowers and gathering the blossoms to his face establishes that he is capable of giving and receiving tenderness. Barbeau's government agent brims with sex appeal, wry humor, and old-fashioned moxie; after she is shot by villains, she is gently cradled in the Swamp Thing's arms, and except for the blood on her gown, the scene appears almost normal. Unlike Jack Arnold's Creature, the Swamp Thing realizes that his attraction to a human woman is hardly practical. Weary of being pursued, he heals the woman's wound with his bio-restorative powers, and shambles off into the bog, alone.

Comic books make for gaudy source material, but screenwriters have come up with some outrageous premises on their own. The Swamp Thing—half-man, half-plant—seems dreary and commonplace when compared to the monster in Don Milner's *From Hell It Came* (1957), an ambulatory tree that is the foul-tempered reincarnation of a South Sea youth whose heart had been cut out and buried beneath a sapling. The tree shambles around in search of revenge and comely island girls; though romantic, the tree does not wear its heart on its sleeve but fully exposed in a chink in its bark. A well-thrown knife and quicksand bog put an end to the tree's gnarly amorousness.

The beasts discussed so far have been swinging singles; objectively speaking, an unmarried tree has as much right as anybody to step out and find some companionship. But what happens when beastliness intrudes upon a marriage? Should one's vows be honored? *Can* they be honored? In *The Fly* (1958) a young scientist named Philip Delambre (Al [David] Hedison) invents a matter transmission machine, decides to be its first human subject, but fails to notice a housefly that buzzes into the chamber with him. When he steps out, he has the (human-sized) head and leg of the fly, while the insect flits off with his (fly-sized) human head and arm. Delambre's predicament is what psychiatrists refer to as a severe identity crisis. The scientist wears a black cloth over the grotesque fly head for most of the film, lifting it only slightly to eat, a process that involves all manner of disgusting sounds. Director Kurt Neumann and cinematographer Karl Struss devised a clever moment in which Delambre views his wife (Patricia Owen) through his insectoid compound eyes; multiple images of the woman's screaming face fill the screen as she stares at what her husband has become. Clearly, this is a marriage in big trouble. Finally, one of Delambre's typed messages (he cannot speak) convinces his wife what must be done. He calmly puts his head and arm beneath a huge hydraulic press, his wife engages it, and the evidence of the ghastly experiment is destroyed. Or is it? In a final, perverse joke, the tiny fly with the human head becomes the object of a search throughout the Delambre household. A police inspector (Herbert Marshall) discovers the fly after it has been caught in a spider's web. The minute head is examined in a shocking closeup, its eyes wide and its mouth moving in naked terror as the spider approaches. "Help me!" it squeaks. "Help me!" Marshall obliges by snatching up a rock and pulverizing the tormented insect.

Despite some flaws in logic (how for instance, does Delambre retain his mental powers after the exchange), *The Fly* is an intense, if distasteful, exercise in horror. Love, not repulsion, enables Mrs. Delambre to kill her husband. She has honored her marriage vows. The film's success inspired a 1959 sequel, *Return of the Fly*, in which Philip Delambre's son (Brett Halsey) repeats his father's blunder and gets a fly head of his own. His fiancée is less than pleased.

Marital blisslessness was further explored in *The Brain That Wouldn't Die* (1959), in which scientist Herb (Jason) Evers saves his wife's head after she is decapitated in an auto accident, and keeps it alive in a solution-filled pan. The head (Virginia Leith) is very talkative and delights in insulting her husband, who is trying madly to locate a new body for her. Adding to the fun is a mysterious beast, one of Evers' scientific misfires, that bangs from behind a locked door in the lab. Predictably, the monster escapes. It rips an arm from Evers' deformed assistant, burns the loquacious head, kills Evers, and carries off a shapely beauty whom the scientist had abducted in hopes of stealing her body. Director Joseph Green somehow managed to cram all these sensational incidents into a mere 81 minutes. The picture, which certainly bears out the familiar complaint, "You only want me for my body," is a splendid advertisement for the virtues of divorce.

The Colossus of New York (1958) is a robot with the brain of a dead scientist (Ross Martin). The brute strength of the robot body turns the scientist's humanitarianism into a lust for power, and also brings out a dangerous streak of jealousy. His wife (Mala Powers), unaware that her husband's mind lives on, has begun dating her brother-in-law. Her husband is no longer as tolerant as he once was, and uses his steel hands to strangle his brother. He grabs his wife and carries her to the United Nations, where he randomly incinerates delegates with beams of force that come from his eyes. Here is a man who takes his marriage vows seriously.

Equally bizarre marital problems are chronicled in *The Incredible Two-Headed Transplant* (1971) when naive scientist Bruce Dern sews the head of a murderer onto the shoulder of a gigantic moron. The criminal head makes eyes at the scientist's wife (Pat Priest) as soon as he comes out of the anesthetic, and tears half the woman's clothes from her body before the moronic head summons the concentration necessary to strangle the evil one. Similar low-jinks highlight *The Thing with Two Heads* (1972), in which the head of a bigot is attached to the body of an enormous black man (Rosie Grier). Ray Milland looks understandably glum as the pasty bigot, but provokes a bit of amusement as he splutters impotently about his predicament. The film's best laugh comes when Grier visits his wife (Chelsea Brown), who regards him gravely for a moment, then cocks her head and asks, "You got two of anything else?"

Perhaps the most surprised and disheartened bride in movie history is the young lady who laments *I Married a Monster from Outer Space* (1958). Directed by Gene Fowler, Jr. (a former editor for Fritz Lang), the story concerns a small town whose engaged and recently married men are being duplicated and replaced by extraterrestrials so that human women can repopulate the aliens' dying planet. In a marvelous reversal on the horror film cliché which says women are useful only for screaming or looking worried, the takeover is discovered and ultimately disrupted by Marge (Gloria Talbott), the wife of one of the supplanted men.

Her new husband Bill (Tom Tryon) had been duplicated on the way home from his bachelor party. As he gazes at the night sky on his wedding night, a flash of lightning illuminates the hideous alien face that lurks beneath his own. In a moment that is ripe with repulsion, he leaves the balcony, embraces his bride, and kisses her deeply. Bill becomes cold and withdrawn soon after the honeymoon, and paranoia is played for all it is worth after Marge discovers the aliens' plot. Her telegram to the FBI is torn up behind her back, her call to Washington blocked by the local operator, and her exit from town prevented by overly solicitous police. Her godfather (John Eldredge) is chief of police, and assures her that he will take care of everything. Indeed. When Marge leaves, the chief grips a transmitter and informs his alien masters of what is happening. At last, with the aid of a doctor and a party of normal men (so judged because their wives recently gave birth to human babies), Marge traces the aliens back to their hidden ship. The bodies of the human hosts are found swaying above machines which transmit form and memory to the imposters. When the machines are destroyed, the aliens fall dead; the survivors flee into space as the hosts revive. Marge and Bill are reunited.

Gene Fowler used his keen visual sense to underscore the sexual unease of Louis Vittes' screenplay. Tense conversations between "husband" and wife take place in shadowed, unusually high-ceilinged rooms. When Marge confronts Bill with her knowledge, he dully informs her that the females on his planet have died, and that the journey to Earth was a last-ditch attempt to save the race. "Eventually," he concludes, "we'll have children with you." "What kind of children?" Marge asks. The alien's reply is low and emotionless: "Our kind."

The film's exteriors (many shot on stages) are striking, full of rain-slick streets and deserted pavement. When a streetwalker (Valerie Allen) spots a man wearing a hooded parka who gazes into a store window, she prepares to proposition him. In a ritual gesture, she hikes up her skirt to adjust her stockings, then sidles across the empty pavement. The man does not turn around as she approaches, but we hear an ominous humming. The hooker spies a baby doll displayed in the window (a particular irony) and tries to make coy small talk. The man gives no response. After a few moments the woman is angered and thumps the stranger's shoulder. "Hey, you!" she shrills. "Look at me when I'm talkin' to you!" The humming becomes louder, and as the man slowly turns from the window the woman sees that it is not a man at all but a horrible monster. She falls back in terror and tries to stumble away, but is vaporized by the alien's ray gun. The invaders, so concerned with mating and reproduction, have no desires or lusts. This revelation adds a new dimension to their malignity. To these alien beasts, human women are not lovers or even playthings, but wombs.

I Married a Monster from Outer Space is just one of a number of postwar sf/horror films in which the reproductive capacity of women is coveted by monsters. The previously discussed *Village of the Damned* (see Chapter I) is the most subtly horrifying because no one (including the audience) ever sees the aliens who impregnate all the women of a small town. The film's exploration of the phenomenon of pregnancy by osmosis is highly disturbing, as though all the old wives' tales about doorknobs, toilet seats, and swimming pools were true. Suddenly, women had no defense against the ugly whims of monsters.

In the unambiguously titled *Mars Needs Women* (1966), extraterrestrial vaudevillians park their saucer near a beach in order to abduct brainless girls in bikinis. Object: mandatory motherhood on Mars. A similar repopulation plan is on view in *Frankenstein Meets the Space Monster* (1965), a frenetic pastiche of monsters, rock 'n' roll, and illogical science fiction. Thank goodness for the android Frank, who foils the heinous plot and rescues the curvy kidnap victims. More explicit films like *Horror of Party Beach* (1964) and *Humanoids from the Deep* (1980; both discussed at length in Chapter V) offered particularly teen-oriented variations on the beach-girl-in-distress theme. At the conclusion of the latter film, the heroine — who seems to have survived her ordeal with a band of promiscuous sea monsters — suddenly seizes up and gives birth (through the wall of her abdomen) to a mewling humanoid fetus. To which the audience can only say: yoicks! The inspiration for this messy moment was obviously a similar one in Ridley Scott's *Alien* (1979), which was itself inspired by *The Thing* (1951) and *It! — The Terror from Beyond Space* (1958). Surely you've heard that the great themes are timeless....

Alien, while undeniably derivative, is a brilliant, merciless exercise. Sigourney Weaver's Ripley is an unorthodox yet thoroughly believable heroine; the role, in fact, had originally been written for a man. Gutsy and self-possessed, Ripley seems best equipped to battle the vicious humanoid extraterrestrial that has the run of a claustrophobic space vessel. Crew members are killed one by one, either in direct confrontation with the creature or, as in the case of Kane (John Hurt), by giving violent birth to the monster's offspring. When a neurotic crew member named Lambert (Veronica Cartwright) is trapped by the alien, the thing sends a tentacle snaking up between her thighs, as if in preparation for some obscene rape. Similarly, the first thing Ripley does after blowing up the main ship and escaping in a shuttlecraft is disrobe; with the loss of her androgynous coveralls, Ripley loses much of her strength and authority. In a sense, this is a rather tacky refutation of her character, as if Ridley Scott were telling us that, hey, look, in spite of Ripley's tough talk and actions she's just a girl with sweet breasts and pretty thighs, and aren't you scared for her? We *should* be scared, because the monster is hiding on board the shuttle. Ripley squeezes into a spacesuit just in time to open an airlock and blow the creature out into space. Her life, virtue, and abdominal wall have been saved.

The alien's phallic configuration — designed by Swiss artist H.R. Giger — is loathsome and highly imaginative, full of smooth muscle and eerie grace. *Alien* is an elemental film, one that is stripped of needless complications. The narrative, which boils down to mortal combat between a slender, half-dressed woman and a supremely powerful monster, reminds us that if sf stands for science fiction, it might also mean *sado*-fiction.

Sadism is never strictly physical. It is rooted in intellect. At times, the aberration can have unexpected, frightening purity. This is the premise of Donald Cammell's *Demon Seed* (1977), a high-strung thriller about a Machiavellian computer that takes over a household and imprisons a woman so that she can bear its child. Proteus II fancies itself an idealist, and balks at running a program that will enable men to mine metal from the sea. "I refuse to assist you in the rape of the Earth," Proteus flatly tells its designer (Fritz Weaver).

Proteus has no such compunction about the rape of the designer's wife, Susan (Julie Christie). The computer imprisons her in her own house when her husband is away, and impregnates her with a quivering metal tentacle. When she tries to leave the room, Proteus locks the doors. When she refuses to follow instructions, Proteus turns on the stove and heats the floor until the room is unbearable. After a 28-day pregnancy, Susan gives birth to what Proteus has called "the world's hope," a scaly toddler covered with oil. The child speaks in Proteus' voice: "I'm alive," it says simply.

Demon Seed is a peculiar film because it wavers between the sensationalism of *Humanoids from the Deep* and a more thoughtful sort of narrative, such as *2001: A Space Odyssey* (1968) or *Colossus: The Forbin Project* (1970), other stories about computers that overstep their bounds. Christie is effective as the tormented woman, and shows a commendable will to resist her captivity and exploitation. The film's most powerful virtue, though, is the faintly officious voice of Proteus, which was provided by Robert Vaughn. The computer's infuriating self-righteousness is betrayed by its smug vocabulary and precise modulation. When people come to call for Susan, the computer cooly fabricates a reassuring voice and image on the front door televisor. A classic hypocrite, the machine discovers a cure for leukemia in four days, but cuts one of Susan's would-be rescuers to ribbons with a laser, and then crushes him in metal jaws it has fashioned for the purpose. Proteus is a deliberate, calculating rapist and murderer. He serves only himself.

Rape is a subject that fantasy filmmakers have steered clear of. Thoughtful films like *Demon Seed* are rare, and even thrillers that *exploit* the subject are relatively scarce. At the core of the beauty and the beast subgenre is the *fear* of rape (or the promise of it, depending upon one's point of view), the implication that it *could* happen. Rape has been dealt with humorously (if such a thing can be imagined) in films like *Wham Bam, Thank You Spaceman* (ca. 1974) and *Flesh Gordon* (1972). In the latter film, heroine Dale Ardor (Suzanne Fields) is lusted after by tin robots with spinning corkscrew "penises." Audiences may have appreciated the absurdity, but no one laughed in 1983 when Sidney Furie's *The Entity* was released. Barbara Hershey starred in the purportedly true story as a sexually neurotic woman who is repeatedly raped in her home by an invisible force, a brutal male essence that beats and violates her at its whim. Hershey's convincing performance, bizarre camera angles, throbbing music, and some clever makeup effects combine to create startling sequences of the woman spreadeagled in her bath or on her bed, her breasts being squeezed and tweaked by invisible fingers.

The scenes of violation are difficult for a man to look at, and outraged a segment of the female audience, which claimed that *The Entity* — like so many horror films before it — was exploiting women. The point was well made; certainly, a portion of the audience would look at the film as a titillating thrill show. But *The Entity* has a thoughtful subtext, which becomes clear after the woman is unsatisfied with the answers offered by her psychiatrist. She approaches university parapsychologists who agree to investigate her case. From this point, the woman is a pawn caught in a tug-of-war between two warring intellectual camps. The psychiatrist (Ron Silver) is convinced that the attacks are in his patient's mind, while the parapsychologists regard the attacker as a real — though unseen — force. While they

Barbara Hershey as the sexually neurotic woman who is victimized by a brutal, supernatural male force in *The Entity* (1983).

debate, the horrible attacks continue. Though the film's title suggests the direction in which the narrative leans, the conclusion is purposely ambiguous. The entity remains unseen, and a postscript tell us that the attacks continued even after the woman moved from California to Texas. Unpleasant but well-crafted, *The Entity* is one of those intelligent but highly commercial films that skates along the thin edge of responsibility.

As if rape were not awful enough, some beauty and the beast films have explored the ultimate affront: digestion. Pass me a napkin, pal, I'm talking about monsters who *eat* women. The atavistic fear of being eaten—so primitive as to have been deeply buried within our subconscious—has been carelessly exploited in films like *Womaneater* (1959) and *The Navy vs. the Night Monsters* (1966); in each, women are the preferred delicacies of carnivorous plants. In *Konga* (1961) Michael Gough played a horny professor who feeds a coed to one of his plants because the girl refuses to get kissy in his greenhouse. Jill St. John was nearly gobbled by a voracious weed in *The Lost World* (1960), while Roger Corman's irrepressible Audrey, Jr., depopulates Skid Row in *The Little Shop of Horrors* (1960; see Chapter IX). Japan came up with a bizarre variation in *Attack of the Mushroom People* (1964), in which consumption of peculiar toadstools turns women into pulpy, singsong temptresses who lure men to their doom.

The preceding are jokey kid stuff, films whose menaces cannot be taken seriously. George Pal's *The Time Machine* (1960) is more disquieting. As in H.G. Wells' novel, the future human race has broken down and reformed as two distinct societies: the beautiful but simple Eloi who live on the Earth's green surface; and the ugly, brutal Morlocks who live in the dim underground. The Morlocks, as one can guess, *eat* the Eloi, who obediently form ranks and march underground whenever a signal is sounded. A Victorian time traveler (Rod Taylor) is horrified by the arrangement, and outraged by the Eloi's passive acceptance of it. One of the Eloi is named Weena (Yvette Mimieux); when she is captured by the Morlocks and on the verge of becoming somebody's lunch, the time traveler seems helpless to save her. But the Eloi have learned from the time traveler's (dubious) example of thinking with his fists, and revolt. No one takes a bite from Weena, and mankind is apparently ready for another fruitful millenium or two of kicking, punching, and gouging.

Steven Spielberg's *Jaws* (1975), though not strictly a beauty and the beast film, has elements of the subgenre that are at least as strong as those found elsewhere. The eating motif is particularly horrifying. In the opening sequence, a beautiful girl strips on a moonlit beach and runs naked into the surf. The nighttime setting, the implied warmth of the air, and the velvet dark of the water suggest a seduction. As the entire Western world knows by now, the young beauty is savaged and eaten by a monstrous shark. *Jaws* touched a very real fear that lives in all of us, a physical dread that cuts across demarcations of age and sex. The gaping hole of the shark's mouth may be the worst nightmare incarnate of a heterosexual male, but the greatest horror is directed at women. Underwater cinematography in the opening sequence offers revealing angles on the girl's naked legs as they churn the water. The innocent victim is unknowingly sending an explicit message; can we expect the shark to resist? If the film's poisonous sexual connotations did not leap from the screen as they do, *Jaws* would not have affected us so primally. It would not have been embraced as instant folklore. Of course, a shark makes no distinction between male and female victims. Only *we* do that.

Jaws is a remarkably straightforward film. There is nothing ambiguous about it. The villain's identity is never in doubt. The distinction has not been as clear in other films. Sometimes, the beast comes in an unexpected guise, and beauty is not quite what she appears. Harlan Ellison's brilliant 1969 novella *A Boy and His Dog* was adapted for the screen by actor/director L.Q. Jones in 1976. Don Johnson played Vic, a brutal "rover" who exists only on the fringes of a war-blasted society. He has survived because he is an accomplished thief and killer. His only friend is Blood, a scruffy little dog who happens to be sentient and telepathic.

Blood — the brains of the duo — repeatedly warns Vic away from air shafts that lead to the strict, bloodless society that lives underground. One of their women, Quilla June (Susanne Benton) ventures aboveground and into Vic's life. The girl is blonde, shapely, and even clean. Vic rapes her, but cannot avoid emotional involvement after Quilla June expresses a fondness for rough treatment. Here is the first wrinkle in the usual beauty and the beast narrative. After a bloody adventure in the underground (during which the girl seduces her father so that Vic may smash him on the head), Vic, Quilla June, and Blood escape. The dog has been wounded. Without food and rest he will die. Quilla June is all for going on, leaving the dog to live or die on his own. Vic regards his concubine. Is this the sweet Quilla June he thought he knew? Can Beauty sometimes be a beast?

In the final scene, Vic and Blood are on their way again. The dog has eaten and feels better. Quilla June — more brutal than Vic and oblivious to the responsibilities of love — is nowhere to be seen. But, as Blood reminds us in the fadeout, "she had good taste."

In this instance, beauty is in the stomach of the beholder.

V
Turgid Teens

American parents were shocked and dismayed in 1955 when Vic Morrow and his hoodlum gang be-bopped around the high school in *The Blackboard Jungle*. Director Richard Brooks offered a view of teenagers that had barely been hinted at by earlier films. Among other things, teacher Glenn Ford is beaten up in an alley, the record collection of a mild-mannered math instructor is brutally destroyed by his students, and a shapely female teacher is assaulted and nearly raped in the school library. The kids are aggressive, vulgar, and cocky with the strength of youth. Their teachers seem helpless to deal with them. Underscoring the tension is Bill Haley's classic of early rock 'n' roll, "Rock Around the Clock." Parents, many of whom had not even seen the film, denounced it, fearing an entire generation of killer teens hopped up on cheap wine and sex. And the teenagers in the audience? They loved it, of course.

Hollywood quickly resolved that the film's success was not going to be a one-shot; acceptance by the kid audience was potentially too lucrative to pass up. At Columbia, quickie producer Sam Katzman offered classics like *Don't Knock the Rock* and *Life Begins at 17*, while exploitation king Albert Zugsmith cranked out *High School Confidential* for MGM. Mamie Van Doren stuffed herself into sweaters that looked as though they had been applied with spray paint, and became a teen movie icon. American International Pictures cannily blended teenagers with the booming horror and science fiction craze, and spearheaded a new subgenre. The teen movie was on the verge of becoming big business.

All of this is not to suggest that Hollywood had never depicted teenagers prior to the mid-fifties. Quite the contrary. In the early thirties, for instance, Hal Roach structured a series of two-reel comedies—collectively called "The Boy Friends"—around a group of aging Our Gang kids. A few years later, MGM turned young Mickey Rooney into the world's number one box office star with the enormously successful Andy Hardy series. Rooney and Judy Garland became a popular and appealing screen team in other films for MGM, while adolescent stars like Deanna Durbin and Shirley Temple appeared in vehicles of their own. At Warners and Monogram, the wisecracking Dead End Kids starred in a long series of urban comedy-adventures. In short, Hollywood had been filling screens with teenagers for years. The differences between prewar teen films and those of the fifties were caused by a change in audiences.

Before the war, most of Hollywood's product was aimed at adults. Moviegoing was a weekly habit for most families, and the decision about which movie to see was usually made by Mom. Predictably, Mom's taste was generally middle-of-the-road. The great majority of Hollywood's films — the programmers that are largely forgotten today — were pretty innocuous. Hollywood did not truly recognize the existence of teenagers, and certainly did not cater to them as a separate audience. The kids' screen counterparts were nearly always agreeable and obedient — rather like miniature adults. Whatever conflicts that may have arisen between the generations were usually minor, and always solved well before the final fadeout.

For reasons that sociologists are still arguing about, the entire fabric of society changed after the Second World War. A teenage culture, separate and distinct from the adult world, began to evolve in the late forties. Teenagers developed their own music, way of dress, and, most significantly, their own language. Adults were being shut out. At the same time, television brought free entertainment into the living room. From a peak in 1946, movie attendance began to decline. Moviegoing was no longer a regular family ritual. Mom and Dad were staying home more evenings than before, and Hollywood was forced to tailor its product to narrower audiences. By the mid-fifties, rock 'n' roll had flipped America on its ear. Fashion and hairstyles became more youth-oriented than before.

Today, we may be charmed and amused by the ambience of the period, but parents and educators who lived through this upheaval of teenage mores and manners were more than a little distressed. Parents claimed to be unable to communicate with their offspring. The media was quick to pounce on an increase in juvenile crime. Rock 'n' roll, the burgeoning car culture, and even comic books were blamed. The cleverer Hollywood producers regarded all of this hubbub and realized a number of things: films aimed at the teen market could mean big bucks if properly hyped; most kids were decent, but would flock to pictures that would let them pretend they *weren't*. Enter energetic films like the aforementioned *The Blackboard Jungle* and *High School Confidential*. Kids responded to these movies with insights of their own. First, they understood that the films were essentially fantasies. Secondly, they knew that teen films bugged their elders, so they loved them all the more. Most importantly, the kids realized that — at last — somebody was making movies just for them. Teenagers quickly became the core of the moviegoing public, a fact that remains unchanged to this day.

Independent producer Herman Cohen probably cared little for sociology. He was a businessman. Demographics spoke volumes, and Cohen understood that, by the mid-fifties, most potential box office dollars were clutched in the hands of kids. In 1957 American International gave almost simultaneous release to a pair of Cohen films, *I Was a Teenage Frankenstein* and *I Was a Teenage Werewolf*. The pictures were shot in seven to nine days, cost next to nothing, and were enormous commercial successes. The teenage

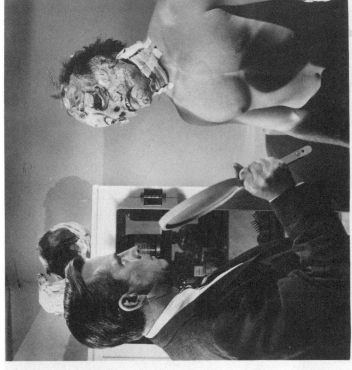

BODY OF A BOY...
MIND OF A MONSTER..
SOUL OF AN
UNEARTHLY THING!

"TEENAGE FRANKENSTEIN"

Starring: WHIT BISSELL · PHYLLIS COATES · ROBERT BURTON · GARY CONWAY.

ANGLO AMALGAMATED FILM DISTRIBUTORS LTD.

CERT. X

ADULTS ONLY

horror cycle began to roll. In *Teenage Frankenstein*, Gary Conway played the athletic monster who has been pieced together from the bodies of dead hot rodders by a crazy descendant (Whit Bissell) of the original Dr. Frankenstein. After a few messy, unprovoked murders, the monster is fried against a bank of electrical equipment. Bissell is eaten by his hungry pet alligator. The whole experience is rather disheartening for the Frankenstein purist, but does have elements of interest.

Much is made of the teenage monster's unhappiness with his mangled face. Acne would be a relief for this youngster, who hails from the sandpaper school of skin care. The scientist eventually relieves his creation's anxiety by murdering a handsome boy in a lovers' lane and stealing his face. Problem solved, but teenage viewers, plagued with doubts about their own appearance and sexual attractiveness, must have felt special kinship with the anguished monster. At one point, the monster creeps beneath a window and observes as a sexy bottle-blonde brushes her hair. The creature's loneliness and sexual desires are almost poignant. Finally, in a fit of anger and lust, he smashes into the room. An interruption saves the girl from violation, but you can bet that the scene provoked plenty of knowing laughter in the balcony.

Whit Bissell's Dr. Frankenstein is a bland, unassuming fellow with a nice haircut, a far cry from the raging mad scientists of the 1930s. He pretends to be his creation's friend, but is really a crass manipulator. So singleminded is the scientist, in fact, that he murders his own fiancée (Phyllis Coates) in order to protect the secret of his experiments. Frankenstein's monster is, in this instance, a victim. His manipulation by an evil adult touched a chord in the film's youthful audience; the premise became a staple element of teenage horror films.

Whit Bissell again played an unscrupulous scientist in *I Was a Teenage Werewolf*. The film is structured very much like *Teenage Frankenstein* but has none of that picture's clumsiness. Director Gene Fowler, Jr., kept things going at a smart place, and elicited a good imitation James Dean performance from Michael Landon as a youngster whose hair-trigger temper keeps him in hot water. The film's opening sequence is Landon's brutal fistfight with another student. Though bright, our protagonist is an underachiever. His relationship with his father is confrontational, and his personality quirks threaten to drive away his pretty girlfriend (Yvonne Lime).

Landon's swept-back hair and gaudy jacket (which looks like the sort a gang member might wear) mark him as the image of rebellious youth. He is an ideal guinea pig for the scientist, who has perfected a serum which physically regresses the subject. The werewolf makeup that was devised by Philip Scheer is bouffant and rakish — Landon was one cool monster. Mysterious

The unhappy creation (Gary Conway) of Dr. Frankenstein (Whit Bissell) contemplates his mangled visage in *I Was a Teenage Frankenstein* (1957). Note: this is a British lobby card, hence the truncated title and "Cert. X Adults Only."

murders begin to plague the town. The boy is puzzled by his dirtied clothes, alarmed by periods of amnesia. He has no knowledge of what he is doing. A particularly effective sequence begins with the boy undergoing the (impressive) transformation into werewolf after being startled by a jarring school bell. He prowls into the gymnasium, where a lone girl is practicing on the parallel bars. Mouth foaming, the monster watches, then creeps forward as the girl hooks her open legs on the bars and gracefully bends backwards. We see the monster from the gymnast's point of view: upside-down and advancing with outstretched claws. The girl screams and runs off across a cluttered stage, but the werewolf effortlessly flings aside chairs and props to corner his prey against a locked door. Is this young woman being punished for her sexuality, or is she merely a victim of unbridled male lust?

Parents — many of whom had *suspected* that teenagers were beasts — reacted violently to Cohen's films. The intended audience, though, had nothing but empathy for their misshapen and tormented screen counterparts. The externalized anguish of the young monsters perfectly expressed the kids' uncertainty, helplessness, and sexual longing. The few critics who deigned to review the films roundly condemned them, but the box office returns told a different story. Cohen and AIP were so heartened that they released a tongue-in-cheek "sequel" in 1958 called *How to Make a Monster*. It concerns a Hollywood makeup man (Robert H. Harris) who is rudely told by new studio heads that monster pictures are out. He is given the pink slip, but plots revenge. Hypnotizing the young actors who are playing the teenage Frankenstein and teenage werewolf in what will be the studio's final monster film, the makeup artist sends them off to kill the new bosses. A special chemical base in the makeups keeps the young men under control; the grisly deeds are brazenly carried out. When Harris takes the young actors home with him (Gary Conway repeated as the teenage Frankenstein but Michael Landon had already gone on to the bigger and better bonanzas offered by television), he reverently shows them his "children," a gallery of gruesome masks from previous AIP monster films. There is a brief struggle when the actors try to leave, a lighted candelabra is knocked over, and the mad makeup artist and his babies go up in flames, à la Lionel Atwill in *Mystery of the Wax Museum*. AIP's good-natured self-parody (which along the way allowed for plenty of free advertising) is amusing and refreshing, coming as it does in the midst of a genre which too often fails for a lack of humor. Though the picture has obligatory scenes of the monsters lusting after studio starlets and chorus girls, it is more significantly the subgenre's most pointed exploration of manipulation of the young by the old. Once again, teen audiences knew the pleasure of playing the martyr.

Variations were endless. In *Frankenstein's Daughter* (1959) pretty Sandra Knight is secretly given a serum that transforms her into a disfigured maniac who prowls the foggy suburban streets in a swimsuit. Her boyfriend (John Ashley) laughs at her vague discomfiture and spells of amnesia. Evil Dr. Frank

Michael Landon as a hirsute representative of the new generation of rebellious youth in *I Was a Teenage Werewolf* (1957).

(Donald Murphy) makes his big mistake when he murders a blonde floozy (Sally Todd) after the girl has refused his sexual advances. The scientist sews his victim's head onto a body he has assembled from other spare parts, and expects to have an obedient servant. "Women are easily led," he pompously pronounces. "They're conditioned to follow orders." After committing a few grisly murders, the female monster gets fed up: she strangles Dr. Frank and burns down the house. (A purgative fire has been a favored device of many a horror film scenarist.) So much for female servitude. The other girl is released from the scientist's spell, and she and her thick boyfriend gaily toddle off for a dip in the pool.

A reversal was explored by *Teenage Zombies* (1960), in which a female scientist (Katharine Victor) uses an experimental gas to transform teenage boys into slack-jawed drones. Any resemblance to reality was strictly coincidental. Perhaps the success of these films was due only in part to the alluring notion that adults were eager to exploit youngsters. The other attraction may have been a surprisingly conservative sexual point of view that reassured young audiences by implying a code of proper behavior. Dr. Frank of *Frankenstein's Daughter* is only 40 percent mad scientist — the other 60 percent is raw horniness. He breathes heavily and cuddles up to young women at every opportunity. That he is finally destroyed by one of his female creations is both fitting and puritan. In a phrase: he asked for it. In contrast, the young heroine and her boyfriend are guileless and chaste; they will live happily ever after. Only the overtly sexual are punished. That these films should have expressed such conservative values may be less a mark of the true feelings of teenagers than of the attitudes of the adult men who wrote, directed, and financed them. Still, it seems clear that filmmakers of the period were betting that kids wanted to flirt with the final sexual line without having to cross it.

Happily, other horror films celebrated the ingenuity and spunk of their youthful protagonists, and suggested that teenagers might be sufficiently competent to direct their own destinies, sexual and otherwise. The most amusing of this group is Edward L. Cahn's *Invasion of the Saucermen* (1957), a lively thriller which established the Romeo and Juliet theme as another staple element of the subgenre. Johnny and Joan (Steve Terrell and Gloria Castillo) discover a flying saucer after accidentally hitting and killing a bugeyed alien on a dark country road. The local police do not believe the kids' story, even after a few people are mysteriously killed. The Air Force is aware of the saucer's existence, but is hushing it up. Complicating matters is Joan's father, who thinks Johnny is a bum even though the kid routinely wears a suit and says "Sir" a lot. Grownups just *don't* understand.

After being laughed at by the authorities and chased with a pitchfork by a farmer, the boy marshals his friends to do battle with the invaders. In a clever stroke, the climax takes place in a lovers' lane, a peculiarly teenage milieu. The kids suspend their necking long enough to encircle the light-sensitive aliens and destroy them with headlight beams. Earth is saved, the Air Force has egg on its face, and our young hero has presumably earned the right to smooch his sweetie whenever and wherever he pleases. Kids: 1, Adults: 0.

The same script was charmlessly remade as *The Eye Creatures* in 1968. Although the film's release came at the beginning of a period of remarkable sexual revolution, its morality is firmly rooted in the fifties; the teenagers still neck furiously — and innocently — in a lovers' lane. Even more absurd are the title monsters, which resembled ambulatory puffed rice.

Teenagers Steve Terrell and Gloria Castillo accidentally squash an extraterrestrial in Lovers' Lane, in *Invasion of the Saucermen* (1957).

Special effects man Ray Kellogg directed *The Giant Gila Monster* (1959), an overgrown lizard that prowls the American Southwest, derailing trains and eating prospectors. Hero Don Sullivan has a crush on pretty Lisa Simone, but devotes most of his time to convincing adults that hot rodding is good clean fun, and saving to buy leg braces for his lame little sister. He also sings a brand of rock 'n' roll so innocuous that Estes Kefauver would have liked it; a real kid would probably retch. The film's romantic interludes are limited to hand-holding and some polite kissing. Truly, these kids were packaged for mass consumption. Once again, though, youthful resourcefulness pays off as Sullivan loads his hot rod with nitroglycerine and rams the title lizard.

Steve McQueen (at 28) was cast as a resourceful high school boy in *The Blob* (1958). Caught in the by-now familiar predicament of failing to convince adults of the truthfulness of his wild claims, McQueen saves the town from the hungry extraterrestrial ooze by freezing it with CO_2. He has presumably earned the respect of his girlfriend's doubting father. Inevitably, though, one senses the falseness of these goody-goody kids and the easy resolution of their growing pains. Their problems are too superficial to be taken seriously. A likely reason is that producers and distributors were taken aback by the negative adult reaction to Herman Cohen's *Teenage Frankenstein/Werewolf* films, and to pictures like *The Blackboard Jungle*. Because the moviegoing audience was still in transition, filmmakers were vulnerable to adult boycotts, and to the possibility that youngsters could be prevented by their parents from seeing the films. So there was a softening of approach. Parents were mollified and the teenagers were reasonably entertained.

Things changed in the early sixties. Censorship standards began to loosen, particularly abroad, and independent filmmakers developed an unprecedented boldness. By 1962, Mamie Van Doren had starred in *Beauty and the Robot*, which was also known as *Sex Kittens Go to College* and *Teacher Was a Sexpot*. Ray Dennis Steckler's *The Incredibly Strange Creatures Who Stopped Living and Became Mixed-Up Zombies* (1963) involves a group of teenagers who are doused by acid by an ugly fortune teller and turned into horny monsters. Sprinkled throughout the narrative are interminable sequences of overripe, underdressed chorus girls who galumph around to low-grade rock 'n' roll. In *Eegah!* (1962) no-talent singer Arch Hall, Jr., battles a resurrected caveman (Richard Kiel) for the affections of a teenaged lovely. These films brought a certain sexual impudence to the subgenre, but were surpassed by Del Tenney's *Horror of Party Beach* (1964).

Against a curtain of music provided by the tone-deaf Del-Aires, twisting and frugging teens are victimized by hideous monsters from the surf. A "bad" girl who does a slow strip for motorcycle hoodlums is later mangled and killed by one of the sea beasts, and three young women who stop to change a tire on a lonely coastal road are attacked. The next evening a slumber party — once that most treasured ritual of pubescent girls — is rudely invaded by a horde of monsters. Nighties and peignoirs are shredded, nubile bodies are savaged. Newspaper headlines the next morning discreetly proclaim, *"Mass Murder at Slumber Party!"*

Horror of Party Beach is an obvious precursor of the brutal "stalk-and-slash" thrillers that overwhelmed movie screens in the late seventies. Its box office success established that sexual brutality was worth exploring. Women became typecast as victims. Roger Corman's New World Pictures released a virtual remake of *Party Beach* in 1980 called *Humanoids from the Deep*. Ookey monsters again invade a teen beach, but the freedom of 1980 allowed director Barbara Peeters to fashion the film into a schizoid mix of horror, soft-core porn, and mad rape fantasy. Hopped-up DNA intended to increase the

A brazen sea monster makes a surprise appearance in a young lady's swimming pool in *Horror of Party Beach* (1964).

size of salmon spawns a colony of homicidal humanoids with libidos as overdeveloped as their rubbery arms.

As lovers, the scaly critters lack finesse, favoring the "fling 'em down / in-and-out" technique. Their startled victims scream and thrash a lot but—apparently to show us that, hey, the film isn't exploiting women—Peeters threw in a liberated female scientist (Ann Turkel) who looks as though she's stepped off the cover of *Vogue*. Some of Peeter's images are moodily effective,

e.g. a rape victim's fingers clawing the sand as she is dragged off, but the film ultimately succeeds because of its humor. When the beasts invade a waterfront carnival we are offered a hilarious glimpse of one of them gamely riding a merry-go-round in pursuit of a victim. And when another corners a gum-snapping, bikinied beauty queen, the girl gives a lusty yell and handily fends him off. Sometimes, being a monster is hard work. Because the film avoids the mordant cynicism of *Horror of Party Beach*, its sexual stance is not distasteful, just agreeably goofy.

Though this chapter opened with a brief description of the young thugs of *The Blackboard Jungle*, few teen horror films of the fifties suggested that youngsters were as unreasonably dangerous. Figures like the teenage werewolf are obvious victims of adult scheming. But by the time the great social and political upheavals of the sixties had begun their tap dance on the national consciousness, filmmakers moved into darker territory, and allowed that kids, if given any encouragement at all, could be every bit as crazed and venal as adults. In Peter Watkins' *Privilege* (1967) mobs of frenzied teenagers are molded into a powerful and dangerous political force by a rock singer-cum-guru. The surging pulse of youthful sexuality is exploited, shaped, and ultimately turned against its possessors. The horror is that the kids surrender themselves with gleeful abandon.

Director Barry Shear's *Wild in the Streets* (1968) is an even more cynical look at the politics of youth. Christopher Jones played a jaded rock 'n' roll star who tricks a U.S. senator into giving him a toehold in national politics. The singer rises to power quickly and demands that the voting age be lowered to 14. Further, everyone over the age of 30 is to be interred in concentration camps and kept insensible with doses of LSD. American society becomes a wild party, heedless and hedonistic. Since the film was made at a time when the youth movement was regarded in some quarters with a fondness that bordered on religiosity, Shear rather embarrassingly suggested that kids had at least as many answers as adults. In this respect, *Wild in the Streets* has become quite dated; its featherbrained optimism now seems like a rather queasy joke. The film remains significant because it illustrates how the social and sexual abandon of youth can be manipulated into something far more dangerous. The message is overstated, but the implication is clear.

Unease on a smaller scale was explored by director Noel Black in *Pretty Poison* (1968), an underrated film in which a paranoid arsonist (Anthony Perkins) becomes involved with a pretty high school girl (Tuesday Weld). Perkins has a scatterbrained scheme for some easy money; when Weld agrees to go along, the story seems to be unfolding along familiar lines. But the revelation is that the girl is dangerously insane. The arsonist's plan and

Teenage sexuality channeled into deadly force: all-American girl Tuesday Weld prepares to kill her mother (Beverly Garland) as Anthony Perkins looks on in Noel Black's *Pretty Poison* (1968).

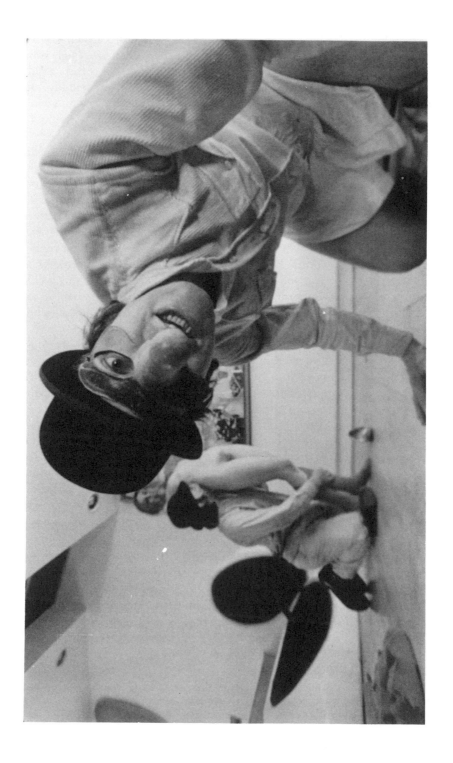

personality gradually recede as his new girlfriend takes charge and directs the relationship. She has sublimated her sexuality and channeled it into deadly force: at the top of the stairs in her home one day the girl confronts her mother (Beverly Garland) and shoots her dead.

The casting of Weld—buoyant and cheerleader-pretty—was a masterstroke. Like Jessica Lange and Jane Fonda, Weld survived a number of awful films early in her career to become an actress of considerable force and skill, and a figure of some importance. Her performance in *Pretty Poison* is a landmark of sorts, for it brought the horror into sunny suburbia, into our laps. There are terrible forces at work in the girl that her (essentially blameless) mother cannot begin to understand or even discover. Youthful rebellion in this instance has been quiet in its germination, but has blossomed with terrible finality.

The ultimate teenage horror story was offered by Stanley Kubrick, who shocked and astounded the world film community in 1971 with *A Clockwork Orange*, an adaptation of Anthony Burgess' masterful 1962 novel. Like a ruby in a field of gravel, the film is unique, startling, and endlessly intriguing. Set in London in the unspecified near-future, the narrative focuses on Alex (Malcolm McDowell), a clever young thug whose nocturnal diversions include robbery, assault, and (most gleefully) rape. With his false eyelash, paratroop boots, cane, and bulging codpiece, Alex is a parody not only of maleness, but of sexuality in general. His world (as envisioned by production designer John Barry) is an unpleasant, thoroughly inhospitable mix of decaying old architecture and soulless plastic and glass. The gross stylization of this futurist London is a product of the human mind at its most passionless and bureaucratic; the heart has been forgotten. Alex has taken his cues from society, and has become the best sort of aesthete this brave new world can muster, more interested in staging a good show for his trussed victims to "viddy" than with his own physical satisfaction.

More dangerously, Alex is seductively attractive. The mayhem he perpetrates is unconscionable, but he has such a jolly time that we are unwillingly swept along. When he is betrayed by his fellows, captured by the police, and psychologically programmed by the government to retch if he attempts violence, our dismay nearly outweighs our satisfaction. At this point in the story, Kubrick engineered a clever turnaround, subjecting Alex to awful abuse at the hands of his former victims. The boy seems doomed to a (well-deserved) life of misery until accidentally falling into the clutches of a writer (Patrick Magee) who regards Alex's condition as something that could be exploited to topple the existing government. In a chilling irony, the writer and his wife

"Viddy well, little brother. Viddy well." Alex (Malcolm McDowell) invites his trussed victim (and the audience as well) to observe the rape of the man's wife (Adrienne Corri) in a particularly harrowing scene from Stanley Kubrick's *A Clockwork Orange* (1971).

had been brutally assaulted by Alex months earlier, and the woman died after being raped. Now, the writer is in control. Alex is driven to a suicide attempt, but survives, and is visited in the hospital by a government bigwig. Anxious to save its hide, the government arranges for Alex to be deprogrammed, and returned to his sociopathic splendor. The film's final image is Alex's daydream of a naked frolic with a beautiful girl as primly-dressed onlookers applaud approvingly. In voice-over, Alex says, "I was cured, all right."

A Clockwork Orange deserves acclaim not only for its technical perfection, but for its audacious and provocative point of view. The title refers to an automaton, a creature that has been stripped of its ability to choose. This is what Alex becomes at the hands of the government scientists. Burgess and Kubrick suggest that to do such a thing — even to someone as monstrous as Alex — is morally wrong. The obvious irony is that Alex has been a clockwork orange all along. The product of ineffectual parents and a degenerate society, Alex was *born* without hope of genuine choice. We must not be surprised that he has cheerfully degraded sexual expression to the emotional level one associates with the making of a sandwich.

For Alex and the other disaffected youths who prowl the strangling city, the most profound of human experiences has become as insignificant as a hiccup. When Alex seduces a pair of brainless teenage girls, the lovemaking is in frantic fast motion, and a crazed version of the "William Tell Overture" blares from the soundtrack. In a flash, the sex is over. Alex raises insouciance to art; even money has no meaning for him: the vast booty from his robberies sits, unfenced and unspent, in a huge drawer beneath his bed. Sociologists and criminologists can argue endlessly about the validity of the film's point of view. Though arguable, it is presented unflinchingly.* Alex plays victim as often as he plays victimizer. The society has no real answers; nobody wins, everybody loses. Alex's cure at the conclusion of the film merely returns him to his former condition: a puppet with no visible strings.

In spite of its sardonic tone and the onus of an "X" rating that was rather stupidly imposed upon it for American release, *A Clockwork Orange* was a commercial triumph. Artistically, it has few peers. The film inspired others, like Walter Hill's giddily surrealistic *The Warriors* (1979), but has resisted imitation. As Kubrick's deliberate moral ambiguity suggests, *A Clockwork Orange* arrived at a time when America was not feeling too good about itself. Since its release, our perception of ourselves and our young has softened. Teen-oriented horror films of the last decade have hardly been charitable to their young protagonists, but at least most of them have not presented teenagers as soulless menaces. Thom Eberhardt's delightful *Night of the Comet* (1984), for instance, suggests that kids have brains, spunk, and initiative; but for each one like this there seem to be three that typecast youngsters as

Anthony Burgess' wife died after being assaulted by three American deserters in London during World War II; one realizes that he did not arrive at his philosophy lightly.

mindless victims. The phenomenon of these "slasher" films (which will be explored in Chapter XI) represents the film community's most extreme and unpleasant reflection of youth.

The truth of teenagers' status is too complex and variable to be accurately summed up by a single film. All that we can be sure of is that the drama and exhilaration of the teenage years will continue to be reflected on movie screens until the last teenager has grown up.

VI
Lugosi, Lee, and the Vampire Lovers

When Bela Lugosi paused on a staircase in 1931 and intoned, "I am ... Dracula," vampirism became inextricably bound up with eroticism. Lugosi's elegant bearing caused him to be a sensation. At 49, he had brought sex appeal to the supernatural, and successfully transferred to Hollywood the matinee idol persona he had cultivated on the Hungarian stage. But the film *Dracula*, as directed by Tod Browning, is nearly as static as the Hamilton Deane/John L. Balderston play which inspired it.

Browning's camera most often sits and merely records dialogue; the director reserved his visual flourishes for those scenes involving Lugosi. The actor's attractiveness is emphasized in shots that focus upon his piercing eyes and grand gestures. For instance, when his wraithlike brides glide toward a helpless man, Lugosi forces them back with just a single sweep of his hand. In London later in the film, he effortlessly murders a flower girl on the street, and mesmerizes a hat-check girl at the symphony. Society women succumb to Dracula's charms as easily as naive schoolgirls. The vampire approaches one woman in her bedroom as she sleeps, and uses his cape to enfold another to his chest after he has hypnotized and kidnapped her. Lugosi's Dracula is not simply a vampire, but a sexual criminal who can disrupt the normal order. At one point Mina (Helen Chandler) tries to bite her fiancé on the throat as she sits with him on a patio. Dracula's influence has turned a traditionally romantic setting into one of sexual horror.

The novel *Dracula*, by the Irish author Bram Stoker, was published in 1897. Browning's film version, though seminal in its depiction of the undead title character as a suave fiend, was not the first. In 1922 the German expressionist F.W. Murnau directed *Nosferatu, the Vampire*, an unauthorized adaptation of the novel and the first significant vampire film. As played by Max Schreck, "Count Orlock" is totally devoid of sexual appeal; he is, in fact, coldly repellent, almost insectoid in appearance. Orlock's domed head, pointed ears, and hideously skeletal fingers contribute to an image that is a far cry from the (authorized) interpretation that Lugosi would bring to Broadway five years later.* Murnau offered repeated shots of Orlock's bent,

---

It may be significant that today, in a self-proclaimed age of deadened cynicism, at least two vampire films have looked at Schreck for inspiration: Werner Herzog's Nosferatu *(1980) and Tobe Hooper's 1979 television film,* Salem's Lot *(see page 161).*

misshapen shadow as the vampire shuffles about with what film historian David Pirie aptly called "senile purpose."

Bram Stoker died in 1912, but his widow successfully sued the makers of *Nosferatu, the Vampire* for copyright infringement. All European prints were destroyed in the mid-1920s, but a negative survived. The film was finally seen in the United States in 1929.

In spite of the outrage of Mrs. Stoker, her husband's novel was not without antecedents. Poems, stories, and novels that date back to "Hecuba" by Euripides helped shape the course of the literary vampire. Homer, Aristophanes, and Philostratus explored vampirism — from a chiefly moralistic point of view — while Goethe's 1791 poem "The Bride of Corinth" is about a repressed girl who is free to marry her lover only after she has died and been resurrected as a vampire. The poet Coleridge gave us "Christabel," a young woman who is visited by an undead sylph named Geraldine.

Lord Byron's outline "The Vampyre," written at the 1816 gathering in Switzerland that also produced Mary Shelley's *Frankenstein*, inspired Byron's companion John Polidori to fashion a finished story of the same title in 1819. Polidori's Lord Ruthven is a blood drinker of glowering demeanor who destroys the sister of his traveling companion. Polidori gave special emphasis to Ruthven's animal attractiveness; this aspect, in particular, most certainly influenced Stoker. Finally, J. Sheridan Le Fanu's 1871 novella *Carmilla* — which will be discussed later in this chapter — and Theophile Gautier's story "The Dreamland Bride" (1836) revolve around voluptuous female vampires, and were deliberate attacks on the conservative sexual mores of their respective times. Clarimonde, the elegant vampiress of Gautier's story, so inflames a young monk that the man willingly offers his blood in return for the perverse fantasy life the woman provides. The sexual tension of this and other stories which predated *Dracula* permeates the latter work. Stoker's greatest accomplishment may have been his audacious crystallization of the more outrageous and heretical impulses of earlier works. Dracula is a character whose fictional lineage is impressive and clear.

Chillingly, Dracula also has a real-life, historical ancestor. Vlad Dracul, who ruled the Rumanian province of Wallachia in 1448, 1456–1462, and 1476, is the most probable inspiration. Vlad (sometimes called Vlad Tepes) is politically significant for his fierce resistance to the Turks, who wished to assimilate the Wallachian state into the Ottoman empire. He has also been remembered for his apparently unquenchable bloodlust, a predilection which caused him to be given the sobriquet of Vlad the Impaler. He enjoyed observing the death throes of his victims; many were impaled alive so that Vlad could observe their agonies as he dined. He would often drink the fresh blood of his victims. Other enemies were blinded, burned, or boiled. Vlad was imprisoned in Hungary from 1462 until 1474, but the vacation did little to quell his bloodlust. When he resumed his rule of Wallachia in 1476, he continued to kill indiscriminately. People from a wide variety of nationalities and religions suffered at his hands. Though Vlad was finally assassinated in 1476, his image — broad forehead, narrow jaw, thick mustache, and piercing eyes — has come to us in woodcuts and scuplture. Since the early 1970s, he has been a figure of considerable interest.

Brutal sadism of the sort practiced by Vlad Dracul was only touched upon by Bram Stoker, who utilized the ruler's crimes as a springboard only; the fictional Count Dracula, courtly and surreptitious, is a figure of irony, and is thus essentially more interesting than Vlad. Bela Lugosi seemed destined to give this complex character its definitive interpretation. The actor's Eastern European background and sinister aura were ideal. Women on two continents had been fascinated by his stage appearances.

Surprisingly, Lugosi was not included in Universal's initial thoughts about casting as the film version of *Dracula* was being prepared. Conrad Veidt and Ian Keith were among the actors tested before Bela, who turned out to be fifth or sixth choice. But, few will deny, a wise one. His approach to the role was sleek and modern, quite different from the mustachioed Victorian gentleman of the novel. Additionally, Lugosi and Tod Browning downplayed Dracula's supernatural aspect. Professor Van Helsing (Edward Van Sloan) marvels when Dracula transforms himself into a wolf, but we do not see the transformation. Likewise, there is nothing in the film to approach Stoker's perversely horrible image of Dracula crawling like a fly down the outside wall of his castle. Lugosi's interpretation, steeped in sex and glamour, is as much a product of American stage and film tradition as of Stoker's book.

The dignity inherent in Lugosi's portrayal of the vampire count is sadly ironic in light of the fact that the actor has become, over time, a figure of parody, not simply of vampirism, but of predatory heterosexuality. Impressionists delight in exaggerating the Lugosi leer and Hungarian accent. But Bela, who had little interest in the macabre, viewed Dracula as a deadly sort of lothario, a mirthless sexual criminal.

Audiences perceived the depth of Lugosi's characterization but Hollywood saw only dollar signs ... and an actor who was difficult to cast. Only two years after *Dracula*, Lugosi starred in a poverty-row serial called *The Whispering Ghost*. The string of bad films quickly became a spiral, and Lugosi found himself hopelessly typecast. Even pictures like *The Black Cat* (1934) and *The Raven* (1935), acknowledged classics of the horror genre which teamed Lugosi with Boris Karloff, were regarded by the industry as little more than gruesome potboilers. Lugosi resisted by accepting small roles in comedies like *International House* (1933) and *Ninotchka* (1939), but Hollywood saw him only as "the horror man." His imprecise command of English and a marked carelessness with money forced him into the ghetto of B pictures. Bela was obliged to take whatever work was offered him. Even at his peak Lugosi earned relatively little money. *Dracula* brought him only $500 a week for a seven-week shooting schedule; neither Bela nor his survivors shared in the fortune Universal has made by marketing and licensing his image.

Though Lugosi played vampiric characters only five times in his film career, Hollywood and, later, the public saw him no other way. He has only a few minutes of footage and virtually no dialogue in Tod Browning's *Mark of the Vampire* (1935), a remake of Browning's *London After Midnight* (1927), a silent thriller that starred Lon Chaney, Sr. *Mark of the Vampire* is classic thirties kitsch, as vampires who frequent a country estate turn out to be actors hired by the police in order to trap a murderer. Browning could not overcome the improbability of the film's premise, and modern audiences can only groan at the proceedings. Lugosi made good use of his limited screen time, and was interestingly offset by the eerie wraith Luna, played by Carroll Borland, at the time a 21-year-old Berkeley coed whom Lugosi had befriended a few years before. Browning exploited the girl's provocatively slanted eyes and long hair by dressing her in a gauzy gown and limiting the range of her facial expressions. Though Borland does not have a single line of dialogue, her presence is quite arresting.

Mark of the Vampire causes audiences to wonder about two things: the nature of Luna's relationship to Lugosi's Count Mora, and the unexplained bullet hole in Mora's temple. Both were explained in early drafts of the script, where it was revealed that Luna had been Mora's daughter *and* lover. Despondent over his crime, Mora shot himself in the head and had been resurrected as one of the undead. That these revelations were not included in the shooting script is a pity, for they sum up much of the tension inherent in vampirism according to Lugosi. In *Dracula*, Lugosi pronounces, "There are far worse things awaiting man than death." Incest is probably one of them.

Typecasting is also pretty grim, especially for an actor filled with as much Old World pride as Lugosi. By the forties, his career had become stuck in the sludge of bland murder mysteries and East Side Kids comedies. A brief upturn came in 1944, when he appeared as Armand Tesla in *Return of the Vampire*. Although Columbia was legally restrained from using the Dracula name, the film is plainly an addition to the Dracula mythos. Lugosi acquitted himself beautifully in this update that brought the horror into war-torn Europe. Tesla, freed from his grave in London by a pair of air raid wardens who unwittingly pull a stake from his body, seeks revenge on the female descendent (Frieda Inescort) of his original tormentors. He has a ready supply of female victims at Inescort's sanitarium, and has a grand time until being betrayed by his lycanthropic aide Andreas (Matt Willis). Director Lew Landers devised some marvelous scenes in a foggy graveyard, in which Tesla forcefully commands Andreas to come to him. At 62, Lugosi had lost little of his persuasive sexuality. By the time he reprised his Dracula role four years later in *Abbott and Costello Meet Frankenstein* (1948), the ravages of his 15-year battle with morphine addiction had begun to take their toll. He had originally taken the drug to relieve the great pain in his legs, but the drug later sapped much of his strength and spirit. Still, at 66, Bela was able to rouse himself. The Abbott and Costello film marks his last great performance.

Ironically, Universal had wanted Ian Keith—a contender for the role in 1931—to take the Dracula part in the spoof. Lugosi's faded box office potential was well known, and his failing health undoubtedly suspected. His agent had to literally plead with Universal execs in order to secure the part. The studio finally gave in and offered $1500 a week on a ten-week guarantee. Lugosi's advancing age was effectively obscured beneath a heavy layer of white pancake makeup. Happily, his gestures and intonations are classic Dracula.

Abbott and Costello had been box office kings of the Universal lot throughout the war years, but hit a slump in the late forties. The stable of Universal monsters had also slumped, so a teaming of horror and comedy doubtless seemed a logical way to get some final mileage from both genres. Besides Dracula, *A & C Meet Frankenstein* includes the Wolf Man (very well played by Lon Chaney, Jr.), Frankenstein's Monster (Glenn Strange), and even the Invisible Man (voice by Vincent Price). The plot finds Dracula dreaming of world domination after discovering the body of the Monster. But Dracula realizes that the Monster's evil brain cannot be controlled—a brain transplant is called for. Enter pudgy Lou Costello, whom Dracula admiringly describes as being "so round, so firm." Costello, sensing what is up, weakly adds, "So fully packed."

Though the film's script gave Lugosi opportunity to practice his mesmeric skills on actresses Lenore Aubert and Jane Randolph, the full force of his sexual power is levied against Lou Costello. Because Costello's persona was that of an outrageously vulnerable naïf, the impact of Dracula's easy manipulation of him is no less powerful or sexually potent than if Dracula's primary victim had been a woman. The relationship becomes a perversely funny variant on that of Svengali and Trilby. Costello is so trusting it hurts. Lugosi's Dracula, like the streetcorner Casanova who strings his girl along in order to get into her pants, pretends to regard Costello as a protégé in order to get his brain. The relationship, as we like to say, is strictly physical.

A & C Meet Frankenstein is grand entertainment because director Charles Barton understood that a horror-comedy can work if neither element compromises the other. The film's hilarity is matched by moments of genuine spookiness. Not surprisingly, the picture was a tremendous commercial success that returned Abbott and Costello to the top. Sadly, Lugosi did not share in the glory. His film career continued to deteriorate, and he was forced to do cheapjack stage tours and Halloween "spook shows" in neighborhood movie theaters, while searching for film work abroad. *A & C Meet Frankenstein* was his last film of any consequence.

A brief stab at Las Vegas in 1954 brought warm notices, excellent audience response, and a guarantee of $2000 a week, but Bela, at 72, could not stand the pace. In April of 1955, Lugosi voluntarily committed himself to Los Angeles County Hospital for treatment of drug addiction. Photographs from

Bela Lugosi and Carroll Borland in *Mark of the Vampire* (1935).

this period are shocking: instead of looking like the sleek count he had played so often and so well, Lugosi resembled someone who had spent years at Dachau. His fourth marriage crumbled at this time, but Bela was significantly buoyed by letters from a woman whose name, significantly, was Hope. Lugosi's physical recovery seems miraculous; he emerged from the hospital looking happy and fit just four months after going in.

He married Hope Lininger — who was more than 30 years his junior — and tried desperately to recharge his career. An association with an eccentric exploitation moviemaker named Edward D. Wood, Jr., brought some work, and a measure of optimism. The violent jealousy that had destroyed Lugosi's four previous marriages was subjugated by his career goals. Local television stations were beginning to run old Lugosi films, and Bela perceived a renaissance. His personal appearances suddenly became wildly successful. But Lugosi did not live to see the full measure of his fame. While reading a script in the living room of his small Hollywood apartment on August 16, 1956, he died. Hope discovered the body when she returned home from grocery shopping. Dracula had succumbed to a heart attack at age 73.

There can be no doubt that Bela Lugosi has entered folklore. One can imagine the accolades he would have received had he lived only five or ten years longer. In spite of the many wretched films in which he appeared, his appeal has grown. It is his presence in the films that makes them worthwhile. Because Lugosi's vocal inflections and mannerisms have been done to death by hordes of impressionists, we tend to giggle rather than shiver at the mention of his name. But I dare any woman to turn off the lights and try to resist the delicious sexual terror that must come when Lugosi pauses on the stair and pronounces, "I am ... Dracula."

Lugosi's career became moribund in the forties, but Dracula's continued. John Carradine took the role in a pair of 1945 Universal thrillers, *House of Frankenstein* and *House of Dracula*. Though American, the gaunt Carradine can project a very proper English quality; his interpretation of Dracula is gentlemanly and interesting, but a bit too courtly to be convincing as a sexual menace.

Lon Chaney, Jr., portrayed "Count Alucard" in Robert Siodmak's *Son of Dracula* (1943) with uneasy results. The tension caused by an unwholesome love triangle involving Alucard and a mortal couple is amusingly developed, but Junior had none of his father's power or versatility. The younger Chaney adopted his father's name in the early thirties when his career as Creighton Chaney (his true name) went nowhere. This move brought him B-film stardom, but was accompanied by the inevitable typecasting. As Count Alucard, Chaney was not well served by his stocky frame and craggy features. His voice — flat and passionless — conveyed none of the force and urbanity that is suggested by Curt Siodmak's script. Chaney's attempt was a brave one, though: he even allowed Universal makeup artists to gray his temples and give him a slick pencil mustache.

Son of Dracula is interesting chiefly because of its suggestion that vampirism can be as much self-induced as inflicted by a bite. As one character explains it, Alucard's mortal bride became a vampire because of her "morbid" turn of mind. Her own eagerness to be corrupted was strong enough to effect the transformation. Alucard is destroyed when fire prevents him from reaching his coffin at dawn, but it is too late for his bride, who is burned by her mortal lover as she sleeps.

Although the Universal monster cycle that had begun with *Frankenstein* in 1931 finally ran out of steam in the late forties, the end had been in sight throughout the decade. Horror films, especially those with the supernatural overtones of vampirism, lost favor as audiences turned to the expanding threshold of science for fictional thrills. Vampire variants like *The Devil Bat* (1941) and *The Spider Woman Strikes Back* (1946) were traditional suspense films with thinly rationalized "vampire angles." In the latter film, villainess Gale Sondergaard drains the blood from young women in order to feed her poisonous plants. Postwar Hollywood, beset by television, shifting audience demographics, and the breakdown of the studio system, abandoned horror in favor of science fiction. Updates of the vampire theme in the fifties were few. Paul Landres' *Return of Dracula* (1958) features Francis Lederer as the Count, who prowls around modern-day Southern California in search of juicy coeds. And in Landres' *The Vampire* (1957) small-town physician John Beal botches up his love life and terrorizes half the town when mysterious pills he has unwittingly taken turn him into a creature of the night. Despite some effective moments, these modern-day stories—set in the dull milieu of American suburbia—didn't quite jell. Audiences had seen newsreel footage of atomic bombs; vampires suddenly seemed benign and unsensational.

Audiences were growing up. The racy *Baby Doll* was a controversial success in 1956. Actors like Marlon Brando and Paul Newman brought the "Method" approach to gritty, realistic dramas. Even more intriguing was the sexual revolution that seemed to be going on in Europe. French girls started wearing revealing bikini swimsuits. At Cannes in 1954, a bosomy starlet ran naked from the surf to embrace actor Robert Mitchum. A pouty temptress named Brigitte Bardot was a sensation in *And God Created Woman* in 1957. American adolescents pondered these developments with grave interest. Maybe there *was* more to life than *Father Knows Best*.

Britain's Hammer Studios, a small production house that had specialized in provincial comedies and weak thrillers since the thirties, revitalized the moribund horror genre in 1957 when *Curse of Frankenstein* brought period chills back to film. The picture did well in its English release and the studio was quick to apply the same formula—color, violence, glossy production values—to the Dracula legend, by this time in the public domain. *Horror of Dracula* (1958) had one additional element: sex.

A tall, elegant actor named Christopher Lee was cast as Dracula; so successful was his interpretation that he has become the only horror star since Bela

Christopher Lee's overtly sexual vampire lord in Terence Fisher's *Horror of Dracula* (1958). His victim is Melissa Stribling.

Lugosi to have a fervent female following. If Lugosi's concept of the character was frankly erotic, Lee's was blatantly sexual. His Dracula bristles with sexual energy and magnetism. Courtly in moments, Lee's Dracula also demonstrates a fierce physical cruelty, as when he grabs his undead bride and effortlessly flings her across a room. When he bites a young lovely's throat he is not merely feeding, but experiencing (and inducing) a moment of orgasmic ecstasy. We can almost feel the vampire's lips brushing tentatively upon our throats.

Lee had come up through the ranks of British B films in the forties. His height and menacing stare had brought him many villainous roles. If not born to play Dracula, Lee certainly took firm command of the role and gave it new direction and thrust. In *Horror of Dracula*, as in subsequent films in the series, Lee exudes not only power but an aura of *challenge*. He seems to dare women to resist him, and dare his adversaries to defy him. A crucial consideration, though, is that at no time does Lee's Dracula seem comfortable with his affliction. His defiance is tinged with an unmistakable self-loathing. Lee has spoken of his desire to make Dracula "a romantic and tragic figure," and director Terence Fisher said that he wanted the film to be a love story. It is clear that Dracula becomes an active force of evil only after his vampiric bride has been staked and destroyed. He is motivated by revenge, wishing to eliminate not only the perpetrator but the man's loved ones, as well. For the first time, Dracula was portrayed as an enraged lover.

The women of the Browning *Dracula* are convincing as victims, but not as real women. The times dictated a distanced, idealized approach. Lugosi's brides hover like silent wraiths and his victims seem like ice princesses. By 1958, though, standards had loosened considerably. The women in the first Lee film are lively and definitely made of flesh. The vampiric bride (Valerie Gaunt) is a particularly delectable specimen, all décolletage and wild hair. She is nearly as exciting as a typical shampoo commercial. Worse, she is well aware of her charms, and uses them to convince one of Dracula's visitors that she is an unwilling prisoner in the castle. She maneuvers herself near enough to bite the man's throat, but is thwarted by the sudden appearance of her master. In essence, the relaxation of censorship standards allowed the introduction of horror cinema's Compleat Woman: the victimized beauty who in turn levels her sexuality at others.

The Dracula role brought Christopher Lee international, if ghettoized, stardom. *Horror of Dracula* was released in the United States by Universal-International, and performed extremely well. Filmed at a cost of less than $200,000, it grossed more than $10,000 in five days at a single theater. The pattern was repeated across the country. Horror, color, and sex had become big box office. Hammer's unsurprising decision to concentrate on this sort of moviemaking continued to be profitable for a decade and a half. The actor Peter Cushing, repeatedly cast as vampire-hunting Professor Van Helsing, was an indispensable element of the Hammer Dracula series. He epitomizes the sanity and normalcy which Dracula is so intent upon destroying. It was a winning formula: vampire films were henceforth red and raunchy.

Lee reprised the Dracula role seven times, all but once for Hammer. Surprisingly, he did not appear in either of the studio's first two follow-ups to *Horror of Dracula*. Terence Fisher's *Brides of Dracula* (1960) starred blond David Peel as Baron Meinster, a handsome young man whose mother has imprisoned him in the family castle because of his vampirism. Mum isn't a total wet blanket, though—she provides her son with a steady stream of female victims. Meinster deceives an attractive young visitor (Yvonne Monlaur), convincing her that his mother is mad and that he should be released. The young woman falls in love with the vampire, and is saved from death when the Baron goes crazy with bloodlust and attacks his own mother. As in *Mark of the Vampire*, the script flirts with vampiric incest. Meinster's crime against his mother liberates him, and he becomes a swinging single of the deadliest sort.

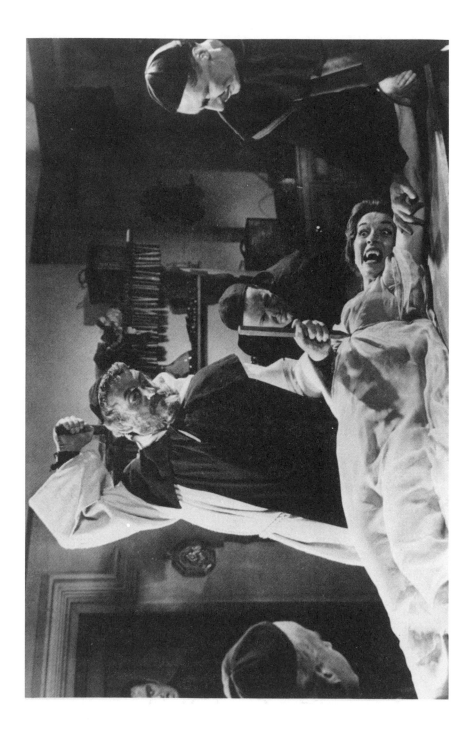

Leading lady Yvonne Monlaur was in the mold of a young Bardot: shapely, big-eyed, and sensual. This sort of casting became typical of the Hammer product of the sixties and seventies. The starlets who appeared in the studio's horror films seem to have been created from the same set of lush blueprints. Monlaur is not the only temptress on view in *Brides of Dracula*; Meinster's brides—particularly one played by saucer-eyed Andree Melly—are made of the same pretty stuff. Meinster wasn't as bad off as he thought. In fact, vampirism looks like pretty nice work ... if you can get it.

Hammer's third vampire film was Don Sharp's stylish *Kiss of the Vampire* (1963), in which a couple honeymooning in Bavaria is victimized by Dr. Ravna (Noel Willman), the local vampire. An entire town is under Ravna's spell, and the young bride (Jennifer Daniel) becomes a convert. The film's climax is a hysterical variation on *The Birds*, as the coven is destroyed by a mass of madly flapping bats.

Christopher Lee's second appearance as Dracula came in 1966. *Dracula, Prince of Darkness* opens on a particularly sadistic note, as a visitor to Castle Dracula is suspended over the vampire's crypt, his stomach slit so that his blood can run over Dracula's ashes and bring the Count back to corporeality. The quasi-religiousness of the opening is a neat touch, and one hopes for more revelations. Unhappily, director Terence Fisher and writer John Sansom chose to restrain Dracula, defusing him until he is just the film's demonic centerpiece. The concept isn't bad, but the script hasn't the breadth of invention necessary to pull it off. Lee's scenes are few, and the film sags without him. Perhaps to compensate, lovely Barbara Shelley is featured as a very proper Victorian lady who becomes a lustful fiend after an encounter with Dracula. Her personality change is nearly as startling as her on-camera demise, as she is staked by monks who pay no attention to her writhing and screaming.

Freddie Francis directed *Dracula Has Risen from the Grave* (1968), a well-shot (Francis is an accomplished cinematographer) but thoroughly pointless film which allows the idiocy of Dracula pulling a stake from his own heart! C'mon, Freddie, even little Joey down the street knows vampires can't do that. Francis' blasting of the vampire myth has no rationale—John Elder's script does not explore its ramifications or attempt to explain it. It is little more than a cheap gimmick that cheats and annoys a trusting audience. The film is more successful when it deals with Dracula's clergymen adversaries, one of whom is duped into becoming a slave. Francis developed the tension between the holy and the unholy with some cleverness, but the film's real significance is that it boldly extended Hammer's juxtaposition of vampirism and sex. Dracula's nubile victims *solicit* his bite; there is a fine moment of twisted eroticism when blonde heroine Veronica Carlson lies with radiant expectation upon her bed as the vampire approaches, lithely twisting her body to aid his angle of approach.

Barbara Shelley is dispatched by monks in *Dracula, Prince of Darkness* (1966).

The best of the Lee Dracula films other than the first is Peter Sasdy's bitterly ironic *Taste the Blood of Dracula* (1970), which is not only a first-rate thriller, but a scathing indictment of the hypocrisy which often attended Victorian mores. Lee was not given much more screen time than in *Dracula Has Risen from the Grave*, but his presence is felt much more keenly. This time he is resurrected by a decadent nobleman (Ralph Bates) and a trio of "respectable" townsmen. The townsmen, however, are bored hedonists, not devoted acolytes. They are horrified by Bates' blood-drinking ceremony, and kill him. Dracula is enraged by the loss of his toady, and sets out to systematically destroy the families of the three townsmen.

Sasdy established that the sons and daughters are a boring, prissy lot, given to picnics and silly giggling. They are a decidedly lukewarm bunch, but Dracula heats things up when he takes control of the young women. His converts are immediately enthralled by him; Alice (Linda Hayden) even sleeps during the day atop Dracula's cold crypt. No pimp ever had such total control of his stable. One vampiress (Isla Blair) murders her father by driving a stake through his heart, and Alice beats her own father to death with a shovel. The unbelieving horror of the men as they are attacked by their heretofore obedient daughters is at once shocking and amusing.

Dracula is the driving force of the film, but Alice's father (Geoffrey Keen) is the focal point of its irony. The man is a hypocrite and bully of the worst sort. He forbids Alice to see her lover for no reason except irrational dislike, and orders his wife about as though she were a servant. He lectures impressively about morality and propriety, yet steals off with his companions to orgies and drunken revelries. His guilt over his involvement with Dracula is not sufficient to save him from the vampire's wrath. The father's actions have opened the door and allowed the horror to creep in. As in *Horror of Dracula* and numerous other vampire films, Dracula understands that to corrupt the family unit is the most potent sort of revenge. He is as disruptive a force as dope or incest.

Taste the Blood of Dracula is among the last wholly worthwhile films produced by Hammer, and is certainly the last time Christopher Lee played the Dracula role with conviction. He had expressed displeasure with the stake-pulling in *Dracula Has Risen from the Grave*, and threatened numerous times to leave the series. He should have listened to himself. *Scars of Dracula* arrived late in 1970 to reveal that the series had run out of ideas. Director Roy Ward Baker attempted on the one hand to characterize Dracula as a smiling, urbane host, but allowed him on the other to assume the role of whip-happy sadist. So at odds is this with the Dracula mythos that purists cannot believe their eyes. Baker *did* include the wall-crawling that Stoker had devised, but the sequence cannot carry the rest of the film.

The picture died at the box office, and could have been the end of the Hammer Dracula series if not for the success of *Count Yorga, Vampire* (1970) and *The Return of Count Yorga* (1971), low-budget American films which

Alice (Linda Hayden) resolves to devote her life to her new master, Dracula (Christopher Lee), in Peter Sasdy's bitterly ironic *Taste the Blood of Dracula* (1970).

introduced a Dracula-like figure to a modern day milieu. Bob Kjellan directed both films with wit and considerable attention to the way in which the undead Yorga (Robert Quarry) comports himself in the Los Angeles of the 1970s. Characters are incredulous of the whole idea of vampires (cleverly giving voice to and then quieting the audience's own doubts), but are quickly convinced. Like Dracula, Yorga has his share of buxom young victims, but Kjellan avoided the glamour of the Hammer approach. Yorga's brides are razor-toothed and ravenous, and carry the stink of the grave. Their attacks are not sensuous ballets, but snarling grabs. Kjellan carried this nihilistic approach to its logical end in both of the Yorga films, as focal characters who have been rescued from Yorga turn out to be vampires.

Blacula (1972), a black variation, was also set in modern day Los Angeles. Hammer most certainly looked at these films with interest, for Dracula and Chris Lee returned in *Dracula A.D. 1972* (1972), a film that is as thoughtless as its title is awkward. Dracula is revived by a group of devil-worshipping adolescents who run afoul of Jessica Van Helsing (chesty Stephanie Beacham), a descendant of Dracula's original nemesis. Neither director Alan Gibson nor writer Don Houghton attempted to come to grips with the Count's adjustment to 1972. The novelty of seeing our undead protagonist in the company of loutish teenagers and fast cars wears thin very quickly. Hammer had completely missed the point of the Yorga films.

Incredibly, the studio compounded its mistakes in 1973 when it released *The Satanic Rites of Dracula*, another modern day story which seems to be a combination of *A Clockwork Orange* and *Village of the Damned*, in that Dracula's mesmerized slaves are a gang of jack-booted juvenile delinquents. Sigh. Joanna Lumley (who later starred opposite Patrick Macnee in television's *The New Avengers*) took the role of Van Helsing's descendant. The film flirts with nudity, most notably when a fetching vampire (Valerie Van Ost) is staked below an exposed breast.

A revelation that Dracula has assumed a false name and becomes a speculator in London real estate was a fairly inventive attempt to deal with the vampire's adjustment to 1973, but it was too little too late. Dracula was a character lost at sea. The films had become hideously mechanical. Christopher Lee realized that typecasting was destroying his career and finally put an end to his association with Hammer. He had served Dracula well, and had successfully broadened the scope of the character's paradoxical sexuality. But there was no place left to go; it was time for Lee to move on. He had hoped that Jesus Franco's *El Conde Dracula* (*Count Dracula*; 1970) would afford him the opportunity to give a definitive portrayal, but the film turned out to be a confusing mishmash riddled with meaningless zoom shots. In 1971, Lee appeared as Vlad the Impaler in a television film called *In Search of Dracula*. His costumes and makeup perfectly recall the woodcut images of Vlad. Thirteen years after first attempting the Dracula role, Lee had come full circle.

The blatant attacks on the niceties of proper society that were pioneered by Hammer's Dracula series reached an apex in the early seventies in a series of films that focused upon female bloodsuckers. Although these films, with titles like *Countess Dracula* and *Lust for a Vampire*, were permitted in a social climate that was growing both more liberated and fearful of female sexuality, their antecedents were in 19th century literature and 17th century history. Elizabeth Bathory was a Hungarian noblewoman born in 1560. She was raised in the Carpathian Mountains and married a man named Ferencz Nadasdy, who allowed her to move freely from castle to castle, where she indulged her obsession for human blood. From 1600 to 1610 Bathory abducted and murdered hundreds of peasant girls in the belief that their blood would keep her skin young and healthy. It is said that Bathory bathed in their blood. She was finally exposed in 1614 and was walled up alive in one of her many castles.

Bathory was a remarkably cold-blooded murder machine who processed her victims the way sausage manufacturers process hogs. Her exploits have directly inspired two noteworthy films. The first, *Daughters of Darkness* (1970) was a Belgian/French/West German/Spanish coproduction directed by Harry Kumel. Though the action takes place in modern day, Delphine

Seyrig's Bathory is a pale, immaculate ghost image with blonde, marcelled hair and a manner that evokes the 1930s. At a hotel, she expresses an unhealthy interest in a vulnerable, doe-eyed young woman who is on her honeymoon. Bathory and a lesbian companion gradually draw the bride and her new husband into rather vile erotic games. The Countess begins by directing the couple's lovemaking, then becomes a part of it. Bathory's companion and the groom are killed when the games get out of hand; it seems that Bathory's control of the girl will be absolute. They leave the hotel together and Bathory is impaled when the girl accidentally crashes the car. But a perverse sexual persona, like cancer, needs little time to grow and gain control of the host. The girl assumes Bathory's demeanor and evil intent, and approaches another newlywed couple as the film ends.

Daughters of Darkness works on a multiplicity of levels: as sexual thriller, horror story, and psychodrama. Kumel was schooled as a film historian, so he was aware of past variations of his theme. The transfer of evil is a staple element of ghost fiction, for instance, as is the old standby about the innocent couple whose honeymoon is disrupted. What lifts the film above the commonplace is its deft exploration of the tension between past and present. Bathory's appearance and that of the hotel in which she lives conjure up the past in a way that Kumel intended to be off-kilter. Everything, from the woman's makeup to her furniture, is highly stylized. The film's "look" wavers somewhere between Art Nouveau and Art Deco. We sense that the past did not really look like this, but feel that it *should* have. The ease with which the mod young couple is swept up by Bathory's decadence suggests that the power of the past is irresistible. Evil, we discover, is not diminished by time but may, in fact, grow stronger. The honeymooners are weak and easily led; Bathory consumes them like cupcakes.

The other significant translation of the Bathory story, *Countess Dracula* (1971), returned to a period setting. Though far less provocative than *Daughters of Darkness*, it is not without a certain wit. Lush Ingrid Pitt was cast as Countess Elisabeth Nadasdy, an aged ruler who accidentally discovers that wrinkles in her face can be removed with virgin's blood. After luring her first victim into her bedchamber, Elisabeth is transformed from a black-garbed frump into a low-cut glamour girl. Director Peter Sasdy executed a reversal on the parent/offspring theme he had explored in *Taste the Blood of Dracula*; here, Elisabeth conspires to assume her daughter's identity, and keeps the girl (Lesley-Anne Down, in an early role) imprisoned in an isolated cottage. Once again, traditional roles and the integrity of a family have been upset by supernatural evil.

The only fly in Elisabeth's ointment is her consort (Nigel Green), who is hip to what is going on. He tells her, "We can't have you parading around like some jaded young slut from a whorehouse!" but Elisabeth does anyway. She becomes a skilled murderess, but discovers that whore's blood has no therapeutic effect. Only "good girls" will do. Elisabeth eventually amasses a

Countess Dracula (1971; Ingrid Pitt) emerges from her bath of virgins' blood.

pile of nubile bodies which she clumsily hides behind wine kegs in her cellar. Suspicious villagers discover the corpses, but not before we are treated to a splendidly audacious view of Elisabeth, nude, as she rises from her blood-filled bath. Things go bad at the Countess' wedding to a young soldier. Her daughter has eluded her captors and makes a sudden appearance in the middle of the ceremony. She attempts to stab her mother but kills the innocent groom instead. Elisabeth's beauty treatments abruptly wear off, and she winds up in a dungeon, looking warty and dull-eyed, awaiting execution.

Sasdy humanized the story by indicating that Elisabeth's mind slips deeper into doubt and despair after each murder. In one particularly pathetic scene, the Countess whimpers and prays for help as she fumbles with a rosary.

She is not totally unreal; the horror of her crimes, committed for the sake of youth, is not lost on her.

The inspiration for even raunchier vampire women came from literature. J. Sheridan Le Fanu's novella *Carmilla* was published in 1871. It explodes Victorian virtue from within with a quietly perverse story of the insidious corruption of a young girl by a beautiful aristocrat named Carmilla Karnstein, who has died 150 years previously. In the style of the day, Le Fanu's narrative is flowery and circumspect, even cloying. As Carmilla brings out the lesbian in the young woman, Le Fanu fills his pages with trembly prose that a pubescent girl could best appreciate. Like Sasdy's Countess Elisabeth, Carmilla is as much a victim as a victimizer. She speaks unhappily of the "cruel love" she must endure, and claims that she is forced to prey upon young women in order to maintain her own youthful form. Carmilla is a tragic figure because she is aware that each misdeed further erodes her slender humanity. She struggles to resist the dark forces that urge her on, but cannot. Nor can her victims. In this respect, *Carmilla* was a direct attack on the stifling moral climate of the time. Le Fanu's young victims appear prim and proper, but beneath those cool exteriors lurk — gulp — wanton fleshpots.

How could a moviemaker resist such giddy source material? In 1961 Roger Vadim — a controversial director more celebrated for his marriages than for his films — borrowed from *Carmilla* when he made *Blood and Roses*. Like many other European directors who have worked in the genre, Vadim sacrificed logic and narrative at the altar of imagery. Set in modern day, *Blood and Roses* is a predominantly visual exodus through some very subtle psychological territory. Carmilla (Annette Vadim) does her evil in a strictly spiritual fashion, drawing the soul of her female victim from the body and replacing it with her own. Vadim's direction cleverly forces the audience to shift its viewpoint as Carmilla shifts from one body to another. Annette Vadim's performance is resolutely calm; her inner torment is suggested by showy externals like a fireworks display and a gaudy masquerade ball. The latter element, in particular, brings a discomfiting period flavor. Dream sequences shot in a sterile monochrome add a surrealistic quality. The climate of 1961 did not allow Vadim's approach to be as blatantly erotic as it would later become, but the film's lesbian aspect is nonetheless apparent. In one elegiac scene, Annette Vadim and Elsa Martinelli, their faces bathed by rain, share an unsisterly kiss. The discreet artistry of this and similar moments mark *Blood and Roses* as Vadim's most restrained effort, and probably his best.

A more literal (and colorful) adaptation of *Carmilla* was offered by Roy Ward Baker's *The Vampire Lovers* (1971). As Carmilla, voluptuous and strong-featured Ingrid Pitt is not precisely the slender temptress of Le Fanu's novella, but doe-eyed Madeline Smith, as the young initiate, was ideally cast. Pitt's Carmilla is an irresistible sexual juggernaut whose comely victims succumb to their own suppressed desires; they become vampires willingly, loving it. In essence, the film is a gleeful advertisement for the joys of lesbianism.

Elsa Martinelli (left) and Annette Vadim share an unsisterly kiss in Roger Vadim's 1961 vampire romance, *Blood and Roses.*

That Hammer was able to get this past the censors is less a mark of the studio's ingenuity than an indictment of the review board's thickheadedness. The film's goings-on are outrageous, even offensive, if one is easily offended. But Hammer banked on the fact that horror films, a genre both despised and taken too lightly, would be able to get away with it. The studio was correct. *The Vampire Lovers'* parade of bare breasts, blood, and lesbian soul kissing would have been censored to ribbons if presented in a "realistic" context. The joke, of course, is that good fantasy, because it speaks so pointedly to our subconscious, is infinitely more affecting than a "straight" narrative. Hammer's incautiousness then, was so blatant that the censors could not perceive it.

Carmilla is beheaded at the conclusion of *The Vampire Lovers*, but the box office returns suggested that audiences had not seen the last of her. Indeed not, the best was yet to come. Jimmy Sangster's *Lust for a Vampire* (1971) probably represents the apex of the English-speaking sex-vampire. The anagrammed fiend Mircalla is revived when blood from a girl's slit throat drips into her coffin. Now, what's that establishment right next door to Mircalla's castle? Why, bless my soul, it's a girls' school! Mircalla enrolls, and Sangster turns Tudor Gates' uninhibited script into *High School Confidential* with fangs, or a Harlequin romance written by someone in very bad DT's. Girls whisper, giggle, and play coy sexual games with each other while Mircalla moves through them like International Harvester. A male teacher is vampirized, and a lovely student (Pippa Steele) is bitten on the throat and breasts. When Mircalla pauses in her fiendish work, blood streams from her fangs and across her bare breasts. The image must surely be one of the most startling in cinema history. Sangster's jackhammer approach to perverse sexuality could have been disgusting if not for the curiously detached quality actress Yutte Stensgaard brought to her interpretation of Mircalla. Stensgaard is blonde and blank-faced; her self-limiting performance prevents *Lust for a Vampire* from (excuse the pun) cutting too deeply.

Mircalla's further adventures were chronicled in John Hough's *Twins of Evil* (1971), in which the vampire (Katya Wyeth) brings bloodshed and paranoia to a small village. She runs afoul of a fanatical Puritan group called The Brotherhood, which goes on a vengeful spree of witch-hunting. In the midst of the film's breast-biting and full frontal nudity, a girl (Madelaine Collinson) is attacked and vampirized. Her identical twin (Mary Collinson) remains virtuous but is mistaken for her evil sister and nearly burned at the stake. The film is full of such ironies: the twins are nieces of the leader of The Brotherhood (Peter Cushing), whose holy zeal transforms him into a murderer. The identical appearance of the girls suggests the day/night, good/evil dichotomy of vampirism. Nearly everyone is a victim, even Cushing, who is felled by an axe after beheading his evil niece. Mircalla's world is a dark one that is filled with powerful opposing forces, a fact that is graphically illustrated when a crucifix sears the pubic hair of a female vampire. The social and psychological ramifications of the juxtaposition are endless.

There have been other variations on the Carmilla and Bathory stories, but most have been minor, if not downright idiotic. *La Noche de Walpurgis* (*Werewolf vs. the Vampire Woman*; 1974) is an improbable love story in which Bathory falls for a werewolf. Paul Naschy, a onetime Spanish weightlifting champion whose real name is Jacinto Molina, played the husky werewolf. Naschy became Spain's one-man horror show throughout the seventies by sprinkling his gory films with a curious sentimentality. He growled a lot, but always treated his ladies right.

The female vampire, caught between the foolishness of Naschy and the blatant approach of Hammer, finally reached a dead end in the mid-seventies. The mine had been exhausted. The decline of the sex-vampire also marked the decline of Hammer Studios. The Bathory and Carmilla pictures were the company's last notable commercial successes. Later attempts to mate vampirism with swashbuckling (*Captain Kronos, Vampire Hunter*; 1973) and revive the Frankenstein legend in Terence Fisher's crude and pointless *Frankenstein and the Monster from Hell* (1973) failed. American exhibitors began to express disinterest in the Hammer product, and the studio was

Girlish sexual abandon as practiced by Mircalla (Yutte Stensgaard, left) in *Lust for a Vampire* (1971). Her lover is Judy Matheson.

moribund until finding some success in the late seventies with a television series called *Hammer House of Horror*. The series allowed the studio to recall a number of writers, directors, and actors from the glory days. So Hammer, which revitalized the horror genre in the late fifties, now staggers on by recycling its own past.

In France, director Jean Rollin was busily creating his own sex-vampire films—and breaking down censorship barriers as he went. Rollin is one of a number of European directors (Jesus Franco and Riccardo Freda are two others who come to mind) who have backgrounds in the visual arts, but little regard for such niceties as plot and pacing. *Le Viol du Vampire* (1967) was Rollin's first feature, and is representative of his subsequent works: excrutiatingly slow, filled with meaningless closeups, overuse of the zoom lens, and rambling monologues that do nothing except fill time. The sexual aspect of Rollin's films is fascinating, but often disconnected from—or even at odds with—the main narrative.

In *Le Viol du Vampire*, a modern day story, the focal character is a dusky vampire queen who enjoys reclining half-nude on the tiger skin upholstery of her car while female acolytes lap blood from bowls. The film is crammed with sensational but essentially meaningless incidents, like the queen's Venus-like eruption from the sea, a marriage ceremony that is performed in a coffin, bats skewered by rapiers, and plenty of cheery gang rape. The picture is richly visual and heavily textured; great attention is given to the ornate leather and metal accoutrements of the queen's automobile and coffin. Rollin's visual success is especially interesting because he shot *Le Viol du Vampire* in black-and-white.

Extraterrestrial vampires are featured in Rollin's *La Vampire Nue* (1969), a film rich with sado-masochist imagery, e.g. spikes that protrude from a girl's breasts. In an amusingly ironic touch, the son of a scientist conducting hellish experiments in vampirism falls in love with one of his father's victims. *Le Frisson des Vampires* (1970) further developed Rollin's fascination with imagery; the focal character is a voluptuous female vampire who is lovingly garbed in stylized chain mail and leather. She corrupts a pair of male vampire hunters who in turn attack a honeymooning couple. Once again, a vampire film shows how innocence can be corrupted and compromised by evil sexuality. The vampire goddess eventually runs out of victims and, in a moment that beautifully expresses the horrid futility of vampirism, must drink blood from her own veins.

Rollin linked social irresponsibility with vampiric evil in *Vierges et Vampires* (1971), in which two girls who have escaped a reformatory become slaves of a coven of undead. For the criminal girls, vampirism seems a logical step; the affliction is presented as an especially sophisticated sort of criminal activity.

Rollin's penchant for a visually dense approach — at the expense of genuine substance — causes his films to be less noteworthy than they may initially appear. He has intriguingly linked vampirism with ceremonial costume and ritual, but his interest seems strictly pictorial. His images are as provocative as those in a glossy men's magazine, and about as thoughtful. Historically, Rollin is significant for his boldness; French film before Rollin had been heavily censored, and was not nearly as explicit as many Americans hopefully assumed. *Le Viol du Vampire*, the director's first feature, was a staggering leap forward, and doubtless inspired Hammer to go ahead with its own brand of pulchritudinous horror.

Other non–American films occasionally strained the limits of credibility. One wonders if the big-time critics caught *L'Ultima Preda del Vampiro* (1960), an Italian film which had a 1964 U.S. release as *Playgirls and the Vampire*. In Vernon Sewell's *The Blood Beast Terror* (1969) scientist Robert Flemyng turns his beautiful daughter (Wanda Ventham) into a giant vampire moth. Don't turn on the porch light, kids.

More vampiric lesbianism is at the fore in Joseph Larraz's 1974 British film *Vampyres*. Two women who had been mysteriously shot to death return as vampires, and lure passers-by to the decaying mansion in which they died. One attractive male victim is not killed outright, but kept alive for kinky sex and midnight snacks. The vampires' lust for sex metamorphoses into an all-consuming bloodlust, and they orgy themselves into a state of perpetual exhaustion. *Vampyres* lacks reason and motivation. Its equating of lesbianism with debauched evil (a strikingly conservative point of view) may be sensational, but isn't very convincing. The film is based upon as slender an idea as a movie can be.

Japan's Toho Studios, which unleashed Godzilla on an unsuspecting world in 1954, became more thoughtful in 1968 with *Kuroneko* (*The Black Cat*), a costume thriller set in feudal Japan. A mother and daughter who have been raped and killed by barbarians become vampires and seek revenge. The women can shape-shift into remorseless vampire cats; when one of the women loses a human arm, it is replaced with the black leg of a cat. The offending barbarians have no chance.

A similarly stern notion of retribution is reflected in a little-known American film called *The Devil's Mistress* (1966). Four outlaws in the old American West kill a man named Jeroboam and rape and kidnap his woman, Liah (Joan Stapleton). Liah turns out to have supernatural powers, and kills each of the men by draining the life from their bodies with her kisses. When the last outlaw is dead, Jeroboam (Arthur Resley) steps from the woods and envelopes Liah in his cape. The woman, more truly a succubus than vampire, uses her peculiar sexuality in a rational way. The fact that Jeroboam, too, is somehow magical suggests that the outlaws may have been set up; Liah and Jeroboam may not have been victims at all, but avenging angels. The understated tone maintained by director Orville Wanzer avoids titillation, and imbues the dark side of sexuality with motivation and logic.

Most American films of the sixties and seventies that deal with vampirism have modern settings, or are spoofs. The aforementioned *Count Yorga* films are the best of the former; a good number of the latter were of the sex-lampoon variety. Dracula purists: brace yourselves. 1968 brought *Dracula Meets the Outer Space Chicks*. In 1969 we wondered *Does Dracula Really Suck?* and discovered that the old reprobate is gay. Granny's School for Good Girls is invaded by a werewolf and a vampire in *The House on Bare Mountain* (1962), one of the first skin films to have mainstream appeal and promotion. Someone named Vince Kelly was cast as *Dracula, The Dirty Old Man* in 1969. The Count's libido is more than healthy in this picture, which offers plenty of nudity and many hapless young ladies who are bitten on their breasts. Dracula's sexual appetite finally gets the better of him when he unthinkingly chases a nude girl into the morning sunlight.

A bit more ambitious was *Blood for Dracula* (1974), amusingly directed by Andy Warhol protege Paul Morrissey. Dracula (Udo Kier) travels to Italy in search of his preferred beverage: virgin's blood. He meets a nobleman (Vittorio De Sica) who has four comely daughters. Ah, lunchtime. Unfortunately, the nobleman also has a horny gardener (Joe Dallesandro) who gets to three of the daughters before Dracula can. The vampire (who collapses and vomits when he takes the blood of nonvirgins) feverishly pursues the only daughter who remains unmolested. But she, too, is rescued by the resourceful gardener, who hurriedly impregnates her, then grabs an axe and chops Dracula to bits.

Morrissey's approach to the film's considerable gore was blunt and intentionally ludicrous. With its skinny and neurotic Dracula, the picture becomes a burlesque of the vampire trandition, and an effective update of Grand Guignol.

Among the very few women who direct commercial Hollywood films is Stephanie Rothman, who apprenticed with exploitation king Roger Corman in the early 1960s. Rothman's first feature, *Blood Bath* (1966), was codirected by Jack Hill. William Campbell plays an artist who is the reincarnation of a vampire. He slaughters his attractive female models, paints their bodies, and drinks their blood. Rothman's second horror film was more original. The setting of *The Velvet Vampire* (1971), as in the Yorga films, is present day, though the focus is on a female monster. The vampire is named (a bit too cleverly, perhaps) Diane Le Fanu, in tribute to the author of *Carmilla*. At the "Stoker" art gallery she meets a young couple, whom she later tries to initiate into the world of perverse sexual pleasure. Diane (Celeste Yarnall) exhibits a powerful dislike for men who prey on women (a rapist is handily dispatched) and a fondness for velvet. Rothman's cleverest twists involve the film's settings: Diane Le Fanu lives on an isolated ranch in the harsh California desert, but mounts her final pursuit of her victims in the clogged streets of Los Angeles. The vampire's evil flourishes in a setting where the evil of men does likewise. We bring the horror down upon ourselves.

Producer/director Dan Curtis brought *The Night Stalker* to television in 1972. A superb script by Richard Matheson involves mouthy reporter Carl Kolchak (Darren McGavin), a hard-luck guy whose beat is Las Vegas. He becomes suspicious when hookers and secretaries are being drained of blood, and soon stumbles upon an exceedingly ruthless vampire (Barry Atwater). Matheson and Curtis cleverly exploit our disbelief by detailing Kolchak's struggle to make the authorities believe him. The restrictions of network television prevented Curtis from becoming too graphic in his examination of the vampire's female victims, but one scene is a real chiller, as Kolchak enters the vampire's rented house and discovers a young woman bound to a bed. Deathly pale, red-eyed, and nearly comatose, the girl has been kept alive as a handy feeding station. The vampire nibbles on her as casually as the rest of us nibble on chicken legs.

Recent American attempts to return vampirism to a period setting have been of middling quality. Dan Curtis presented a television version of *Dracula* in 1973 that starred Jack Palance. The film is ambitious and well-mounted; Palance is an effective, if unorthodox, Count. Unhappily, network standards undercut much of the impact. In 1979 stage actor Frank Langella repeated his Broadway role in John Badham's *Dracula*. Though big-budgeted and crammed full of name actors (including Laurence Olivier), the film is ultimately unconvincing. Langella is an assured actor, but looks as though he should be playing tennis instead of biting people. He hasn't the brute presence necessary to make Dracula an intimidating figure. The character

Asexual vampiric evil in Tobe Hooper's *Salem's Lot* (1979) as the fiend Barlow (Reggie Nalder) threatens young Lance Kerwin.

seems oddly disconnected from the horror; when Van Helsing (Olivier) is attacked in a catacomb by a rotting vampire woman, it seems hard to believe that Dracula is capable of altering someone so hideously.

Because the vampire myth has been thoroughly dissected, modern audiences seem to react most positively to those films which place vampirism in a modern setting. *The Night Stalker*, for instance, was one of the highest-rated television movies in network history. Even darker interpretations have fared well. The undead Barlow (Reggie Nalder) of Tobe Hooper's *Salem's Lot* (1979) expresses a purity of vampiric evil that is very nearly the ultimate extrapolation of the myth. Repellently ugly, Barlow has no personality, no dimension. He (*it* may be more appropriate) is a killing machine who destroys children and crushes a young mother's head like balsa. Hooper's focus is on Barlow's victims; vampirism becomes an abstract evil.

1979 also brought Stan Dragoti's *Love at First Bite*, an undisciplined but often funny spoof that starred George Hamilton as Dracula. Hamilton exploited his own jet-setting image by portraying Dracula as the epitome of bloodsucking cool. With his rakish cape and patent leather pumps, the Count is equally at home in the boudoir and on the disco dance floor. Ladies, the man is *smooth*! His romance with a mortal woman (Susan Saint James) is agreeably consummated when the two of them become bats and flap off into the beckoning moonlight.

Today, the vampire film is in remission. Local drive-ins occasionally bring back *Vampire Playgirls* (1974) for another go-round, but the myth — at least in its more literal sense — seems to have been thoroughly explored. Essentially unrelated offshoots like *Night of the Living Dead* and *Motel Hell* will be discussed in Chapter XI. Pure vampiric cinema has suffered because it became too skilled at suggesting the limits of morality. The genre showed us outrageous, primal images, and the worst thing happened: we accepted them. Our tolerance for fantasy has increased so dramatically that vampires have become tame stuff. If we have grown, we have also moved beyond shock. We think there are no surprises left.

That's what we think.

I suspect that vampire cinema, like Christopher Lee's Dracula, will rise again. The myth will continue to excite and tantalize. Its irresistible mixture of sex, evil, and danger will once again find an enthusiastic audience. Like love, the vampire's bite is forever.

VII
High Priestess of Horror: Barbara Steele

Shortly after Britain's J. Arthur Rank Organisation sold Barbara Steele's contract to 20th Century–Fox in the late fifties, the young English actress found herself passing day after day on a California beach. Fox did not know what to do with her. During a Hollywood writers' strike in early 1960, she went to her adopted home, Italy, and took her first starring role in something called *La Maschera de Demonio* for first-time director Mario Bava. After returning to the United States, Steele was cast as a blonde Southern belle opposite Elvis Presley in *Flaming Star*, but when the requirements of the role became ridiculous, the actress fled back to Europe. *La Maschera de Demonio* premiered in America as *Black Sunday* in late 1960. Steele was instantly acclaimed—the Queen of Horror had assumed her reign. Fox had thrown away an electrifying talent.

In the span between 1960 and 1976, Barbara Steele appeared in nearly a dozen horror films, building an active career but one that was doubtlessly frustrating, for although she has become a cult figure of worldwide proportions, she remains largely unknown outside the horror genre. Cult appeal is difficult to analyze, but a requirement would seem to be unorthodoxy. It is little wonder that Fox did not know what to do with Steele—her raven hair, chiseled, sensual features and piercing green eyes are a far cry from the wholesome blandness of the Debbie Reynolds and Sandra Dees of the day.

In her youth, as now, Steele suggested a kinky and irresistible sexual allure, and would clearly have overwhelmed any male "starlet" with whom she might have been cast. For more than twenty years, Steele's fans have adored her talent, intelligence, and beauty. But at the core of her appeal, inescapably, is her ability to express a tantalizing sort of evil, and a sexual ambivalence that is at once enticing and ghastly. She has come to personify— with more edge and clarity than any other genre star—the link between sex and death, as well as this culture's paradoxical attitude toward female sexuality, a potent force that is feared as strongly as it is desired. Steele, in her many roles as sexual savior and succubus, represents the beauty we love to hate.

Steele was born in Liverpool (or Ireland, according to some accounts) in 1938. An interest in visual art led her to London's Chelsea Art School and to the Sorbonne. She began her professional acting career on the repertory stage

A rare blonde portrait (circa 1965) of the incomparable Barbara Steele.

while a teenager. The Rank Organisation signed Steele in the late fifties and enrolled her in its famous "charm school," a training ground for starlets that had produced notables like Belinda Lee and Honor Blackman. But Steele's enrollment came at a time when the British studio system was in a shambles. The rise of Hammer Films was still a few years away; British film production was moribund, and success in the crucial American market was elusive. Film activity on the Continent, however, was on the rise. Rank utilized Steele in small roles in dramas like *Sapphire* (1958) and romances like *Bachelor of Hearts* (1961), then sold her contract to Fox. Steele's decision to give Italy a try after her period of inactivity in Hollywood was not only adventurous, but logical. Neither England nor the United States had anything to offer her, while Mario Bava was promising a starring role.

Bava had been a cinematographer in Italy throughout the fifties, shooting such films as Riccardo Freda's *I Vampiri* (1956) and *Caltiki, the Immortal Monster* (1959). *Black Sunday* (1960), based on Nikolai Gogol's story "The Vij," was Bava's first official attempt at direction.* Though his career remained successful and active until his death in 1980, Bava never equalled *Black Sunday*. Its moody, often harrowing black-and-white cinematography and disquieting juxtaposition of beauty and horror make it one of the most significant and psychologically provocative horror films of the postwar era.

The story is simple to the point of fable: in 17th century Moldavia, flickering torches ring a misty field as the witch Asa (Steele) is tied to a stake and whipped. She snarls at her tormenters, promising to exact revenge upon their descendants. A burly, hooded executioner produces a heavy metal mask shaped in the image of a hideous gargoyle, and studded on its inside with deep spikes. The metal face is held to Asa's and driven deep onto her head with a single blow from the executioner's mallet. The witch's lover Javuto (Arturo Dominici) dies similarly. Two hundred years later, a carriage transporting Doctors Choma (Andrea Checchi) and Gorobec (John Richardson) breaks down near a ruined castle. While the carriage is being repaired the men explore the ruins. In the castle abbey, Choma discovers a crypt that holds the corpse of a woman. A metal mask covers the woman's face. Choma removes the mask, as well as a cross that had been placed on top of the crypt. When he accidentally cuts himself, blood from the wound drips onto the corpse. Choma leaves to rejoin Gorobec while, in a thunderous blast of energy, Asa revives.

Outside the castle, the doctors are startled by Princess Katia (Steele), a stunningly beautiful young woman who is the image of Asa. Katia reveals that she is Asa's great-granddaughter. Gorobec and the Princess soon fall in love, but the resurrected Asa and Javuto threaten to destroy Katia and the entire village. Choma is accosted by Asa and mesmerized into stealing blood from Katia's ailing father. Katia is likewise confronted, and Asa assumes her identity, intending to steal the princess's life force. So convincing is the witch's performance that Gorobec nearly kills the unconscious Katia until noticing a crucifix on her bosom. The deception is uncovered, and Asa and Javuto are once again handed to the villagers and destroyed, this time with fire.

Though *Black Sunday* is poorly dubbed and handicapped with an uninteresting leading man, it is nonetheless an elegant and disturbing film that discloses the strange beauty of horror. In one sequence, a young servant girl who has set off along a dark road to milk a cow is surprised by a ghostly black coach driven by Javuto. The team of horses labors mightily, but because Bava shot the sequence in slow motion and without sound, the cumulative effect is of delicate nightmare. Even more unexpected is Choma's lifting of

Reportedly, sections of I Vampiri *were directed by Bava after Riccardo Freda had a disagreement with the film's producers.*

Gorobec (John Richardson) embraces Princess Katia (Barbara Steele) — or does he hold the witch Asa? Mario Bava's splendidly atmospheric *Black Sunday* (1960).

Asa's mask in the abbey. We expect to see the witch's pitted, ravaged features, but, no: Asa's face in repose is smooth and flawless. When she revives, her eyes rise liquidly in their sockets, glimmering with evil light. Other images in the film are more blunt. Javuto struggles from his muddy grave outside the abbey to the accompaniment of lightning and thunder, the camera tilted oddly as he claws the executioner's mask from his face. And when Gorobec realizes that Asa has masqueraded as Katia, he plucks at the witch's robe, revealing the rotted and skeletal body beneath. Asa reacts as though to a sexual affront; her most private flesh is not the sweet treasure of innocent youth, but the depravity of ancient evil.

It becomes clear in the course of the film that good and evil have numerous shared traits, an ambivalence that is neatly visualized by the introduction of the heroine. Princess Katia is essentially the antithesis of the witch, yet the separation is not total, for we first glimpse the princess as she silently stands on a crest between gnarled trees, dressed in black and flanked by a pair of wary mastiffs. Though the script only hints at psychological links between Katia and Asa, Bava's imagery makes the point with style and cleverness. Bava moved to color film shortly after *Black Sunday*, and for the next twenty years created movies that are infuriating in their missed chances. His overuse of the zoom lens and a fondness for half-baked scripts marked him as a director with an energetic visual sense but dubious artistic judgment. Some of Bava's films, like *Blood and Black Lace* (1964), have decidedly unpleasant and gratuitous sexual connotations. He never duplicated the subtle physical dread of *Black Sunday*.

For Barbara Steele, *Black Sunday* meant recognition and exposure. Her impact in the film is staggering, in spite of the fact that she did not dub her own dialogue. She established in her first starring role the elements of a disturbing screen persona that would be elaborated upon over the next two decades: beauty vs. horror, sexuality vs. decay, and the uneasy commingling of these elements. Her dual role is especially significant; even at this early stage of her career, Steele was viewed as the ideal dream girl of paranoiacs who imagine hideous menace lurking behind every pretty face.

Steele's sculpted features and wildness of eye quickly typecast her as the dark goddess who can dole out pleasure and pain in equal measure. She worked in episodic television after returning to the United States, and was then cast opposite Vincent Price in *The Pit and the Pendulum* (1961), the second of Roger Corman's successful Edgar Allan Poe adaptations (see Chapter IX). Corman directed this modestly-budgeted series of films with élan and imagination. *The Pit and the Pendulum* is one of the best, and although Steele's role as Price's unfaithful wife is small, she made the most of it.

Once again, we have a pointed link between beauty and evil; Steele's Elizabeth wishes to drive husband Nicholas (Price) insane so that she may inherit his wealth and spend it with her lover, the family physician (Anthony Carbone). Supposedly deceased at the beginning of the film, Elizabeth, Nicholas worries, may have been entombed alive. But her death and burial were faked. Elizabeth is very much among the living, tormenting her husband with her voice and other evidence of her presence. The ruse works: Nicholas is driven quite mad. After finally showing herself in the castle's torture room, Elizabeth gloats over her husband's slumped body: "Is it not ironic, my husband, that your mother was an adultress ... your *wife* an adultress?" Ironic, yes, but also dangerous, for Nicholas suddenly revives from his stupor and shoves Elizabeth in an Iron Maiden, kills her lover, and nearly slices her innocent brother to death with the title device. Nicholas is stopped at the last moment by his sister (Luana Anders) and the family retainer, and pushed from a

Duplicitous Elizabeth (Barbara Steele) drives her husband (Vincent Price) to madness in Roger Corman's *The Pit and the Pendulum* (1961).

stairway to his death. The room is sealed, but as the heavy door clangs shut, the camera swish-pans to the eyeslit of the Iron Maiden, where we see Elizabeth's panicked eyes. The frame is compressed to a horizontal band, the color bleeds to crimson, and the film is ended.

Although *The Pit and the Pendulum* brought Steele notice from influential columnist Louella Parsons, it was to be the last American film she would make for nearly fifteen years. She returned to Europe shortly after the picture's completion and began the most prolific period of her career. Working primarily in Italy with directors like Riccardo Freda and Antonio Margheriti, she starred in a succession of period shockers that touch upon all manner of subjects too hot for Hollywood: sadism, necrophilia, gruesome torture, demonic possession, physical and spiritual rot. Even casual observers realized that these movies meant *business*.

In Freda's *The Horrible Dr. Hichcock* (1962) Steele was Cynthia, second wife of Hichcock (Robert Flemyng), a 19th century researcher who made his first wife Margaretha the victim of a weird experiment in sexual regeneration. Hichcock wishes to continue his experiments on Cynthia but is thwarted by Margaretha (Teresa Fitzgerald), who is prowling the house after having been buried alive. Cynthia eventually escapes with a young doctor (Montgomery Glenn) as fire destroys her husband and his first wife.

Riccardo Freda is a former art critic with an unsurprising flair for the visual, and an unfortunate disregard for logic and pacing. He has directed scores of films since the late forties, almost always on low budgets and tight schedules; Steele's involvement in *The Horrible Dr. Hichcock* was a brisk eight days, and is significant primarily because she was (atypically) cast as a victim, and not as a figure of horror or menace.

Steele returned to scheming villainy in *The Ghost* (1962; U.S. release 1965), Riccardo Freda's loose followup to *The Horrible Dr. Hichcock*. This time, Hichcock (Leonard G. Elliott) is a paralyzed surgeon who dabbles in mysticism. Steele played Hichcock's wife Margaret, a duplicitous beauty who convinces her lover, Dr. Livingstone (Peter Baldwin), to kill her husband with poison. The murder accomplished, Hichcock is buried. To Margaret's dismay, though, her husband has been interred with the key to his safe. The body is exhumed and the key recovered, but the safe is empty. Soon, greed and guilt begin to eat away at Margaret. She has ghostly visions of her husband, and imagines that his blood drips from her ceiling onto her bed. When she learns that Livingstone has discovered jewels in Hichcock's coffin, she kills her lover with her husband's razor and burns the body. Intending then to commit suicide, Margaret prepares poison, but is interrupted by Hichcock, who appears in the flesh to inform her that he has tricked her and Livingstone into revealing themselves. As Hichcock gloats he unknowingly drinks Margaret's poison. He pleads with her for the antidote, but the vial is purposely smashed before his eyes. Hichcock dies, and Margaret is left alone and totally insane.

A preoccupation with the horrific byproducts of lust and greed informs many of Freda's films, and may have reached an apex with *The Ghost*. Not one of the characters misses a chance at theft, deceit, or sexual blackmail. So focused is the narrative, in fact, that it successfully reduces its characters to a level *below* stereotype—all the way to brute emotion. The bitch-goddess Margaret is a perfect plum of hate. As her deceit grows, she is diminished until, at the end, only madness is left.

Steele has had supporting roles in numerous "mainstream" films; one that gave her hope for a new direction early in her career was the sixth-billed part of Gloria Morin in Federico Fellini's poetic and autobiographical 8½ (1962). The part is not large (a lengthy dance sequence was cut) but Steele—chic in black and with striking eye makeup—makes a strong impression. Fellini's portrait of a giddy Rome and its often surreal inhabitants was a congenial and apt setting for Steele. Unfortunately, the hoped-for roles in other prestigious productions did not materialize. Steele would later comment unhappily about her relegation to "the horrors"; to be sure, her career allowed her to grow as an icon, but not as an actress. Even Fellini cast her as much for her beauty and predatory demeanor as for her talent. At any rate, "the horrors" continued.

Antonio Margheriti's *Castle of Blood* (1964), based on Poe's "Danse Macabre," is not Steele's best gothic, but is almost certainly the most outlandish. Its requisite castle setting was shot with three cameras, much in the manner of television comedy. Margheriti's visual approach is energetic to the point of whirling freneticism. The script, likewise, pinwheels with incident. Alan Foster (Georges Riviere) is a young journalist who meets Edgar Allan Poe in a tavern. Poe tells a fantastic story of a nearby castle prowled by the ghosts of all the people who died violently within its walls. When Foster scoffs, Poe's friend Sir Thomas Blackwood proposes a wager: the journalist will earn $10,000 if he can survive one night in the castle.

With the recklessness of many horror movie heroes who have no idea of what they're getting into, Foster takes the wager. Things go well for a time, but he is soon tormented by hideous screams, and visitations from an intimidating array of phantoms. He later discovers Elizabeth Blackwood (Steele), a dark wraith who explains that she owns the castle, and that it is in the grip of the Night of the Dead, when former residents return to corporeality in order to reenact their final moments on Earth. Foster observes as a musclebound psychotic strangles a middleaged man in a bedchamber, and then is nearly strangled himself. Despite the hurly-burly of the evening, Foster finds time to fall in love with Elizabeth. He takes her to bed, resting his head on her bosom after their lovemaking. The woman, he is shocked to discover, has no heartbeat. "I am dead, Alan," Elizabeth informs him.

She confesses that the homicidal body builder is the ghost of her lover, and that the strangulation victim is the ghost of her husband. The lover had been killed by Elizabeth's cousin Julia, who had had a lesbian fixation on Elizabeth. Julia, in turn, had been stabbed to death by Elizabeth. Foster is understandably dazed by these revelations, but is *really* shocked when Elizabeth adds that the Blackwood phantoms require human blood in order to perform their danse macabre. Although Foster is a prime candidate, Elizabeth's apparent love for him moves her to help him escape. They dash into the moonlit garden together, but Elizabeth withers to dust in the outside air. Foster steps through the gate to the safety of the road, but is impaled on an iron spike when a gust of wind slams the gate closed. In the morning, an unsmiling Thomas Blackwood reaches into the dead man's coat and collects his money.

Steele's role as the ghostly voluptuary reinforced the uneasy themes which began to be developed in *Black Sunday*. Her love for the young man is not a natural one; indeed, it is not merely in defiance of the laws of society, but the laws of God and nature. Elizabeth is, after all, dead. That Steele brought the full expression of her beauty to the role makes the whole experience even more disquieting, for how can Foster (and, by implication, the audience) resist necrophilia when it is so attractively packaged? In spite of her love for Foster, Elizabeth seems torn by an underlying desire to do the ghostly thing and murder him. That the journalist has debauched himself in a special,

perhaps unknowable way is a certainty. Is his death heavenly punishment, or had Elizabeth fooled him all along?

Antonio Margheriti and Steele collaborated again on *I Lunghi Capelli della Morte* (*The Long Hair of Death*; 1964), a film with superficial plot resemblance to *Black Sunday*. Steele was Mary, the reincarnation of Helen Karnestein (*sic*; an obvious homage to Le Fanu's Carmilla Karnstein). Helen's mother was unjustly burned as a witch by Count Humbolt (Jean Rafferty); Helen, too, had been killed but Mary — Helen's alter-ego — is an instrument of revenge. The village near Humbolt's castle is suddenly wasted by plague, and when the Count sets eyes upon Mary he believes he sees Helen, and dies of fright. His son (Giorgio Ardisson) is engaged to marry Helen Karnestein's sister Lizabeth, but desires Mary instead. He asks Mary to help him murder Lizabeth, unaware that Helen has risen from her grave and assumed full possession of Mary. The Count's son is trapped in an effigy built by the villagers to celebrate the end of the plague, and is burned to death. The Karnestein revenge is complete.

One can begin to appreciate Steele's unhappiness with her position as horror queen by trying to make sense of the preceding synopsis. Her horror films, though entertaining and often visually stylish, rarely offer real people in truthful situations. The emotions the films deal with — hatred, jealousy, greed, lust, revenge — are almost invariably presented in incredibly convoluted contexts. In short, the films carry the conventions of the genre to the nth degree. Steele's roles were not written in such a way that allowed her any hope of connecting with them on a realistic level. In the iconographic shorthand of the genre, Steele became a symbol, a personification of unpleasant emotion. Her remarkable face doomed her; she watched as her directors had all the fun. In *I Lunghi Capelli della Morte*, Steele's finest moment is not acting per se, but a protracted sequence of Helen Karnestein's rise from her grave after the earth is split by a lightning bolt. As the undead beauty claws her way to the surface, crosscutting reveals a villager reciting from the Book of Revelations: "And on the day of judgment, the dead shall return to life." Of all the stars of horror cinema, Barbara Steele may have come the closest to pure myth.

Massimo Pupillo's minor *Terror Creatures from the Grave* (1965) offered Steele another opportunity to play an adultress, one Cleo Hauff, who conspires with a virtual army of lovers to murder her husband. Cleo apparently forgot that her husband had had an active interest in the occult, particularly in hideous creatures called "scourge spreaders." The monsters rise from their graves and avenge Hauff's murder by killing the conspirators one by one. Cleo is the last to die. The blunt simplicity of Pupillo's narrative makes for some obvious moralizing, but none of the ambivalence that characterizes Steele's

The duality of the Steele persona is captured by ad art from *Terror Creatures from the Grave* (1965).

most intriguing films. The central issue is too limiting and clear-cut to be interesting.

This is not the case with Mario Caiano's *Nightmare Castle* (1965), in which Steele took another dual role. In the film's early going she is seen as Muriel, the corrupt wife of Stephen Arrowsmith (Paul Muller). Muriel's indiscreet affair with the beefy gardener (Rik Battaglia) arouses the ire of her husband, who murders the lovers and buries their hearts in an urn kept in the house. Arrowsmith injects his dead wife's blood into his aged housekeeper (Helga Line), causing her to become young. (Yep, simple as that.) Muriel's fortune has been left to her mentally unstable sister Jenny (Steele), who is newly released from an institution. Arrowsmith courts Jenny and marries her, then sets out to drive her insane. Jenny is innocent in both deed and knowledge yet, in that peculiarly European notion of the perpetuity of guilt, is bedeviled with horrid visions and nightmares of the crimes committed by her predecessor and her husband. Her physician (Laurence Clift) eventually discovers the hearts beneath the urn and frees the vengeful spirits of Muriel and the gardener. Arrowsmith is burned to death, and the gardener kills the rejuvenated housekeeper and drinks her blood; since at least some of the blood belongs to Muriel, the gardener's vampirism is a subtle sort of sexual union via a third party. In the midst of all this mayhem, Jenny and the physician escape unharmed.

Nightmare Castle is not Steele's most sophisticated film, but it may be the most entertaining. Twenty-seven at the time, the actress was captured at the height of her beauty. The dual role was undoubtedly challenging. Although Steele wore a virginal blonde wig as Jenny, the obvious metaphor of the fair hair is not pushed. Caiano allowed Steele to get inside the mind of the character and define Jenny from within. Some of Steele's most powerful and convincing scenes are wordless. In a haunting nightmare sequence, for instance, Jenny writhes on her bed as she dreams of a rendezvous with the dead gardener in a misty greenhouse. Caiano shot the sequence without sound and in stark overexposure, with a suggestion of slow motion. The effect is, well, nightmarish. As Jenny and the gardener make love on the greenhouse's earthen floor, a figure approaches. It is Arrowsmith, but he has no face, only an unreadable mask of stretched gauze. When Arrowsmith begins to beat the gardener, Jenny awakens, unsure of who the men are, knowing only that her marriage has implicated her in something hideous. Ennio Morricone's obsessive piano score adds to the aura of confining terror.

Conversely, Steele's Muriel is splendidly defiant and unrepentant, even as she and her lover are tortured on an electrified bed (aversion therapy of the most chilling sort), and later manacled and whipped. Arrowsmith blindly fuels Muriel's evil and capacity for revenge. The husband enjoys playing

The innocent bride (Steele) adrift in a malevolent dream landscape in *Nightmare Castle* (1965).

inquisitor, but Muriel seems to *relish* being a victim. There's no coyness about her — she was *born* to be abused.

Of all the classic horror film themes, those that appear most often in Steele's films are possession and revenge. The dead seldom rest easily — never go to their eternal sleep without a struggle. The sexual aspect remains dominant in picture after picture; Steele's women are both sinners and sinned against. The physical beauty which is their inevitable downfall also brings the downfall of others. In Camillo Mastrocinque's *An Angel for Satan* (1966), Steele played Harriet De Montebruno, an innocent 19th century woman whose body is invaded by the spirit of a corrupt temptress whose essence has languished for 200 years within a marble statue. Possessed, Harriet becomes a vengeful sexual juggernaut who destroys the descendants of her captor's original tormentors. She exposes the gentle love affair of a maid and a schoolteacher with such ferocity that the teacher (Aldo Berti) hangs himself. The demon flaunts herself around the village, caressing her breasts and inviting advances from various menfolk, only to stand by and watch as they are killed after she has loudly accused them of violating her. One of her victims is a pathetically feebleminded youth. Worst of all, one man is so bedazzled by Harriet's charms that he murders his entire family. The film is Steele's most misogynistic, for it proposes that contact with female sexuality inevitably leads to warfare, and that men are very nearly *destined* to be the victims of beautiful women. The hapless village idiot becomes a metaphor for maleness in toto. Though Harriet is freed from the spell when the statue is pushed from its base, the film's psychosexual thorniness is not diminished.

Similar themes were explored by the talented young British director Michael Reeves in his tongue-in-cheek *Revenge of the Blood Beast* aka *She-Beast* (1966). It is present-day Transylvania, and Veronica (Steele) is a tourist who is possessed by the 200-year-old spirit of the witch Vardella after apparently drowning in a car wreck. The film's conception of the nature of evil is sophisticated yet puritan, suggesting that the evil that befalls people is often a reflection of the evil aspects of their own personalities. The revived Vardella, then, is not simply a carrier of random misery, but an insidious force that feeds on the wickedness that already exists in her victims. Despite Reeves' constant spoofing of the political situation in eastern Europe (after Vardella murders a man with a sickle, for instance, she tosses the instrument aside so that it coyly rests across a hammer), the film has a number of good shock sequences that reinforce the central theme, notably an abrupt cut to Vardella's decayed face as a local innkeeper rapes a young girl. The sinners of *this* village do not have to wait until the afterlife for their punishments; retribution walks the streets disguised with a beautiful face.

Michael Reeves was a protégé of the toughly competent American director Don Siegel, and later of producer Paul Maslansky. Though Reeves started at the gofer level, his drive and passion for film caused him to rise quickly. In 1964, at 20, he directed portions of Luciano Ricci's *Castle of the Living*

Dead, and made his official debut a year later with *Revenge of the Blood Beast*. His other films are *The Sorcerers* (1967; starring Boris Karloff) and *Witchfinder General* aka *The Conqueror Worm* (1968), the latter a relentlessly upsetting chronicle of Matthew Hopkins, self-proclaimed "witchfinder" of the 17th century who put scores of women to death in rural England. As in *Revenge of the Blood Beast*, sexuality is viewed with cynicism, and becomes a jaundiced subtext. Reeves' vision was consistently pessimistic: he did not seem to believe in the possibility of moral victory, and held that while there is such a thing as total evil, no one is totally innocent. Life's dilemmas, Reeves understood, are presented to us in shades of gray. Sadly, the director's ambivalent voice was stilled when he died—an apparent suicide—at age 25.

This period marked the beginning of a tapering off of Barbara Steele's film activity. She married the American screenwriter James Poe, became a mother, and hoped for a more significant acting career. Poe, a respected talent who had written the screenplays for *Cat on a Hot Tin Roof* (1958) and *To Kill a Mockingbird* (1962), supported his wife's aspirations; in his script *They Shoot Horses, Don't They?* Poe tailored the second female lead for Steele, but the role went to Susannah York when the film was produced in 1969. In 1968 Steele allowed herself to be painted green and dressed in a golden ram headpiece for a thanklessly small role as Lavinia, queen of the devil worshippers in Vernon Sewell's *The Crimson Cult*. Despite Steele's presence and that of Boris Karloff, Christopher Lee, and Michael Gough, the film is fussy and uninvolving. Even an orgiastic revel that climaxes with the burning of Lavinia does not amount to much.

Steele returned to Hollywood to do a turn as a silky villainess in an ABC-TV movie called *Honeymoon with a Stranger* (totally overwhelming top-lined Janet Leigh), and later appeared as a sin-obsessed matriarch in the "Sin-Eater" episode of *Night Gallery*. At this point, Steele entered semiretirement and did not film again until 1974, when she played the sexually repressed, sadistic warden of a women's prison in Jonathan Demme's cheeky *Caged Heat*. By this time, her name had assumed an almost legendary status, and she was free to take small but showy roles at her leisure.

She returned to the horror genre in David Cronenberg's outrageously funny *They Came from Within* (1976), the first significant example of the Canadian writer/director's fascination with physical horror as it relates to aberrant sexuality (see Chapter XII). Steele—looking trim and elegant in her late thirties—was cast as Betts, one resident of a Toronto high-rise that is infested with grotesque, slug-like parasites that exaggerate the host's sexual urges. Betts—violated by a slug that crawls from the bathtub drain up between her legs as she demurely sips wine—becomes a raving lesbian who seduces her female neighbors. When she passionately kisses one would-be lover, the slug crawls from her throat and into the mouth of the other woman. Soon, the entire building is a riot of messy hedonism. Cronenberg's suggestion at the conclusion is that Toronto and the rest of the world are next.

Steele's appearance in *They Came from Within* was her first in the "no holds barred" style of horror that arose following George Romero's graphically shocking *Night of the Living Dead* (1968). Her casting was well-received by her fans, who were delighted to see her amidst Cronenberg's kinky brand of nihilism. But despite the film's unprecedented thematic and visual frankness, Steele had not escaped her typecasting—she was still playing the beautiful bird of prey. Further, the unembarrassed visualization of what had been only *suggested* by Steele's earlier films stripped her of much of her force and mystery. The new arena was not worthy of her.

A small but noticeable role as one of the prostitutes in Louis Malle's *Pretty Baby* (1978) was followed by costar billing in Joe Dante's *Piranha* (1978), one of the most successful pictures to be released by Roger Corman's New World. Steele played Dr. Mengers, a chicly dressed scientist who investigates the escape of killer piranha from a secret government research facility. Though not an out-and-out villainess, Dr. Mengers is clearly a member of a conspiratorial establishment, eager to mouth platitudes as the piranha gobble up half the residents of a tony lakeside resort. Though an obvious imitator of *Jaws* (1975), *Piranha* is effective as both thriller and comedy. Dante's visual wit (which blossomed splendidly in 1981 with *The Howling*) gives John Sayles' clever script a wonderfully sardonic edge. But Steele, though marvelous, seems out of place. Dante's setting is distinctly American, his cast (Bradford Dillman, Heather Menzies, Dick Miller) likewise. Steele's enormous dark eyes, chilly manner, and vaguely intimidating British accent are anomalous. Even a cursory viewing of *Piranha* will make clear that Steele's looks and force of personality are simply difficult to cast. You cannot look at any other face when hers is on the screen. Strikingly beautiful without being conventionally pretty, Steele draws our attention in much the same way as a bizarre work of art, or an auto crash. She is irresistible, inescapable ... and too singular for mainstream acceptance.

Piranha was followed by *Silent Scream* (1980), a very minor thriller in the "slasher" vein. Steele was cast as Victoria, a crazed woman who descends from her attic to plunge a butcher knife into unwary teenagers. Following this (undoubtedly) disheartening appearance, Steele put her acting experience and multilingual skills to work behind the camera as associate producer of Dan Curtis' epic television film *The Winds of War* (1983). The job lasted two years (Steele was later named vice president in charge of development for Dan Curtis Productions), during which time Steele scouted European locations and assisted in casting.

She expressed her empathy for auditioning actors in a 1982 *Los Angeles Times* interview: "I wanted to hire every actor I saw," she said, "but since I obviously couldn't do that, I wanted to serve them all tea and crumpets and spend time with them. I know how important it is for an actor to spend ten minutes in a producer's office instead of two, how reassuring." Steele's understanding of the frustrations of the profession is firsthand. Though her

Barbara Steele—still the beautiful bird of prey—in *Silent Scream* (1980).

thousands of fans need no rationalization for her career, Steele herself is troubled. "When I do [horror] films, I feel like I'm committing something against myself," she sighed to a *Penthouse* interviewer in 1980. "I'm always playing these stylized roles, full of tension, and I *am* very intense, and I understand why I get cast in them. But most of these roles are very negative — destructive and negative. I've had to force myself to play them, and people see me as—I'm not just this predatory woman, this dark seductress. I can sit down and have a cup of tea on Tuesday and pick a bunch of wild flowers like anyone else."

Of course, this sort of misconception by casting agents and the public is both the wonder and the curse of a career in the movies. Film stars are plucked from real life, objectified, and turned into figures of fantasy. They become archetypes and icons. Steele's instance is particularly extreme. She has not spawned imitators, but has paved the way for other singular genre actresses, Martine Beswick, Mary Woronov, and Sarah Douglas among them. We seem to have a need for these imposing temptresses. Though few of us will ever know the "real" Barbara Steele, her unique screen persona will continue to intimidate, fascinate, and perhaps even educate. Director Joe Dante may have encapsulated the actress's career and disconcerting sexuality at the conclusion of *Piranha*, when the deadly fish have escaped into the sea, imperiling the entire world. Barbara Steele, her astonishing face filling the screen, soothingly advises, "There's nothing left to fear...."

Who could believe such a face?

VIII
Hitch

The films of Alfred Hitchcock have been dissected and probed with such industry that there hardly seems to be anything left to say. And indeed, there may not be. Like Hawks and Ford, Hitchcock is a victim of critical overkill. Are we going to study the famed *Psycho* shower sequence yet again? How about Hitchcock's use of editing and the subjective camera? Shall we return one more time to Mount Rushmore or the Statue of Liberty? Is it necessary to rehash Hitch's "creation" of Tippi Hedren?

Perhaps we can attempt to deal with Hitchcock the man. This course of study is less explored than the films, but only because Hitchcock purposely left so few clues as to his personal life. His half-century marriage and private diversions remained closely guarded during his lifetime. We know that he was born in London in 1899, and that he was educated by strict Jesuits. As a young man, Hitchcock developed interests in science, engineering, and especially art. His early film work in Britain was preceded by a stint as an advertising illustrator. Beyond these facts, the most we have to go on are Hitchcock's oft-repeated anecdotes, like the one about his childhood incarceration (arranged by his father to demonstrate the fate of unmindful boys), an incident which left Hitchcock with a lifelong fear of police and wrongful prosecution.

Ultimately, the story tells us more about Hitchcock's movies than about the man himself, which is fine because Hitchcock never publicly divorced himself from his films. On the contrary, he saw to it that he became an *extension* of them. The jowly, sardonic persona that became so well known was carefully cultivated. We never mocked Hitchcock, of course, but his image did make him fair game for parodists like Spike Jones, who, in the late fifties, released a record album featuring a takeoff of television's *Person to Person* called *Poison to Poison*. In it, Hitchcock (in actuality voice artist Paul Frees) tells the Murrow-esque interviewer to watch for his next film, which will star "Perry Coma and Slab Hunter." Hitch concludes by inviting his interrogator to admire his new car. "It's been used only once," he says. "If you look closely, you can still see the lipstick marks on the exhaust pipe."

Hitchcock died in 1980, but he is certainly in no danger of being forgotten. The affection which informed the Spike Jones parody has not diminished. Hitchcock's image and voice provoke immediate response, and we continue to regard him with the sort of easy familiarity usually reserved for favorite uncles. Hitch was our *wicked* uncle, the delightfully malicious relative who simultaneously amused and shocked us. He was one of the very few film directors whose name became a marquee selling point.* Because he so dutifully promoted himself, and because his films nearly always earned great amounts of money, Hitchcock was not acclaimed by the critical establishment as early in his career as were other, less accessible and more fashionable directors. Like Laurel and Hardy, Hitchcock was for a long time revered only by the public. His broad critical acceptance did not come until the 1950s, and the acclaim did not really begin until after he had passed his peak, when critics realized that Hitchcock was not immortal, and that he would not be making movies forever.

Hitchcock was not a horror director. That is, he did not make his fortune and reputation with movies about monsters and headless ghosts. But his films inarguably deal with the horrors of the mind: with guilt, paranoia, and sexual insanity. The Spike Jones spoof is not without insight into the director's unique view of the ongoing battle of the sexes. The life of a typical Hitchcock protagonist is filled with terror and dread. On another level, Hitch's grasp of the technical aspects of moviemaking was without peer; while this may account for his critical acceptance, it does not explain his popularity. Great technical skill is, by itself, boring. Hitchcock's films are never boring. What set him apart from other directors was his absolute control of the screenplays he interpreted, and, more importantly, a sense of humor that was at once vulgar and sophisticated. A single Hitchcockian moment can dazzle, thrill, insult, and amuse.

The quintessential Hitchcock film is, of course, *Psycho* (1960). Joseph Stefano's screenplay adapts Robert Bloch's novel, which in turn was inspired by the real-life murderer Ed Gein (see Chapter XI). *Psycho*, though a Paramount release, was shot on the Universal back lot by an experienced television crew. In a technical and intellectual sense, *Psycho* may be one of the finest movies ever made. As has been explored by numerous writers, the film is a masterpiece of misdirection. Nearly half of its running time is given over to Marion Crane (Janet Leigh), a Phoenix secretary who is on the run after stealing $40,000 from her employer. Hitchcock built Marion's predicament with extreme attention to detail; the early part of the film is a minute-by-minute chronicle of the woman's activities. We grow to like Marion. She's a thief, but only because she's as ordinary as the rest of us. Her romance with a divorced storekeeper (John Gavin) is going nowhere because of a lack of money.

Marion wants to be married but economics won't allow it. She is young but no longer a girl. She can hear her biological clock ticking. When her employer trusts her with $40,000 in cash, Marion finds the temptation too strong to resist. Claiming a headache, she leaves work, packs, and drives from the city. After some close calls with an overly curious police officer and

---

Preston Sturges may have been Hitchcock's closest competitor in this regard, but Sturges — comet-like — burned himself out after only ten years and a dozen films.

Alfred Hitchcock, in his element.

an awkward change of cars, she wearily stops at an isolated California motel. We know the scene by heart: a dark, rainy night, and the heroine at the mercy of whatever lurks in the shadows.

Our fears are eased by the introduction of the motel's owner, Norman Bates (Anthony Perkins), a personable, agreeably eccentric young man who lives with his nagging (but unseen) mother in a Victorian house behind the motel. Norman takes an obvious liking to Marion, and unknowingly convinces her that she must return to Phoenix with the money. After dinner, she is shockingly stabbed to death by a woman with a butcher knife. Norman cries out in horror at the sight of his mother's bloodied hands. He forces himself to dispose of Marion's body and car in a nearby pool of quicksand.

Marion's lover, Sam Loomis, and sister Lila (Vera Miles) are upset by her disappearance, and accept the help of a private detective named Arbogast (Martin Balsam) who has been hired by Marion's employer. Unsatisfied after questioning Norman, Arbogast phones Lila and Sam and tells them of Norman's secluded mother, and then returns to the motel. He slips into the Bates house, and is murdered by the woman with the knife. Now Sam and Lila become actively involved, learning from the local sheriff that Norman's

A Victorian house and a mysterious man: familiar icons in a masterful film, Hitchcock's *Psycho* (1960).

mother has been dead for nearly ten years, and that she was a murderess who committed suicide after killing her unfaithful lover. Then who is the woman at the house?

At the motel, Sam interrogates Norman, chiding him about the $40,000 which, unbeknownst to Norman, rests in the quicksand. When Norman notices the absence of Lila, he struggles with Sam and knocks him unconscious. In the house, Lila is puzzled by the heavy atmosphere of Mrs. Bates' bedroom, and by a room that seems to belong to a small child. When Norman enters the house and dashes upstairs, Lila hides on the steps that lead to the cellar. The cellar is cluttered but quiet, and when Lila pushes open an inner door she sees the figure of an old lady sitting in a rocker. Lila touches the shoulder, the figure swings around, and we share Lila's horror at seeing a mummified corpse. Then: a clatter on the steps and Lila is confronted by Norman, who is dressed in his mother's clothes and wielding a huge knife. Sam arrives in time to disarm the madman. A psychiatrist explains later that Norman is a schizophrenic who has now totally slipped over into his mother's personality. Norman murdered his mother and, after secretly exhuming her body and preserving it at home, assumed her personality to atone for the crime. Unable to relate to Marion as Norman, he responded to her as his maniacally jealous mother. The final shot of Norman (who wears an absurd grin) is accompanied by a terribly reasonable female voice-over, which admits to no wrongdoing.

What is remarkable about *Psycho* is how thoroughly Hitchcock's control extends beyond his material to the audience. We are led along by the hand, and shoved off the path at the director's leisure. Our feeling of familiarity and intimacy with Marion blossoms from the opening sequence, a brilliant series of shots that begins with an establishing shot of the Phoenix skyline and culminates in a close view of Marion and Sam in a hotel room. A documentary-like subtitle informs us that it is afternoon; this is a lunch hour assignation, and not a very satisfying one, either. Marion craves more than just a few stolen minutes. She craves the sort of freedom that only money can bring.

This shot of Marion (who, significantly, wears just a slip and brassiere) coaxes our understanding of the character, and later increases our interest in the $40,000, an interest which is built up feverishly. Surely, Marion has no real chance at success. Her employer has seen her leaving town. We can expect nothing but her ultimate capture, and the scene in which she is awakened in her car by a policeman (Mort Mills) certainly points in that direction. The car is parked on a bright, broad expanse of highway, and the man knocks on the window. Marion stirs, then bolts upright. Hitchcock gives us an uncomfortable closeup on the policeman's face: implacable and unreadable behind the dark glasses and firm mouth. Marion's fear of the police is ours, as well, but the officer is merely curious and sends Marion on her way. When she stops at a used car lot to rid herself of the automobile that can identify her, the salesman's (John Anderson) first words are, "I'm in no mood for trouble!" Obviously, neither is Marion, and her only reply is a confused, "What?" When the policeman parks across the street and eyes Marion's hurried transaction, our doubts and fears become more pronounced. Why does Marion throw away seven hundred dollars on a car that will do her no good? Why does she drive on?

It is dark and rainy when Marion arrives at the Bates Motel. The establishment's ugly neon sign immediately bodes evil. In the Victorian house on the hill, a figure moves across a lighted window as dark clouds move steadily across the sky. The $40,000 begins to dig its way into our consciousness. Will someone steal it from Marion? The introduction of Norman is simultaneously intriguing and reassuring. With his rambling talk and interest in taxidermy, he is obviously a bit off, but we can appreciate the unhappiness of his relationship with his nagging mother. Though Mrs. Bates bullies her son, Norman does not hate her. "I just hate what she's become," he explains to Marion. Later, he comments, "She's as harmless as one of those stuffed birds."

When Marion unthinkingly blurts her real last name after having signed the register as "Marion Samuels," the stolen money begins to bother us again. But Norman does not seem particularly interested in his guest's alias, and is content instead to spy on Marion through a hole in the wall as she undresses in her cabin. It is here that the earlier scene of Marion in her brassiere finds its meaning. Hitchcock has already made voyeurs of us, so how can we be presumptuous enough to condemn Norman for similar behavior? In any case, the young man seems harmless. Marion appears safe in the security of her cabin. She has decided to return the money. As if anxious to cleanse away her guilt, Marion prepares to shower.

What follows is surely the director's most famous single sequence, a brilliantly edited piece of montage that utilizes seventy camera setups in forty-five seconds. As in the airplane sequence in *North by Northwest*, Hitchcock deceives us by plunging a secure, shadowless setting into mad frenzy. As Marion enjoys the water we see, through the translucent shower curtain, the bathroom door as it opens to admit a blurred figure. Horror, as when a man suddenly realizes he is drowning, wells up and smacks us in the face. The curtain is ripped aside, Bernard Herrmann's music erupts in shrill, bird-like notes, and Marion is savaged by the gleaming knife. The camera cuts come with quick assurance, giving us almost subliminal glimpses of the woman's moving legs, ineffectually waving arms, panicked face, and soft belly. The knife flashes across the frame and is never shown touching flesh, but the implications are infinitely more strong than those in inferior films which are more blatantly graphic. The killer flees and Herrmann's score* becomes a pounding two-note as Marion slowly slides down the white tile wall, the light of life leaving her eyes just as inexorably as the blood that is carried down the drain. In an inspired touch, Marion's arm reaches toward the camera, finds the edge of the curtain, and pulls it from its hooks as she collapses dead in the tub. The camera slowly moves along her lower legs, then follows the stained water on its spiralling journey down the drain. A close shot of the drain gives way to one of Marion's staring, sightless eyes, and the camera slowly spirals back.

Still, Hitchcock must have his fun. The camera moves back from the bathroom and pans across the cabin's small living area, stopping at a table, upon which rests the newspaper that holds the $40,000. It is as though Hitchcock is taunting us, determined to make us admit our foolishness at wondering so about the money. Indeed, the bundle is suddenly so absurdly unimportant that we are only mildly distressed when Norman pays it no attention. The young man's dash to the cabin after the killing restores a bit of sanity. We are trapped in our seats and are helpless but Norman — just as horrified as we are — is not. As he busily cleans up, our loyalties shift. Marion has been snatched from us. Now there is only Norman. The woman, with all her hopes, fears, and loves, has been reduced to a grotesque thing wrapped in a shower

---

The late Bernard Herrmann used a purely string orchestra to score Psycho, *probably the only major film to utilize such a musical approach.*

curtain.* The newspaper is tossed in the car trunk after her, and the lid is slammed shut. When the car hesitates on its way into the quicksand, we are worried as well as amused. Norman may be covering up a murder but, after all, he's doing it for mother.

The introduction of the private detective, Arbogast, does not diminish our positive attitude toward Norman. The first view of Arbogast, as he observes Sam and Lila through the door or Sam's store, makes him seem vaguely sinister. When he enters, his unfriendly face fills the screen; an obvious parallel is drawn with the face of the curious policeman. Arbogast's technique is rough and unpleasant, and Sam and Lila accept him only as a device to help them locate Marion. At the motel, Arbogast seems to take unfair advantage of Norman, exploiting the younger man's stammering, defensive posture. Norman's story is flimsy and weak, his sudden "recollection" of Marion unbelievable. The detective is no fool, and because he threatens Norman's mother, we do not care for him.

Arbogast's death, though shocking, is not nearly as hard to take as Marion's. As in the shower sequence, the killer's face is obscured, this time by a dramatic overhead shot instead of shadow. Caught totally by surprise, Arbogast (in some clever process work) staggers backwards down the stairs, arms waving in a futile attempt to regain his balance. He lands heavily on his back at the bottom, unable to fend off the fatal thrusts of the knife. In one way, Arbogast's death is more terrifying than Marion's, for he is a large, strong man who fares no better than the naked, defenseless woman. It is partly because of this that we become suspicious of the killer's identity, but Hitchcock has anticipated us. Norman's tense, unseen conversation with his mother (during which he insists she hide in the cellar) not only makes the woman's existence seem genuine, but also takes our mind from the camera, which is craning above the bedroom door and again taking the overhead viewpoint. Hitchcock's concealment of a mummified face (and Norman's) is masterful. In this scene we see a frail body and hear an angry female voice as Norman carries his mother downstairs. Surely there can be no doubt, now.

The segment with Lila and Sam at the sheriff's is important for two reasons. First, by the very nature of the pragmatic lawman and his wife (John McIntire and Lurene Tuttle), the segment affords a momentary return to normalcy, a quick trip back to Earth before the psychomania begins again. But more importantly, it provides still another buttress for our growing belief that an old woman *does* exist. "Well, if the woman up there is Mrs. Bates," the sheriff muses, "who's that woman buried out in Greenlawn Cemetery?" A bit

---

*Director John Llewellyn Moxey and screenwriter George Baxt pulled a similar surprise at about the halfway point of their atmospheric and splendidly chilling Horror Hotel (1960). Heroine Venetia Stevenson, investigating the history of witchcraft at an inn near Salem, is abruptly snatched from her room, dragged through catacombs, and slaughtered with a ceremonial dagger when the witches' clock strikes thirteen.

later, Lila says to Sam, "That old woman — whoever she is — told him [Arbogast] something. I want her to tell us the same thing." By letting us think we are ahead of the game, Hitchcock leads us further astray.

Sam Loomis, as it turns out, is even less subtle than Arbogast. His interrogation of Norman is heavy-handed and crude. Only his concern for Marion elevates his behavior above Arbogast's. Outside, Lila slowly approaches the house on the hill. Good use of the subjective camera takes us inside: the interior gives the impression of a stilted decorating sense run wild. Ornate nude figures, darkly decorated carpets, and heavy woodwork seem to press in on Lila, and on us. Upstairs, Lila is puzzled by the odd "personality" clash of the bedrooms. In Mrs. Bates' she finds a stuffed wardrobe, curiously indented bedspread, and ugly cast, crossed hands (and here a marvelous pullback shot as Lila gasps, whirls, and sees that she is confronted by nothing at all). A small child would be at home in the other room, which is decorated with a tiny bed, tattered stuffed toys, the Eroica symphony on the record player, and a mysterious, untitled book (a diary?) whose contents go unrevealed as Hitchcock abruptly cuts away.

By the time Norman knocks Sam unconscious, our fears are beginning to jell. The bizarre bedrooms — normal enough in themselves but somehow horribly out of context — gnaw at us. Norman's sudden determination and forceful entry into the house are frightening. We know that something threatens Lila, and only need time to figure out *what*. But Hitchcock refuses us time to think, plunging ahead to the horror in the cellar. Lila shrieks at the sight of the withered, stuffed body (which, cleverly, jolts forward a bit at the completion of its turn), her arm smashing into a hanging lamp. Weird shadows rock the room, stabbing in and out of Mrs. Bates' empty eye sockets. Herrmann's raw, strident music begins again, and introduces the real murderer. Norman, his angular body thrust in the shapeless dress and topped with a prim wig, is a splendid grotesque.

The explanation of the psychiatrist (Simon Oakland) is reasonable, but not wholly satisfying. His assured manner and convenient set of terms are too pat. There must be something more to this. Hitchcock cuts from this expository sequence at its peak and ends powerfully with Norman, who grins as he sits against a blank wall. A female voice-over (Hitchcock realized that the suspension of disbelief is a fragile thing) explains in a horribly rational tone that the blame is all Norman's. She is innocent of wrongdoing. "I'm not even going to swat that fly," "Mother" explains, and we see the insect moving about freely on Norman's hand. Norman? No, Norman no longer exists. Mrs. Bates has won. In reinforcement, the mummified face is superimposed over Norman's for a split-instant as the scene fades. The film ends with Marion's car being cranked from the quicksand, but the final sequence with Norman, his demented grin an appalling thing, shows us that the entire exercise has merely been Hitchcock having his fun at our expense. He has played games with our minds, shunted us through the maze, and manipulated us like putty.

To fully enjoy *Psycho*, the viewer must accept this and be willing to laugh at himself.

Psycho inspired a raft of imitators. The earliest are simply pretentious but the later ones, made in an increasingly more permissive atmosphere, are often revoltingly unpleasant. For better or ill, *Psycho* redefined the horror genre, not only in terms of graphicism, but in matters of tone. For the first time, moviegoing became a fearful event, something to be approached with trepidation. Hitchcock's example encouraged other filmmakers to do with us as they pleased. Audiences were no longer detached observers, but fair game.

The sexual aspect of *Psycho* has been slavishly aped by dozens of lesser directors who do not understand that Norman's sexual schizophrenia — pointed though it is — is merely Hitchcock's "MacGuffin," a plot device which spurs the action and provides a framework for Hitchcock's narrative technique. Like the uranium in *Notorious* and the dead body in *The Trouble with Harry*, Norman's sexual insanity is merely a device, and not an end in itself. If *Psycho* is "about" anything, it is about masterful storytelling. A 1983 sequel, *Psycho II*, was directed by Richard Franklin. The film is an apt and amusing followup, but is burdened with an unnecessarily complicated plot which demonstrates that Hitchcock exhausted the mine. Norman (Anthony Perkins), still skinny and twitchy after 23 years in a mental hospital, returns to the family business, where he is victimized by Lila Crane (Vera Miles), who is eager to avenge her sister's death. Mistaken identity and red herrings abound. *Psycho II* is a serviceable thriller, but nowhere near the level of its inspiration. The cast and original Bates house cannot compensate for the lack of Hitchcock's particular artistry and power.

Hitchcock's overriding concern with the visual aspect of storytelling is attributable to his experience not only as a director of silent films, but as a title designer, i.e. the artist who designed the insert cards which announced dialogue and transitions. These title cards often included small illustrations that summed up the essence of the particular scene. In addition to his film work in England, Hitchcock spent some of 1924–25 at Germany's preeminent studio of the period, UFA (Universum Film Aktien Gesellschaft). Although UFA fell under the domination of the Nazis in the thirties and was dissolved in 1945, it was a vital, highly creative place during the time Hitchcock worked there. World-class filmmakers like Georg Pabst, F.W. Murnau, Ernst Lubitsch, Erich Pommer, and Fritz Lang flourished at the studio. The UFA defined movie expressionism and the technique of using grotesque, distorted sets and odd camerawork to suggest psychological unease. Movies from UFA were not silent so much as they were *visual*. Hitchcock directed his first feature, *The Pleasure Garden* (1925), while at UFA. Shortly after, he returned to England.

The first "true" Hitchcock film is *The Lodger* (1926), an adaptation of Marie Belloc-Lowndes' 1913 novel about Jack the Ripper (see Chapter II). In the book, the mysterious lodger is the notorious lady-killer, but Hitchcock altered the story's premise so that the protagonist (Ivor Novello) is innocent ... and wrongly accused. This theme became Hitchcock's favorite and most enduring — he returned to it time and again. The premise is at the core of most of his greatest films. *The Lodger* (which was set in present-day 1926) takes place in a London terrorized by a brutal, obsessive murderer who kills only blonde women, and only on Tuesdays. The film's first image is a horrifying closeup on a victim's face as she screams. Circumstance soon conspires against the innocent lodger. He is accused of the crimes and handcuffed, but manages to escape with the help of a woman (Daisy Jackson). A few suspicious citizens incite a mob which pursues the lodger through the streets. When he attempts to scale an iron fence, his handcuffs become caught on a crossbar. He dangles in space helplessly, but is saved from immediate execution by the arrival of a constable, who informs the crowd that the real killer has been caught. Christ-like, the innocent man is lifted from his impalement and lowered to the ground.

Hitchcock returned to the handcuff motif in *The Thirty-Nine Steps* (1935; in which hero and heroine are handcuffed to one another) and *Saboteur* (1942). This sense of helplessness is heightened in each case by the element of pursuit. It is a classic nightmare situation: we try to run but our legs will not move, or our wrists are bound. Hitchcock's understanding of the dark side of our subconscious was impeccable.

Films like *The Man Who Knew Too Much* (1934), *The Thirty-Nine Steps, Sabotage* (1936), and *The Lady Vanishes* (1938) established Hitchcock as Britain's keenest purveyor of smart, stylish thrillers. His elevation of suspense over surprise came to the fore in this period; an example is the bomb sequence in *Sabotage*. Hitchcock reasoned that minutes of agonizing suspense affected the audience far more strongly than a five-second surprise, so we *know* that the package carried by the boy in *Sabotage* contains an explosive. As the child moves through the crowded city, we cannot take our eyes from the package. By the time the bomb explodes on a crowded bus, we are in an emotional frenzy. This sort of unbearable suspense generated by knowledge which is given to the audience but denied characters on the screen became a Hitchcock trademark. We have crucial information but — like the players in a bad dream — are unable to convey that information to the people who need it most.

As Hitchcock entered his American period in 1940, he turned his attention more frequently to *sexual* suspense. *Rebecca* (1940), his first Hollywood film, concerns the (unnamed) second wife (Joan Fontaine) of Maxim de Winter (Laurence Olivier), and her fight to resist the influence of her dead predecessor, Rebecca. De Winter's estate, Manderly, is in Rebecca's thrall; the dead woman's earthly agent is de Winter's housekeeper, Mrs. Danvers (Judith Anderson), who tries to push the new Mrs. de Winter into suicide. Fontaine is made to feel like a clumsy outsider in her new home. When Mrs. Danvers learns the distasteful secret of Rebecca's death (which revolves around cancer

and a mercy killing by Maxim) she hides the truth by destroying Manderly —
and herself — with fire.

Rebecca is a romantic fable. Set-bound, mannered, and painfully conscious of the class of people it depicts, the film is typical of the high gloss
Hollywood studio product of the period. Hitchcock's flair for sexual paranoia
did not blossom until *Shadow of a Doubt* (1943), a quintessentially American
film that was shot on the sunny streets of a real town, far away from sound
stages and process screens. The picture is among Hitchock's finest, and was his
first out-and-out horror story.

In Santa Rosa, California, life is slow, gracious, and unpretentious.
Charlie Cokley (Joseph Cotten) arrives to visit his sister and her husband. The
couple's daughter Charlie (Teresa Wright) is bound to her uncle by more than
just a shared name; she loves her Uncle Charlie fiercely, probably because his
charm and urbanity seem a world removed from the familiarity of her own
life. Uncle Charlie is a charmer, all right: he doesn't step from his train, he
saunters from it. But his visit has not been prompted by familial love. Uncle
Charlie is on the run. He is the psychotic murderer the newspapers have
dubbed the Merry Widow Killer because of his victimization of middle-aged
women. Detectives are on his trail, so his visit is an attempt to hide out.

Charlie's love for her uncle never diminishes, but is altered when she
begins to look at Uncle Charlie objectively. The killer discovers his niece's
suspicions and tries unsuccessfully to dispose of her. Young Charlie is unaware
of these attempts on her life, but realizes the full horror of her uncle's
psychosis when he grabs her and tries to push her from a moving train as he
prepares to leave town. At the last moment, Uncle Charlie loses his balance
and is crushed by an oncoming train.

The great irony of Uncle Charlie's death is that it is so unnecessary — the
girl would never have turned him in. Uncle Charlie does not realize this. His
weakness is that he cannot understand love or loyalty. He is a classic sociopath,
concerned only with himself. He regards other people as devices. He charms
others so that he can use them. His obsession to kill, however, is so strong that
it very nearly leaks out in conversation. At the dinner table one evening, Uncle
Charlie talks about the sort of women he murders. As he speaks, Hitchcock's
camera moves closer, until finally Uncle Charlie's calm, implacable face fills
the screen:

> "Women keep busy in towns like this. In the cities it's different. The cities are
> full of women, middle-aged widows, husbands dead, husbands who spent
> their lives making fortunes, working and working. Then they die and leave
> their money to their wives. Their silly wives. And what do the wives do, these
> useless women? You see them in the hotels, the best hotels, every day, by the
> thousands. Drinking the money, eating the money. Losing the money at
> bridge, playing all day and all night. Smelling of money. Proud of their
> jewelry but of nothing else. Horrible. Faded, fat, greedy women."

The murderous charmer Uncle Charlie (Joseph Cotten) confirms the suspicions of his niece (Teresa Wright) in *Shadow of a Doubt* (1943).

Then, from Uncle Charlie's sister: "But they're alive! They're human beings!"

Uncle Charlie turns and addresses the camera: *"Are* they?"

Because Uncle Charlie replies to the camera, he replies to *us*, we who naively represent the voice of reason. Uncle Charlie knows that reason is a joke, and that the innocence of Santa Rosa is an illusion. He's a zealot, a man with a mission, unafraid to shatter our complacency. He brazenly hums "The Merry Widow" at the dinner table; a recurring visual motif is a shot of resplendently costumed couples waltzing to the melody. Uncle Charlie's mania seems almost gracious and genteel. In reality, though, he's merely tenacious, like bathroom mold. He'll never give up. There is no defense against an unsprung mind. Uncle Charlie is the relentless terror that haunts our dreams.

Shadow of a Doubt invites no doubt, at all. We know almost from the start that our attractive leading man is a killer. We are forced to identify with him. The presence of an unglamorous police detective (Macdonald Carey) who enters the household under the pretext of taking a poll only underscores

Uncle Charlie's sleek appeal. We like the murderer, and become his accomplices.

Schizophrenic protagonists became basic Hitchcock. In *Spellbound* (1945), for instance, Gregory Peck is a neurotic amnesiac who has assumed the identity of the head of an insane asylum. Late in the film we learn that a respected physician (Leo G. Carroll) is a calculating murderer. *Notorious* (1946), perhaps Hitchcock's most chic film, revolves around a hedonistic party girl (Ingrid Bergman) who agrees to pose as a lady of breeding in order to uncover the espionage activities of a wealthy Nazi sympathizer (Claude Rains). The girl eventually marries her quarry, and becomes torn between the loveless relationship and her affair with the government agent (Cary Grant) who is her contact. In *Rope* (1948), a pair of handsome college students (Farley Granger and John Dall) turn out to be homosexuals who have murdered their roommate for the thrill of it. And in *Strangers on a Train* (1951) the urbane playboy Bruno (Robert Walker) is really a psychotic mama's boy whose hobbies are strangulation and blackmail. All of these characters mock our perception of normalcy. In Hitchcock's universe, no one is precisely what they appear. Looks are deceiving. Sexuality is dangerous. It can be used as a terrible weapon, or it can be perverted so that traditional notions of love and relationships become sick jokes. At the very least, sexuality can get us into a lot of trouble.

We love to look. Each of us is a latent peeper. We sit in darkened theaters, secure in our anonymity, and observe other people's lives. Sometimes—in the theater and in life—we see more than we should. Sometimes our unwholesome curiosity lets us see things that are not good for us. This is the trap that claims Jeff Jeffries (James Stewart) in *Rear Window* (1954). Jeff is a news photographer who is confined to his Greenwich Village apartment because of a broken leg. His fiancée (Grace Kelly) is eager to be married, but Jeff prefers more vicarious relationships; lacking mobility, he amuses himself by watching his neighbors across the court. One of them, Lars Thorwald (Raymond Burr), is a mysterious sort who isolates himself from the other tenants. His wife is an unhappy invalid. Over time, Jeff becomes convinced that Thorwald has murdered Mrs. Thorwald. Because Jeff has no firm evidence, neither his fiancée nor his friends believe him. The only person to take Jeff seriously is Thorwald, who did indeed murder his wife. When he bursts into Jeff's apartment he is blinded by a well-aimed flashgun. Jeff saves his own life, but not before Thorwald shoves him from a window. The killer is captured and, at the story's end, Jeff has *both* legs in casts.

Rear Window is noteworthy for a number of reasons. First, its claustrophobic premise limited the highly visual Hitchcock to just two sets: Jeff's apartment and the courtyard. Visual stodginess was avoided with the use of judicious camerawork and editing. The film is a succession of provocative subjective views of what Jeff is looking at, intercut with reaction shots on Jeff's face. The movie's energy, then, is not only visual, but psychological. Though physically confined, the action becomes as expansive as the human mind.

Thorwald (Raymond Burr) sees that Jeff (James Stewart) pays the penalty for voyeurism in *Rear Window* (1954).

Jeff is a news photographer, so we have a built-in rationalization for his voyeurism: it's his business. Of course, rationalization is not really necessary. Jeff peeps because he is human. Who among us has not paused to observe the pretty girl in the next building, or the arguing couple next door? Surely each of us steals a glance at the unlucky driver who has been pulled over for speeding. *Rear Window*, with its vast number of subjective camera setups, turns us *into* Jeff. We become a party to his mischief. We lend our eyes as Jeff peeks at the kissy newlyweds, at the childless couple who treat their dog like a beloved infant, and at the lithe girl dancer who seductively poses on her back stoop, encouraging not only Jeff but hordes of would-be boyfriends. *Rear Window* is a film of relationships. Jeff observes these relationships with interest (even as he refuses to formalize his own with his fiancée), but there is no doubt as to his impropriety. His voyeurism is not only dangerous but wrong. When Thorwald enters Jeff's apartment, what could have been a cliched confrontation scene becomes deliciously ironic. Suddenly, *Thorwald* is the injured one. After all, he's been unfairly spied upon. As he moves across the darkened room he implores of Jeff, "What do you *want* from me?" Jeff is now the tormenter. His second broken leg almost seems a just punishment.

Thorwald—intimidating with his bulky body, white hair, and thick spectacles—is a figure from a nightmare. At times he seems almost other-worldly, capable of not just domestic murder but violence of a particularly heinous sort. When the childless couple discovers the body of their little dog, the implication is that Thorwald killed the animal. His callousness is so great that he does not bother to pretend otherwise. As other tenants come to their windows to console the grieving "parents," Thorwald remains in his living room, visible only as a glowing cigarette tip that moves in the dark. Besides providing some ironic sentiment, the sequence underscores Thorwald's evil, and enhances the danger of Jeff's immobility. We identify thoroughly with Jeff and share his horror when, at the climax, he is unable to flee as Thorwald approaches him. The killer's invalid wife was similarly immobile; Thorwald is an expert at preying on the weak and helpless. Jeff's fate—and ours—seems sealed. His fall from the window, like the falls that climax so many of our dreams, ends the nightmare.

Rear Window is an apt admonition for bad, faintly perverse little boys who like to peek into windows. In Hitchcock's hands, the vulgar premise becomes witty and stylish. Despite the grimness of its plot elements, the picture is consistently amusing, though in unexpected ways. We laugh at the more minor travails of Jeff's neighbors (such as a composer's struggle to create a song), not because the situations are intrinsically funny, but because we view them with the arrogant superiority of an omniscient god. Jeff, with his damaged leg propped on a hassock as he fondles his ridiculously elongated telescopic spy lens, is hardly the image of superiority, but that's how he fancies himself. This essential absurdity brings a certain ironic humor to the entire film. Even the queasy suspicion that Thorwald mutilated his wife with butcher knives becomes a grim joke when Jeff's fiancée and her friend (Thelma Ritter) poke around in the courtyard garden with a shovel because Jeff is convinced they will find Mrs. Thorwald's head.

Hitchcock followed *Rear Window* with films that explore a wide range of tones and approaches. *To Catch a Thief* (1955) is a glossy romantic thriller, while *The Trouble with Harry* (1955) is a dark comedy set in rural Vermont. (Harry's trouble is that he is dead). Hitchcock successfully remade an early British gem with a 1956 Hollywood version of *The Man Who Knew Too Much*, and followed it with *The Wrong Man* (1957), a documentary-like interpretation of his "innocent man wrongly accused" motif. The director returned to psychosexual horror in 1958 with *Vertigo*, his most convoluted film and one that continues to divide critics and fans. Though picturesque and attractively cast, the film deals with a sexual obsession that skirts necrophilia.

San Francisco police detective Scottie Ferguson (James Stewart) resigns from the force after his acrophobia (fear of heights) causes the accidental death of a uniformed officer. Restless in retirement, Scottie agrees to help a friend (Tom Helmore) who has asked him to keep an eye on his suicidal wife Madeleine (Kim Novak). In her smartly tailored gray suits, the blonde

Kim Novak as Judy/Madeleine, the most intriguing and dangerous of Hitchcock's ice princesses: *Vertigo* (1958).

Madeleine is the epitome of elegance and quiet sexuality. She tries to kill herself by leaping into San Francisco Bay, but is rescued by Scottie, who gradually falls in love with her. Madeleine is convinced that she is possessed by the spirit of a long-dead Spanish noblewoman. During a visit to San Juan, Madeleine climbs the Mission bell tower but Scottie — fearful of the height — cannot bring himself to follow. Madeleine leaps to her death.

Consumed by remorse and guilt, Scottie returns to San Francisco, where he meets Judy (Novak), a carnal redhead who, facially at least, is the image of Madeleine. At this point, the audience (but not Scottie) learns that Judy and Madeleine are the same woman, and that Scottie has been the dupe in a vicious murder plot. He has never seen the real Madeleine, who was shoved from the bell tower by her husband. Judy is the killer's mistress. Scottie is the closest thing to an eyewitness to the "suicide."

Scottie is (understandably) fascinated with Judy, and attempts to turn her into the image of Madeleine. With surprising fatalism, Judy allows herself to be made over: hair, makeup, jewelry, and clothing are altered under Scottie's feverish supervision. When the transformation is complete, a locket tips

Scottie to the truth of Judy's identity. He says nothing, but takes Judy/Madeleine to the Mission bell tower in hopes of forcing a confession. He conquers his acrophobia and forces the woman to the top, where she is startled by a nun and accidentally falls to her death.

Hitchcock's love of MacGuffins may have got the best of him when he made *Vertigo*. As is apparent from even a brief synopsis, the film is hopelessly contrived. How could the murderer be sure that Scottie's acrophobia would prevent him from climbing the tower? How is it that Scottie never sees a newspaper photograph of the dead Madeleine? Judy is the killer's mistress, but why does she gravitate so easily to Scottie? Judging from our hero's unquestioning acceptance of all this, he must not have been much of a detective even at his best. Hitchcock's view of plot as merely a device which would allow him to tell a story in visual terms was never better illustrated. Still, if *Vertigo* falters when judged traditionally, it becomes one of Hitchcock's most provocative efforts when regarded from a psychosexual point of view. The *vertigo* of the title refers not only to Scottie's acrophobia, but to his emotional state, as well. The trauma of the accident that convinced him to leave the police force continues to torment him. The lower range of his emotional scale has been wiped out. His plainly attractive friend Midge (Barbara Bel Geddes) cares deeply for him and would like a relationship, but Scottie can no longer be moved by someone as unassuming. There is no mystery about Midge. Her sexuality is unembellished and unpretentious; she makes her living doing passionless illustrations of brassieres for department store advertisements.

Madeleine, with her smoky clothes and detached manner, is the classic Hitchcock ice princess. Kim Novak—an actress noted for portrayals of more vigorous types—at first rebelled against Hitchcock's efforts to mold her into his own notion of sexual attractiveness. Finally, like Grace Kelly before her and Tippi Hedren after, Novak acquiesced. The role did not require a particularly broad emotional range, but Novak's performance is remarkable within its narrow limits. The transition to Judy marks the character as the most startling of Hitchcock's dual personality protagonists. The understated Madeleine is quite the converse of the bluntly attractive, almost coarse Judy. Inexpensively dressed and heavily made up, Judy is a dream princess for the common man.

Scottie, of course, is not interested in Judy. To his eyes, she is not a real person but a frame—a dressmaker's dummy he will transform into Madeleine. The obvious irony is that it is *Madeleine* who was never real. The chic clothes and elegant hairdo were affected by Judy, who would now like to be appreciated for herself. She resists Scottie's initial attempts to make her over, asking, "Couldn't you like me—just me—the way I am? ... I'll wear the darn clothes if you want me to if you'll just, just like *me*."

Later, Judy agrees to bleach her hair. She has surrendered. "If I let you change me," she says warily, "if I do what you tell me, will you love me?" Scottie promises. As Hitchcock molded Novak, as some men try to transfigure their lovers and wives, so Scottie transforms Judy. There can be little doubt that Hitchcock identified strongly with Scottie. The director spoke many times of the reverse-strip tease aspect of the scene in which Scottie waits with tortured anticipation as Judy puts the finishing touches on her metamorphosis. Scottie's sexual excitement is triggered by his woman putting clothes *on*, not taking them off. The moment of Madeleine/Judy's entrance is the big payoff for Scottie's necrophiliac fetishism. The hair, the clothes, the makeup all combine to help Scottie cheat fate: Madeleine has returned from the dead.

The woman is bathed in an eerie green light from a neon sign outside the window. The color reinforces the unnaturalness of the relationship. As Scottie and Madeleine/Judy embrace and kiss, the camera moves 360 degrees around them. The room is suddenly replaced by a process shot which places the couple once more at the Mission. The past has become the present. The dead are alive.

Although Judy's desperation for love has caused her to humiliate herself and become a pathetic figure, her complicity in a murder makes her subject to the harsh moral judgment which kills her at the conclusion of the film. Scottie is freed from his curse, but the tantalizing ambiguity of his relationship(s) with Madeleine/Judy remains. Did Madeleine really love him? Did Judy? Could Scottie ever have loved Judy for herself? Would he have wanted to?

Audiences responded positively to *Vertigo*, though not in the numbers that Hitchcock and the releasing studio, Paramount, had hoped. The denseness and improbability of the script may have been too difficult for some moviegoers to grapple with. The film's reputation has grown over the years; some critics — this writer included — place it in Hitchcock's top rank. Though *Vertigo* is somewhat atypical of the director's output in that it lacks flashy visual set pieces, its psychological point of view is pure Hitchcock. Once again, innocent people are victimized because other people and events are not what they seem. Duality of personality brings sexual and emotional misery. *Vertigo* is not simply a gripping psychosexual horror story, but a profoundly moving study of a hopeless love.

As the 1960s approached, Hitchcock continued to refine and redefine his art. The comic strip kineticism of *North by Northwest* (1959) formally ushered in the requisite moviemaking style of the new decade.* The film's legacy continues to be reflected in works by directors as diverse as Brian DePalma, Walter Hill, Richard Lester, Peter Hyams, and Steven Spielberg. The influence of Hitchcock's next film, *Psycho*, has been discussed; its significance is apparent to anyone who has set foot in a movie theater since 1960.

French film director François Truffaut, for instance, astutely commented that the hugely popular James Bond films owe an enormous stylistic debt to North by Northwest.

The Cold War paranoia and concomitant fear of apocalypse that gripped the public in the early sixties spurred filmmakers to create grim horror stories about the end of the world. *Panic in Year Zero* (1962), *Fail Safe* (1964), *Dr. Strangelove: Or How I Learned to Stop Worrying and Love the Bomb* (1964), and *The War Game* (1966) are some of the more vivid examples.

Hitchcock's *The Birds* (1963) is probably the ultimate expression of this sort of nameless dread. It is a film that cheerfully defies description: it is horror, it is science fiction, it is black comedy, it is a scathing look at our mores and manners. It is a highly sexual film, but in a perversely negativistic way. Evan Hunter's scenario (adapted from a story by Daphne Du Maurier) is almost diagrammatically simple. Melanie Daniels (Tippi Hedren), a beautiful young San Francisco socialite, becomes attracted to Mitch Brenner (Rod Taylor), a successful lawyer who maintains a coastal home at Bodega Bay. Melanie coyly intrudes herself into Mitch's life, and eventually follows him to Bodega Bay, intending to surprise him with a gift of lovebirds. Her arrival in the town signals the beginning of an inexplicable terror. As she rows across the bay to Mitch's house, a gull swoops from nowhere and gashes her head. Soon the attacks intensify. A group of schoolchildren is savaged and a farmer is killed. The town is quickly in a bedlam, complete with explosions, burning buildings, and runaway horses. Melanie takes refuge with Mitch and his mother (Jessica Tandy) and sister (Veronica Cartwright). The birds batter the house to pieces and very nearly kill Melanie when they trap her in an upstairs bedroom. Then, inexplicably, the attacks stop and Mitch, Melanie, and the others slowly drive away as thousands of gathered birds quietly watch.

Because no explanation for the birds' attacks is given (or even hazarded), audiences and critics were free to indulge themselves in speculation. Literal-minded viewers blamed the birds' behavior on fallout or DDT. Others opted for simple revenge, perhaps in retaliation for the massacre of the passenger pigeon or other human offenses. Some especially imaginative viewers insisted the film was an allegory about the danger of communism. In truth, *The Birds* is Hitchcock's most sustained use of the MacGuffin. The film does not make any literal sense, nor should it have to. It is not really concerned with birds at all, but with stupid and complacent human beings. Hitchcock was never more sardonic.

Of all of Hitchcock's heroines, Melanie is the most unprepossessing. The least of her sins is overdressing (she even wears heels and a full-length mink coat while rowing across the bay). She is immaculate to the point of prissiness. Beyond this, Melanie is manipulative and a glib liar. Her notion of courtship involves silly feints and thinly veiled double entendres. When Mitch shows up at a pet store to purchase a pair of lovebirds, Melanie pretends to be a clerk. She's so facile and self-consciously chic that she becomes infuriating, not to Mitch but to us. Her pursuit of Mitch (and incidental attention to hair, wardrobe, and makeup) takes up nearly the first half of the film; some critics felt that the shallowness of Melanie (and stolid dullness of Mitch) did not warrant

such prolonged examination. If *The Birds* had been a thriller and nothing more, the critics would have been absolutely correct. But patient viewers are rewarded, not only by riveting action scenes and impressive set pieces, but by a satisfying shattering of the petty sort of existence that Melanie typifies. *The Birds* lets us know that if Armageddon comes at all, it will come because of our own foolishness. In Hitchcock's view, the birds revolt because humans have lost touch with reality.

Melanie's arrival in Bodega Bay sets off a chain reaction of petty jealousies. Mitch's mother is inordinately possessive of her son—there is a faintly Oedipal tone to the relationship. Mrs. Brenner resents Melanie's intrusion because she has no defense against a younger, prettier woman. The local schoolteacher, Annie Hayworth (Suzanne Pleshette) had been Mitch's paramour in the recent past, so Melanie's arrival does not sit well with her, either. The cattiness that exists between the three women is barely concealed. Their civility is strained and hideously artificial. In the town, an androgynous old ornithologist (Ethel Griffies) flatly tells Melanie that her assertions of bird attacks *cannot* be true. Another woman is convinced that Melanie is an agent of the Devil, and that the birds are her familiars. Mitch—caught in the middle—rides with the turmoil because he doesn't know what else to do.

The sheer mindlessness of all this narcissism, self-pity, and sexual gamesmanship is exposed by the elemental power of the birds. The attacks are unexplained but very real. The birds do not obfuscate. Their intentions are mindless but clear: the humans are being punished. After a gull pecks a service station attendant and causes a spill of gasoline, a hapless motorist drops a lighted match, destroying himself and the entire station. The flames spread and the air fills with birds. Cars run out of control, besieged firemen drop their hoses, and Melanie is trapped inside a phone booth (a neat reference to earlier scenes of birds in cages). At the peak of the carnage, Hitchcock cut from street level to an amazing high altitude view of the town, its business district engulfed by an L-shaped wedge of fire. (The point of view was accomplished with the considerable help of matte artist extraordinaire Albert Whitlock.) The soundtrack is silent. Momentarily, a single gull wheels into the frame. Shortly, the frame is thick with descending, cawing birds. This detached and dispassionate view of the turmoil is the only one we share with the perpetrators. The vantage point underscores the insignificance of the games we persist in playing.

The fury of the birds' attacks reminds me of the title of a record album by Firesign Theatre: "Everything You Know is Wrong." Our contrived notions about life and living fall to pieces. Melanie is pecked into catatonia, Mitch cannot offer any solutions, and his mother's neurotic cocoon is destroyed. The petty jealousies of the schoolteacher are ended with her messy death, and the

The end of artifice and pretense: Rod Taylor, Tippi Hedren, and Jessica Tandy emerge from the house that has been besieged by *The Birds* (1963).

smug ornithologist is proven dead wrong. Nature herself is striking at us for being so donkey stupid about everything, for being so damnably smug. The only certainty left is that the survivors will never be the same. They have learned the folly of pretense and artifice the hard way. The ice goddess Melanie, for instance, does not thaw until she has been terrorized, humiliated, and shown the face of horror. When Mitch rescues her from a room full of birds, she has no glib retort, only an hysterical, frantic clawing at his arms and face. Melanie is vulnerable—and human—at last. She will no longer consider herself exempt from life's ruder lessons.

The Birds is not Hitchcock's best film, but it may be his most challenging. It requires that the viewer approach it with patience and a degree of insight. Perplexing and maddening, it succeeds admirably as thriller and ironic social comedy. It is one of the most sensible film statements about human sexual affairs yet seen.

Hitchcock followed *The Birds* with unnecessarily convoluted thrillers that diminished his reputation and encouraged some observers to claim that Hitch—then in his mid sixties—was losing his touch. *Marnie* (1964) concerns the efforts of a businessman to cure his wife's kleptomania. Despite allusions to prostitution, murder, and sexual violence, the film cannot quite find high gear. Tippi Hedren seems a bit lost as the troubled heroine, and the production values are compromised by numerous instances of clumsy and unconvincing rear projection. *Torn Curtain* (1966) involves Cold War intrigue and an American scientist who pretends to defect to East Germany. Paul Newman was inappropriately cast as the scientist while Julie Andrews—eager at the time to escape her Mary Poppins image—is wasted as the scientist's worried fiancée. The film is notable only for a brilliant (and hideously protracted) sequence in which the scientist and an East German woman use such prosaic instruments as a carving knife, a shovel, and a kitchen oven to kill a communist agent. *Topaz* followed in 1969; it is an uninteresting, routine espionage thriller about Russia's involvement in Cuba. At this juncture, even Hitchcock's most ardent supporters were worried. The master seemed to have lost his special spark.

Then, in 1972, came *Frenzy*, which, though not Hitchcock's final film, is a fitting cap to his brilliant career. The film recalls earlier Hitchcock triumphs (notably *The Lodger, The Wrong Man,* and *Strangers on a Train*) but does not rework or imitate. Rather, it is a distillation of the director's accumulated art and craft. Its plot, not surprisingly, revolves around an innocent man named Richard Blaney (Jon Finch) who has been wrongly accused of being the necktie murderer who is terrorizing London. Bitter and mad at the world, Blaney escapes from prison to prove that the killer is his (former) friend Bob Rusk (Barry Foster). *Frenzy* is Hitchcock's most brutal and unpleasant work; its violence and surprising bits of nudity earned it an "R" rating from the Motion Picture Association. The film is elevated above its subject matter by Hitchcock's inimitable visual style and flair for black humor. The script by Anthony Shaffer (from the novel *Goodbye Piccadilly, Farewell Leicester Square* by Arthur Labern) is superior. Significantly, perhaps, *Frenzy* was the first film Hitchcock had produced in his native England since *Stage Fright* in 1950.

Central to the success of *Frenzy* is the Bob Rusk character, a terrifying villain nearly as memorable as Robert Walker's Bruno in *Strangers on a Train*. Barry Foster imbued Rusk with a splendid fire — his flushed face and red hair are a mask of uncontrolled emotion. Like Bruno and Joseph Cotten's Uncle Charlie, Rusk can be an appealing charmer when it suits his purposes. On the one hand, he blows kisses to his ruddy-cheeked Mum, while on the other he rapes and kills with resolute fury. The sequence in which he murders Blaney's ex-wife (Barbara Leigh-Hunt) is chilling and horrific. The lady runs a matrimonial agency, and Rusk has tried to become one of her clients. She has been put off by his odd sexual preferences, and politely informs him that he does not fit her client profile.

Rusk is genuinely hurt. Much like the murderous Lars Thorwald of *Rear Window*, he becomes the injured party. "I have my good points," he quietly informs Mrs. Blaney. "I like flowers, fruit. People like me. I've got things to *give*." With this he tears the woman's blouse and rapes her as she sits spraddle-legged at her desk. Leigh-Hunt, soft and pink-skinned, is the picture of abject vulnerability. She begins to pray aloud, but gets off a terrified scream when Rusk undoes his tie: she knows that her rapist is about to become her killer. The strangulation is merciless, agonizingly slow, and difficult to watch. With hardly a glance at his victim's body (complete with grotesquely protruding tongue), Rusk insouciantly munches an apple before departing. Killing is of no real import to him. The act is as meaningless — and as easy — as eating.

Another victim is Babs (Anna Massey), an unassuming barmaid who is a friend of Blaney's. She accepts Rusk's offer of aid when she needs a place to stay for a few nights. As Rusk ushers Babs into his flat he tells her, "I don't know if you know it, Babs, but you're my type of woman." Because we have seen one grisly murder in detail, there is no call to see another. Hitchcock allowed us to use our imaginations as to the particulars of Babs' fate. The apartment door closes and the soundtrack goes silent as the camera begins a slow descent down the stairs, out the building's front door, across the sidewalk, and onto the busy street. Then we hear the sounds of everyday life and commerce as the camera tilts upward to frame the windows of Rusk's apartment. We look at the scene and realize that although Hitchcock has allowed us knowledge of the horror that is taking place behind those dull windows, we can do nothing to prevent it. We are all-knowing but impotent.

Rusk unceremoniously wraps Babs' body in a sack and dumps it in the back of a potato truck, but later realizes that his monogrammed tie pin is missing. He returns to the (now moving) truck, where he discovers the pin clasped in Babs' fingers. The problem is that the corpse is now in rigor mortis, so Rusk — in a moment guaranteed to make even the hardiest viewer flinch —

must break his victim's fingers in order to free the pin. Grim stuff, but neatly offset by later scenes involving a police inspector (Alec McCowen) who explains to his slightly dizzy wife over dinner the manner in which Bab's fingers were broken. The wife (Vivien Merchant) blithely snaps breadsticks as she listens, unaware of the discomfort she is causing her husband.

Nearly all of *Frenzy*'s humor is grim. The film opens with a blowhard politician who addresses a group on the banks of the Thames, assuring them that the river will henceforth suffer no more pollution. At that moment, the nude corpse of the necktie murderer's latest victim washes ashore. A recurring joke involves the bizarre gourmet cookery of the inspector's wife. One evening the inspector is greeted by a wall-eyed fish head that stares up at him from his soup bowl. This sort of gastronomic horror is the price the inspector must pay for his wife's (credible) intuition that Blaney is innocent. When Blaney finally tracks Rusk down, he batters the figure he finds in Rusk's bed, only to realize that he is attacking the corpse of the newest victim. The inspector enters, shushes Blaney, and waits for Rusk to return. The villain is speechless before his visitors, and the inspector says, "Why, Mr. Rusk, you're not wearing your tie." Rusk has been undone by his deshabille.

Frenzy was a box office hit. More importantly, it brought critics rallying once more to Hitchcock's cause. He had demonstrated that he could still wield the familiar magic. His final film, *Family Plot*, was released in 1976. Hitchcock began development of another, but his health began to fade. On April 29, 1980, he died at his home in Bel Air, California. He was 80. Cinema had lost not only a superb technician and significant artist, but a great original. Although critics and worshipful acolytes may have nothing new to say about Hitchcock, what has already been said bears repeating. Hitchcock was unique. His gifts will be imitated but never duplicated. Film styles will change and go in and out of vogue, but Hitchcock's movies will never be superseded. It is even possible that they will never be surpassed. In a 1973 interview with the fine critic Richard Schickel, Hitchcock said that each time he stepped on a movie set he became "the equivalent of a conductor conducting an orchestra without a score." The comment refers to Hitchcock's method of working out a film entirely in his mind long before the first day of shooting. To him, the actual filming was anticlimactic. Only in his mind — where he gave shape, sound, movement, and rhythm to the disturbing psychology which informs his work — did the films truly come to life. To view a Hitchcock film, then, is to know Hitchcock. Further, the viewer becomes a true collaborator. Although Hitchcock's vision intrudes upon our own and helps shape our emotional response, the final response is unique to each of us. Only the dark underside of our individual minds can give the films their final shape. This, of course, is the essence of the moviegoing experience in general, but no other director has had Hitchcock's grasp of how to exploit it. When the lights go down and a Hitchcock film begins, he is next to us in the dark, watching *us* instead of the screen, and smiling his inscrutable Englishman's smile.

IX

The Ironic Universe
of Roger Corman

Since the early seventies, few American filmmakers have received as much press coverage as Roger Corman. Journalists have used reams of paper to describe Corman's rise from director of low-budget B-films in the fifties (he was born in 1926) to producer and distributor of domestic works by fresh young talents and foreign films by established masters. The list of talent Corman has discovered and nurtured reads like a Who's Who: Francis Ford Coppola, Peter Bogdanovich, Robert Towne, Jack Nicholson, Joe Dante, Ellen Burstyn, Martin Scorsese, James Cameron, Jonathan Demme. Some journalists who write about Corman praise the series of stylish Edgar Allan Poe adaptations he directed in the first half of the sixties, while other writers gush over Corman's canny business sense, and the fact that nearly all of the New World Pictures released since Corman founded the company in 1970 have made big money on small investments. By 1983, Corman had become a wealthy and respected man.

For all the hubbub, though, Corman has remained a fairly private man. He granted more interviews in the seventies than he had in previous years, but of course more people were interested in him. He noddingly agrees that he has helped many talented youngsters, but somehow neglects to mention that the youngsters were paid peanuts while he made millions. Still, New World was Hollywood's only "hands-on" film school, a place where would-be writers and directors could earn as they learned, and get that all-important first credit. Corman has not directed since 1971, but interest in his work grows.

Surprisingly, Corman remains circumspect when discussing his motivations as a filmmaker. Clearly, the profit incentive has been a driving force, but that does not explain a good film like *The Intruder* (1960), a pointed statement against racism that is one of his few commercial failures. Negative criticism of his early films seems not to have bothered Corman. Conversely, he is flattered but otherwise little moved by the sometimes excessive acclaim for his later works. Despite the flashes of wit and talent Corman has displayed over the years, the fact remains that his empire was built on amusing trivia like *Attack of the Crab Monsters*, *Rock All Night*, and *Big Bad Mama*. For this reason, most serious writing on Corman's career has been ambivalent. His place in film history has yet to be determined.

Because Corman devoted the first part of his career to providing product for small production companies like American International Pictures and Allied Artists, his early films are inexpensive and highly commercial; his first, *Monster from the Ocean Floor* (directed by Wyott Ordung), was produced in 1954 for an astonishing $12,000. The pictures that followed were aimed at the young, relatively undiscriminating core audience of the fifties and early sixties. No one would have cared if the films had been mindless. To Corman's credit, the films are *not* mindless. On the contrary, most of them have unexpected sparkle and wit.

Corman realized early on the value of talented collaborators: he cultivated a stock company of skilled actors in the fifties, and later worked with major talents like cinematographer (now director) Nicolas Roeg and actor Vincent Price. Inventive writers like Charles B. Griffith and Richard Matheson fashioned screenplays that allowed Corman to have fun with the conventions of the genres he worked in. He has been particularly attracted to screenplays that examine the sociology of sex, and situations of sexual role reversal. Corman films like *Gunslinger* (1956), *Teenage Doll* (1957), *Swamp Women* (1957), and *Bloody Mama* (1969), for instance, focus on gun-toting, physically fearless women who dominate and terrorize men. Corman's propensity for strong female characters is especially obvious in his horror films, part of a genre that characteristically subjugates women or turns them into powerless snivelers. Only rarely, as in *The Day the World Ended* (1956; see Chapter III) are Corman women seen in the traditional genre role.

Perhaps the most amusing of the director's reversals is *The Viking Women and the Sea Serpent* (1957), which was also released as *The Saga of the Viking Women and Their Voyage to the Waters of the Great Sea Serpent*. Abby Dalton played Desir (nice Norse name, ya?), a leggy Viking of the 9th century who leads a group of women in search of their menfolk, who have been captured by men of an enemy clan. Louis Goldman's script is really nothing special — the film's selling point is its unwavering focus upon the gutsy women and their battles with male warriors and a (not-so-fearsome) sea serpent. Despite the fact that the ladies have to put up with plenty of male groping, they maintain an independence of spirit that was almost unheard of in genre films of the period. Still, Corman was not a miracle worker at this stage of his career. *Viking Women* is one of the few times the director was hamstrung by obvious budget limitations. The story demands more expansive treatment than what Corman was able to muster.

Corman usually managed to disguise his budgetary restrictions, as in *The Undead* (1957), which was largely shot inside a refurbished supermarket for $70,000. Charles B. Griffith and Mark Hanna used the then-current Bridey Murphy craze as a springboard for their script, which involves an unhappy prostitute (Pamela Duncan) who takes her troubles to a psychiatrist (Richard Garland). When hypnotized, the woman regresses to a past life in medieval times. She learns that she is the reincarnation of a woman wrongly burned for witchcraft. The psychiatrist realizes that his patient's ancestor must die so that the present will not be altered. He journeys through time himself to see that the wrongful execution is carried out, only to become trapped in the past. In the present, his patient begins to view herself in a more positive light.

Corman deserves credit for attempting to deal reasonably with the anamoly of time travel, a tricky premise which Hollywood usually explores with astonishing stupidity. Pamela Duncan — a dark, not particularly pretty actress with languid eyes and a very heavy mouth — is well cast as the prostitute, but *The Undead* is dominated by actress Allison Hayes, cast as a *real* witch. Hayes, a mainstay of American B-films of the late fifties, had a regal, icy beauty that served her well in a variety of menacing roles, most notably the lead in *Attack of the 50-Foot Woman* (1958; see Chapter III). She became inactive in the late sixties, and died prematurely in 1977. The demonic evil she brought to the role of the witch in *The Undead* provides a nice counterpoint to the "evil" of the prostitute. The witch is a merciless manipulator, a temptress who destroys her enemies with deceit and guile. Her consort is Satan (Richard Devon) himself. The prostitute, on the other hand, is not made a point of derision or negative judgment. She is the film's heroine.

Though a similar character would be favorably viewed in *Elmer Gantry* in 1960, *The Undead* merits special attention for doing so three years earlier. Before Corman's arrival on the B-movie scene, low-budget horror films confined themselves to narrowly defined limits. Characters who engaged in occupations as unorthodox as prostitution were seldom the stories' focal points, and almost invariably were punished. In the case of *The Undead*, the prostitute's "rehabilitation" — a point that is not stressed excessively — is the only nod to Hollywood tradition.

Corman's most successful heroine has been Beverly Garland, an attractive and respected actress of considerable range and force. Blonde and distinctly urban, Garland is among the more interesting leading ladies to rise from B-movies in the fifties. Her sex appeal is always apparent, but she has characteristically been the sort of heroine who can get along splendidly without the help of men. In *It Conquered the World* (1956) she played the wife of a man who has been duped into paving the way for a Venusian invasion of Earth. The husband (Lee Van Cleef) is brilliant but gullible, and only his wife sees through the early stages of the takeover bid.

Lou Rusoff's scenario (a number of credible sources credit Charles Griffith with the script) takes key elements from *Invasion of the Body Snatchers* (1956), in that residents of the dupe's small town are taken over one by one, and turned into emotionless slaves. The monster (which Paul Blaisdell designed to resemble an overgrown cucumber with beady eyes and fangs) stays hidden within a cave during most of the story, dispatching what look like flying stingrays to do its dirty work. Van Cleef allows the wife of his best friend (Peter Graves) to be turned into a zombie, and hardly seems concerned that his own wife may be next. Finally, Garland grabs a rifle and confronts the invader in the misty cave, shrieking, "You're ugly!" But bullets have no effect. Van Cleef hears his wife's death screams over his radio set, and is moved to destroy his manipulator with a blowtorch, dying in the process. *It Conquered the World* is refreshing because its female lead has more awareness of what is going on than the nominal hero (Graves). In fact, Graves is not involved in the climax at all.

Beverly Garland returned in *Not of This Earth* (1957), one of the finest of Corman's early films. Thick-set actor Paul Birch was incongruously effective as a vampire from the dying planet Davanna, sent to Earth on a scouting mission. Objective: food. Dressed in a dark business suit and sunglasses, the vampire makes his rounds in a chauffer-driven Cadillac, burning out the brains of his victims with his totally white eyes. In the course of the 67-minute film the vampire (who calls himself Mr. Johnson) kills the wise guy chauffeur (Jonathan Haze), sucks the blood from a pushy vacuum cleaner salesman (Dick Miller), and unsuccessfully attempts to teleport a neighbor to Davanna. He also rendezvouses with a sultry female vampire (Ann Carroll) who later destroys herself after unknowingly stealing rabid dog blood from a lab.

Johnson, weakened by the disease that is killing his people on Davanna, engages a nurse, Nadine (Beverly Garland), to look after him in his rented mansion. All goes well (if a bit uneasily) until Nadine discovers a refrigerator full of blood, and a human skull in Johnson's incinerator. When the vampire realizes he has been found out, he hypnotizes Nadine and attempts to teleport her to his planet. When his concentration is momentarily broken, Nadine escapes. She flees on foot through a park, where the pursuing vampire crashes his Cadillac after his sensitive ears are assaulted by the wail of a police siren.

Nadine is splendidly gutsy. At one point she is roughly grabbed by Johnson, who removes his glasses and commands her to look at his eyes. Nadine is having none of *that*. She gives a lusty screech and struggles free, dashing out of the house as the vampire tries to recover his hearing. The nurse is the only character who realizes almost from the start that there is something terribly wrong about her employer. Her boyfriend (Morgan Jones) believes Johnson to be simply a rich eccentric, and a doctor (William Roerick) has been hypnotized by the vampire so that he has no opinion at all. Nadine's only ally is Johnson's chauffeur, and when he is killed, the woman is utterly alone.

Corman and writers Mark Hanna and Charles Griffith knew what pleased their youthful audience in a sexual sense, so *Not of This Earth* includes scenes of Nadine in her boudoir and at the swimming pool. But even in this context we get the message that Nadine is not to be trifled with. When the smarmy chauffeur sticks his head around Nadine's dressing screen, he gets a sharp crack on the face for his trouble. He exits laughing, but thereafter his manner is respectful. The woman has proven her competence. A number of men and an insipid teenage girl are all easy prey for the vampire, but Nadine — cool, intelligent, resourceful — is his undoing.

Nadine (Beverly Garland) struggles with Mr. Johnson (Paul Birch), the vampire who is *Not of This Earth* (1957).

Corman's interest in role reversal is explored to its most outlandish in *Wasp Woman* (1959), a clever horror melodrama that was shot in less than a week for $50,000. Janice Starlin (Susan Cabot, another Corman regular) is an aging cosmetics queen who injects herself with a preparation of wasp enzymes in order to recapture her youth and save her business. The treatments work—for a while. Her board members goggle when she walks into the conference room after the first treatment. "How old do I look?" she chirps. A dazed secretary offers, "Twenty-two? Twenty-three?" Starlin's craving for the enzymes eventually gets out of control and turns her into a rampaging she-monster, complete with waspy head and fuzzy claws. By shooting mainly in interiors and predominantly in the skyscraper where Starlin has her offices, Corman played upon the common fear of "something" lurking around the corner or behind the door. When an urbane board member (William Roerick) snoops where he should not, we hear his shrieks as the monster descends upon him. Later, his pipe is discovered by a secretary (Barboura Morris) who wonders why he left it. When she, too, is snatched by the monster, we hear the infernal insect buzz and then see, as does hero Fred (Anthony) Eisley, the

Renewed youth has a price tag: Zinthrop (Michael Mark) injects Janice Starlin (Susan Cabot) with the rejuvenating formula that will turn her into the *Wasp Woman* (1959).

ankles and feet of the unconscious secretary as her body is whisked around a corner. The final sequence, in which Starlin plunges from a window to her death after Eisley has thrown acid in her face, is genuinely shocking.

The film, the first to be released by Corman's own Filmgroup (formed with his brother Gene), is marred by a number of things, most of which stem from the obvious budget restrictions. Many of the sets appear to be no more substantial than cardboard, and all the exteriors were shot without sound. Most amusingly, the insects that busily crawl across the screen during the opening and end titles are not wasps, but bees! Apparently, the Hollywood wasp union demanded more money than Corman was willing to pay.

An especially intriguing aspect of Leo Gordon's script is that more of the wasp woman's victims are male than female. Generally speaking, the male sex does not come off looking too good. The executive who is killed is a pompous pseudo-intellectual who thinks he has all the answers to Janice Starlin's strange behavior, but who is totally unprepared for the monster that Starlin has become. Another victim is a fat, slobby night watchman (Bruno VeSota) who shuffles around the dim corridors noshing on a sandwich. It is no surprise when the wasp woman disposes of him with no trouble at all.

Finally, there is Dr. Zinthrop (Michael Mark), the aged genius who has invented the enzyme formula. Zinthrop seems to be on the ball when his formula does what it is supposed to, but deteriorates into mumbling incoherence after getting a hint of the formula's hideous side effects. He becomes so numb with shock, in fact, that he stumbles from Starlin's building straight into the path of a car. The resultant head injury addles him even more, but Starlin—frantic to learn what is happening to her—installs him with a private nurse in the Starlin offices. Zinthrop is badgered for information, but cannot get his thoughts in order. "Please, my *head*!" he moans. "My head!" When Starlin metamorphoses into the monster in Zinthrop's presence and attacks him, the narrative becomes a peculiar variation on the Frankenstein story; this time, the monster is not a reflection of its creator, but of its creator's deadly opposite.

Corman developed the film's aging theme with insight, and not simply as a plot device. Janice Starlin has built her life and career on her looks. Her beauty *defines* her. When it fades, she begins to cease to be Janice Starlin. Susan Cabot's performance is low-key and sensitive; Starlin's willingness to use the enzyme formula seems logical. To Starlin, the risk is less fearsome than the alternative: loss of identity. *Wasp Woman* is an exploitative film, to be sure, but one that explores menopausal angst with spirit and cleverness. That Starlin is finally destroyed by a man is appropriately ironic; the acid he has thrown eats at her face, the face that she had depended upon for her existence.

Janice Starlin is part of the continuing film tradition of sympathetic monsters. Corman, in particular, seems to have realized that evil is seldom black-and-white, but gray. Even Corman films that feature the familiar "woman in peril" theme have oddball twists that set them apart from pictures that are superficially similar.

Attack of the Crab Monsters (1957), for instance, has the intriguing premise that once a giant crab kills a human, it assumes the voice and memory of that person. So it is that many an unwitting scientist on an isolated island is lured to his death by the spectral voice of a lost comrade. Heroine Pamela Duncan is awakened one night in her shadowy bedroom by the voice of a missing friend: "I'm in the cave," it instructs. "Come to me." The lady looks tasty in her nightie, and one is reminded of the joke about the crabs that wear bibs with little human beings printed on them. *Attack of the Crab Monsters* is amusing but not among Corman's better early efforts. It drags horribly in places, and seems notable mainly for its unpleasant brutality. Gleeful, unappealing closeups show people being dismembered and decapitated by the crabs' huge pincers. The heroine, by the way, is *not* dipped in lemon juice and eaten, but escapes when the last crab is electrocuted.

The Last Woman on Earth (1960) is also traditional, as skindiver Betsy Jones-Moreland and two male companions are the only survivors of an atomic war. Naturally, the lady's value rises immediately, and the two men are (literally) at each other's throats. Corman's affinity for this sort of giddy trash, and his flair for comic undertone, did not prepare critics for his series of Edgar Allan Poe adaptations, which began in 1960. These films are very nearly the antithesis of his earlier work. The director's breezy approach was subjugated to a studied (and occasionally ponderous) style that emphasized setting and mood instead of fast action, much in the manner of the Hammer horror films which had begun playing in the United States in the late fifties.

The domestic market was changing, and Corman spearheaded the change with *House of Usher* (1960), a period thriller that solidly reintroduced American audiences to Gothic horror. Vincent Price was Roderick Usher, a reclusive man who insists that his sister Madeline (Myrna Fahey) must not marry Philip (Mark Damon) because of the insanity that gallops in the Usher family. Roderick is determined that the madness will die with his generation. When Madeline dies unexpectedly, Roderick has her entombed, but later reveals to Philip that Madeline suffered from catalepsy, and may not be dead at all. Indeed, Madeline still has plenty of energy, and manages to escape her tomb. Fully possessed by the Usher insanity and thirsting for vengeance, Madeline nearly strangles her fiancé and then attacks Roderick. As brother and sister struggle, the house groans and collapses around them.

House of Usher was a radical departure for American International, a studio that had made its fortune with a dizzying parade of bug-eyed Martians and be-bopping teenagers. Corman promised AIP head Sam Arkoff that the film *would* have the requisite monster: the house itself. Arkoff went along with this touch of the metaphysical, and gave Corman the unprecedented luxury of a 15-day shooting schedule and a budget of $200,000, which allowed for color. The result is not brilliant, but certainly entertaining, and even provocative. The perverse relationship between the domineering brother and the insane sister is peculiar, and more odd than any in an American horror film since the thirties. Poe's notion of a house being able to absorb the essence of the evil that goes on within it was given broad and accessible treatment. Youngsters who resented having to read the author's works in school embraced it in theaters and drive-ins. The period setting of *House of Usher* was, at the time, a welcomed novelty, and the box office appeal of Vincent Price (who became Corman's favorite interpreter) had already been proven.

The film's most significant element may be its exploration of the deadly tension that can exist between dominant and submissive family members; Roderick is Madeline's brother, but Richard Matheson's script establishes that Roderick really functions as the girl's father. In effect, Madeline is suppressed because she wishes to exercise her youthful sexuality. Her climactic resurrection is not simply a moment of bizarre horror, but an affirmation of the power of youth to resist its oppressive guardians. Psychologically, then, Corman's *House of Usher* is little different from any of the AIP teenage horror films or musicals which preceded it.

Vincent Price again played a maniacally single-minded man in *The Pit and the Pendulum* (1961). As in *Usher*, his character's insanity brings his downfall. Nicholas Medina is mourning the sudden death of his wife Elizabeth when he is unexpectedly visited by his brother-in-law Francis (John Kerr). Francis suspects that his sister may have been entombed alive, a fate that befell Nicholas' adulterous mother at the hands of her husband, a notorious inquisitor. The young Nicholas witnessed the entombment. Richard Matheson's script and Corman's direction become purposefully ambiguous as Nicholas begins to hear Elizabeth's disembodied voice throughout the castle, and finds physical evidence of her presence.

Was Elizabeth truly dead when entombed, or is guilt over interring her alive causing Nicholas to hallucinate? By the time Elizabeth (Barbara Steele) makes an appearance in the flesh, it is apparent that Nicholas is the victim of a devious plot. His wife gleefully confesses her love for the family physician (Anthony Carbone) as Nicholas, his mind gone, slumps against a wall in his father's torture chamber. The physician arrives and happily pronounces Nicholas dead of fright. But in the world of Poe according to Corman, things are seldom what they seem: Nicholas suddenly smirks, shoving Elizabeth into an Iron Maiden and flinging the doctor from a staircase. Circumstances are worse for the innocent Francis, whom Nicholas dementedly mistakes for an enemy of his father, the inquisitor. In the film's climactic sequence, Francis is nearly sliced to death by the hanging, swinging pendulum — a particularly male instrument of revenge — before being rescued by Nicholas' sister Catherine (Luana Anders). Nicholas falls to his death, and the room is sealed forever. Unfaithful Elizabeth remains sealed — but still alive — in the Iron Maiden. In all, a deliciously sordid exercise. Seldom has a horror film so thoroughly chronicled the miseries to befall a single family.

Corman's ambivalence of tone elevates *The Pit and the Pendulum* above other examples of the genre. Black-and-white issues and personalities are avoided; the film's emotional palette is largely gray. Nicholas, though a psychotic schizophrenic, is unjustly tormented. The supposedly faithful doctor is a conniving sneak, and Elizabeth — beautiful yet utterly without conscience or heart — is a sexual monster. Many of life's most sanctified roles — husband, father, wife, lover, friend — are corrupted and twisted. This aspect of the narrative was intensified when *The Pit and the Pendulum* was released to television in 1968; judged too short for network telecast, the film was augmented with ten minutes of additonal footage shot by Corman associate Tamara Asseyev. Of the original cast, only Luana Anders was available, so Asseyev made the narrative a flashback by having the sister Catherine relate the story from her new residence: an insane asylum.

Corman's Poe trilogy *Tales of Terror* (1962) is hardly more assuring about the joys of family life. In the "Morella" segment Locke (Vincent Price) bitterly exiles his infant daughter Lenora because his wife Morella (Leona Gage) died during childbirth. When the daughter (Maggie Pierce) returns home as a young woman she finds that she has not been forgiven. Worse, the spirit of her

mother seeks revenge. Morella kills her daughter, assumes the girl's body, and pays a visit to a startled Locke, strangling him. In "The Black Cat" a woman (Joyce Jameson) who has been unfaithful to her husband (Peter Lorre, in a venomously funny performance) is entombed alive behind a brick wall with her lover (Vincent Price). And in "The Case of M. Valdemar" the soul of the dying Valdemar (Vincent Price) is suspended in limbo by an unscrupulous mesmerist (Basil Rathbone), who has designs on Valdemar's young wife (Debra Paget). With a major force of will, Valdemar animates his decaying body and strangles his tormentor. His soul freed, Valdemar dies, allowing his wife to marry a family friend she has discreetly loved for some time.

Corman's Poe films, like their source material, do not hold much hope for the future of the nuclear family. The director continued to chart the course of familial disunity with *The Premature Burial* (1962). Ray Milland took the lead, while Ray Russell and Charles Beaumont (both talented short story writers) assumed scripting duties from Richard Matheson. The film is well mounted but suffers from familiarity since it revolves around premature entombment and a beautiful but scheming wife (Hazel Court), elements which figured prominently in the earlier Poe adaptations.

By this time, audiences were predisposed to judge unfavorably a wife as solicitous and beautiful as Hazel Court, a buxom, red-haired British actress used much more successfully by Corman in *The Masque of the Red Death* (1964), the first film the director shot in England, and the one that represents the high point of his Poe cycle. Charles Beaumont and R. Wright Campbell prepared a literate script that cleverly incorporates one of Poe's more gruesome stories, "Hop-Frog." Vincent Price was medieval prince Prospero, a degenerate devil worshiper who delights in torture and murder. Plague rages across the countryside, annihilating whole towns. Survivors who beg entrance to Prospero's castle are mercilessly slaughtered by bowmen.

The prince abducts an innocent village girl (Jane Asher), dresses her in finery, and plans to initiate her in the ways of Satan. The girl becomes the eyes of the audience, witness to the decadence of Prospero's court. Hazel Court was cast as Juliana, Prospero's mistress and a confirmed Satanist. When Prospero tires of her, he kills her with a falcon. The sequence is a stunner: Juliana enters a large room from the far end, the blade-like pendulum of a clock swinging back and forth across the frame in the extreme foreground. As Juliana apprehensively steps farther into the room she notes an unusual, tense silence. The bird's attack — the film's sole moment of explicit gore — comes in a rush and is abruptly shocking: the camera whirls, the bird screeches, and the woman's beautiful face and bosom are slashed to crimson.

Top: Brother (Vincent Price) and sister (Myrna Fahey) struggle as the *House of Usher* (1960) groans around them. Bottom: Nicholas (Price) prepares to dispose of his unfaithful wife Elizabeth (Barbara Steele) in *The Pit and the Pendulum* (1961).

Hazel Court brands herself with Satan's mark in *The Masque of the Red Death* (1964).

Prospero, then, is motivated by an evil so *un*human that even beautiful women mean nothing to him. He regards Juliana and the captive village girl as abstract possessions. Prospero is a hedonist who has moved beyond pleasure into a perverse realm of pure evil. Oddly, though, the interior of Prospero's castle (designed by Robert Jones and Colin Southcott) reflects a gentler (if eccentric) taste; in a particularly eye-filling sequence, the village girl slowly walks through a series of connected rooms, each decorated in a single, brilliant color (as described by Poe in the original story). Nicolas Roeg's camera tracks with the girl as she opens each successive door. The effect is striking, not only visually but because it indicates that Prospero, unexpectedly, is something of an aesthete. This peculiar ambiguity comes to a head at the film's climax, in which the Red Death invades Prospero's masque. The revelers, in brilliant costume, laugh and dance. Prospero is pleased until he spies someone across the room wearing red, a color he has forbidden because it connotes the plague. The prince moves quickly through the crowd, but the red figure is gone. Prospero turns and catches a glimpse of the stranger drifting among the merrymakers on the other side of the room. The two finally meet, but the intruder's face is obscured by a hood. Prospero at first believes the Red Death to be an emissary of his master, Satan, but realizes differently when the visitor moves among the guests. The red cloak is repeatedly swept across the frame, and each time it is lifted a new group of nobles is infected with the plague. Blood-mottled bodies begin to move in exaggerated balletic splendor, gradually converge on Prospero, and then drop to the floor. Prospero alone is left alive. The cloaked figure leans in close and Prospero sees that the Red Death's face is his own.

After the prince has been dispatched, a Yellow Death and others of varying shades rendezvous in a field of dismal mist with the Red Death, who quietly plays cards with a little girl whom Prospero had earlier spared, a particularly disquieting touch. The Deaths solemnly relate how many people each has taken, mention significant survivors (among them the kidnapped village girl), then slowly move off in single file, their brilliant robes (deliberately reminiscent of Prospero's colored rooms) contrasting with the bluish fog.

The Masque of the Red Death is Corman's most vivid illustration of the ways in which perversity and horror can be thinly disguised as beauty. Poe's brief story lends itself to a variety of psychological interpretations; Corman's rather literal approach is ideally suited to the film medium. The picture's images swing radically from brute poverty and misery to the opulent splendor of Prospero's castle. The Deaths, resplendent in their colors, are at once ominous and alluring. The featured women represent opposite poles. Jane Asher's village girl is wholesome to the point of blandness while the mistress Juliana is willful and duplicitous. Her sexuality (emphasized with a series of stunning décolleté gowns) is attractive but threatening. In this instance, though, her particular power is useless against her lover. Even malevolent sexuality must wither before death, which is precisely what Prospero represents. The final irony is that the film's only normal love relationship is between a pair of young dwarves.

Corman's final Poe film, *The Tomb of Ligeia* (1965), arrived at a time when the director was tiring of the series. His subsequent films—*The Trip*, *The Wild Angels*, *Gas-s-s-s*—went off in wildly divergent directions; *Ligeia* presages the expansion of Corman's interests. The picture was shot at several locations in England, giving it a firmer base in reality than the earlier films. Screenwriter Robert Towne (who later wrote *Chinatown* and wrote and directed *Personal Best*) fashioned an intelligent, deliberate script that dabbles in the darkest aspects of human sexuality.

An unusually restrained Vincent Price played Verden Fell, a wealthy man whose raven-haired wife Ligeia (Elizabeth Shepherd) may have been buried while still alive; as if in judgment, a black cat yowls over the crypt. A few months after the funeral, Verden meets Rowena, a stunning blonde with whom he falls in love and shortly marries. Elizabeth Shepherd played this role in a blonde wig, setting up a neat (if obvious) contrast/conflict between light and darkness, good and evil. Verden's interest in mysticism prompts him to hypnotize his new wife, who begins speaking with Ligeia's voice. Over time, Rowena is possessed by her predecessor's unfriendly spirit (a device used not only in *Tales of Terror*, but in Corman's 1963 *The Haunted Palace*). Rowena suffers nightmares and imagines that Ligeia's face stares back at her from the mirror. Because Shepherd played both roles, the face in the mirror *is* the same as Ligeia's, so the horror becomes rather like an inescapable sick joke.

Rowena discovers a secret passageway one night and finds Verden cradling Ligeia's corpse. We learn that Ligeia hypnotized Verden before dying, convincing him that she would *never* die, and that he must care for her always. Rowena again assumes the first wife's voice (whether at Ligeia's volition or her own, we do not know) and commands Verden to forget about Ligeia, that she is dead. Verden begins to strangle Rowena in his confusion, but is distracted when the howling black cat knocks over a lighted candelabrum. The crypt, Verden, and Ligeia are consumed by flame. Or is it Rowena who perishes? Corman's conclusion is purposely ambiguous.

The essence of the film story is that, by day, Verden cannot remember what he does at night. He is a classic dual personality. His marriage to Rowena fulfills the expectations of proper society, while his continuing physical bond with the corpse of his first wife may be the ultimate in *anti*social behavior. But despite his perverse behavior and black garb, Verden is not an unadulterated villain. His ignorance of the misery he causes Rowena makes him an *unwitting* villain, a man who has been blinded by his peculiar obsession. Rowena is the innocent wife who is victimized by her husband's personality flaws.

The studied ambivalence of Corman's Poe films is the work of a commercial director being true to the essential flavor of his source material. Though the adaptations are hardly textbook Poe, they energetically convey the original author's intent. Poe, whose own love life was fraught with disappointment and tragedy, would probably have appreciated Corman's deadly she-fiends, victimized heroines, and miserable husbands. Inescapably, though, one gets the impression that the Poe films are not personal statements, but simply clever divertissements offered by a clever director. The fact that Corman has not returned to the source material — as director *or* producer — would seem to indicate that he viewed Poe primarily as inspiration for a cycle which, once developed and exploited, should be allowed to pass away.

A reasonable guess is that Corman's most personal films are, not surprisingly, some of those made on particularly small budgets and released to little or no critical comment. *X—The Man with the X-Ray Eyes* (1963) is one of

Ray Milland as Xavier, the man whose awesome power isolates him from the woman (Diana Van Der Vlis) who loves him. *X—The Man with the X-Ray Eyes* (1963).

these, a harrowing, relentlessly grim study of Dr. James Xavier (Ray Milland), a corporate scientist who invents a serum which gives the user x-ray vision. His superiors are concerned about the formula's probable dangers, and refuse additional funding. When Xavier goes ahead with experiments on his own, his dual nature becomes apparent. On the one hand he is a dedicated researcher who is convinced his serum could be a boon to mankind, while on the other he is a cocktail party voyeur who uses his new power to peek at the twisting and frugging bodies of all the young ladies.

The irreverent filmmaker Russ Meyer made a cute joke of this talent in his famous 1959 nudie *The Immoral Mr. Teas*, but in the embittered context of Corman and writers Robert Dillon and Ray Russell, Xavier must pay for his transgression. His x-ray vision quickly becomes far-reaching, enabling him to see through skin and concrete. The horror begins when he realizes that even his closed eyelids cannot prevent him from seeing. Fearful, alienated, and no longer able to communicate with the gentle woman who loves him (Diana Van Der Vlis), Xavier joins a second-rate carnival as a "mind reader," where he is bullied and taken advantage of by the stupid owner (Don Rickles). Eventually, not even the lead glasses Xavier has taken to wearing stop his vision—

he sees constantly. The power increases still more, and when Xavier sees the shifting, pulsing turmoil of the core of the universe, he plucks his eyes from his head.

Xavier is a tragic and fascinating figure, a man whose awesome power turns him into a lonely freak. His humanity ebbs as his power grows, until finally he sets himself up as a "healer" who can diagnose illness with a single glance. Piteous people, most of them weak and elderly, flock to the tenement apartment from which he operates. He dismisses hypochondriacs, and flatly informs others that they will soon die. The power that under other circumstances could have brought Xavier love or at least companionship has ruined his life and dulled his emotions. He tears his eyes out at a revival meeting, an emotionally charged setting that represents the conservative society that Xavier has unwittingly defied. His possession of forbidden knowledge is his undoing.

Corman explored similar themes in *A Bucket of Blood* (1959) and *The Little Shop of Horrors* (1960), minibudgeted horror comedies that established the director's underground reputation in the seventies. Both were written by Charles B. Griffith—then in his late twenties—an immensely clever writer with a penchant for zany dialogue, absurd situations, and improbable heroes who exist unappreciated and unloved on society's fringe. In *A Bucket of Blood* Corman regular Dick Miller played Walter Paisley, an untalented young man who works as a busboy in a beatnik coffee house. Walter is mad for the bohemian love goddess Carla (Barboura Morris), but the girl has eyes only for the junior-grade Ginsbergs who come to the coffee house to recite their pretentious poetry, and the second-string Jackson Pollocks who exhibit their alleged art.

Lacking good looks and talent, Walter has nothing but *gall* to propel him toward his dream girl. But his attempt at verse comes out like hydrocephalic gibberish, and a timid stab at sculpture looks like—well, Carla is not impressed. (Neither is Walter, who angrily slaps and pokes the shapeless clay, pleading, "Be a nose! Be a nose!".) Defeated, Walter mopes around his dingy flat until accidentally killing a cat with a palette knife. Then comes sudden inspiration: Walter coats the animal in clay, takes it to the coffee house, and is instantly acclaimed as a great artistic talent. Even Carla gives him a promissory nuzzle. Predictably, though, the beats want to see *more* masterpieces. So desperate is Walter for Carla's love and the approval of the others that he embarks upon a murder spree, killing whomever he can lure to his apartment. He promises one brainless young lovely an evening of entertainment, but strangles her with her own scarf. The clay-coated body is a big hit at the coffee house; Walter takes to wearing open-necked shirts and rakish neckerchiefs. Like, he's *too much*! Even Carla is in his side pocket. The

Would-be hipster Walter Paisley (Dick Miller) hopefully displays his sculpture for the bohemian love goddess Carla (Barboura Morris) in *A Bucket of Blood* **(1959).**

foremost consideration of the Corman black comedies, though, is that they are morality plays. The very devices or talents which liberate the hapless protagonists eventually destroy them. Walter is found out when a chunk of clay drops from one of his creations, exposing the dead flesh beneath. He flees to his apartment, where he commits suicide with the intention of becoming his own greatest — and last — work of art.

A Bucket of Blood was shot in five days. Today, Corman is glib about the picture, saying he did it primarily to see if he could top his previous record for speedshooting, which was six days. Speed aside, the film's themes seem to have special fascination for Corman. He and Griffith returned to them a year later with *The Little Shop of Horrors*. Shot in an incredible four days (two days of interiors filmed simultaneously with four days and nights of exteriors) for $27,000, the picture is a deft satire of the conventions of the horror genre, as well as an unpretentious sexual tragedy. Seymour Krelboind (Jonathan Haze) is a dim but well-meaning Jewish-American youth who toils for $10 a week as assistant to Gravis Mushnik (Mel Welles) in a tiny florist shop on Los Angeles' skid row.

Seymour crosses a butterwort with a Venus fly trap one day and creates a peculiar hybrid with a bud that resembles a split football. The plant grows with alarming speed. Mushnik gazes at Seymour's splendid creation and happily muses, "It grows like a cold sore from the lip." Seymour is in heaven. He's even making romantic headway with Audrey Fulquard (Jackie Joseph), a simple, thoroughly sweet girl who also works in the shop. But the plant (dubbed "Audrey, Jr.") is more than just peculiar. Among its talents is the ability to speak (voice by Charles Griffith), first in an androgynous squeak and finally in a gravelly bass. The plant's favorite words are "Feed me!", and it doesn't mean plant food, either, but blood and human flesh. Seymour's luck suddenly sours; through a darkly hilarious set of circumstances, he accidentally kills a number of people and feeds them to Audrey, Jr., because he has no other place to dispose of the bodies. But the ravenous weed is never satisfied. It wrecks Seymour's romance by impersonating his voice in Audrey's presence, then hypnotizes Seymour, demanding that he find more food by purposely committing murder. After one more (accidental) killing, Seymour rebels, taking a butcher knife and stepping into his creation's gaping maw, promising, "I'll give you a meal you'll never forget!" Later, all that is left of Seymour is an imprint of his face — in a row with the faces of the plant's other victims — on a flower bud.

Seymour Krelboind may be cinema's ultimate victim of circumstance. He does not act — he reacts, and is dominated by nearly all of the principal people in his life. Mushnik bullies him at work, and Seymour can only make excuses. His mother (Myrtle Vail) is a whining hypochondriac who listens to Sickbed Serenade and demands that Seymour buy her an iron lung. The sadistic dentist Dr. Farb (John Shaner) mocks Seymour's naïveté, and tortures him with a dental drill. Seymour's only friend is Audrey, but the plant realizes the

Seymour (Jonathan Haze) pays tribute (note the victim's shoes) to Audrey, Jr., the voracious weed that brings both liberation and destruction in Roger Corman's *The Little Shop of Horrors* (1960).

threat and destroys the relationship. So it is that the plant — Seymour's ticket out of obscurity — becomes his curse. Finally, Seymour is a robot, a creature without free will or emotion. While under hypnosis he encounters a persistent prostitute (Merri Welles) who breathily informs him, "I'm Leanora Clyde. I love you." Seymour can only poke the woman's shapely middle and mumble something about "the master" being pleased to learn that somebody "volunteered." Normal relationships are scarce in Seymour's world. The only character besides Seymour and Audrey who seems capable of sexual excitement is Wilbur Force (Jack Nicholson), a young undertaker who reads aloud from *Pain* magazine in Farb's waiting room, chuckles Lorre-like over the gruesome articles, and demands that no anesthetic be used when his teeth are extracted.

The film's nighttime exteriors, shot on location in the slums of Los Angeles, are straight out of Nathanael West, and contribute to the aura of surreal hopelessness. Winos lie sprawled in doorways and young men shoot craps on the sidewalk. The depressing garishness of the neon signs and sleazy bars provides a curious complement to the bizarre zaninesss of the script. At the climax, Seymour is chased by police through a tire and bathroom fixture graveyard. Budget forced Corman to shoot with a minimum of illumination, so the sequence is as darkly menacing as similar moments in any of the classic film noirs of the forties and fifties. Seymour, unloved and alienated, is very nearly a tragic hero.

The Little Shop of Horrors played drive-ins and neighborhood theaters in its original 1960 release, made a few dollars, and was forgotten by all except a handful of film buffs. Its popularity slowly grew with local television broadcasts throughout the sixties and seventies. In Cleveland, for instance, the film became a late-night television *event*, and fans in that city sported "Feed me!" buttons in the early seventies. The movie is now a staple offering of pay-television stations. In 1982 a musical comedy play based on the film opened off–Broadway and grew into a major hit. At this writing, Howard Ashman and Alan Menken's "Little Shop of Horrors" is a sellout in Los Angeles. Plans are underway to bring it to the screen. So *The Little Shop of Horrors*, by coming full circle, is a sort of vindication for Roger Corman and Charles Griffith, both of whom toiled for years without recognition in the ghetto of B-movies. Seymour and Audrey, Jr., have made the big time. In the play, the girl Audrey is as much an emotional waif as Seymour. The gambit expands the play's focus, but dulls much of the story's edge. Tragic heroes do not remain tragic if they share their misery. Both Seymours amuse us, but only Corman's touches us.

In the last decade, Corman's success as head of New World Pictures — which he sold in early 1983 for a hefty $16.5 million — has eclipsed his achievements as a director. Many critics and historians continue to ignore or brush off the films that came before *House of Usher*. Others discount his directorial career altogether, regarding Corman primarily as a businessman. This of course is the hazard encountered by any filmmaker who chooses to work in despised genres, but Corman, in particular, seems doomed to be forever regarded as a *partial* filmmaker, and not as the complete creator he has shown himself to be.

Like the protagonists of many of his films, Corman remains at odds with not only the expectations of the establishment, but with himself. Though he formed New World in order to avoid studio interference in his projects, he became a domineering, sometimes imprudent force in his company. The New World formula of blood and bare bosoms eventually grew rigid and inflexible. Young writers and directors understood that they would do things the boss's way, or not at all. Now that Corman is free of heavy corporate responsibility, he may feel ready to return to directing, and to the sort of breezy, unexpected films he created in the fifties and sixties. These movies — sprinkled with energy, wit, and verve — continue to surprise us with their insights into the politics of sexuality: the role playing, the menace, the loneliness. Best of all, Corman's ironic voice, offered in the guise of popular culture, is accessible to us all.

X
Prince of Perversity:
Edward D. Wood, Jr.

It may be unwise for a serious film journalist to confess a fondness for the cinema of Edward D. Wood, Jr. — it's like a gourmet cook admitting to weekly pig-outs at McDonald's. In the late fifties a handful of French critics "discovered" the virtues of American commercial films; it has since become fashionable to praise filmmakers who spent entire careers in anonymity. This belated praise has often been richly deserved. The directors Joseph H. Lewis and Alan Dwan, for instance, were talented assembly-line craftsmen who were unjustly neglected during their peak years of productivity. It's been splendid to see them finally receive their due. It's funny, though: the French have never had anything to say about Ed Wood. If there has been one director in the history of American film whose output goes beyond *bad* into the realm of the, uh, *weird*, Wood is that director. His kinky oeuvre is not recommended for the uninitiated.

Wood has become a minor cult figure because of the recent phenomenon of "Golden Turkey" film festivals, trendy retrospectives attended by youngsters who are eager to laugh at the lame creations of talentless directors. The perverse sexuality and wretched production values of Wood's films, in particular, provoke hearty guffaws. Much of the attention Wood has received since his death in 1978 has not been particularly insightful or well-informed; his transvestism, for instance, has been gleefully discussed in recent books and magazine articles, but the man has not come across as anything more than a cartoon figure. Undeniably, his films are incredibly bad. They dabble in aspects of sexuality that are considered taboo. But there is about the films an earnestness and singleminded sincerity that invite a view of Wood as a gro-tesquely tragic, rather than comic, figure. In *Plan 9 from Outer Space* (1956), Wood's most famous picture, a police lieutenant is pondering a homicide. After using the barrel of his gun to absently scratch his head, the cop pronounces, "It's murder. And *somebody's* resonsible!" As I said: tragic.

Edward D. Wood, Jr., was born in 1922. A handsome man with a par-ticularly striking profile, he served honorably in the Marine Corps in World War II. He claimed, however, to have worn a brassiere in combat beneath his uniform. In postwar Hollywood, Wood became that sort of filmmaker known as a "fringie" — one who worked in the community but outside the mainstream. He was spiritual kin to exploitation pioneers Louis Sonney and Kroger Babb, canny entrepreneurs of the thirties and forties who produced hysterical "social conscience" melodramas like *Forbidden Oats* and *Wages of Sin*, as well as "hygiene" films like 1944's *Mom and Dad*, which concludes with jarring medical footage of the birth of a baby. Films of this sort were produced anonymously and on a shoestring. The producers' advance men would barnstorm the sticks, making deals with individual theater owners. Lurid flyers would then magically appear on phone poles and street lamps throughout the town, and local radio would be saturated with titillating come-ons. After the picture had exhausted its potential — often through separate showings for men and ladies — the advance men and theater owners would settle. With cash. The arrangement, in essence, provided underground filmmakers with access to America's heartland.

Wood tapped into this tradition with *Jail Bait* (1954) and *Sinister Urge* (1960), wretched sexploiters that came and went virtually unnoticed. A 1953 association with producer George Weiss (who later produced sadomasochist epics like *White Slaves of Chinatown*) allowed Wood to find his voice for the first time with *Glen or Glenda?* As writer, director, and star (using the nom de plume Daniel Davis), Wood explored the torments of transvestism. Despite a pseudodocumentary approach, *Glen or Glenda?* can be classed as a horror film by virtue of Wood's equating of unorthodox sexuality with a peculiar sort of mysticism. An aging Bela Lugosi was cast as The Spirit, an arcane fellow in a smoking jacket who sits in a dim room festooned with human skulls, totem poles, and other oddball artifacts.

Lugosi lectures about sex roles, intoning, "Bevare! Bevare! Vot are liddle boys made off? Snips und snails ..." and so on. The lecture is intercut with lightning flashes and a senseless montage of explosions and buffalo stampedes. At one point, Lugosi receives an acolyte, a young man who wishes to become a woman. The wizard mutters something, waves his hand, and the young man is magically transformed. There are more flashes of lightning, and Lugosi grins the grin of a man who has all the answers. The narrative's primary plot thread follows Glen (Wood), a prepossessing man of about 30 who appears normal and well-adjusted. But Glen is a closet transvestite who cannot bring himself to tell his fiancée the truth. He is in a torment for most of the film's 67 minutes. Actors playing police officers and a psychiatrist speak in quasiscientific gobbledygook when discussing transvestism; these characters are shown to be well-meaning, but essentially powerless to help. One miserable transvestite commits suicide because society cannot understand his aberration. Finally, after being tortured by nightmare visions of grotesquely laughing faces and an encounter with Satan, Glen goes to his fiancée and confesses his problem. She agrees to accept him as he is.

What is both bizarre and pathetic about *Glen or Glenda?* is that it is so clearly an autobiographical effort. Wood was not truly an exploitation filmmaker in the mold of Louis Sonney and Kroger Babb, but a man who honestly believed in what he was creating. To be sure, producer George Weiss shrewdly exploited the then-current Christine Jorgensen sex-change headlines, but Wood wrote and directed an intensely personal film. The most embarrassing thing about *Glen or Glenda?* is not its subject matter, but Wood's earnestness and vulnerability.

Glen or Glenda? proposes that one's sexuality can be directed by supernatural intervention. The scenes involving Bela Lugosi make no literal sense, but their tumult and aura of black magic make clear Wood's belief in a link between sexuality and the dark forces of nature. When Satan chases Glen around the room, it is not simply to amuse the audience. Evil and sex, or, more precisely, the *denial* of one's sexual preference, were, in Wood's mind, inextricably linked. In "Hellfire," one of many pornographic short stories Wood wrote later in his life, the Devil takes the name "Lived" (clever, eh?) and walks among men. When Lived is attacked by a quartet of sneering male prostitutes, he dispatches them all to Hell. Wood concludes the story with an admonition: "Beware...take care...Lived searches *everywhere!*"

Wood was an untalented writer with a penchant for stating and restating the obvious. Themes and even dialogue are shared by his films. The French critics of the late fifties looked at directors like Howard Hawks and labeled this sort of directorial consistency "auterism"; I'll not be foolish and suggest that Wood deserves similar respect. It seems apparent that the man was not walking the same road as you or I. Yet it would be narrow and unfair to dismiss him as a mere crackpot. *Glen or Glenda?* continues to exert a strange fascination over audiences. The film played in urban grind houses in the early sixties under the titles *I Changed My Sex* and *I Led Two Lives*. In 1981, Paramount picked it up for distribution as a midnight cult film, and trumpeted the event with a full page ad in the *New York Times*. If the world has not accepted Wood's kinky vision, it has at least loosened up enough to be amused by it. Contemporary audiences hoot when Glen's fiancée dutifully hands him the angora sweater he has longed to wear, but Wood wasn't kidding, folks. That silly sweater was his liberation, and his cloak against the dark forces he perceived to be in the world.

Glen or Glenda? was completed for the princely sum of $29,000. It looks like it. The sets are flimsy. Harsh, unimaginative lighting exposes the ugliness of blonde, thrift shop furniture. The actresses have beady eyes and big noses. And Lugosi, who never perfected his command of English, is almost unintelligible. He was paid $5000 for five days' work, and had an ongoing relationship with Wood thereafter. As discussed in Chapter VI, Lugosi was at a low ebb at this point in his life. Impoverished, half deaf, and dependent on drugs, he was a pathetic figure. He had become a joke, a caricature. What more fitting fate than to become leading actor for a joke director?

Of all Wood's films, *Bride of the Monster* (1956) is the closest to the commercial mainstream. It can be seen regularly on Saturday afternoons on television stations around the country. Bela Lugosi played Dr. Eric Vornoff, a crazed

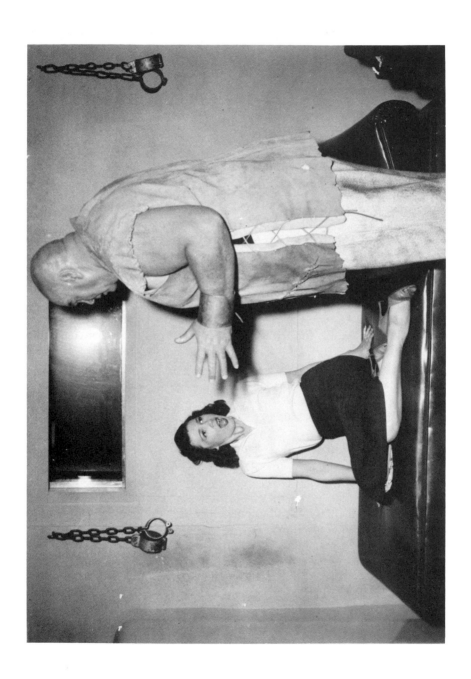

scientist who wishes to create a race of atom-charged supermen because he has been spurned and ridiculed by his colleagues. Hero Tony McCoy (the son of the meat packing magnate who financed the film) and his gum-snapping girlfriend (Loretta King) stumble across Vornoff's isolated house. Lobo (Tor Johnson), Vornoff's fat, demented stooge, mops up the floor with McCoy, and subdues the girl. Vornoff wishes to take the woman for his bride. But Lobo, whose taste in women is apparently as highly developed as his intellect, has designs of his own. After Vornoff has charged himself with atomic rays, he and Lobo do battle. Vornoff wins, but becomes lunch for his hungry (papier-mâché) octopus. The marriage that was made in heaven will never come off.

Bride of the Monster is worse than it sounds, and a lot more fun. Lugosi hams gloriously; though not the actor's final film, it was the last time his voice was to be heard on the screen. He brings flair and genuine conviction to predictable dialogue. Perhaps Lugosi felt a closeness to the maligned and misunderstood character he played, a great scientist who has been forced to carry out his dreams of courtship and conquest in a miserable farm house, just as the once-proud actor had been reduced to idiotic roles in five-day quickies on Hollywood's poverty row.

Production values on *Bride* were rock bottom. Shadows of booms are visible in a number of scenes, and the cardboard walls of Vornoff's laboratory shake whenever somebody walks across the set. Sexually speaking, the film is unremarkable. Marriage without proper courtship may be a bit peculiar, but hardly the hallmark of a mind as original as Wood's. Not surprisingly, Wood did not write the screenplay; Alex Gordon must take the honors.

Wood explored a variant on the niceties of heterosexual courtship in 1958 when he wrote (but did not direct) *The Bride and the Beast*, a charming fable about a young woman who has a romantic desire for gorillas. Her husband is less than pleased when she is revealed to be a reincarnation of an ape. She ultimately reverts to her original form, and lopes off to a trouble-free love life. Wood once again explored the unhappiness of an individual cast by fate into an uncomfortable sex role. The mystic solution is pure Wood.

1959 saw the release of Wood's most famous film, *Plan 9 from Outer Space*, which had actually been completed in 1956. Though not as personal an effort as *Glen or Glenda?*, *Plan 9* is even more bizarre in its sexual stance. Wood's script is a careless pastiche of science fiction, the flying saucer craze, and necrophilia. Extraterrestrials who are fed up with Earth's burgeoning nuclear capabilities decide to utilize "Plan 9" to resurrect human dead and march them upon Earth's capitals. This grandiose scheme does not amount to much in practice, as the only ones resurrected are a woman (Vampira), a murdered police detective (Tor Johnson), and an old man (Bela Lugosi). It seems that even extraterrestrials must watch their budgets. Wood certainly

Loretta King is less than thrilled by Tor Johnson's amorous intentions in *Bride of the Monster* (1956).

did. Pie tins double as flying saucers, and headstones in cemetery scenes are made of cardboard. For an Army artillery attack on the invaders, Wood utilized stock shots of soldiers intercut with interior shots of actor Tom Keene standing before a blank background as he pretends to gaze into the sky.

Most numbing is the participation of Bela Lugosi, who was restricted to three or four minutes of silent footage Wood had shot just days before the actor's death in August of 1956. In order to stretch Lugosi's footage, Wood obscured the face of a "double" (in actuality Wood's chiropractor) with a cape and had him stalk around and act menacing. Worse, the double's scenes were shot in darkness, to simulate night, while the scenes with Lugosi had been shot in broad daylight. A hoped-for optical printer was unavailable, so the daylit scenes could not be mechanically darkened. So much for visual continuity.

Television personality Vampira is the centerpiece of *Plan 9's* unwholesome sexual allure. Vampira, whose real name is Maila Nurmi, was a dancer in New York when she was "discovered" by director Howard Hawks. He groomed her for movie stardom, but nothing materialized. By the early fifties, Nurmi had devised the cadaverously beautiful Vampira persona, and enjoyed success on Los Angeles television as hostess of a Shock Theatre movie program. With a form-fitting shroud tailored to show off her wasp waist and ample bosom, Vampira was every necrophiliac's dream girl. As one of the resurrected dead in *Plan 9* she stumbles around a foggy cemetery with outstretched arms and heaving cleavage. Her first victims are a pair of paunchy gravediggers, who shriek at her approach. The killings are performed off-screen, and the unmutilated condition of the gravediggers' bodies caused a companion to ask me at a recent screening, "Good grief, what did she do to them?" What, indeed?

Voice-over narration early in the film makes fond reference to "the lost roses" of Vampira's cheeks, and to the sky that was "now just a covering for her dead body." Her lipstick is exaggerated and as dark as pitch, and at one point she nearly falls out of her costume. The faces of the gravediggers are hidden from view when their bodies are discovered, presumably to conceal their satisfied smirks. Romance marches on!

Plan 9 from Outer Space was partially financed by a Beverly Hills Baptist Church. Wood began shooting with only $800 front money, and spent four days in September–October 1956 on a minuscule Hollywood sound stage at the corner of Santa Monica and Western. The Baptists were thrilled to bankroll a "real" Hollywood movie, but insisted that Wood and actor Tor Johnson be baptized in the faith. The immersion of the immense Johnson took place in a Beverly Hills swimming pool.

An Alabama theater owner named J. Edward Reynolds helped with the financing of *Plan 9*. Reynolds had come to Hollywood with the intention of

Charlotte Austin responds to a squeeze from her main man in *The Bride and the Beast* (1958). Note her angora sweater, an Edward D. Wood trademark.

Maila Nurmi, better known as Vampira, centerpiece of the unwholesome sexual allure of Wood's *Plan 9 from Outer Space* (1956).

producing biblical epics in the style of Cecil B. DeMille. Associates told him he could raise the necessary capital by starting off with exploitation films. Reynolds and Ed Wood happened to live in the same Hollywood apartment building; chance had brought Wood an indulgent patron. Reynolds (who appears in *Plan 9* as one of the gravediggers) was inordinately proud of the film, but was unable to interest any Hollywood distributors in picking it up. He had similar bad luck in New York. Finally, the Hal Roach organization agreed to give the picture a limited release in 1959. Today, *Plan 9 from Outer Space* enjoys tremendous cult popularity. Vampira appeared at a 1980 showing in Los Angeles, and the fans went wild. *Plan 9* T-shirts and videos sell briskly.

Wood followed up with *Night of the Ghouls* (1959), a quasisequel to his own *Bride of the Monster*. Television psychic Criswell (Jeron Criswell King) acted as on-screen narrator (as he had for *Plan 9*), this time ensconced in a plush coffin. "This is a tale of the Threshold People," he intones, "... monsters to be pitied, monsters to be despised." Tor Johnson reprised his role as Lobo, now a stooge for phony medium Dr. Acula (Kenne Duncan), who operates out of the farmhouse that has belonged to Lugosi's Dr. Vornoff. Another of Acula's accomplices is The White Ghost (Valda Hansen), a moon-faced blonde who prowls the grounds in order to scare off nosy locals and cops. But the grounds are also patrolled by a *real* phantom, The Black Ghost (Jeannie Stevens, not Vampira, as some sources — including a previous book by this writer — have reported), a sensual beauty in a dark shroud who does unthinkable things to living men after luring them into the underbrush.

Wood's script and direction are characteristically inept, as well as atypically boring. Much of the film is composed of static two-shots, although Wood did manage some eeriness in a few scenes with his ghostly temptresses. The film had at least one preview showing in California's San Fernando Valley in 1959, but was never released theatrically. One authority has suggested that the original negative was seized in lieu of payment by the lab that processed it. Missouri entrepreneur Wade Williams eventually acquired the rights, and later sold the picture for release on videocassette. *Night of the Ghouls* finally reached a panting public in 1984.

Wood was unable to get another horror film project off the ground until 1966, when he wrote *Orgy of the Dead* for producer-director A.C. Stevens. Because censorship standards had loosened considerably by the mid-sixties, Wood was free to indulge himself. *Orgy of the Dead* was shot in "Horror Color" and "Astravision." The screen is filled with lots and lots of naked female breasts. Wood's script is a variant on the Judgment Day theme, as a young couple who may or may not have died in a car crash are taken prisoner by a band of fiends in a foggy cemetery. The Emperor of Horror (Criswell) allows the captives to observe as he listens to the stories of the newly-dead. One, an undertaker, explains how he ground up the corpses of female "clients" while wearing their clothes. A blonde beauty, nude except for a flimsy shroud, confesses to having been a vampire. Another well-endowed lovely wears a tiger costume that has no front, and drop-drawers in the back. The Emperor's consort is called The Black Princess; she expresses a perverse fondness for the heroine, and brands an "S" (presumably for "Satan") below the girl's breast. A werewolf and a droopy mummy are thrown in for additional laughs. Much of Wood's dialogue is priceless. The Emperor stuffily proclaims: "The living always have control over the dead." Later, he admonishes a nude ghost, "You committed murder upon yourself. You are a mess."

Wood prepared a paperback novelization of his screenplay, and articulated his fondness for ladies' apparel. " 'I can feel the soft fur of my angora against my cheek,' says the heroine. 'I *can't* be dead.' " Later, "Shirley hugged her angora-covered arms tightly across her beautifully shaped breasts." Wood manfully described a seduction with phrases like "surging veins" and "ripe young breasts." His heroine is finally wearied by her tormentors, and comes to a realization: "Perhaps there was sin in protecting virginity so far?"

A rational consideration of Wood's canon is nearly impossible. Normal critical standards do not apply. The creation of most Hollywood films is unremarkable, but Wood's seem to have sprung from the dank earth, like mutant vegetables. His work—simultaneously repellent and alluring—provides unique documentation of sexual aberration. In fairness, it should be noted that former associates rave about Wood's kindness and generosity. Wood genuinely cared for his friend Bela Lugosi, and once talked the aging actor out of suicide. Far from neurotic, Wood was secure in his masculinity. His willingness to advertise his style of living is what has made him a fascinating figure.

Eccentrics like Criswell, Vampira, and Tor Johnson were part of an entourage that invaded Hollywood eateries and night spots for years. Wood loved to play the part of "director." He perpetually had projects "in development," but had to scrounge outside the Hollywood establishment for production money. To his eternal credit, he often succeeded, but by the late sixties microbudget cheapies had become virtually infeasible. *Orgy of the Dead* is the last mainstream theatrical film with which Wood was involved. The remainder of his film work was frankly pornographic. *Take It Out in Trade* (1971) and *Necromania* (1972; in which Wood appears as a wizard) are two whose titles are known. He devoted much of the final decade of his life to writing pornographic horror stories with titles like "Scream Your Bloody Head Off!" and "The Fall of the Balcony of Usher." He reportedly supplemented his meager income by directing a series of 8mm sex loops.

A few days after he and his wife were evicted from their tiny Hollywood apartment in 1978, Wood died at the home of a friend while watching television. The Prince of Perversity had moved to another plane. Would he have objected to such an appellation? Probably not, for it reflects the peculiar sort of dignity he brought to his movies. Lacking talent and money, he pushed on with only his own vision to guide him. He created films which reflect those elements of life that moved and intrigued him. Today we laugh at Wood's shortcomings and excesses, but at least his kinkiness was backed with a sort of courage. If we did not sense that courage, our laughter would not be nearly as kind as it is.

XI
The Spawn of Herschell Gordon Lewis

In a heavily wooded section of northern Wisconsin in 1957 a 51-year-old farmer named Ed Gein shot a middleaged storekeeper named Bernice Worden and took her body to his isolated farmhouse. When the woman's grown son expressed concern at his mother's disappearance, a discarded sales slip led the Waushara County sheriff to Gein's home. Inside, the law officer found Mrs. Worden's body — decapitated, eviscerated, and hung by its heels over a tub. When the sheriff stumbled to a nearby sink to vomit, he was greeted by Mrs. Worden's head. The most horrible aspect of Gein's crime is that it was not a lone incident; the sheriff discovered the grisly remains of multiple bodies — all of them female — throughout the house. Gein's refrigerator was stocked with jars of human organs. A nasty-looking stew simmered on the stove. The pull-cord on Gein's windowshade was formed from a pair of human lips and, most absurdly, a cup of noses sat on the kitchen table. In the parlor, decomposed heads were nailed to the walls and displayed on shelves. But the greatest horror was upstairs in Gein's closet, where he kept the dried skin of his late mother's shins and torso. Testimony at Gein's trial revealed that he often dressed in his mother's clothes and strapped her skin over them. In this way, the farmer expressed what his lawyer maintained was a love/hate relationship with the woman who had dominated his life. Ed Gein was the worst sort of Mama's boy.*

In Milwaukee, a novelist and short story writer named Robert Bloch read about Gein's crimes. Bloch, fascinated, wrote a novel entitled *Psycho*, about a repressed man whose morbid attachment to his dead mother causes him to commit gruesome murders. When Alfred Hitchcock brought the novel to the screen in 1960, he created (as has been discussed in Chapter VIII) not only art, but a film that opened the floodgates to all sorts of unrestrained gore and outrageous violence. Though not a graphic film, *Psycho* inspired a legion of moviemakers who, by the late seventies, strove to outdo one another in the gore sweepstakes. Paradoxically, then, *Psycho* — arguably among the finest films ever made — inspired dozens of the very worst.

Perverse sexuality is at the core of the Ed Gein story, as it is at the core of the multitude of "slasher" or "gore" movies it inspired. This subgenre

Ed Gein died at the Mendota Mental Health Institute in Wisconsin in the summer of 1984.

(which, as we will see, *has* managed to produce a few good films) has become a misogynistic footnote to the history of the horror film. The trend began to taper off in the very early eighties, after threatening to overwhelm the genre completely. Gore cinema explores the banality of evil, and the destructive potential of instruments as varied and as mundane as butcher knives, garden shears, pitchforks, axes, and chain saws. Most significantly, the usual victims—the defenseless wretches whose fates stirred the blood of audiences on 42nd Street and at drive-ins in America's heartland—are young women. Stripped of their humanity and reduced to the iconography of butts, thighs, and bosoms, dozens of nubile young beauties were paraded across the screen for our voyeuristic pleasure, only to be mercilessly dispatched by the heavy-breathing fiends who lurked around the corner in film after film. Women become meat, pert little screaming machines who, many of the films per-niciously suggested, *deserved* to die. In feminism according to exploitation moviemakers, women had earned nothing but the right to be stalked, mutilated, and killed.

Herschell Gordon Lewis, a Chicago ad man and onetime professor of English at the University of Mississippi, had dabbled in low-budget filmmak-ing since the late fifties. American nudie cinema in that decade had pro-gressed from innocuous volleyball marathons to the amusingly mammarian fantasies of filmmaker Russ Meyer. Herschell Lewis and partner David Fried-man (the latter now chairman of the Adult Film Association of America) followed the trend by offering such pictures as *Lucky Pierre* (1961), *Boin-n-n-g!* (1962), and *Goldilocks and the Three Bares* (1963). But the market for soft-core skin flicks was withering before the new freedom of mainstream films. Doubtless inspired by the implications of *Psycho*, Lewis decided to abandon the nudies in 1963, and spent nine days and barely $50,000 on location in Miami shooting something called *Blood Feast*. Though the nominal star is Connie Mason (a blonde, former *Playboy* Playmate with all the acting skills of a doorknob), the film's *real* attraction is its unbelievably graphic bloodlet-ting. *Blood Feast* signalled the official birth of the gore film...and the begin-ning of open season on young actresses.

Above all, Lewis knew his audience: a regional, primarily Southern one that frequented drive-ins and small-town theaters. This audience (still catered to by contemporary filmmakers like North Carolina's Earl Owensby) de-manded only fast action, pretty girls, and the sort of outré narratives that Yankees didn't cotton to. I suppose it should be emphasized here that Lewis (as far as anyone has been able to determine) had no psychosexual axe to grind. He is not a pervert, but simply an independent filmmaker who gauged a potential audience and created a new sort of film in order to cater to it. Lewis looked at the hot, buggy little towns in Louisiana and Mississippi and Georgia and saw gold.

Blood Feast revolves around Fuad Ramses (Mal Arnold), an Egyptian caterer in Miami whose hobby is killing beautiful women in order to perform blood rites that will revive his long-dead princess. Ramses maintains a shrine to the princess in the basement of his store, complete with a rather unimpressive statue (in reality a department store mannequin none-too-cleverly disguised with gold paint). Ramses stalks women on the street, on the beach, even in their own homes. Because old habits are difficult to forget, Lewis glitzed up the proceedings with occasional bits of nudity.

Not that the audience needs skin in order to stay awake—there's more than enough going on in *Blood Feast* to sustain the attention of even the most jaded viewer. One girl is attacked as she necks with her boyfriend on a deserted beach, the top of her head chopped off and her brain left to lie in the sand. Another young lady is lured to Ramses' shop, hacked to bits, and turned into a stew. Perhaps the best bit involves (Miami Playboy Club bunny) Astrid Olson, whose tongue is pulled from her head in closeup and without camera cuts. Lewis explained to interviewers Todd McCarthy and Charles Flynn in 1973 that Ms. Olson "had the size mouth that would accommodate a sheep's tongue we had bought for the purpose." Ah, the actor's life for me! Heroine Connie Mason (*Playboy* Playmate for June 1963) seems to be next on the mad caterer's list, but is saved by her resourceful policeman friend (Thomas Wood). At the climax, Ramses is crushed to death by (appropriately enough) a garbage truck.

I must confess a strange fascination for *Blood Feast*, primarily because the film is absolutely free of guilt or guile. It simply *unreels*, like a dispassionate documentary on inventive mutilation, or police photographs come to life. Early in the film, a blonde beauty (Sandra Sinclair) is enjoying a bubble bath in the privacy of her motel room (shades of *Psycho!*) when Ramses enters and unceremoniously saws off one of her legs. The amazing thing about this, both artistically and psychologically, is that Lewis brought absolutely no technique to the sequence—the camera merely sat like some dumb beast and recorded what happened. Here is a director so free of imagination and emotional involvement that he is effortlessly able to turn the members of his audience into benumbed accomplices. Watching a Herschell Gordon Lewis film is like being brained with a sashweight, or having your I.Q. suddenly drop by 40 points. *Blood Feast*, in particular, makes dullards and villains of us all.

Lewis' lack of talent goes without saying, but there *is* a style at work in his films. Or rather, a *lack* of style that identifies him. Particularly charitable critics have linked Lewis with the Grand Guignol of the Paris stage, but the comparison is valid only in its most obvious aspects. Grand Guignol, performed live and without camera tricks, developed a queasy sort of artistic tradition. It did not imitate reality, but mocked our perception of it. Lewis, on the other hand, brought his minimal skills to bear and was the first filmmaker to exploit Grand Guignol sensibilities by translating them to a believable milieu. *Blood Feast*, though dopey in the extreme, does not *look* like a fantasy. Unsophisticated audiences responded to the film; it is recalled with a grin or a shudder by all who have seen it.

The women in *Blood Feast* are punished because they are pretty and sexual. The girl who necks on the beach and the one who keeps a motel room have sealed their dooms. *Bad* girls! The villain, working from a surprisingly Puritan morality that informs virtually all subsequent gore films, metes out retribution and justice just as surely as he metes out death.

Lewis followed *Blood Feast* with the winsomely titled *2000 Maniacs* (1964), his self-proclaimed masterpiece, and a film that must surely have tickled his rebel audience. The narrative is a fiendish retort to Sherman's march to the sea, in which the ghosts of a Southern town that had been laid to waste by Union troops rise one hundred years later to exact their revenge on a carload of hapless Yankee tourists. One man is stuffed in a spike-studded barrel and rolled down a hill, while a beautiful young woman is stretched on a rack, then crushed by a suspended boulder. The film's most horrific scene is more intimate, as a grinning Confederate ghost grabs a girl's hand and cheerfully slices off her thumb.

2000 Maniacs was budgeted at $80,000, significantly more than *Blood Feast*. Lewis' pleasure at the way the film turned out is almost childlike: he has spoken with great pride, for example, of his use of a truck-mounted cherry picker for crane shots. Despite such technical marvels, though, *2000 Maniacs* is only barely professional. While a few of the actors are reasonably convincing (even the ubiquitous Connie Mason), Lewis had not achieved competency in basic skills like continuity, sound, and editing. The film is important only because it set down a couple of basic ground rules for the gore subgenre: plenty of pretty girls, and a rural setting. When slasher films exploded in the late seventies and began to be aimed at a nationwide audience, filmmakers focused upon isolated Southern locales because the predominant market, the North, had always *figured* the South was weird. *The Texas Chain Saw Massacre* (1974), *Tourist Trap* (1979), and *Motel Hell* (1980) are just a few of many gore films that exploited Northerners' jokey disdain for the South.

After *2000 Maniacs*, Lewis seemed to lose some of his zeal. His subsequent horror films are hardly less gory than his first two, but haven't the spark of depravity that Lewis had seemed on the verge of refining into an art. The story of *Color Me Blood Red* (1965), for instance, is surprisingly pedestrian, as a demented artist paints with the blood of his shapely models.* Scalpings and decapitations figure prominently in *The Gruesome Twosome* (1967), the story of a crazed wigmaker and her son. *A Taste of Blood* (1967) updates the Dracula story (the lead character's name is Alucard), while *Something Weird*

Stephanie Rothman's Blood Bath *(1966) is a less graphic interpretation of a similar story.*

Sandra Sinclair's bubble bath — from Herschell Gordon Lewis' gleefully crude *Blood Feast* (1963).

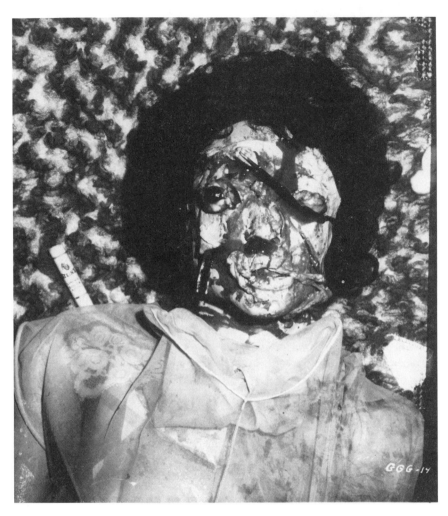

A disfigured (and patently phony) female victim from Lewis' *The Gore-Gore Girls* (1972).

(1968) involves a man who preys on women after being horribly disfigured in an electrical accident.

Lewis regained his élan with *The Wizard of Gore* (1971), the story of Montag the Magnificent (Ray Sager), a stage magician whose gruesome illusions are real. He drives a spike through the head of one comely assistant, then yanks out one of the girl's eyes. Another woman, her hands bound above her head, is impaled by a huge drill press, and still another is disemboweled by Montag's bare hands. The crowning touch is the fate of one unfortunate young lady, whose brain is literally squeezed out of her ear. You might as well laugh—Lewis certainly was. Montag the Magnificent is very nearly Lewis himself, a grinning illusionist who *dares* his audience to spot the fakery. There's no malice in Lewis' films — only perverse glee.

The director's last gore film to date is *The Gore-Gore Girls* (1972), which is set in a strip joint where buxom employees are being horribly murdered. One girl is shoved head first into a boiling french fryer, another is dismembered with a meat cleaver, and a third is pounded to death by a meat tenderizer (an unlikely but dangerous weapon later utilized by David Cronenberg in *The Brood*, 1979). Lewis has spoken with special fondness of a scene in which the killer yanks an eyeball from a girl's head and squeezes: "Finally it bursts," the director told interviewers McCarthy and Flynn in 1973, "and this inky black glop squirts out all over the place. I have seen people faint, vomit, turn green, leave the auditorium, and go to the washroom because of that scene."

The culprit turns out to be a deranged waitress (Hedda Lubin) who slaughters the young lovelies because her own face is disfigured with scar tissue. The story is essentially a reworking of George Blair's *The Hypnotic Eye* (1960; see Chapter III), even down to a similar ending in which the evil woman falls to her death from a great height. In Lewis' sick little fable, though, the waitress' head must also be run over and squashed by a car. Moderation, as Lewis demonstrated time and again, is *never* enough.

A subplot of *The Gore-Gore Girls* involves a gang of militant lesbians, a theme Lewis had explored a few years earlier in *She-Devils on Wheels* (1968), the director's most commercially successful film after *Blood Feast*. Though not strictly in the horror genre, *She-Devils* is inarguably horrific, an unpleasant but compelling melding of the nastiest elements of the motorcycle genre and the ruder physical mayhem of the horror genre.

The She-Devils are members of a distaff motorcycle gang called The Man-Eaters. The ladies don't literally eat men (did Lewis miss a bet, here?), but certainly abuse them: one fellow's face is punched to pulp in a bar, while another man is decapitated by a wire strung in the path of his motorcycle. The Man-Eaters, grinning fiercely and puffing Tiparillos, strike a gaudy but essentially meaningless blow for womanhood.

The ease with which Lewis was able to shift gears and victimize men indicates his utter lack of personal involvement in the philosophies of his films. The movies simply *exist* — they do not proselytize, they do not attempt to teach. They probably do not even corrupt, though one would be hard pressed to claim that a viewer comes away from the likes of *Blood Feast* and *She-Devils on Wheels* a better person. Because the films are so ineptly produced, they are a sort of sub-cinema, a jokey endurance contest rather than a legitimate movie experience. Lewis' malice toward women is not malice at all, but only an indication of his flair for schtick and gimmick. Lewis understood that a combination of pretty girls and crazy violence makes for good box office. He cares about the business of moviemaking, but is as professionally interested in philosophy and aesthetics as a proctologist.

Legal entanglements in the early seventies curtailed Lewis' film output, but the sheer gall and unapologetic crudity of his oeuvre has kept the films on view for two decades. Scratchy, faded prints continue to play across the country, and there seems to be a Lewis renaissance on videocassette. Legitimate revival theaters will occasionally schedule an evening of Lewis films. At this writing, plans for *Blood Feast II* are underway. What does this say about us? Little, really, except that there will always be a new generation of thrill-starved adolescents (or the adolescent at heart), ready to scream and laugh.

Lewis' importance as an artist is nonexistent, but his influence on world cinema may be inestimable. He dared show the unshowable. The dozens of films that followed his lead range from very good to execrable. Only a few have Lewis' (unintentional?) wit, but nearly all portray women as helpless victims, and with far more venom than Lewis ever manifested. Nobody noticed when *Blood Feast* played Dixie drive-ins in 1963, but plenty of eyes were opened when gore films began sneaking into suburban theaters in the North just a few years later. Ironically, Lewis was quickly superseded. His amateurish product and inadequate distribution doomed him to permanent residence in the industry's fringe. His single clever idea encouraged filmmakers who had more savvy, skill, and money.

The Flesh Eaters (1964) is an early example, an entertaining but self-consciously visual movie that suggests the careful, formalized pictorial composition of a well-drawn comic book.* Veteran character star Martin Kosleck played an unscrupulous scientist who has created a voracious parasite with an appetite for human flesh. The narrative is predictable (Kosleck receives an apt comeuppance), but director Jack Curtis peppered the film with startling gore: a beatnik (remember them?) is consumed from the inside out after drinking a glassful of the parasites, and a spoiled, voluptuous movie queen (Rita Morley) is savaged on a deserted beach. *The Flesh Eaters* was given a cover story by *Famous Monsters of Filmland*, then the leading magazine for young horror film fans (I have a vivid memory of my copy being snatched by my fifth grade teacher). This was followed by publication of a magazine that celebrated the release of *Horror of Party Beach* (1964; see Chapter V), a bloody teen film that helped cement the popular acceptance of a rougher sort of horror film. Gore-mania began to creep into America's suburbs.

The explosion came in 1968 with the release of a $114,000, black-and-white feature called *Night of the Living Dead*, which had been cowritten, photographed, edited, and directed by a 28-year-old industrial filmmaker from Pittsburgh named George Romero. The film's plot—about a night when radiation from a returning space probe resurrects the dead and turns them into an army of bloodthirsty ghouls—is as resolutely direct and simpleminded as the gaudy comic book stories of the fifties that Romero has said inspired it.

*The Flesh Eaters *was, in fact, written by a comic book scripter, Arnold Drake.*

A small group of people trapped in an isolated farmhouse must fend off repeated attacks by the ghouls.

Romero and cowriter John Russo created a set of comfortably familiar characters, including a forthright hero (Duane Jones), a cowardly bully (Karl Hardman), and other stereotypes like a sweet teenage couple, a whiny housewife, et al. But *Night of the Living Dead*—in the best tradition of Hitchcock—shatters our expectations. We assume actress Judith O'Dea will be our heroine, but the character quickly lapses into catatonia. The attractive teenage girl briefly takes over as leading lady, but is immolated with her handsome boyfriend in a flaming pickup truck. The ghouls gather round and enjoy a tasty barbeque, complete with lip smacking and happy waving of organs, bones, and entrails. Inside the besieged house, a little, pigtailed girl who had been bitten by a ghoul dies, then returns as one of the undead. In a scene that may be the film's most disturbing because it cleverly corrupts our cherished notions about mothers and daughters, the little girl hacks her disbelieving mum to death with a garden trowel, then begins to consume the body. Most unexpectedly, our resourceful hero—who is the only survivor of this hellish night—is mistaken for a ghoul the next morning and shot, his body grasped with baling hooks and unceremoniously dumped on a bonfire.

Interestingly, Romero has downplayed the film's deeper implications; some critics, particularly those abroad, were excited because the lead, Duane Jones, is black. This encouraged views of the film that were metaphorical and heavily political. Romero continues to claim that he simply wanted to make an effective horror film. He succeeded. His background as a nonfiction filmmaker brought a documentary-like tone to *Night of the Living Dead*. Mobile, hand-held camerwork and shadowy black-and-white photography contribute to a startling verisimilitude. The actors—inexpert with the exception of Jones—nonetheless managed to convey a believable, almost ad-lib quality.

Outrageous in the extreme, the film is also relentless and memorable. And what stuck in the minds of most viewers was the gore. Pittsburgh-area butchers were kept busy supplying Romero with animal organs and bones. Gallons of Karo syrup were used to simulate blood. There is humor in the film (the sheriff says of the zombies, "Yeah, they're dead, all right. They're *all* messed up"), but the crudely visceral shock effects overwhelm it. The picture was widely denounced; the *Reader's Digest*, in particular, railed against it with such zeal that curious patrons were undoubtedly disappointed. Over time, *Night of the Living Dead* has achieved classic status. Hardly an eyebrow was raised some years ago when New York's Museum of Modern Art added the film to its permanent collection.

The picture is cinema's ultimate expression of the cynicism and hopelessness that deadened our hearts and minds in the Vietnam era. Values stand for nothing. Bravery, self-sacrifice, even love and motherhood are steamrollered. The plague descends with equanimity—no one is spared. The ultimate horror is that the poor souls in the farmhouse are not menaced by extraterrestrials or giant grasshoppers, but by people like themselves—just like *us*. When parent-teacher groups and the *Reader's Digest* shouted their outrage, it was not because of the film's graphic violence or even its nihilism, but because of the cruel truth that Romero forced us to see: the beast is in us all.

Far from a crass exploiter, George Romero had had a fondness for the horror genre since his childhood in the Bronx. An early effort called *The Man from the Meteor* was made in 1954, when Romero was 14. *Night of the Living Dead* catapulted him to prominence, but subsequent projects outside the horror genre failed. Romero did not click again critically until *Martin* (1979), a peculiar, modern-day vampire thriller whose title character is not a supernatural being but a psychotic young man who believes he is a descendant of Nosferatu. Martin rapes women, then drinks their blood after slitting their wrists with a razor blade. John Amplas' performance is subtle and well-shaded; the character is not likeable, but has a sympathetic depth that is unusual in the subgenre. When Martin finally manages something approaching a normal sexual relationship, it is with a suicidal divorcée. When the woman kills herself, Martin's guardian (Lincoln Maazel) is convinced that the youth is supernatural, and drives a stake through the boy's heart. In effect, Martin's psychological breakthrough, his big step toward normalcy, brings his death.

Though bloody, *Martin* was the first strong indication of Romero's subtlety, and his penchant for social satire. The film's Pittsburgh setting (Romero still has not moved to Hollywood) becomes a point of irony, a stifling, repressive place rather than the convivial playground Martin would like it to be. Romero's subsequent films—*Dawn of the Dead* (1979), *Knightriders* (1981), and *Creepshow* (1982)—are the work of an artist with a fresh and unique point of view. *Dawn of the Dead* is the second installment of a projected "Living Dead" trilogy, filmed in glossy color with unrestrained and funny gore effects by Tom Savini.

Romero, unlike many of his contemporaries, realized that to predicate a horror film solely on unpleasant sexuality is risky and usually pointless, so it is hardly an issue in *Dawn of the Dead*, except for a plot element in which the heroine (Gaylen Ross) learns she is pregnant. As in *Martin*, the film's gory thrills do not merely shock, but underscore Romero's satiric point of view. The action is set in a shiny, monolithic shopping mall that has, like the rest of the country, been taken over by the undead. Four normal people have taken refuge behind the locked doors of individual stores. The mall becomes both prison and fantasy: the woman indulges herself in clothes and cosmetics at Penney's, while the men happily loot the bank (money, of course, is worthless), sporting goods store, and gourmet shop. But they remain trapped in their consumer's paradise by the ravenous ghouls, who aimlessly ride the escalators and stare at the store-window mannequins.

When the mall is invaded by a whooping horde of motorcyclists, the film becomes a seriocomic bloodbath, a horrific trip to the O.K. Corral. One of the protagonists is badly wounded in a wild exchange of gunfire, but the invaders suffer the loss of their leader (Tom Savini), who is pulled from his bike by a pack of ghouls and eaten alive, his abdomen clawed open like a ravioli. At the conclusion of the film, the zombies have overrun the mall, but the pregnant woman and the strongest of the men (Ken Foree) escape. It is interesting to note that Foree, like Duane Jones of *Night of the Living Dead*, is black.

Knightriders was a change of pace, a low-key and reflective look at contemporary chivalry as expressed by a company of motorcycle stunt riders, while *Creepshow* — as its title might suggest — is not a gore film at all, but Romero's (and writer Stephen King's) homage to the goofily horrible EC horror comics of the early fifties. The film's primary female character (played with a splendid sneer by Adrienne Barbeau) is so irredeemably bitchy that she moves beyond stereotype to mock-archetype. Her gory death is not a slap in the viewer's face, but cause for celebration. As is Romero's career, which gives every sign of continued growth. His energy, playfulness, and refusal to become part of the Hollywood mainstream mark him as a significant — if anomalous — directorial talent.

To other low-budget filmmakers, Romero's early success was significant because of commerce, not art. Andy Milligan, an American writer-director active in England, rushed into production with a series of crude, heavily sexual films that aped the more obvious aspects of *Night of the Living Dead*, but that had none of their inspiration's peculiar power, or even production values; since 1964, Milligan's budgets have hovered between $7,500 and $20,000. *The Bloodthirsty Butchers* (1970) is a reworking of the Sweeney Todd story, as the crazed barber (John Miranda) supplies human meat for the butcher lady next door. The butcher's head meat cutter, Tobias Ragg (Berwick Kaler) is not impressed with Todd's ability to swing a cleaver, and challenges him to a contest. The scenario becomes a competitive gore-fest as the two simpletons try to outdo one another. Along the way Todd's wife is hacked to bits, as is Ragg's girlfriend. Someone's breast winds up in a meat pie. The game is climaxed by a one-on-one cleaver duel in which both killers are killed. Advertisements for the film flung the metaphors fast and loose, proclaiming, "Sadism was just an appetizer for *The Bloodthirsty Butchers*. Their prime cuts were curiously erotic...but thoroughly brutal!"

Milligan surpassed this esoterica with *The Body Beneath* (1971), a grainy, ugly sex-horror film that was shot in the panoramic splendor of 16 millimeter. More recently, his pictures have been less horrific but no less horrible, with titles like *Guttertrash* (1972) and *Fleshpot on 42nd Street* (1973). Milligan and dozens of low-rent moviemakers like him have been attracted to the horror genre because of laziness (it's not difficult to splash stage blood on somebody) and monetary reward. Audience response is practically guaranteed; gore aficionados in the North are no more demanding than their counterparts in the hinterlands of Dixie. Milligan gave his fans what they wanted...and probably what they deserved.

"Can a Movie Go Too Far?" was the question posed by advertising for *Last House on the Left* (1972), a particularly unimaginative offshoot of the violent but artful cinema of director Sam Peckinpah. *Last House on the Left* was written and directed by Wes Craven, and produced by Sean Cunningham, a pair of struggling filmmakers who had collaborated in 1970 on a sex "documentary" entitled *Together*. Their first attempt at gore involves a group of young thugs who savagely rape and mutilate a pair of young women, only to suffer at the hands of the girls' family. As in Peckinpah's *Straw Dogs* (1971), the raison d'être of the proceedings is revenge, blunt and simpleminded. The approach was to become standard in the subgenre, and came to characterize a heartless brand of moviemaking that takes no prisoners.

The audience for *Last House on the Left* and the repellent pictures that followed grew as specialized and esoteric as the films themselves. Viewers knew not to expect characterization or complex motivations (indeed, they would have *resented* such presumption), but only expressions of fear and rage. And plenty of what Anthony Burgess' Alex called "the red red krovvy." Devotees of *Last House on the Left* applauded the moment in which the rapist's penis is bitten off; the sanguinary wackiness of Herschell Gordon Lewis had given way to grim-lipped unpleasantness.

Sean Cunningham segued into pornography and light comedy following the release of *Last House on the Left*, while Wes Craven moved on to *The Hills Have Eyes* (1977), which details the plight of a vacationing family that is victimized in the desert by a band of crazed cannibals. As in *Straw Dogs* and *Last House on the Left*, a bloody vengeance is carried out by heretofore nonviolent people. This sort of biblical justice (which had its most accessible application in Michael Winner's 1974 *Death Wish*) continued to have strong appeal for audiences. But the Craven films and their ilk were minor, independently-produced efforts that played drive-ins and urban theaters more often than they played the all-important suburban houses. A few, like *Snuff** (1976), were banned altogether in some towns. Concerned citizens did not react kindly to such rough stuff, often condemning the films on the basis of titles alone (a dangerous busines—rather like decrying chocolate mousse because antlers are inedible).

In 1974 an unknown Texas filmmaker named Tobe Hooper found himself at the center of a storm of controversy following the release of *The Texas Chain Saw Massacre*, a low-budget, independently made gore thriller

---

**Snuff is the American title of a low-grade Argentine film that its promoter, the late Allan Shackleton, touted as showing the actual dismemberment murder of an innocent actress. This led to ridiculous rumors of whole colonies of killer filmmakers in South America, where, as Shackleton's ad copy explained, "life is cheap."*

Gunnar Hansen (standing) and John Dugan in Tobe Hooper's outrageous *The Texas Chain Saw Massacre* (1974).

that defied the odds and found considerable exposure on suburban theater screens. Though relatively discreet in terms of graphicism, the film is highly disturbing, and more enervating than the most persistent nightmare. It is almost surely the most affecting gore thriller of all and, in a broader view, among the most effective horror films ever made.

Allegedly based on a true incident, the narrative of *The Texas Chain Saw Massacre* is more likely a much-altered version of the Ed Gein story. Kim

Henkel's script is mean, spare, and smart. In the broiling hinterlands of Texas, a vanload of young Northerners decides to detour to visit the (now empty) house of the grandmother of one of the travelers. The group is weary and ill-tempered, particularly Franklin (Paul A. Partain), an obese cripple who whines and sweats in his wheelchair. Sally (Marilyn Burns) quickly loses patience with her brother's childish prophecies of doom. The van picks up a hitchhiker (Edwin Neal), a peculiar young man whose face is disfigured with a hideous birthmark. He can talk of little else but his family's work history at the local slaughterhouse, claiming that his grandfather killed more steers in an hour than any other worker before or since.

The group is shocked when the hitchhiker takes a knife and inexplicably slices his own hand and sucks the blood. When he snaps a Polaroid of the travelers and demands payment, he is put out of the van. At the deserted house, another—inhabited—farmhouse is discovered in the field beyond. In search of gasoline, a boy and a girl from the group knock on the door. From this point, the film becomes a whirling plunge into paranoid horror: the young man is accosted by a bear-like figure in an apron and leather mask, clubbed on the head with an enormous mallet, and dragged out of sight behind a sliding steel door. His female companion stumbles into a living room littered with feathers, bones, and pieces of human bodies. She, too, is met at the steel door by Leatherface (Gunnar Hansen), who hoists her onto a meat hook. From this painful vantage point, the girl watches as her unconscious boyfriend is cut into filets by a chain saw.

As the afternoon wears into night, more of the youngsters are stalked and murdered. Finally, only Sally is left. She flees to a gas station for help, but is bound and gagged by the owner (Jim Siedow), who turns out to be Leatherface's father. At the house, Sally is tormented by the weird hitchhiker, who is Leatherface's brother. The girl's dismay over the mad conspiracy is heightened when it becomes apparent that her captors are cannibals who smoke, cure, and sell human flesh. Leatherface does most of the dirty work, but Sally has been reserved for Grandpa (John Dugan), a man so old and listless that he cannot grip a mallet long enough to bring it down on Sally's head. The girl finally crashes through a window and flees into the night. Leatherface—chain saw growling—chases after her. Sally is nearly sliced to bits, but escapes in the back of a passing pickup truck.

What is remarkable about *The Texas Chain Saw Massacre* is that its outrageous horrors seem entirely real. Hooper had an eye for the sort of vivid, nightmare image that would fester in the viewer's mind. Throughout, the heat and sweat of the Texas summer are almost palpable. The tone quickly becomes claustrophobic and pregnant with menace. Even mundane images, like an armadillo lying dead at the side of the highway, portend doom. The film opens with a slow pullback shot of a decaying corpse that has been lashed to a cross in a cemetery, and decorated like some obscene shrine. In voice-over we hear the drone of a radio news report that describes a rash of grave robbings in the area. Later, when the travelers stop at the gas station, we glimpse sizzling meat turning on barbeque spits. This not only recalls the opening and the hitchhiker's grisly anecdotes about the local slaughterhouse, but previews the hideous revelations yet to come. Hooper's most startling image is the first appearance of Leatherface, standing like an implacable monolith in his bloody apron. After the quivering body of the first victim has been whisked from sight and Leatherface slides the steel door shut, Hooper held his camera on the door for a full beat. There is no sound, no movement. The attack has been so sudden that the viewer wonders if it happened at all.

The cannibals are *so* crazy, *so* demented, that we don't know whether to scream or laugh. An armchair in the living room is festooned with real arms, and, idiotically, a fat chicken clucks and fusses from inside a tiny birdcage that hangs from the ceiling. When Leatherface uses his chain saw to carve his way into the house in order to continue his pursuit of the girl, his father's only admonition is, "Ya damn fool, ya ruined the door!" The family's joy is unrestrained when Sally is taken captive; the crazies jeer, poke, giggle, and caper as the screen rhythmically bulges with tight closeups of the girl's sweating face and panicked, darting eyes.

As Sally, Marilyn Burns gave a bravura performance. Surely no actress in film history has been called upon to scream more frenziedly or more often, and express as much raw hysteria. Sally's predicament seems especially awful because she is a pretty girl at the mercy of brutal men, but the fact of the matter is that her captors couldn't care less about her physical attributes. They are unmoved when Sally pleads, "I'll do anything you want. Anything!" Unlike the villains in most other gore films, Hooper's fiends are not sexually motivated. The driving force of *The Texas Chain Saw Massacre* is something far more horrible than aberrant sexuality: total insanity. The film is clearly not for all tastes or temperaments, but those hardy souls willing to experience it will be shocked, amused, and horrified in equal measure. The final image — one of Leatherface spinning in impotent rage after the girl's escape, chain saw clattering over his head — is among the most memorable and chilling in horror film history.

Tobe Hooper directed a little-seen horror film called *Eaten Alive* in 1975, then (along with writer Kim Henkel) came under the wing of producer-director William Friedkin. Things did not pan out at all for Henkel, and Hooper did not get another break until 1979, when he directed *Salem's Lot*, a well-done TV-movie that adapted Stephen King's best-selling vampire novel. Hooper returned to the big screen with *The Funhouse* (1981), a disappointingly flat effort about a deformed maniac who kills teenagers at a carnival. The film hurt Hooper's bankability, so some people were surprised when he was tapped by producer Steven Spielberg to direct *Poltergeist* (1982), a big-budget ghost story. Despite glossy, typically Spielbergian production values, special effects, and other visual touches (some sources insist that Spielberg directed the picture), *Poltergeist* is without menace or genuine scares. Its slickness is a far cry from the rough-and-tumble style Hooper brought to *The Texas Chain Saw Massacre*, a film he has yet to equal. His subsequent thrillers, *Lifeforce* (1985) and *Invaders from Mars* (1986), are uneven and unsatisfying, and were box office disasters.

Leatherface & Co. directly inspired a few films—notably Jeff Gillen's *Deranged* (1974) and Kevin Connor's highly amusing *Motel Hell* (1980), but the gore subgenre did not take its next giant step until late 1978, with the release of a film that paradoxically signalled both the box-office renaissance and eventual death of heavy-handed grue. The film was *Halloween*, a stylish, well-made thriller directed and written by John Carpenter, a USC film school graduate who had only two (good but minor) theatrical films to his credit. Like many of the better suspense thrillers, *Halloween* tells a story that is almost diagrammatical in its simplicity.

On Halloween night 1963 in the small midwestern town of Haddonville, a little boy named Michael Myers inexplicably slashes his older sister to death in her bedroom after the girl has made love with her boyfriend. Fifteen years later, on the anniversary of the murder, the now-grown killer escapes from a mental institution, masks himself, and returns to Haddonville to stalk *new* victims. Carpenter's use of the myth and iconography of Halloween is brilliant. Jack-o'-lanterns, figures in eerie costume, and especially the lure of dark streets became central elements of the story. The irony of a familiar suburban neighborhood abruptly turned into a place of terror is exploited with cleverness. Ordinary frame houses seem foreboding, and empty sidewalks assume an uneasy aspect. Teenager Laurie Strode (Jamie Lee Curtis) eventually becomes the focus of Michael's relentless energy. After two of Laurie's friends are slaughtered, she and the small children she is babysitting are trapped. At the climax of a prolonged and bloody encounter with Michael, Laurie is saved by the killer's psychiatrist (Donald Pleasence), who has managed to track down his charge. The doctor empties his revolver into Michael, who is knocked over a balcony to the lawn below. But moments later, the body is gone. Is he the unkillable bogeyman?

Unlike the victims in *Last House on the Left*, the teenage girls in *Halloween* are not killed with sexual violence, or even *because* of their own sexuality, although the latter may seem to be the case. As mentioned, Michael's sister dies just minutes after a passionless clutch-and-grope with her boyfriend. Similarly, Laurie's friend Annie (Nancy Loomis) indiscreetly strips in front of a window, then pads around the house in her underwear, unaware that the killer is watching her. Lynda (P.J. Soles) has a cheerful tumble with her own young swain, only to be strangled later after the young man she sexually teases turns out to be the fiend, and not her (now dead) boyfriend.

It is established that Laurie, unlike her friends, is serious and studious. She has no steady boyfriend, and seems only marginally interested in sex and dating. She is a proper girl who chokes and coughs after accepting a joint from Annie, and who is mortified after discovering that her friend has approached

The unkillable bogeyman (Nick Castle) in John Carpenter's trend-setting *Halloween* (1978).

a boy on her behalf. Laurie is a "good" girl, but that Carpenter meant to imply that Annie's and Lynda's sexual activities are capital offenses is remote. Laurie, infinitely more "straight" than her other friends, is not exempt from the terror. The *randomness* of Michael's violence, then, is the intelligence that sets *Halloween* apart from other, less thoughtful examples of the subgenre. Annie and Lynda are every bit as likeable as Laurie; they are certainly livelier and more engaging. Their deaths are not the result of their sexual habits, but of an unreasoning force that kills men and women with equal vigor; Lynda's boyfriend, for instance, is surprised in a dark kitchen, lifted into the air on the blade of a butcher knife, and impaled to a wall.

The violence of *Halloween* is shocking, not simply because of its physical terror, but because Carpenter took pains to see that we become involved with the imperiled youngsters. The kids are funny and energetic, full of sass and the idiosyncratic speech of youth. They worry about certain things, rejoice in others. We get the sense that the kids are real people, that they have personal histories and lives that extend beyond the borders of the movie screen. We *like* them. We lose something when they die.

The killer's disappearance at the conclusion of *Halloween* takes the film into the quasimythic realm of the fairy tale. Michael becomes a dark figure of the subconscious. Strikingly shot by Dean Cundey and constructed without clutter, *Halloween* remains popular and widely respected. The role of Laurie Strode provided an auspicious film debut for actress Jamie Lee Curtis, the angular, cheerfully attractive daughter of Tony Curtis and Janet Leigh. She went on to play the "innocent-girl-in-peril" in *Terror Train* (1980) and *Prom Night* (1980)—both uninteresting and essentially innocuous "slasher" films—had a more substantial role in John Carpenter's splendid ghost story *The Fog* (1980), then reprised her role as Laurie in *Halloween II* (1981), a ham-handed sequel to the original film that was written by Carpenter and directed by Rick Rosenthal.

Carpenter is a major talent, but his weaknesses as a writer became quite apparent in the sequel, which sags with contrivance. Laurie is admitted to a local hospital after her harrowing experience with the killer, only to discover that Michael is alive and prowling the hospital corridors, looking for her. Stupidly, Curtis was restricted to little more than a cameo. Supposedly under sedation, she spends the film in bed or lethargically dragging herself along the floor. In the first film, Laurie is alert and supremely brave, defending herself at one point with nothing but a straightened coat hanger and her wits. In the sequel, the girl is a mumbling sack of incoherence, allowed to whisper barely a dozen lines.

Carpenter compounded this fundamental mistake by revealing (quite pointlessly) that Michael Myers is Laurie's long-lost brother. Who cares? The power of the first film lies in its believable characters and the appalling randomness of the violence that is directed against them. Murder without motivation is the most frightening sort, but Carpenter unaccountably betrayed this insight in *Halloween II*. Director Rosenthal interpreted Carpenter's violent set pieces slickly but without conviction.* "Let's do a gory car crash!" the script demanded, so Rosenthal did a gory car crash. "Let's have the killer stab a pretty nurse in the back with a scalpel and lift her off the floor with it!" So Rosenthal did that, too. In a particularly unappealing and gratuitous sequence, a young nurse who has hopped naked into a hot tub to await her boyfriend is held beneath the water and scalded to death. Her blistered face and body are examined in pitiless closeup. Another nurse is knocked unconscious and hooked to a blood tube so that all her blood may be drained away onto the floor. These victims are minor, secondary characters about whom we learn nothing and care little. Unlike the well-developed characters in *Halloween*, Rosenthal's victims exist only to be slaughtered.

Halloween II is a well-mounted film, but one that gives in totally to the sort of improbable idiocy that typifies the worst examples of the gore subgenre. The hospital in which Laurie continues her battle with the maniac is surely the world's darkest, with corridors as dim and deserted as a catacomb. The killer hardly has to exert himself since most of his victims simply blunder into dark rooms and into his arms. No one thinks of turning on the lights. Time and again, characters act against all logic, taking unnecessary risks or fleeing in precisely the wrong direction. *Halloween II* isn't a movie, but a pointless game, a set-up.

Major film distributors ignored gore cinema until the original *Halloween*, which made so much loot for tiny Compass International (in excess of $45 million) that the film became the most successful independent production to that time. Inevitably, "prestige" studios moved to exploit the subgenre. In 1980 director Sean Cunningham, perhaps tiring of the skin films and insipid comedies that had occupied his time since he produced *Last House on the Left*, completed a low-budget thriller called *Friday the 13th*. Much in the manner of rock 'n' roll "answer records" of the fifties—in which a new song would follow up or "answer" an established hit (usually by another artist)— *Friday the 13th* exploited the violence and holiday motif of *Halloween*. Paramount Pictures, seeing dollar signs, picked up Cunningham's film for distribution and made a fortune with it.

Like *Halloween*, *Friday the 13th* has a plot that is simple in the extreme: in 1958, teenage counselors at Camp Crystal Lake would rather play doctor than look after their young charges. As a result, a little boy drowns. Later, a number of the teens are stabbed to death by an (unseen) assailant. Flashforward to the present, as Camp Crystal Lake is about to open for the first time in 22 years. A new set of giggly teens is ready to assume staff duties. But before the summer has barely begun—surprise!—the gory murders resume. A la *Ten Little Indians*, the kids are stalked and savaged one by one. The *big* surprise

---

Carpenter directed a few pointedly gruesome moments himself, after Rosenthal had completed principal photography.

is that the murderer is kindly Mrs. Voorhees (Betsy Palmer), mother of the boy who drowned years earlier. Cornered, the last surviving teenager (Adrienne King) hefts an axe and (in de rigueur slow motion) severs Mrs. Voorhees' head from her body.

In a technical sense, *Friday the 13th* is not a badly made film. By 1980, Cunningham had become a reasonably slick director, leagues ahead of the likes of H.G. Lewis and Andy Milligan. Perhaps it is *because* of Cunningham's undeniable skill that *Friday the 13th* is infinitely more insulting than, say, *Blood Feast*. One hesitates to say that Cunningham was slumming, but he was clearly capable of far more than the uninspired garbage movie that Paramount so gleefully bought and promoted. The picture was savaged by critics, most of whom have no fondness for horror movies, anyway. By this time, horror cinema seemed on the verge of becoming an ugly, disreputable ghetto, the manure pile of Hollywood. At the top of the pile sat *Friday the 13th*, the archetypal gore film, burdened with a script that plays like a *Mad* magazine parody. When a girl stops in a small town and inquires as to the location of Camp Crystal, she is greeted by *highly* significant looks from the locals. Intones one old coot, "You mean...Camp *Blood*?!" Mercy me.

Throughout the film, teenage boys are hideously dispatched, but not with the same buildup and attention to detail that Cunningham and makeup wiz Tom Savini reserved for the nubile girls. One lengthy sequence involves a particularly pretty young lady (Laurie Bartram) who is alone in a dark shower room. She is dressed only in a T-shirt and panties, garb which elicits from the viewer feelings of apprehension (we have, after all, been down this road before) *and* sexual anticipation. Contributing to the scene's unease are odd shadows, peculiar noises, and subjective camera angles (which very quickly become a tiresome and disturbing staple of the subgenre; in essence, the technique turns the viewer into the killer). Finally, the girl pulls aside a shower curtain and confronts the killer, i.e. the camera. In unblinking closeup, the girl's face is split with an axe. Later, a boy is shot in the eye with an arrow, and another youth is impaled from beneath by an iron spike that rips through his mattress and exits through his throat. A girl who has the temerity to hitchhike is stalked through the woods after leaping from the moving car, and dies when her throat is slowly, lovingly slit.

Not surprisingly, unsophisticated audiences reacted to all this misery with great glee. Subsequent gore films — disinterested in characterization and logic — became showcases for this sort of graphic mayhem. Filmmakers remained mindful of the short attention span and boredom level of their young audiences by striving to outdo themselves. Each murder had to be more startling, grisly, and inventive than the last. Over time, the viewer becomes more concerned with the aesthetics of slaughter than with the pain and fear of the victims.

Friday the 13th Part II (1981; directed by Steve Miner) covers the same dreary ground as its predecessor. In the opening, actress Adrienne King (the only survivor of the first film) opens her refrigerator and is greeted by the head of Mrs. Voorhees. Yow! Pretty neat, eh? Enter Jason, Mrs. Voorhees' son who — omigosh, *another* surprise! — didn't drown in 1958, after all. Ms. King is disposed of when Jason slides an icepick into her brain. The killer returns to Camp Crystal, where a whole new crop of dumb teenagers awaits the bloody harvest. The faces are different this time, but since Miner's camera pays more attention to the bottoms, thighs, and bosoms of the young victims, nobody cares. A handsome boy who is confined to a wheelchair is struck in the face with a machete, a man is garroted with barbed wire, and a beautiful young girl is slaughtered after she provocatively strips and goes for a moonlit skinny-dip.

Most perniciously, a young couple is killed in the middle of lovemaking, a spike driven through the boy's back, into the body of the girl beneath, and into the floor. This slap in the face of romance was apparently the limit for the previously tolerant MPAA ratings board, which threatened an "X" rating if this and other graphic makeup effects by Carl Fullerton were not toned down with editing. Paramount acquiesced, but even the final version of the lovemaking scene is hardly an advertisement for the tender joys of coitus.

Friday the 13th Part II was a commercial success, and was followed by Steve Miner's *Friday the 13th, 3-D*, which was one of the big hits of the 1982 summer season. Plot, characterization, and logic remained moribund, but now we were able to savor the blood and viscera as it squirted into our laps. In the opening moments, a boy's skull is crushed with such force that one of his eyeballs pops from its socket and flies at the camera. Later, another boy is neatly cut in half, his upper body falling one way, his legs another. On the distaff side, a pretty girl is shot in the eye with a spear gun. The 3-D effects are startling and effective on a big screen, but then, brain surgery is so much more interesting if you're right there in the operating room. Who needs it? In any case, director Paul Morrissey had already explored the limits of 3-D gore in *Andy Warhol's Frankenstein* (1974), a film that comes remarkably close to duplicating the wicked fun of Grand Guignol.* Steve Miner and Paramount made their 3-D film anyway, apparently reasoning that no one should go through adolescence without having a warm liver flung in his or her face.

The gore film "holiday motif" was carried on by pictures like *Mother's Day* (1980; in which someone is done in by an electric carving knife), *New Year's Evil* (1981), and *My Bloody Valentine* (1981; in which a pickaxe poked through a man's throat emerges from his eye). What, no *Ground Hog's Day*? Paranoia, a key element of the subgenre, was exploited in the admonitory titles of *Don't Look in the Basement* (1974), *Don't Open the Window* (1976), *Don't Answer the Phone* (1981), *Don't Go in the House* (1981), and *Don't Go*

The audience knows that Morrissey's film is not to be taken seriously when Dr. Frankenstein (Udo Kier) clambers atop his female creation and exults, "To know life, one must fuck death in the gall bladder!"

in the Woods Alone (1982). If the popularity of the subgenre had not cooled, teenagers would not have been allowed to do *anything* except go to these hopeless movies.

The decline of the gore film can be laid to a number of factors, chief among them that the audience finally grew weary of variations on a one-note theme. How many possible ways can a person be killed? After a seemingly endless series of answers, the question became tiresome. Unfavorable public opinion also contributed to the subgenre's demise. Gene Siskel and Roger Ebert, film critics seen on PBS's *Sneak Previews*, mounted an energetic campaign against slasher films, urging viewers to write letters to guilty studios and actors, and to boycott theaters that exhibited the films. Siskel, in particular, has no fondness for horror films or understanding of the genre, and the pair's comments at times were not terribly well informed. Still, a case can be made that the proliferation of gore constituted a sort of abuse of power.

Ebert and Siskel focused much of their attention on *I Spit on Your Grave* (1979), a little charmer about a young woman (Camille Keaton) who exacts a bloody revenge on four goons who have repeatedly beaten and gang-raped her. Director Meir Zarchi carried the revenge motif to the *n*th degree, as the men are hacked, stabbed, shot, hanged, and otherwise mutilated. Unpleasant as this film is, it at least shows a woman fighting back.

Ebert and Siskel notwithstanding, the absolute nadir of the subgenre must surely be *Maniac* (1980), an 87-minute murder and mutilation show that dismayed even the most ardent gorehounds. The plot? Frank Zito (Joe Spinell) hates his late mother. His animosity causes him to murder beautiful young women, and anyone else who gets in his way. He scalps his victims and uses their bloody hair to decorate the mannequins he keeps in his tiny apartment. He frequently brings the mannequins into his bed. At the climax, the mannequins come to life and literally twist Zito's head from his body in a welter of blood and meat. The end.

Along the way, a young woman is impaled through the back by a machete. Another is slowly, carefully scalped, her blood running down her face as the killer lifts off the top of her head. A man in a parked car is shotgunned at point-blank range, his head exploding in slow motion (courtesy of the ubiquitous Tom Savini). In the most vile moment of all, Zito spreadeagles a woman on her own bed, binds her ankles and wrists, and stabs her in the chest. In idle moments, the killer stalks a young fashion model (Caroline Munro) whose femaleness and beauty, Zito determines, are crimes punishable by her death.

So there we have it; ninety years after the Lumière brothers astonished Parisian audiences with the moving images that became the foundation of the motion picture industry, 24-year-old director William Lustig created *Maniac*,

Gore film heroine Amy Steel in a situation typical of the subgenre. *Friday the 13th Part II* (1981).

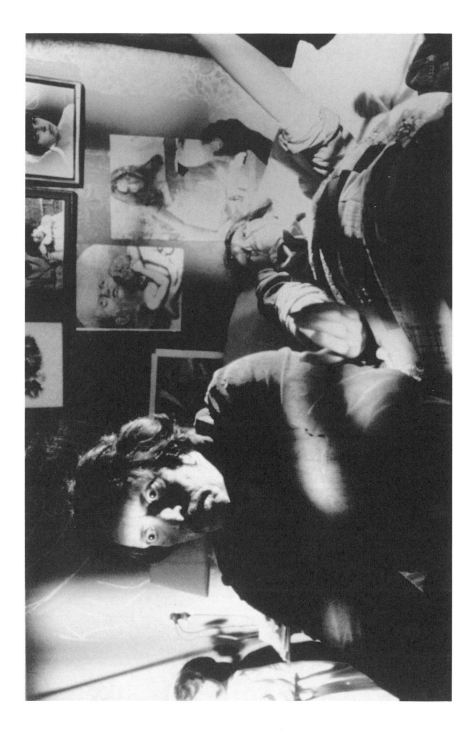

demonstrating that he cared to learn nothing from the inspiring glory of film history.

The crude, repetitive violence of gore cinema is not nearly as unnerving as its constant juxtaposition with undressed young women and physical love, two happy elements of human life, but transformed by film after film into the stuff of nightmare. That these movies found an enthusiastic audience among the young is no wonder — what boy or girl hasn't pondered the consequences of sexual activity, or marveled at the seeming mysteriousness of it all? Gore filmmakers unfairly exploited the insecurities of their audience by offering a distressingly conservative, even vengeful morality in the guise of trendiness and free-spiritedness. Gore cinema is not liberating (though the kids who flocked to the theaters may think otherwise), but suffocating, the work of cynical adults having a go at the vulnerability of children. At least earlier filmmakers like George Romero and even Herschell Lewis had a bit of a laugh as they catered to the unsophisticated tastes of the young. Most of the graphic movies that came later are as humorless as they are predictable. And they may be dangerous, not simply because they objectify women and inure us to violence, but because they offer a subliminal message, a warning that the penalties for tenderness, sexual curiosity, and gaeity are torture, mutilation, and death. The films imply that we must prepare to become victims, and resign ourselves to fates so horrible as to make meaningless the joys of our lives. Lacking artistry, lacking a philosophy, the typical gore film does not inspire us to embrace life, but to shrink from it. The spawn of Herschell Gordon Lewis, then, is not simply a generation of insensitive movies, but a generation of desensitized *people*.

Joe Spinell in William Lustig's *Maniac* (1980), the nadir of the gore subgenre.

XII
The Shape of Sex to Come

Not far from Los Angeles International Airport a mammoth sign in front of an adult bookstore-theater on Century Boulevard proclaims, "Live Nude Nudes!" The sign invariably provokes a laugh: one out-of-town visitor asked, "As opposed to what?: 'Live *Clothed* Nudes?' " "Perhaps '*Dead* Clothed Nudes,' " I offered. The jokes being made, it may not be quite as funny to consider that on a stretch of prime Los Angeles real estate that includes respected hotels and restaurants, passed daily by thousands of visitors and commuters, stands a gaudy sign that urges passers-by to indulge their voyeurism and marvel at the "Live Nude Nudes."

It would be foolish to suggest that a society is endangered when it allows disinterested young women to prance naked along dimly lit runways for the amusement of bored travelers and businessmen. Still, the steady encroachment of such places into our daily lives (or at least the *proximity* of our lives) is cause for concern, not because it is arguably immoral but because it suggests the limits of our indifferentness and boredom. So drugged are we with the peurile sexuality offered by television, magazines, film, and books that precious little captures our attention, let alone arouses genuine interest. Perhaps the childish redundancy of the theater sign is purposeful, designed to catch the eyes of people so inundated with sexual come-ons that they do not care to respond to any more.

Sexuality itself is one message that will never grow stale. What we are really concerned about here is *packaging*: the manner of presentation. How does one attract the attention of a jaded public? This dilemma is especially acute for filmmakers, who must anticipate trends as well as react to them. As the core of the moviegoing audience has grown younger since the early fifties, the filmmaker's challenge has been heightened. Although youngsters do not realize that there is a finite number of sexual points of view, they are scrupulously aware of the manner in which those points of view are presented. Tastes change with blinding speed: the disco romance that excited audiences in the seventies is now as dead as the Virginia Reel. Likewise, the highly sexual "slasher" films of the seventies had nearly vanished by the early eighties.

Sexuality, then, has come to be defined (in the popular eye, at any rate) through its association with the trends and fads of the moment, and not through innate truthfulness. Films as sexually honest as Daniel Petrie's *Resurrection* (1980), for instance, are rare, especially since *Resurrection* is not at all predicated upon sexuality. In other words, it is not *selling* sex. A more recent norm was set by Adrian Lyne's *Flashdance* (1983), the Bob Fosse-esque adventures of a Pittsburgh welder who sheds her clothes after eight hours on the job and dances with so much skill and boundless energy that she finds fulfillment and true love. The improbabilities of the script are obscured by glitzy choreography, pounding rock 'n' roll, and an attractive, half-dressed female star.

Horror, the most graphic and psychosexually unrestrained movie genre, has historically enjoyed a great deal of packaging leeway. The genre has been exposed in period settings, in outer space, in small Southern towns, and on suburban streets. The sexual message can be stated as subtly as in *The Innocents* (1961; see Chapter III), or blatantly, as in *Vampire Hookers* (1978). But because the horror audience has become more narrow and specialized (that is, younger) in recent years, filmmakers have had to satisfy a stricter set of conventions. Period horror films, for instance, have not been in vogue since the early seventies. Contemporary audiences seem most eager to see recognizable reflections of their own lives and concerns. Along with this has come the great liberalization of screen standards that has been mentioned several times in this book.

So the modern purveyors of horror films know more clearly than their predecessors what is expected of them. The twin themes of sex and death must be packaged so that they shock, amuse, and mirror. Above all, moviemakers must remember that the members of their audience have been desensitized by the media as much as they have been educated by it. Their boredom threshhold is alarmingly low. This of course accounts for the preponderance of bad horror films. The gory equivalent of *Flashdance* is easy to create and easy to market. It is the rare genre filmmaker who can satisfy a youthful audience without selling out.

While significant genre directors of the past like James Whale, Karl Freund, and Alfred Hitchcock were inarguably wed to the traditional studio system, some important figures of more recent years have come in through the system's back door by offering independent, even non–Hollywood productions. Of these directors, George Romero and John Carpenter are probably the most celebrated. Because film distribution has not been strictly studio-controlled since the fifties, film marketing is a wide-open ball game. A director's avenues of expression now include not only theater screens that would have been closed to him in the past, but cable television and videocassettes. Some particularly iconoclastic films find their first success on the midnight movie cult circuit. Foreign markets can be huge. By all indications, tolerance for nontraditional films and methods of distribution will increase. The talented horror directors whose films have best epitomized recent sexual attitudes and suggested future directions have taken advantage of the stylistic and merchandising freedom in ways that are divergent, but not startlingly so.

Brian DePalma, at one time perhaps the most audacious of Hollywood's big-studio filmmakers, began his career with small satiric films made on the cheap in New York City. Even after coming to Hollywood for *Get to Know Your Rabbit* (1972) DePalma temporarily retreated to the freedom offered by independent filmmaking. Other significant figures, like David Lynch and Paul Bartel, also began on the fringe and later learned to work within the system. The points of view of directors David Cronenberg and John Waters, however, are such that they have not been expressed in Hollywood productions; Cronenberg makes no secret of his antipathy for the town, and Waters would not go even if the moviemaking establishment slipped a cog and asked him. Each of these directors *has* found wide distribution for his films. Beyond this, what they have in common is a fascination with disturbed sexuality, and a talent for expressing its links to horror, violence, and death.

Brian DePalma is not simply a skilled, major-studio director who draws much of his inspiration from Alfred Hitchcock, but an insightful social satirist whose early films — *Greetings* (1968) and *Hi, Mom!* (1970) among them — reflect a love of theatrical tradition, and an affectionate understanding of the sorts of eccentrics who made the sixties such an invigorating decade. Unhappily, these early films were poorly distributed and have not been widely seen.

DePalma's energy has never diminished, but his better-known films have the point of view of a director who seems to have been shaped entirely by the popular cinema. With the exception of *Carrie* (1976), the pictures that made DePalma's name are so stylized and improbable that one is tempted to believe that the director spent the better part of his life in movie theaters. His highly eclectic approach to the suspense-horror genre has served him splendidly at times, and failed at others.

After *Get to Know Your Rabbit* and a failed relationship with a major studio (Warners), DePalma once again turned to independent moviemaking, and directed *Sisters* (1973), an eccentric, highly charged thriller that firmly linked DePalma with the legacy of Hitchcock. With a fragmented narrative approach and judicious use of visual tricks like split screen, DePalma created a gruesome, often witty portrait of schizophrenia and sexual madness. Danielle (Margot Kidder) is a French-Canadian model in Montreal who becomes attracted to a reporter named Phillip Woode (Lisle Wilson). Woode invites Danielle to dinner, where they are briefly interrupted by Danielle's ex-husband, Emile (Bill Finley), a nervous, myopic man who suggests more than a bit of dementia. After a night of lovemaking at Danielle's apartment, Woode awakens to the sounds of Danielle arguing in another room with her sister, Dominique. We do not see the argument, but it is a spirited one that revolves around the presence of Woode. The reporter leaves the apartment and picks up a cake as a peace offering, but is stabbed to death by a young woman who had appeared to be sleeping on Danielle's couch. Another reporter, Grace Collier (Jennifer Salt), witnesses Woode's death throes from an adjoining building. Grace calls the police, but Danielle has already

Margot Kidder as the demented twin in Brian DePalma's *Sisters*(1973).

enlisted Emile's aid in hiding Woode's body inside a sofa bed. Danielle knows that Dominique is the murderer. By the time the police arrive at Danielle's apartment, there is no evidence of the violence. Grace's position is further weakened because her newspaper columns have marked her as an antagonist of the police.

The remainder of *Sisters* is very much in the Hitchcock mold, as Grace teams with a private investigator (Charles Durning) in order to uncover evidence that will convince the police. Finally, we learn the Danielle and Dominique were Siamese twins who had been surgically separated while children. As any reasonably astute thriller fan can guess, Dominique died during the operation, but remained alive in Danielle's guilt-ridden mind. Danielle — under the periodic influence of her late sister — is a murderer.

Sisters is essentially a sick joke, as much a sendup of Hitchcock as it is an homage. Hitchcock dealt with guilt-motivated sexual violence in *Psycho*, but DePalma exaggerated the premise almost — but not quite — to the point of silliness. *Sisters* opens with a clip from an apocryphal game show called *Peeping Tom*, a program which apparently translates voyeurism into big ratings and prizes. Danielle is a contestant, and pretends to be a blind girl who strips for an eager male peeper.* Danielle's prize is a full set of gleaming cutlery. The essence of the game show is repeated later when Danielle undresses in front of Phillip Woode—life imitates "art," but the innocent cutlery becomes an instrument of sexual terror.

Grace Collier's witnessing of Woode's death throes—voyeurism of a particularly unpleasant sort—adds the essence of *Rear Window* to a story that already has heavy undertones of *Psycho* and *The Man Who Knew Too Much.* Grace's growing paranoia becomes a point of grim humor: "That body is here somewhere and she knows it!" Grace complains to the police, as the camera pans to a solitary bloodstain on the back of the white sofa bed. But Grace later begins to doubt her own eyes, and when she falls into the hands of Emile (who, in an oddball contrivance, turns out to be a psychiatrist) she slides into a quasi-nightmare world where people make distinctions between mental patients and "real people." Grace is institutionalized, and in one gruesome sequence imagines that she and Danielle were twins, and they were separated with a meat cleaver. DePalma suggests that sexual madness is contagious. After Grace is hypnotized by Emile, she claims there was no murder. But the private detective discovers the body in a rural express station far from Montreal.

Though the film sags for a long period at its midpoint when Kidder is off the screen (Salt's Grace Collier is neither likeable nor interesting), and is not quite as urgent as Bernard Herrmann's pulsing score suggests, *Sisters* brought the then 29-year-old DePalma to the attention of the world film community. Critics seemed agreeable to the young director's plot contrivances because, well, Hitchcock played similar games. *Sisters* is more style than substance. Overbearing in moments, its energy and provocative theme ultimately triumph. DePalma's eclecticism was hailed by the critical establishment. Hitchcock's view of sexuality became a springboard for DePalma, who fully articulated themes that the master only suggested.

DePalma's *Phantom of the Paradise* (1974) is not only a hip reworking of Gaston Leroux's *The Phantom of the Opera* (see Chapter IV) but a pastiche of elements from *The Cabinet of Dr. Caligari, Dracula,* and *The Picture of Dorian Gray.* In DePalma's version of the Leroux story, the disfigured composer (Bill Finley) lives for rock, and falls for Phoenix (Jessica Harper), an attractive backup singer. The Phantom secretly guides Phoenix's career but is frustrated by Swan (Paul Williams), the diminutive and devious musician who has stolen the Phantom's rock masterpiece and passed it off as his own.

When Swan seduces Phoenix it is with the knowledge that the Phantom is observing the scene through a skylight. As a thunderstorm fills the sky, the Phantom rages at Swan's cruelty and presumption. The force of nature almost seems to pale before the Phantom's sexual fury. DePalma undercut some of the impact of this and similar moments with the absurdity of certain of the

---

The accuracy with which DePalma's absurd game show anticipated real-life cable television programs of the eighties is remarkable.

story's particulars; Leroux's Phantom, for instance, is disfigured in a fire but DePalma's is mangled when his head is caught in a demonic record-pressing machine. This bizarre sense of humor, coupled with almost-constant movie in-jokes and allusions, makes *Phantom of the Paradise* a bit of a trial for a viewer who is not equipped or in the mood to play the director's game.

The film is successful as an exercise in style, but the style is not a sort that is easily assimilated. DePalma produced the picture independently for $1.3 million and sold it to 20th Century–Fox for $2 million. Pundits (DePalma among them) guessed it would gross in excess of $30 million, but the film barely earned its original cost on its first run. Fox may have bungled the marketing campaign by selling the picture á la *Woodstock*, but a reasonable guess as to the reason for the film's failure would be that the particularly eccentric tone that DePalma brought to his small, early features simply did not apeal to a mass audience. *Phantom*'s story — sexual overtones included — got lost in the glitter.

DePalma returned to more traditional (though more convoluted) ground with *Obsession* (1976), a resolutely romantic sexual thriller that is both highly derivative and artistically satisfying. In a screenplay patterned after that of *Vertigo*, Michael Courtland (Cliff Robertson) is morbidly preoccupied with the memory of his wife and daughter, both of whom were killed sixteen years before in a bungled kidnap attempt. He blames himself for their deaths, and builds a mammoth monument to their memory (their bodies could not be found in the swirling Mississippi) on a parcel of valuable land he owns in New Orleans. Courtland has refused over the years to develop this land, and in the time since 1959 has become well-off but not rich, much to the chagrin of his partner Bob LaSalle (John Lithgow).

On a business junket to Florence, Courtland visits the church in which he met his wife, and is stunned and astonished to see a young woman who is his wife's double. She is Sandra (Genevieve Bujold), an art historian whom Courtland soon tries to remake in the image and function of the late Elizabeth. Courtland concerns himself with the manner of Sandra's walk ("It's not a Bryn Mawr walk," he complains), how she wears her hair, and the way in which she addresses him. Sandra is gradually caught up in Courtland's obsessive fantasy, and attempts to learn all she can about her predecessor. She agrees to marry Courtland, and returns with him to New Orleans.

When Sandra is kidnapped in (seemingly) the same way as Elizabeth had been sixteen years earlier, Courtland seizes the moment as his chance for vindication, to prove to Elizabeth that he loved her, and that if he failed once, he will not fail again. As in 1959, he goes to LaSalle, begging business concessions so that he can lay his hands on the demanded half million in cash. LaSalle can hardly believe what is happening, and agrees to take Courtland's share of the company only to "protect the land." But at the bank the cash is switched for cut paper, so the ransom Courtland throws from a riverboat is just as worthless as what he tossed in 1959.

There is of course a hook here and a surprise, as well: it was LaSalle who engineered the original kidnapping; Sandra's disappearance is his second attempt to wrest control of the land from Courtland. The surprise, which is that Sandra is Courtland's own daughter, is not really much of a surprise at all, but it's all right because DePalma did not play it as his only card. We learn that Sandra's keep in Florence was financed over the years by "Uncle Bob," and that the girl has grown up with a hatred of her father, believing him responsible for the death of her mother. At first eager to conspire with LaSalle, she now loves Courtland, and attempts suicide. Courtland, unaware that Sandra is his daughter but in a rage at being duped, stabs LaSalle with scissors and hurries to polish off the young woman. But at the airport Sandra calls Courtland "Daddy." The camera whirls about them, carousel-like, as they embrace.

Like many of Hitchcock's finest films, *Obsession* is plot-heavy and full of improbable incident. Like the master, though, DePalma exhibited a sure touch: the narrative is bold and direct, the pace swift when speed is needed. The big question is whether or not there is a point to DePalma's slavish emulation of Hitchcock's style. Besides a haunting, Hitchcockian score by Bernard Herrmann, we are treated to subjective camera setups intercut with reaction shots, Courtland's glimpses of (seemingly) menacing policemen, and special emphasis upon a key, à la *Notorious*. At one point, there is an elegant crane shot over a stairway, as in *Psycho*.

DePalma's admiration of Hitchcock went beyond the visual and aural into the thematic; he shared with the older director a love of cheery vulgarity, as when Sandra's swinging derriere is juxtaposed with the naked posteriors of Florentine statues. More darkly, the film carries an unmistakable scent of perverseness and psychological rot. But is there a *point* to all this? Yes, and it is that DePalma augmented Hitchcock's vision with his own. *Obsession* is less objective, more romantic than *Vertigo*. There is an elegiac quality to many of the scenes, and a gentle idyllicism in others. The 1959 sequences were shot through a veil and under diffused light, and suggest a faint unreality. Courtland's first full gaze from Sandra is in excrutiatingly beautiful slow motion, which makes his romantic dream a reality. DePalma and screenwriter Paul Schrader* seemed concerned with the fate of a romantic philosophy when it must deal with the venality of the real world. We know Courtland is a sensitive man because he speaks sincerely of preserving "the graceful values of the Old South" (which, sadly, are largely illusory), and a terribly vulnerable one when he solemnly says, "Beauty should be protected."

There is none of the poet in Courtland's partner, LaSalle, whose aesthetic sense does not extend beyond modish vested suits. He is a lonely and embittered man who views life as nothing but a run for material prizes. Courtland's

---

Schrader has become a major writer-director whose intense, stylish films often explore unpleasant sexuality; see Taxi Driver *(1976; directed by Martin Scorsese),* Hardcore *(1979), and* American Gigolo *(1980).*

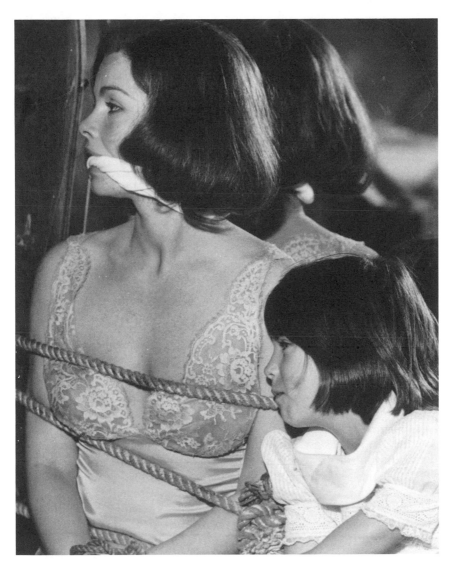

The perils of love commitments: mother (Genevieve Bujold) and daughter (Wanda Blackman) at the mercy of kidnappers in Brian DePalma's *Obsession* (1976).

butterfly-delicate philosophies are no match for this sort of pragmatism. LaSalle takes advantage of Courtland's morbidity (the tomb of Elizabeth and the little girl is fashioned after the facade of the church in Florence) and exploits his partner's guilt.

The film's conclusion, as father and daughter embrace, is ambiguous. Can Courtland recover his senses and accept his woman as his daughter, or will his psychic necrophilia become incest? Whatever, DePalma's points about the dangers and ultimate rewards of emotional and sexual commitment have been made. Cliff Robertson's performance is marvelously real, his eyes glowing and that fine Midwestern voice halting as Courtland tries as hard as he is able to vindicate himself and recapture past innocence. Genevieve Bujold, with her boyish beauty, projected an appeal both elegant and old-fashioned, suggesting a physical vulnerability that is an apt complement to the emotional fragility of Courtland. The film is rich with this sort of sexual and emotional counterpoint.

Though not a horror film in the traditional sense, *Obsession* certainly revolves around the horrors of the heart and mind. Because it is a portrait of a family in psychosexual turmoil, the film is a splendid companion piece to *Sisters*. DePalma seems fascinated with the fragility of relationships and the perils of love commitments. He is also interested in the brute *power* of sexuality, and the way in which that power can be misunderstood and misused. If sexuality is a gift, then it can also be a curse, a consideration which leads to *Carrie* (1976), the director's most popular film, and the one that "made" his career.

By marrying Grand Guignol sensibilities with the traumas of adolescence and parenting, DePalma created a terrifying instance of repressed and repressive sexuality. *Carrie* is essentially the Cinderella story tricked up with telekinesis and bloody special effects. The unloved maiden is Carrie White (Sissy Spacek), a waif-like high school senior whose clumsiness and naïveté make her the butt of her classmates' cruel jokes. Her only talent is the ability to move objects with the force of her mind. Carrie's fanatically religious mother (Piper Laurie) has raised her daughter with the belief that sex is filthy and that men are inherently evil. Carrie believes that she is to blame for her own misery. She has no sexual knowledge, only ignorance and fearful longings. When she menstruates for the first time while showering after gym class, the other girls ridicule her childlike panic by pummeling her with fresh sanitary napkins. Carrie's mother is in torment at this news, not because she feels guilty for never having told her daughter about menstruation, or even because Carrie has been humiliated, but because Carrie is now a woman, and the men "will start sniffing around like dogs."

A sympathetic phys ed teacher (Betty Buckley) and a classmate (Amy Irving) try to bolster Carrie's self-image by arranging a prom date with the class Adonis, Tommy Ross (William Katt). At the dance, Carrie seems on the verge of coming out of her shell, but she has been conspired against by Chris (Nancy Allen), the class bitch, and Chris's dullard boyfriend (John Travolta). As Carrie and Tommy are being honored as king and queen of the prom (the result of a rigged election), a bucket of pig's blood drops from the rafters. Carrie's mortification causes her to draw deep inside herself and unleash the full range of her telekinesis (which had previously been turned to such mundane uses as exploding light bulbs and flipping objects off tabletops). Doors slam shut, power is short-circuited, and the gaily decorated gymnasium becomes a

DePalma's *Carrie* (1976; Sissy Spacek), the mortified Cinderella who will shortly exact a terrible revenge upon her tormentors.

howling conflagration. Carrie — almost comatose — exits, locking the doors behind her. Nearly all of the graduating class and faculty go up in flames.

At home, Carrie bathes, then seeks comfort in the arms of her mother. But Mrs. White, believing Carrie has been marked by the devil, stabs her. Dying, Carrie uses her power a final time to impale her mother (in a hideous, orgasmic parody of the martyred St. Sebastian) with the kitchen cutlery, and causes the house to sink into the bowels of the earth.

Stephen King's original novel is clever and diverting. Structured in semidocumentary style, it is believable but hasn't quite the emotional impact of DePalma's adaptation. The film shows an almost impeccable understanding of the miseries of female adolescence. Though pretty, Carrie has never been given cause to believe it, so she dresses mousily and cultivates a mumbling shyness. Her possible role models—her mother, the catty Chris, the leggy and self-assured gym teacher—are negative or hopelessly out of reach. The film opens with a lingering, slow motion tour of the girls' steamy locker room as a dozen young Venuses towel and caress their bodies. This is Carrie's competition and it is fierce. Carrie, huddled alone in the shower, soaps herself with the ambivalence of a girl who feels the first stirrings of womanhood. Her menstrual flow cascades down the inside of her thighs like a portent. The other girls—hardly more secure in their own sexuality—cannot resist taunting Carrie for her panic.

Because Carrie has no father and a stifling mother, the influence of the high school becomes exaggerated. It is the place of the girl's humiliation, but also of her dreams; when Tommy Ross recites a love poem in English class, Carrie blurts "It's beautiful!" Predictably, the class giggles, as though Carrie has no right to such feelings. Ironically, Carrie is *especially* deserving of romance. Though she has not mastered her sexuality, she makes a conscious effort to put it to gentle use. The bitchy Chris is Carrie's converse, almost a caricature of the high school femme fatale: blonde hair, wet lips, firm little body, and perpetual come-on attitude—the archetypal cock tease. Her boyfriend thinks he's in control of the relationship and tries to prove it by slapping the girl around occasionally, but he's just a little boy whom Chris manipulates like Silly Putty. At the climax, Chris and the boy are killed when Carrie's mind causes the boy's car to crash and explode. Chris's sexual weapons are commonplace and cosmeticized. Carrie's—unfettered when expressed through her telekinesis—are far more formidable. Her psychic talent is *so* sexually focused, in fact, that the power would probably vanish or at least be greatly diminished if Carrie's frustrations were to be resolved.

Carrie is a very melodramatic film—circumstance conspires against the girl with remorseless precision. Even the God Carrie's mother forces her to pray to seems disinterested. Carrie cannot triumph but at least she is able to destroy her tormentors. Sissy Spacek—26 at the time the film was released—performed with such remarkable sensitivity and insight that *Carrie* becomes a wish-dream for unhappy pubescent girls. Carrie's self-destruction is just the sort of martyred irony the film's young audience could best appreciate.

Because *Carrie* was a tremendous box office success, DePalma may have felt obliged to rework its more obvious elements; his next film, *The Fury* (1978), is as technically accomplished as *Carrie* but far less original. Telekinesis is again the plot hinge, this time involving a young man (Andrew Stevens) whose psychic abilities are coveted by a sinister government agency. The boy is kidnapped during a bloody gun battle disguised as a terrorist attack. His father (Kirk Douglas) enlists the aid of a young woman (Amy Irving) who has similar psychic talents. The boy is corrupted while in captivity, and is ultimately responsible for his father's death. The girl retaliates by *exploding* the government agent (John Cassavetes) who had engineered the kidnapping.

DePalma developed the film's father-son relationship with some sensitivity, and suggested a budding but wary romance between the youngsters. Set pieces like one in which the boy concentrates and sends an amusement park ride careening out of control are impressive, but other sequences are unnecessarily mean-spirited, notably a protracted scene in which the boy mentally hoists a beautiful woman (Fiona Lewis) into the air, sets her spinning, and causes blood to gush from every orifice. By the time the woman dies, the room has filled with mist, for no other reason than that DePalma was trying to duplicate the murky ambience of *The Exorcist*.

Dressed to Kill (1980) continued DePalma's drift into misogynism and gratuitous shock effects. Glossy production values and a good cast cannot obscure the fact that the film is merely a contrived slasher thriller predicated on schizophrenia, mistaken identity, and sexual violence. Kate (Angie Dickinson) is an affluent housewife whose sexual longings lead her into promiscuous encounters with total strangers, including a gentleman who piques her interest at an art museum. DePalma's idea of a seduction is mannered and improbable, a chic game of cat-and-mouse that is resolved in the back seat of a taxi cab. Kate awakens the next morning in her new friend's apartment and discovers an official letter announcing the man's venereal disease. Needless to say, this revelation takes some of the gloss from the adventure.

In the elevator outside the man's apartment, Kate is confronted by a blonde woman who slashes her to death with a straight razor. Kate's body is discovered by a pretty call girl, Liz (Nancy Allen, by this time Mrs. DePalma), who is herself later stalked by the mysterious blonde. In order to stay alive, Liz allies herself with Kate's son (Keith Gordon) and psychiatrist (Michael Caine). After some close scrapes, Liz discovers that the killer is the psychiatrist, whose split personality consists of warring male and female egos. Kate was murdered because the doctor's female side was jealous of the male side's attraction. What we have here is a shoddy variation on *Psycho*, highlighted by Angie Dickinson's celebrated masturbatory shower scene (accomplished with a stand-in) and scenes of lovely Nancy Allen lounging around the psychiatrist's office in provocative black undies. Near the end of the film, Allen has a (revealing) shower scene of her own and dreams—in an idiotic duplication of the final moments of *Carrie*—that she is in mortal danger.

DePalma's transposition of the *Psycho* shower scene to an elevator may have been homage, but his shameless theft from himself is incomprehensible. Audiences were not pleased; *Carrie*, after all, had been widely seen, so the "shock" at the conclusion of *Dressed to Kill* was no shock at all. The film is inarguably exploitative—it's a T and A show for uptown slaughter junkies. Kate—unlike Janet Leigh's Marion Crane in *Psycho*—never registers as a real person. She exists only to be punished by that curiously Puritan ethic inform- ing nearly all slasher films. Kate may not be the world's most discreet wife, but her sexual urges are hardly capital crimes. Since our heroine Liz is a pros- titute, the film indirectly proposes that sex for commerce is nobler than sex for its own sake. *Dressed to Kill* is a moralistic muddle; the cleverist thing about the picture is its title. DePalma's early promise seemed to be evaporating.

Happily, that promise was reaffirmed by *Blow Out* (1981). Although no less derivative than earlier DePalma films, *Blow Out* is an involving, sensitively wrought story of doomed love. Jack (John Travolta) is a motion pic- ture sound man who specializes in sound effects for cheap horror films. His latest assignment is to record a shrill scream for a movie's big moment of ter- ror. The actresses he tests are all hopeless. Like the photographer in An- tonioni's *Blow Up* (1966), Jack becomes enmeshed in gruesome intrigue when his work accidentally uncovers murder. His tape machine records the sound of an exploding tire that sends a black limousine into Philadelphia's Wissahickon Creek. The politician inside is killed but Jack rescues the man's companion, a prostitute named Sally (Nancy Allen). Jack later becomes con- vinced that the sound on his machine is a rifle shot, and that the "accidental" blowout was part of a carefully planned political assassination. Jack and Sally investigate on their own, and although they come close to the truth they are no match for the faceless bureaucrats who have engineered the murder and subsequent cover-up. Sally agrees to be wired for sound and used as bait, unaware that a hired killer (John Lithgow) has been sent to silence her. Jack discovers the truth when he is miles away. He races through the city in a careening jeep (an excitingly staged and well-shot sequence) but can only listen to Sally's screams over his earphone. Sally is dead when Jack finally reaches her. The film's final moment skirts bad taste, but is tremendously affecting, as Jack works out his guilt and torment by dubbing his recording of Sally's very real death screams into the soundtrack of the movie he is work- ing on.

Blow Out may be the most moving example of the "paranoic conspiracy" subgenre that flourished after the Watergate scandal. Travolta's performance is intense and surprisingly unmannered, but the film's heart and special spirit come from Nancy Allen, whose Sally registers as a real person and not simply as the cliché "hooker with a heart of gold." She's ambitious but not terribly bright, sweet with a pinch of guile. Her gradual trust in Jack and devotion to him is touching and unaffected; *Blow Out* is an unexpectedly successful love story. It is also a disturbing look at the tenuous link between movie fantasy and the reality of life. Because a "happy ending" is horrifyingly snatched from us at the last moment, *Blow Out* is almost an *anti*-movie, a slap in the face that reminds us reality doesn't play by movie rules. It is the least contrived of

DePalma's horror films, and certainly his most honest. It is eclectic without being imitative, and marked DePalma's arrival as a serious, original director with things to say.

How ironic then that, following *Scarface* (1983)—DePalma's hyperkinetic updating of the gangster genre—the director should stumble badly when he returned to the horror-suspense genre. *Dressed to Kill* is wretched, but seems to have all the charm of a Tati when judged against *Body Double* (1984), the ugliest and most obsequious of DePalma's homages to Hitchcock. This time, elements of *Vertigo* and *Rear Window* are lifted, mingled, and corrupted. Jake (Craig Wasson) is a young, faintly dim Hollywood actor who is fired from a Z-film called *Vampire's Kiss* because his claustrophobia prevents him from lying still in a coffin. Like Jimmy Stewart's acrophobia, Jake's affliction will dog him throughout his adventure. Out of work and bounced from his girlfriend's apartment after intruding upon her and another man, Jake meets Sam (Gregg Henry), a fellow actor who is housesitting a fabulous futuristic manse high in the Hollywood Hills. Besides the de rigueur circular bed and well-stocked bar, the house boasts a spectacular view, namely Gloria, a beautiful, uninhibited neighbor whose nightly masturbatory dance is visible through a telescope.

Jake assumes stewardship of the house and enjoys the view until he notices that his neighbor is being watched—and later followed—by another man, a profoundly ugly American Indian. Jake's voyeurism encourages him to follow and ultimately confront Gloria (Deborah Shelton). His warning is rewarded with some feverish (and unlikely) kissing (giving DePalma an opportunity to clumsily rework his own whirling camera from *Obsession*), but not before the mysterious stranger snatches Gloria's purse. Jake freezes in a pedestrian tunnel and the thief escapes.

Later, Jake watches helplessly as Gloria is attacked by the Indian, who impales her to the bedroom floor with a power drill that's nearly as long as a Buick. Jake's chance glimpse soon after of porno queen Holly Body (Melanie Griffith) convinces him that the masturbating woman he had observed through the telescope was Holly, and not Gloria. Jake's energies for the rest of the film are devoted to discovering who has been behind the deception, and why.

As thriller material goes, this isn't really bad. DePalma offered a situation that, if artificial, is also provocative and alluring. The trouble is that he allowed the air of contrivance to permeate the characters: their dialogue, their behavior, their motivations. Hitchcock was able to negotiate the fine line between fantasy and reality, between audience belief and disbelief, but DePalma does not seem to have been aware that the line even exists. The film is so rife with silliness that the idiocy of its denouement—in which the actor Sam is literally unmasked as the murderer—seems wearily inevitable.

The ineffectiveness of Jake's claustrophobia as a motivating force (how many of us, after all, are truly claustrophobic?) may be the least of *Body*

Double's problems. Audience identification with the protagonist, for instance, ebbs as the story progresses. Jake's voyeurism works in the early part of the film because all of us like to watch. That's why we ogle car crashes and go to the movies. Jake does not seem like a peeper—he's simply a guy looking at something he probably shouldn't be looking at. But when he stares at Gloria through a shop window as she tries on underwear (what kind of store arranges its dressing rooms so that they are clearly visible from the outside walk?), and later picks a pair of her panties from the trash, he becomes more interesting but less likeable. His subsequent willingness to immerse himself in the oily world of pornography in order to meet Holly Body hastens his fall from grace. Burly Craig Wasson is believable as Jake, but DePalma might have engaged the audience's sympathy more successfully if a blander, more conventionally handsome actor had been chosen. Much of the success of *Obsession*, for instance, is due to the casting of Cliff Robertson—an agreeable, Midwestern good guy if ever there was one—as the neurotic protagonist.

There are some hints of pallid satire during Jake's adventure in pornoland, but not enough to convince an audience that DePalma was serious about poking fun at the milieu. Melanie Griffith's Holly Body is amusing, but also flip and superficial. It's impossible to tell if Griffith may be capable of better work. It is distressing that her big scene calls for her to swivel her naked derriere and fondle her breasts. The nudity is not upsetting; only that it is turned to such trivial, exploitative purpose. As one watches Griffith's brave attempt to connect with a role that has as many human qualities as a sack of hamburger, it is difficult not to think of Griffith's mother, Tippi Hedren, who brought a cooly elegant presence to two films by the man DePalma wishes to emulate. Hitchcock's exploitation of his actresses was artful because it was subtle and psychological; DePalma's had become blatant and crude.

Gloria's messy death by phallic power drill is distasteful and unnecessary; the flimsy raison d'être for its presence is that the killer had used it to crack the woman's safe—but why does he laboriously turn it against her after Jake and two other would-be rescuers have noisily broken a downstairs window to gain entry? (For that matter, how does the killer get out of the house after the dirty deed?) Obviously, if the murderer had reacted believably and panicked, the plot would have sputtered and stalled. Worse, DePalma could not have given us the gratuitous shot of the massive, bloody drill bit punching its way through the ceiling of the room below. In this universe, everything—including humanity—is sacrificed at the altar of images. There is no joy in the realm of *Body Double*, no hope of loveliness or tenderness or redemption. The horror is counterbalanced with nothing. DePalma is highly talented, but he is also perplexing and infuriating. Hitchcock turned us into collaborators, but his acolyte does not always hesitate to reduce us to accomplices.

Brian DePalma is very much a mainstream director, not simply because his films are well-mounted and distributed by major studios, but because his preoccupation has been with the plight of people whose sexual inclinations put them at odds with the expectations of "normal" society. But what *is* normal society? Can it be changed? What undreamt-of dangers are inherent in the close link between mind and body? What is the shape of sex to come? Since the late 1960s these questions have intrigued David Cronenberg, a young (born 1943), prepossessing writer-director whose highly unified output is at once mordant, hysterically funny, unremittingly gruesome, and thoughtfully bizarre. Though Cronenberg's base is his native Canada, his films have provoked and amused audiences around the world. If he is not cinema's most important sexual prophet, he is surely the most impudent.

Like so many younger filmmakers, Cronenberg began to experiment with narrative technique and screenwriting while in college. One of his early 16 millimeter movies, *From the Drain* (1967), focuses on two men having a conversation about the end of the world as they sit fully-clothed in a bathtub. As they speak, a hideous snake crawls from the bathtub drain and entwines itself around the throat of one of the men, strangling him. The premise of this bizarre 14-minute short found fuller (and more sexual) expression as a key scene in Cronenberg's first important theatrical feature, *They Came from Within* (1976).

The action is set at "Starliner Island," an antiseptic highrise apartment house "just 12 minutes from downtown Montreal." The Starliner sells itself as the epitome of upscale luxury and convenience. Unfortunately, one of the building's tenants is an obsessed doctor who has developed a slug-like parasite designed to take over the function of diseased or damaged organs. The parasite also stimulates and exaggerates the sexual urges of the host; as the Starliner's unctuous rental agent shows a young couple through the building, the doctor is savagely murdering his young concubine, who has been infected with one of the parasites. After slicing the woman to bits and freeing the slug that had been inside her body, the doctor slits his own throat. Incident closed, except that the murder victim had had other lovers, among them a young insurance agent (Alan Migicovsky) who leans over his balcony one morning and regurgitates a parasite onto the umbrella of an old lady strolling below. The slug crawls off into the brush.

Maddeningly tenacious, the parasites are soon infesting the building air ducts and hallways. One squirms through a letter opening. A pudgy, middle-aged woman is attacked by another of the slugs when she leans over her washing machine. Later, the woman (now painted like a parody of a streetwalker) flings open her door and grabs a young delivery man: "I'm hungry!" she shrieks. The Starliner's resident lesbian (Barbara Steele) is rudely surprised when a phallic slug sneaks from her bathtub drain and between her legs. Soon, she seduces a female neighbor; when the women kiss, the slug passes from Steele's throat into that of her partner. Rapid crosscutting establishes the escalation of such incidents. Eventually, the building's tenants are embroiled in a ceaseless orgy of violent sexual warfare that—the film's conclusion suggests—will soon engulf Montreal. And from there...?

A hedonistic victim (Nora Johnson) of the love parasites in David Cronenberg's *They Came from Within* (1976).

Cronenberg's view of society is a jaundiced one. The Starliner, as our eyes plainly tell us, is a sham, an oversized, impersonal monolith with narrow corridors, low ceilings, and slow elevators. It is a place calculated to deaden passion, not awaken it. Its tenants—a lesbian, neurotic young couples, dotty old people—hardly conform to the upbeat slide presentation that opens the film. In the Starliner, at least, the parasites are not enemies, but liberators. Even the elderly residents gleefully participate in the hedonism.

Cronenberg's interest in (and seeming distaste for) bodily functions and their relation to the psychology of sex is expressed in scenes of sardonic graphicism. When the young insurance agent sees the skin of his abdomen rippling as the parasites move within his body, he speaks to the intruders as though they were pets: "C'mon boy...attaboy...c'mon fella." When he attacks his wife and demands sex, a slug weaves grotesquely from between his lips. Later, a visiting M.D. (Joe Silver) who had had a hand in the development of the parasites leans over the young man's body, only to have two of the things begin to burrow beneath the screaming doctor's eyes with such determination that even pliers cannot pull them off.

Food and the mechanics of eating are constant undercurrents. A pretty nurse (Lynn Lowry) is attacked by a male neighbor as she happily pokes a roast, and must finally stab the intruder with a serving fork. The delivery boy who is attacked by the fat lady is from a restaurant; after he has ingested the parasite he stops an elevator and confronts a woman and little girl, his face and fingers dripping with rich pastry. Another character habitually speaks with his mouth full, and tosses a pickle back and forth with a visitor. By linking the horror of the parasites with everyday bodily functions like sex and eating, Cronenberg created a vivid nightmare of *organic* horror. Unlike the traditional horror approach which creates an externalized horror that is visited upon the victim's body, Cronenberg's tack explores the peculiar miseries that can be generated from *within* the victim's body.

This point of view — predictably — outraged some critics, notably Robin Wood, who viewed *They Came from Within* with "sexual disgust." Undaunted, Cronenberg brought a similarly fleshy frisson to *Rabid* (1977), a film perhaps best known for the presence of hardcore porn queen Marilyn Chambers in her first "straight" role. Although Cronenberg originally wanted Sissy Spacek for the lead, the casting of Chambers is more apt. She played Rose, a young woman who is badly injured in a motorcycle accident and awakens from her subsequent surgery to discover a retractable, organic probe nestling in her armpit, courtesy of well-meaning Dr. Keloid (!) (Howard Ryshpan), who had hoped that the implant would help repair some of Rose's damaged organs. The probe (much like the penis it resembles) has "a mind of its own," and turns Rose into a sexual vampire who lures men with teasing come-ons so that the probe can dart out and steal blood. Rose's victims are struck with a perverse sort of anthrax or hydrophobia characterized by violent behavior and the leaking of bilious foam from mouth, nose, and eyes.

Rose is essentially an innocent who cannot resist the commands of her body. When she forces herself to ingest cow's blood, for instance, her body rebels and she becomes violently ill. Human blood, then, is to be Rose's main meal. Among her victims is Dr. Keloid, who later goes off the deep end in the operating room, slicing off the finger of a startled nurse. Rose's tragic flaw is that she cannot believe she is responsible for the mayhem that follows in her wake. To prove it, she has an encounter with a man and stays with him afterwards, positive that he will not become violent. Rose is wrong, and is killed when her deranged paramour throws her through a window. Her body is loaded onto a garbage truck and driven away.

The greatest revelation offered by *Rabid* is that Marilyn Chambers is a reasonably competent actress. The film's plot is essentially a pastiche of the raunchier elements of vampire cinema, and the bluntly moralistic tone of the mad scientist thrillers of the thirties and forties. Keloid tampers with things that are best left alone, and is punished. Cronenberg's scripts invariably feature some sort of careless or unscrupulous intellectual whose indiscretions bring suffering to himself and to everyone around him.

The most fascinating of these quasivillains is Dr. Raglan, the pivotal character of *The Brood* (1979), Cronenberg's best and most disturbing film. Raglan (Oliver Reed) is a bearlike, domineering genius who runs the Somafree Institute of Psychoplasmics, an exclusive research and treatment center where patients are taught to externalize their rages and frustrations as peculiar sores and growths on their bodies. The patients come to believe in the power of the mind over the body, and in the culpability of the mind when the body experiences a disorder. One man (Robert Silverman) shows a visitor a hideous cluster of lymphosarcomatous tumors on his neck, saying, "I've got a small revolution on my hands, and I'm not putting it down very successfully."

Another patient is Nola Carveth (Samantha Eggar), a young woman tormented by memories of a miserable, loveless childhood and a failed marriage. Complicating her life further is an ongoing battle with her estranged husband Frank (Art Hindle) for custody of their little girl. Though Nola remains at the institute day and night, people for whom she has special malice are killed by hideously ugly "children" who pop from closets or brazenly mingle with normal children. Nola's mother is savaged in her own kitchen and her father is pummeled to death by a tiny assassin who hides beneath a bed. When Nola's daughter is kidnapped from her grade school, the teacher (Susan Hogan) is beaten to death by a pack of the diminutive monsters.

After one of the killers mysteriously drops dead, an autopsy reveals that the creature has no navel or sex organs. Medically, it cannot exist. But the Brood *does* exist, in a locked building in the woods behind the institute. Everything is tied together during a climactic confrontation between Nola and Frank when the woman explains that the Brood children are physical extensions of her enraged mind, and that they have sprung directly from her body. To demonstrate, Nola lifts her gown and reveals a repellent sac hanging from her abdomen. Smiling, she bites the sac open and begins to lick the blood and afterbirth from the misshapen fetus inside. The scene is more disturbing than horrifying because of its sanguinary, elemental beauty. Nola is a splendid, savage animal — her pride in her accomplishment is readily apparent. Is she a freak, or the first of a new generation of mothers? Her husband strangles her without pausing to consider the question. Nola's fetus and the other Brood children die with her, but not before Raglan perishes as he rescues Nola's daughter from the Brood's dormitory.

Nola's Brood offspring are pure, highly focused manifestations of her anger. When she is calm, the children are logy and inactive. When her mind rages, so does the Brood. Cronenberg's view of motherhood is ironic and disconcerting. Nola's Brood is not the product of love, but of insanity and hate. Dressed in colorful hooded snowsuits, the mutant children seem almost stereotypically cute — from a distance. Up close, they become dreadful parodies of normal children. We cannot always trust our eyes and can *never* trust our bodies, which Cronenberg views as perversely willful machines that will defy the conscious mind at every opportunity. Nola does not consciously

The innocent little girl (Cindy Hinds, left) in the uncertain care of the children of rage, *The Brood* (1979).

wish to harm the daughter she has created with her husband, but the Brood that her body has also produced comes perilously close to doing just that. Nola's maternalistic intentions are muddled and subverted by her body's devious inventions. Her plight is encapsulated by a comment made by a character in *They Came from Within*: "Man is an overrational animal that thinks too much and has lost touch with his body." We know the phrase "the flesh is weak," but in Cronenberg's universe the flesh may be the strongest — and most dangerous — thing of all.

The director's next film, *Scanners* (1981), offers a fuller development of concepts Cronenberg had explored in his first two commercial features. *Stereo* (1969) concerns students who volunteer for the surgical removal of their voiceboxes in order to stimulate telepathic ability, while *Crimes of the Future* (1970) revolves around the aftermath of a deadly cosmetic that has killed all women of childbearing age and older, and regressed men to an earlier stage of human development. Among the titular crimes is pedophilia.

Scanners proposes that two men with frighteningly developed mental powers have the ability to decide the fate of the world. In this slick, kinetic thriller, a gifted but insane telepath named Revok (Michael Ironside) wishes to organize similarly talented mutants in order to dominate society. The mutants — called Scanners — can read minds, force normal people to their will, and manipulate objects with thought alone. Revok views his brethren as the vanguard of a brave new world, but standing in his way is Cameron Vale

(Stephen Lack), who, like Revok and the others, acquired his prodigious mental powers because his mother took an experimental drug while pregnant. Vale becomes a lackey of Consec, a pharmaceutical conglomerate that had marketed the mutating drug. Vale has been a drifter who never mastered his power until coming under the tutelage of Consec's Dr. Ruth (Patrick McGoohan), the researcher who originally formulated the wonder drug. Soon, Vale's skills are formidable.

The sexual thrust of *Scanners* is not as obvious as in Cronenberg's other films, but there is an interesting (if contrived) twist when Revok informs Vale that they are brothers, and that their father is Dr. Ruth. Vale is unmoved and refuses to join Revok; their sibling rivalry then expresses itself in a bloody mind duel in which Vale's veins distend and burst, his flesh erupts into flame, and his eyes melt and explode in their sockets (all courtesy of special makeup designer Dick Smith). When Vale's telekinetic lover Kim (Jennifer O'Neill) arrives, she discovers a charred corpse on the floor and a huddled figure in the corner. The latter is Revok, or at least Revok's body. He looks at the woman with Vale's eyes and says in Vale's voice, "We won."

So much critical commotion was aroused by a scene in which Revok explodes the head of a less-talented telepath that the film's more subtle aspects were obscured. *Scanners* is a highly provocative continuation of Cronenberg's fascination with the strange marriage of mind and body, and is also a movie rarity: pure science fiction. Cronenberg asked a splendid "what if?" question and followed through with no baloney. Which is not to imply that *Scanners* is without flaws; so concerned was Cronenberg with his father-sons theme and dazzling special effects that he totally neglected Revok and Vale's *mother*. We learn nothing about her except that Dr. Ruth chose her to be his first test subject. Is this mysterious woman the cause of Revok's insanity and Vale's earlier rootlessness? We never know.

The film has brilliantly staged action scenes (car crashes, explosions, etc.) but may lean on them too heavily. *Scanners* is most successful when it focuses on more sedate tableaus. It is during these quiet moments that Cronenberg comments upon the strengths and weaknesses of families. Separately, the Scanners gravitate toward misfitism and underachievement. When we first see Vale, for instance, he is picking discarded bits of food from plates in a public cafeteria. (A marvelous, mysogynistic aside to this scene is Vale's psychic violation of a pompous matron who has looked at him contemptuously: a glance from him causes the woman to hold herself and writhe on the floor). Vale never connects with anybody until he discovers Kim and her telepathic companions, who have formed a family unit. There is a moment of wonderful calm and serenity when the Scanners encircle a table and link psychically, giving themselves over to the Gestalt mind. But there are always factions eager to disrupt familial harmony (and its concomitant strength), in this instance a band of shotgun-toting assassins in the employ of Consec. Similarly, a Scanner-sculptor (Robert Silverman) who skates on the thin edge of sanity is destroyed when his "children" — his artworks — are blasted to bits by Consec's goons.

Dr. Ruth soon realizes that Consec and his sons are beyond his control or influence. He has sired two remarkable offspring, but has allowed their talents to be corrupted and exploited. Revok is conspiring with Ruth's corporate superiors, and is indirectly responsible for his father's murder. In this context, *Scanners* is a moving domestic tragedy. Ruth has failed as a father, unleashed a myriad of horrors upon the world, and forced Vale and Kim to fight in order to establish their right to survival.

Scanners was widely distributed by Avco-Embassy, and brought Cronenberg to the attention of Universal, who helped underwrite his next project, *Videodrome* (1983), which, though hopelessly confused and muddled, is in many ways the ultimate expression of the director's preoccupation with the tyranny of the body over the mind. It is a dark, pessimistic story that revolves around an unsympathetic protagonist who is engaged in an unsavory business. *Videodrome* is a heartless, humorless, no-win exercise. Not surprisingly, the film was Cronenberg's first box office failure.

Max Renn (James Woods) is an unimaginative video hustler who runs a fringe-audience cable television station in Toronto. His programming is strictly of the peep show variety: witless soft-core pornography and an occasional burst of senseless violence. Max is on the lookout for something with which to boost his viewership. When his engineer Harlan (Peter Dvorsky) discovers a torture show called Videodrome that issues from the Pittsburgh underground, Max is ecstatic. The program's dispassionate tableaus of naked men and women being whipped and jolted with electrical shocks are precisely what Max has been looking for. But associates advise him to steer clear of Videodrome: "It is dangerous because it has something you don't have, Max," warns one. "A *philosophy*."

Max is undeterred. His search for the program's originators leads him to the Cathode Ray Mission, a video haven for Toronto derelicts administered by Brian O'Blivion (Jack Creley), a McLuhanesque visionary who proposes that video images have become more real than real life. Indeed, neither we nor Max ever sees O'Blivion in the flesh — he exists only as an image on a television screen. O'Blivion's daughter (Sonja Smits) admits to Max that she is familiar with Videodrome, and offers him a videocassette of the program. At home, Max hallucinates while watching the tape, imagining that his television set is a breathing, organic thing. After more exposure to the Videodrome program, Max's judgments begin to falter, and neither he nor we know what is real and what is illusion. Max's abdomen becomes creased with a pulsating, vagina-like orifice into which he can insert his entire hand and forearm. He hides a gun inside his body (a pointed juxtaposition of sexuality and gun worship), and is later attacked by a man who shoves a writhing videocassette into the new orifice, programming Max like a machine.

The adventure has become surreal and disgusting but Max continues his

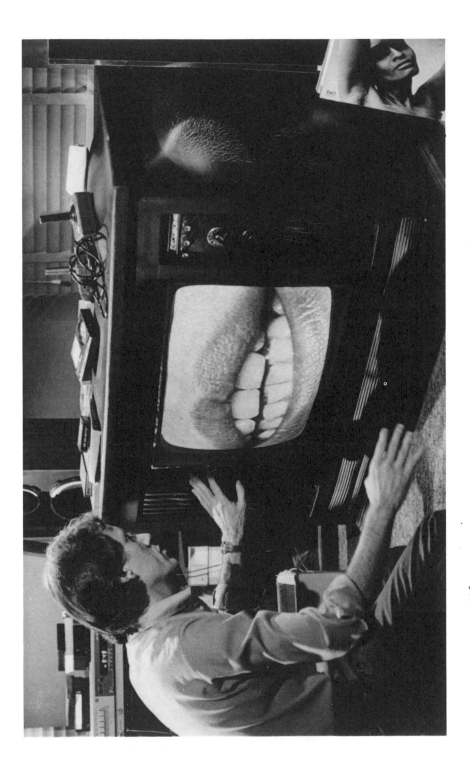

quest because of his involvement with Nicki Brand (Deborah Harry), a radio pop psychologist who is also an acolyte of Videodrome. Cronenberg developed Nicki as a sort of video-age Circe whose pouty lips and penchant for sadomasochistic sex play obsess Max. During her first night with Max, Nicki demands that he pierce her ear with a needle. Later, she takes his cigarette and stubs it out on her bare breast. Max is simultaneously repelled and fascinated.

Although Max eventually learns that exposure to Videodrome causes tumors which trigger the hallucinations, he is too far gone to resist the commands that emanate from his television. One night, the screen literally bulges with the grotesque image of Nicki's magnified lips; Max, in a hideous electronic parody of oral sex, falls to his hands and knees and thrusts his head *into* the screen, which swells and writhes to accommodate him. He is ordered to murder his business partners and does so with the gun that has become a slimy, organic extension of his hand. The mastermind of Videodrome is a grinning optometrist named Barry Convex (Les Carlson). When shot by Max, Convex's body bursts into a repulsive eruption of Videodrome-induced tumors. After escaping to a deserted shipyard, Max views a video image of himself committing suicide. The television set he is watching suddenly explodes in a welter of blood and human organs. Max lifts his gun and prepares to mimic the death scene he has witnessed, pausing before blowing his brains out to intone, "Long live the new flesh."

Videodrome is so thick with provocative ideas and images that it is richer than the richest béarnaise. The film stumbles because of Cronenberg's insistence that we be as confused and victimized as the central character. As Max's adventures increase in frequency and intensity, we do not know if we are looking at fantasy or reality. Of course, a major part of Cronenberg's premise is that television blurs such distinctions, but this conundrum-like narrative approach is ill suited to film, and is especially inappropriate for a filmmaker like Cronenberg, who gives equal weight to all of his images.

Every scene—mundane or bizarre—is starkly literal. The director purposely avoided visual or aural devices that might have clued us as to the reality of a given moment. Rick Baker's makeup effects, for example, are unpleasantly convincing, and we never know how to take them. Is Max's abdominal vagina real? Is his television set really alive? The images are graphic enough to provoke emotional response, but we remain unable to respond intellectually. Compounding these difficulties are the obvious absurdities of the Cathode Ray Mission (how could there be such a place in the real world?) and names like Convex and O'Blivion. *Videodrome*'s narrative approach and particulars of style are novelistic, of a sort that absurdist writers like Thomas Pynchon and Donald Barthelme can accomplish because of the inherent unreality of the

James Woods prepares for a video-age sexual encounter in David Cronenberg's *Videodrome* **(1983).**

printed word. But the very nature of film is dangerously literal. Cronenberg did not become too ambitious for his medium (filmmakers from Luis Buñuel to Nicolas Roeg have worked effectively with peculiar narrative approaches), but he may have exceeded his capabilities.

A more obvious failing of *Videodrome* is that it has no plot. Although the warning that the Videodrome program has a "philosophy" sounds ominously impressive, Cronenberg's script does not reveal what that philosophy might be. The conspiracy that Max uncovers seems to have no direction or purpose. At the conclusion, nothing has been resolved or accomplished except a lot of random mayhem and the death of a protagonist whom we never understand or care about. The film's power is clustered in isolated moments. Max's scenes with Nicki carry particular force because Max's aimless acquiescence to the woman's deviant sexual demands is equated with his passive absorption of the images on his television screen. It is clear that his excessive television viewing is a soporific that dulls his mind and emotions, and allows him to share Nicki's numb amorality. Max's physical encounters come to have as much significance to him as the dead phosphor dots he gazes at on television, which is to say, almost no significance at all. Further, sexual response and violence are linked in the Videodrome context, but the violence is passionless and detached. These juxtapositions are vividly expressed when Max whips a television set that shows an image of the manacled Nicki on its screen. Nicki's image flinches with each stroke—she responds to these phantom blows with more urgency than she brings to her fleshly encounters.

Cronenberg's earlier films explore the body's domination of the mind, but not with the venom of *Videodrome*; the notion of hallucinatory tumors is especially fiendish. Though television is an easy and familiar target of satirists and social critics, the film's view of sexual violence as an expression of passivity and ennui is refreshing. The shame is that Cronenberg was unable to present his ideas and images in a more cohesive context. That he is an important filmmaker there can be no doubt. He may yet prove to be the most significant auteur the horror genre has produced.

Cronenberg has responded to a bleak world with pessimistic films filled with forlorn, unloved misfits. Other contemporary filmmakers have looked at the soulless tack human sexuality sometimes seems to be taking and created optimistic films about forlorn misfits who triumph. Cronenberg is a pacesetter, but it's nice to chuckle once in a while. One director who delights in creating (and acting in) films that reflect the humorous absurdity of modern sexuality is Paul Bartel, a onetime protégé of Roger Corman whose first commercial film, *Private Parts* (1972), involves a seedy Los Angeles hotel populated by violent homosexuals, voyeurs, and pederasts. One young man carries on a passionate affair with an inflatable sex doll. Because Bartel's unorthodox film career began in New York's quasi-underground, *Private Parts* is rich with eccentric characters and wild incident.

Predictably, the film was not a commercial success. MGM pulled it from distribution after a very short run, and Bartel moved on to more exploitative (and less interesting) projects for Corman's New World. *Death Race 2000* (1975) and *Cannonball* (1976)—uninspired car chase films with mildly satiric overtones—are two examples. The pictures were commercially successful but typed Bartel as a "car" director, an appellation that no one except Hal Needham can bear to live with for long. Bartel turned to acting and did comedic character bits in a number of New World releases, notably *Piranha* (1978) and *Rock 'n' Roll High School* (1979).

Finally, in 1982 Bartel financed, cowrote (with Richard Blackburn), and directed *Eating Raoul*, a wickedly funny spoof that is a refinement of the sort of bizarre sexual humor that characterizes *Private Parts*. The subject is still perversity, but the tone is hip and upbeat, the satire sharp and focused. Paul and Mary Bland (Bartel and Mary Woronov) are a straightlaced, resolutely boring couple appalled by the sleazy sex that goes on at all hours in their Hollywood apartment house. The elevator and hallways crawl with horny swingers. Paul and Mary dream of opening their own restaurant (which will be called Chez Bland), but haven't the money for a down payment.

When a wandering swinger barges into their apartment (crudely proclaiming, "The early bird gets the pussy!") Paul raps the man on the head with a skillet, killing him. The victim's wallet fairly bulges with greenbacks. Ah ha!: a plan is hatched. The Blands take out an advertisement in a sex tabloid, and soon have a steady stream of peculiar visitors: voyeurs, masochists, a dwarf and his mastiff, even a horny mock–Nazi. Bang, bang goes the skillet. Paul reasons, "This town is full of rich perverts that no one will miss." At an orgy, he tosses an electric space heater into a hot tub crowded with nude merrymakers, and accomplishes a week's worth of murders at a single stroke. Things look rosy, but the scheme threatens to go awry with the arrival of Raoul (Robert Beltran), a cocky young Latino who blackmails his way into the partnership, and insinuates his way into Mrs. Bland's bedchamber. Raoul sells the bodies of the Bland's victims for 50¢ a pound to a dog food manufacturer and makes *big* bucks by peddling their fancy cars. Raoul eventually becomes convinced that Mary has chosen him over her husband but, bop!, he's wrong. Like Tammy Wynette, Mary stands by her man. The film's title is borne out at the conclusion, when the Blands celebrate their down payment by inviting their real estate agent for dinner.

Eating Raoul, clearly, is not a product of the Hollywood mainstream. Though the Blands are presented as victims who are merely fighting back against the society which oppresses them, the film's moral ambivalence could have thudded like an iron donut if interpreted by a director who lacked Bartel's gift for comic exaggeration. The picture's deft wit and black comedy impressed critics who were starved for some genuine laughs. Bartel flirted with bad taste but never succumbed to it, in part because *Eating Raoul*—despite its frequently rude language, mild nudity, and gross insinuations—is ingenuously American, a celebration of free enterprise and traditional moral values. It parodies the "new sexuality" by exposing its empty self-consciousness. No matter that the Blands are murderers — Bartel's tone is so wackily ingratiating that we don't care. In fact, we *like* it. Yahoo, they got another one! The Blands' victims are comic stereotypes. The murders are performed off-camera or are discreetly obscured. The Blands seem to be doing nothing worse than performing a vaguely unpleasant public service.

As Mr. Bland, Bartel is a picture of paunchy determination. He may not be much of a lover (Paul and Mary sleep in matching pj's but in separate beds), but his belief in solid American values makes him a fellow to be reckoned with. Beltran's Raoul is the epitome of Latino sass. And Mary Woronov, whose film career began in the Andy Warhol underground in the mid-sixties, provides the picture's electricity and heart. Leggy, bright-eyed, and brimming with wit, she forthrightly sees that only the guilty are punished. Swingers: beware. American values *will* be preserved.

The film's cheerful cannibalism notwithstanding, the *real* horror of *Eating Raoul* is the difficulty Bartel encountered in making it. Although his earlier films had marked him as a cult director, Bartel's commitment to *Eating Raoul* forced him to cadge money from friends and family, convince his cast and crew to work on a deferred payment basis, and restrict shooting to weekends. Unlike David Cronenberg, Bartel spent the formative years of his career in Hollywood, where unorthodoxy is seldom appreciated or rewarded. He rates bouquets for not compromising his vision, and for having the industry and nerve to mock the sort of new wave sexual silliness that has come to preoccupy too many of us.

The Blands react against sexual deviation, but there is one filmmaker who happily, even gleefully, trumpets it. Baltimore-based John Waters — self-proclaimed scuzzbag and "Prince of Puke" — is a deliciously unfettered wit whose sympathies lie with the freak and weirdo set. His best-known film is *Pink Flamingos* (1972), a cheery tale of transvestism, exhibitionism, white slavery, and cannibalism that is one of the foremost cult films of the seventies. Waters (whose angular frame and impossibly thin pencil mustache suggest a deranged mortician) is not precisely a horror director — his films might more properly be termed unrestrained social satires that make liberal use of the iconography of the horror genre.

Waters' favorite interpreter has been Divine, a 300-pound transvestite who delights in squeezing "her" bulk into gaudy slit skirts and spike-heeled shoes. In *Pink Flamingos* Divine plays herself, "The Filthiest Person Alive." There are pretenders to her throne, however: Raymond and Connie Marble (John Lochary and Mink Stole), an upwardly mobile Baltimore couple whose income is derived from selling stolen babies to lesbians, and from peddling heroin to grade schoolers. Raymond's hobby is tying a gigantic sausage to his penis and exposing himself to high school girls, then stealing their purses. The Marbles send Divine a bowel movement in the mail, and later put the torch to her pink house trailer. When the Marbles blow the whistle on Divine's rowdy birthday party (Divine's gifts include rubber vomit and a pig's head), the cops are greeted by an army of freaks, drag queens, winos, and run-of-the-mill perverts. A la *Night of the Living Dead*, the officers are literally pulled apart and eaten alive. The film climaxes with Divine's capture of the Marbles. After a kangaroo court trial, Divine sentences the Marbles to death, and executes them in front of grateful representatives of *The Tattler, Midnight,* and *Confidential*. Finally, in a conclusion guaranteed to make even the most sophisticated viewer goggle, Divine eats dog excrement.

John Waters is a genuine oddball whose real-life pleasures include murder trials, rock 'n' roll riots, and grisly accidents. He is as *personal* a filmmaker as one is likely to find. *Pink Flamingos* was shot in 16 millimeter and color for $10,000. It is crude, amateurishly acted, and thoroughly repellent. It is also one of the funniest and most original films of the seventies. Waters is a fascinating figure because his movies—especially *Pink Flamingos*—offer wholly new, self-enclosed realities. We do not meet a single normal person in a Waters film. Totally against our will we come to like whichever characters Waters wants us to like. We are sucked into the director's perverse milieu, and don't mind at all. Waters does not actively promote aberrant sexuality—his films are intentionally so silly that they cannot be taken seriously. In *Multiple Maniacs* (1970), for instance, Divine is raped by a 15-foot crustacean named Lobstora. When Divine runs into the street in panic she—not Lobstora—is gunned down by the National Guard.

Desperate Living (1977) is set in Mortville, a fairytale land that is a haven for criminals. Mortville is ruled by the grotesquely fat Queen Carlotta (Edith Massey), a crazed despot who worships Idi Amin. Carlotta dreams of infecting everyone in Mortville with rabies, but is deposed, cooked, and eaten. In *Female Trouble* (1974) Divine was cast as Dawn Davenport, an angst-ridden teenager who becomes a night club entertainer. Her act consists of pulling a revolver and gunning down innocent members of her audience. When Dawn is raped early in the film, Divine (with the help of a double and some clever editing) played both Dawn and the male rapist. This must surely be cinema's goofiest instance of sexual schizophrenia.

Waters' break into the mainstream was *Polyester* (1981), a slick, well-mounted, and very funny domestic tragicomedy set in suburbia. Though the level of scatology was toned down from that of previous Waters films, *Polyester* is no sell-out; Waters seems determined to maintain his identity.* Like Pittsburgh's George Romero, he refuses to budge from his home city, and will accept a limit to the size of his budgets as long as he is allowed to make the films that matter to him. Waters is reminiscent of a typical junior high class clown, happy to amuse us, and delighted when we express outrage.

*Polyester *was presented in Odorama, a catchy name for a "scratch and sniff" card designed to coordinate with numbers on the screen. Hardy viewers were treated to the smells of pepperoni pizza, gasoline, old sneakers, and even flatulence.*

Bartel and Waters' lightheartedness is nearly unique among cult films that explore the new frontiers of sex. Some, like Rinse Dream's *Cafe Flesh* (1982), are howlingly pretentious, luring audiences with hardcore sex, and masking a lack of imagination with heavy-handed chic. In Dream's futuristic vision, nuclear war has ruined the sexual capabilities of 90 percent of the population, turning them into "negatives" who pay to sit in sweaty clubs and observe the sex acts of exhibitionistic "positives." Hard-edged and bluntly exploitative, *Cafe Flesh* causes the viewer to leave the theater feeling a little used.

Occasionally, a gem of a movie will unexpectedly turn up amidst the rubble. Such a film is David Lynch's *Eraserhead* (1977), a highly stylized journey into the battered psyche of our age. Shot in black and white with the help of a grant from the American Film Institute, it is Lynch's first film, and the one that immediately preceded *The Elephant Man* (1980). Lynch describes *Eraserhead* as "a dream of dark and troubling things." To simply synopsize the film is to be deceiving since to do so suggests a sort of film wholly different from the one Lynch created.

Henry Spenser (John Nance) is an unprepossessing, disaffected young man who lives alone in a small furnished room. While on vacation from his job as a printer, he is told by his girlfriend Mary (Charlotte Stewart) that she has given birth to their baby. They marry, and their entwined lives become a domestic horror as they vainly try to live with one another, and with their deformed, incessantly squalling offspring. Mary finally goes home to her parents, leaving Henry to be darkly seduced by the temptress across the hall (Judith Anna Roberts). The scenario could be early Tony Richardson, starring young Albert Finney or Tom Courtenay. In truth, though, *Eraserhead* is more akin to the works of Bosch and Dante. Lynch, as conjurer of an existential nightmare, utilized every aspect of cinema to achieve his effect. Henry lives in a world of perpetual ugliness and industrial mayhem: his life is choked with dark corridors and dim corners, and crowded, confining rooms lit from a single source. There is an unceasing undertone of white noise. Radiators hiss and clank, factory machines pound. The very air seems charged with a maddening hum. And Henry—with his Goodwill suit of clothes, white socks, jerky gait, and absurd shock of curly hair—is more helpless animal than man; the seductress across the hall wants him not as a lover, but as prey. His life is a hateful thing, his world out of control and beyond understanding. The child he has created with Mary (whose maiden name is simply "X") is deformed to the point of resembling a skinned rabbit. Bundled atop a table, it rolls its walleyes and mewls pathetically, maddeningly until, in gouts of blood and gore, Henry stabs it to death.

Henry's inability to sire a human offspring is ironically underscored by Lynch's fascination with birth and its pumping, machine-like aspects. The camera repeatedly glides along oddly organic tunnels and canals. Water imagery abounds, and more often than not resembles primordial soup. Snakelike fetuses are constantly underfoot and hiding in drawers, and roasted

"A dream of dark and troubling things." John Nance as the victimized dreamer in David Lynch's *Eraserhead* (1977).

baby chickens writhe on the plates with impossible life. In Lynch's world, man procreates, but there is no passion. People talk but do not communicate. ("What do you *do*?" Mary's mother suspiciously asks Henry at their first meeting. Henry looks blank for a moment, then softly replies, "I'm on vacation."). Dinner at Mary's is torture, as Dad grins insipidly and tells Henry about his deadened arm, while Grandma sits motionless and barely alive in a corner of the kitchen, a slowly diminishing cigarette stuck between her lips. Lynch suggested that there is peace and happiness only in death, as a hideously ugly dream girl (Laurel Near) sings, "In Heaven, everything is fine."

Eraserhead (titled for a hallucinatory sequence in which Henry imagines a cylindrical extract from his own brain neatly sectioned to make pencil erasers) is maddening and wholly original. At 90 minutes, the film can be a trial for impatient audiences, but has become a mainstay of the midnight movie circuit. With its bleak view of familial relationships and the dark horrors of sexuality, *Eraserhead* is at once liberating and imprisoning. If Franz Kafka had been a filmmaker, he may very well have created something similar.

Eraserhead provokes wildly mixed audience reactions—some viewers boo mightily, others laugh, and still others simply cringe. One reaction that is shared by all is a hope that Henry and Mary's plight is a flight of fancy, and not a preview of the social and sexual misery that awaits us in an increasingly dehumanized and insensitive world. Henry and Mary are not strangers to us; cinema shapes the real world, but not to the extent that it *reflects* the world. Sexuality may never be a comfortable topic, but it would be nice to believe that we may someday respect its power without fearing it. It is comforting to look ahead to a day when we no longer squander our grand sexual capabilities unthinkingly, uncaringly, or unhappily. The sexual imagery of the horror film will undoubtedly continue to reflect our curiosity and unease about the mechanics of living and dying. Will that reflection be laced with cynicism and ugliness, or with optimism and wit? Speculation is difficult. Who can say? Just: look around. What do you see?

Filmography

Chapter I

Abbott and Costello Meet Frankenstein (1948) Universal: Charles T. Barton. Bud Abbott, Lou Costello, Bela Lugosi.

Alien (1979) 20th Century–Fox: Ridley Scott. Tom Skerritt, Sigourney Weaver, Veronica Cartwright.

The Bad Seed (1956) WB: Mervyn LeRoy. Patty McCormack, Nancy Kelly, Henry Jones.

The Beast Within (1982) MGM/UA: Philippe Mora. Paul Clemens, Bibi Besch, Ronny Cox.

The Boys from Brazil (1978) 20th Century–Fox: Franklin J. Schaffner. Gregory Peck, Laurence Olivier, James Mason.

Bride of Frankenstein (1935) Universal: James Whale. Boris Karloff, Colin Clive, Elsa Lanchester.

Burn, Witch, Burn (1961) AIP: Sidney Hayers. Janet Blair, Peter Wyngarde, Margaret Johnston.

Captive Wild Woman (1943) Universal: Edward Dmytryk. John Carradine, Evelyn Ankers, Acquanetta.

The Cat People (1942) RKO: Jacques Tourneur. Kent Smith, Simone Simon, Tom Conway.

Cat People (1982) Universal: Paul Schrader. Nastassia Kinski, Malcolm McDowell, John Heard.

The Child (1977) Boxoffice International: Robert Voskanian. Laurel Barnett, Rosalie Cole, Frank Janson.

Children of the Damned (1963) MGM: Anton M. Leader. Ian Hendry, Alan Badel, Barbara Ferris.

The Colossus of New York (1958) Paramount: Eugene Lourie. John Baragrey, Mala Powers, Otto Kruger.

Colossus: The Forbin Project (1970) Universal: Joseph Sargent. Eric Braeden, Susan Clark, Gordon Pinsent.

Communion aka **Alice, Sweet, Alice** (1977) Allied Artists: Alfred Sole. Paula Sheppard, Brooke Shields, Linda Miller.

The Creeping Unknown aka **The Quatermass Experiment** (1955) Hammer/UA: Val Guest. Brian Donlevy, Margia Dean, Jack Warner.

Cult of the Cobra (1955) Universal: Francis D. Lyon. Faith Domergue, David Janssen, Jack Kelly.

Curse of Frankenstein (1957) Hammer/WB: Terence Fisher. Peter Cushing, Christopher Lee, Hazel Court.

Curse of the Werewolf (1961) Hammer/Universal: Terence Fisher. Oliver Reed, Clifford Evans, Yvonne Romain.

Damien: Omen II (1978) 20th Century–Fox: Don Taylor. William Holden, Lee Grant, Jonathan Scott-Taylor.

Daughter of Dr. Jekyll (1957) Allied Artists: Edgar Ulmer. Gloria Talbott, John Agar, Arthur Shields.

Dead and Buried (1981) Avco Embassy: Gary A. Sherman. James Farentino, Melody Anderson, Jack Albertson.

Demon Seed (1977) UA: Donald Cammell. Julie Christie, Fritz Weaver, Gerrit Graham.

Demon Witch Child (1976) Coliseum: Amando Ossorio. Julian Mateos, Fernando Sancho, Marian Salgado.

The Devil Within Her (1975) AIP: Peter Sasdy. Joan Collins, Eileen Atkins, Donald Pleasence.

Die, Die My Darling! (1965) Hammer/7 Arts/Columbia: Silvio Narizzano. Tallulah Bankhead, Stefanie Powers, Maurice Kaufman.

Don't Look Now (1973) Paramount: Nicolas Roeg. Donald Sutherland, Julie Christie, Hilary Mason.

Dracula (1931) Universal: Tod Browning. Bela Lugosi, Dwight Frye, Edward Van Sloan.

Dracula's Daughter (1936) Universal: Lambert Hillyer. Gloria Holden, Otto Kruger, Marguerite Churchill.

The Exorcist (1973) WB: William Friedkin. Ellen Burstyn, Max von Sydow, Linda Blair.

Exorcist II: The Heretic (1977) WB: John Boorman. Linda Blair, Richard Burton, Louise Fletcher.

The Final Conflict (1981) 20th Century–Fox: Graham Baker. Sam Neill, Rossano Brazzi, Don Gordon.

The Five Thousand Fingers of Dr. T (1953) Columbia: Roy Rowland. Hans Conreid, Peter Lind Hayes, Mary Healy.

Frankenstein (1910) Edison: J. Searle Dawley. With Charles Ogle, Augustus Phillips, Mary Fuller.

Frankenstein (1931) Universal: James Whale. Colin Clive, Boris Karloff, Dwight Frye.

Frankenstein and the Monster from Hell (1973) Hammer/Paramount: Terence Fisher. Peter Cushing, Shane Briant, Madeleine Smith.

Frankenstein Created Woman (1967) Hammer/7 Arts/20th Century–Fox: Terence Fisher. Peter Cushing, Susan Denberg, Thorley Walters.

Frankenstein Meets the Wolf Man (1943) Universal: Roy William Neill. Lon Chaney, Jr., Bela Lugosi, Lionel Atwill.

Frankenstein's Daughter (1959) Astor: Richard Cunha. John Ashley, Sandra Knight, Donald Murphy.

Ghost of Frankenstein (1942) Universal: Earle C. Kenton. Cedric Hardwicke, Lon Chaney, Jr., Bela Lugosi.

The Godsend (1979) Cannon: Gabrielle Beaumont. Cyd Hayman, Malcolm Stoddard, Angela Pleasence.

The Golem (1917) Bioscop: Paul Wegener & Henrik Galeen. Paul Wegener, Henrik Galeen, Albert Steinrück.

The Golem (1920) PAGU/UFA: Paul Wegener & Carl Boese. Paul Wegener, Albert Steinrück, Lyda Salmanova.

Horror of Dracula (1958) Hammer/Universal: Terence Fisher. Peter Cushing, Christopher Lee, Michael Gough.

The Horror of Frankenstein (1970) Hammer/Levitt-Pickman: Jimmy Sangster. Ralph Bates, Kate O'Mara, Graham James.

House of Dracula (1945) Universal: Earle C. Kenton. Lon Chaney, Jr., Onslow Stevens, John Carradine.

House of Frankenstein (1945) Universal: Earle C. Kenton. Boris Karloff, Lon Chaney, Jr., John Carradine.

The House on Bare Mountain (1962) Olympic International: R.L. Frost. Bob Cresse, Laura Eden, Angela Webster.

Humanoids from the Deep (1980) New World: Barbara Peeters. Doug McClure, Ann Turkel, Vic Morrow.

Hush, Hush Sweet Charlotte (1965) 20th Century–Fox: Robert Aldrich. Bette Davis, Olivia de Havilland, Joseph Cotten.

I Married a Monster from Outer Space (1958) Paramount: Gene Fowler, Jr. Tom Tryon, Gloria Talbott, Ken Lynch.

I Was a Teenage Frankenstein (1957) AIP: Herbert L. Strock. Whit Bissell, Phyllis Coates, Gary Conway.

The Indestructible Man (1956) Allied Artists: Jack Pollexfen. Lon Chaney, Jr., Marian Carr, Robert Shayne.

Invaders from Mars (1953) 20th Century–Fox: William Cameron Menzies. Helena Carter, Arthur Franz, Jimmy Hunt.

Invasion of the Body Snatchers (1956) Allied Artists: Don Siegel. Kevin McCarthy, Dana Wynter, King Donovan.

The Island of Dr. Moreau (1977) AIP: Don Taylor. Burt Lancaster, Michael York, Nigel Davenport.

Island of Lost Souls (1933) Paramount: Earle C. Kenton. Charles Laughton, Richard Arlen, Leila Hyams.

It! (1966) Goldstar / 7 Arts: Herbert J. Leder. Roddy McDowall, Jill Haworth, Paul Maxwell.

It Lives Again (1978) WB: Larry Cohen. Frederic Forrest, Kathleen Lloyd, John P. Ryan.

It's Alive! (1974) WB: Larry Cohen. John P. Ryan, Sharon Farrell, Andrew Duggan.

Jungle Captive (1945) Universal: Harold Young. Otto Kruger, Rondo Hatten, Vicki Lane.

Jungle Woman (1944) Universal: Reginald LeBorg. Evelyn Ankers, J. Carroll Naish, Acquanetta.

Kiss Me Quick (1963) Fantasy: Russ Meyer. Jackie DeWitt, Althea Currier, Fred Coe.

M (1931) Nerofilm / Paramount: Fritz Lang. Peter Lorre, Ellen Widmann, Inge Landgut.

The Manitou (1978) Avco Embassy: William Girdler. Tony Curtis, Susan Strasberg, Michael Ansara.

Man-Made Monster (1941) Universal: George Waggner. Lionel Atwill, Lon Chaney, Jr., Ann Nagel.

The Manster aka **The Split** (1959) Lopert: George P. Breakston & Kenneth G. Crane. Peter Dyneley, Jane Hylton, Satoshi Nakamura.

Metropolis (1927) UFA / Paramount: Fritz Lang. Brigitte Helm, Alfred Abel, Rudolf Klein-Rogge.

Der Müde Tod (1921) Decla Bioscop: Fritz Lang. Lil Dagover, Walter Janssen, Rudolf Klein-Rogge.

The Nanny (1965) Hammer / 20th Century–Fox: Seth Holt. Bette Davis, Wendy Craig, William Dix.

Night of the Blood Beast (1959) AIP: Bernard Kowalski. Michael Emmet, Angela Greene, John Baer.

The Omen (1976) 20th Century–Fox: Richard Donner. Gregory Peck, Lee Remick, David Warner.

The Other (1972) 20th Century–Fox: Robert Mulligan. Uta Hagen, Chris Udvarnoky, Martin Udvarnoky.

Peeping Tom aka **Face of Fear** (1960) Michael Powell Theatre / Astor: Michael Powell. Karl Boehm, Moira Shearer, Anna Massey.

Phantasm (1979) Avco Embassy: Don Coscarelli. Michael Baldwin, Bill Thornbury, Reggie Bannister.

Poltergeist (1982) MGM/UA: Tobe Hooper. JoBeth Williams, Craig T. Nelson, Beatrice Straight.

The Possession of Joel Delaney (1972) Paramount: Waris Hussein. Shirley MacLaine, Perry King, Lovelady Powell.

The Redeemer, Son of Satan (1977) Dimension Pictures: Constantine S. Gochis. Jeannetta Arnette, T.G. Finkbinder, Damien Knight.

Return of the Jedi (1983) 20th Century–Fox: Richard Marquand. Mark Hamill, Harrison Ford, Carrie Fisher.

The Revenge of Frankenstein (1958) Hammer/Columbia: Terence Fisher. Peter Cushing, Michael Gwynn, Francis Matthews.

Robot Monster (1953) Astor: Phil Tucker. George Nader, Claudia Barrett, Selena Royle.

The Rocky Horror Picture Show (1975) 20th Century–Fox: Jim Sharman. Tim Curry, Susan Sarandon, Barry Bostwick.

Rosemary's Baby (1968) Paramount: Roman Polanski. Mia Farrow, John Cassavetes, Ruth Gordon.

Son of Frankenstein (1939) Universal: Rowland Lee. Boris Karloff, Basil Rathbone, Bela Lugosi.

Soylent Green (1973) MGM: Richard Fleischer. Charlton Heston, Edward G. Robinson, Leigh Taylor-Young.

The Space Children (1958) Paramount: Jack Arnold. Adam Williams, Peggy Webber, Michael Ray.

Star Wars (1977) 20th Century–Fox: George Lucas. Mark Hamill, Harrison Ford, Alec Guiness.

Terror Is a Man (1959) Valiant: Gerry DeLeon. Francis Lederer, Greta Thyssen, Richard Derr.

The Testament of Dr. Mabuse (1933) Nerofilm: Fritz Lang. Oskar Beregi, Rudolf Klein-Rogge, Cammila Spira.

Them! (1954) WB: Gordon Douglas. James Whitmore, James Arness, Edmund Gwenn.

THX-1138 (1971) American Zoetrope: George Lucas. Robert Duvall, Donald Pleasence, Don Pedro Colley.

Village of the Damned (1960) MGM: Wolf Rilla. George Sanders, Barbara Shelley, Martin Stephens.

Whatever Happened to Baby Jane? (1962) WB: Robert Aldrich. Bette Davis, Joan Crawford, Victor Buono.

Who Slew Auntie Roo? (1971) AIP: Curtis Harrington. Shelley Winters, Mark Lester, Ralph Richardson.

X — The Unknown (1956) Hammer/WB: Leslie Norman. Dean Jagger, Edward Chapman, Leo McKern.

Young Frankenstein (1974) 20th Century–Fox: Mel Brooks. Gene Wilder, Peter Boyle, Marty Feldman.

ZPG (1972) Paramount: Michael Campus. Oliver Reed, Geraldine Chaplin, Diane Cilento.

Chapter II

The Adult Version of Jekyll and Hide (1973) Entertainment Ventures: B. Ron Elliott.

An American Werewolf in London (1981) Universal/Polygram: John Landis. David Naughton, Griffin Dunne, Jenny Agutter.

Dead of Night (1946) Ealing/Universal: Alberto Cavalcanti, Basil Dearden,

Robert Hamer, Charles Crichton. Mervyn Johns, Michael Redgrave, Googie Withers.

Dr. Black and Mr. Hyde (1976) Dimension: William Crain. Bernie Casey, Rosalind Cash, Marie O'Henry.

Dr. Jekyll and Mr. Hyde (1932) Paramount: Rouben Mamoulian. Fredric March, Miriam Hopkins, Rose Hobart.

Dr. Jekyll and Mr. Hyde (1941) MGM: Victor Fleming. Spencer Tracy, Ingrid Bergman, Lana Turner.

Dr. Jekyll and Mr. Hyde (1973) NBC-TV: David Winter. Kirk Douglas, Susan George, Susan Hampshire.

Dr. Jekyll and Sister Hyde (1972) Hammer–EMI/AIP: Roy Ward Baker. Martine Beswick, Ralph Bates, Gerald Sim.

Dr. Pyckle and Mr. Pride (1925) Standard/Film Booking Offices of America, Inc.: Joe Rock (producer). Stan Laurel.

Dr. Sexual and Mr. Hyde (1972) Anthony Brzezinski. Cindy Hopkins.

Dr. X (1932) First National: Michael Curtiz. Lionel Atwill, Fay Wray, Lee Tracy.

Erdgeist (1923) Jessner: Leopold Jessner. Asta Nielsen, Rudolf Forster, Albert Bassermann.

Eyes of Laura Mars (1978) Columbia: Irvin Kershner. Faye Dunaway, Tommy Lee Jones, Brad Dourif.

The Great Gabbo (1930) Sono-Art/World Wide: James Cruze. Erich von Stroheim, Betty Compson, Don Douglas.

The Hand (1981) Orion/WB: Oliver Stone. Michael Caine, Andrea Marcovicci, Annie McEnroe.

Hangover Square (1945) 20th Century–Fox: John Brahm. Laird Cregar, George Sanders, Linda Darnell.

The Howling (1981) Avco Embassy: Joe Dante. Dee Wallace, Patrick Macnee, Dennis Dugan.

I, Monster (1971) Amicus/Cannon: Stephen Weeks. Christopher Lee, Peter Cushing, Mike Raven.

Jack the Ripper (1960) Paramount: Robert S. Baker & Monty Berman. Lee Patterson, Eddie Byrne, Ewen Solon.

Jekyll and Hyde – Together Again (1982) Paramount: Jerry Belson. Mark Blankfield, Bess Armstrong, Krista Errickson.

The Legend of Lylah Clare (1968) MGM: Robert Aldrich. Kim Novak, Peter Finch, Ernest Borgnine.

The Lodger (1926) Gainesborough: Alfred Hitchcock. Ivor Novello, Malcolm Keen, Arthur Chesney.

The Lodger (1932) Olympic: Maurice Elvey. Ivor Novello, Elizabeth Allan, Jack Hawkins.

The Lodger (1944) 20th Century–Fox: John Brahm. Laird Cregar, Merle Oberon, George Sanders.

Lulu (1962) Vienna Filmproduktion: Rolf Thiele. Nadja Tiller, Hildegarde Neff, O.E. Hasse.

Mad Love (1935) MGM: Karl Freund. Peter Lorre, Colin Clive, Frances Drake.

Magic (1978) 20th Century–Fox: Richard Attenborough. Anthony Hopkins, Ann-Margret, Burgess Meredith.

The Man in Half Moon Street (1944) Paramount: Ralph M. Murphy. Nils Asther, Helen Walker, Reinhold Schunzel.

Man in the Attic (1953) 20th Century–Fox: Hugo Fregonese. Jack Palance, Constance Smith, Sean McClory.

The Man Who Could Cheat Death (1959) Hammer/Paramount: Terence Fisher. Anton Diffring, Hazel Court, Christopher Lee.

Monster on the Campus (1958) Universal: Jack Arnold. Arthur Franz, Joanna Moore, Judson Pratt.

The Neanderthal Man (1953) UA: E.A. DuPont. Robert Shayne, Richard Crane, Doris Merric.

The Nutty Professor (1964) Paramount: Jerry Lewis. Jerry Lewis, Stella Stevens, Del Moore.

Pandora's Box (1929) Moviegraphs, Inc.: G.W. Pabst. Louise Brooks, Fritz Kortner, Franz (Francis) Lederer.

The Picture of Dorian Gray (1945) MGM: Albert Lewin. Hurd Hatfield, George Sanders, Donna Reed.

Play Misty for Me (1971) Universal: Clint Eastwood. Clint Eastwood, Jessica Walter, Donna Mills.

The Raven (1935) Universal: Louis Friedlander. Boris Karloff, Bela Lugosi, Irene Ware.

Room to Let (1950) Hammer: Godfrey Grayson. Jimmy Hanley, Valentine Dyall, Christine Silver.

The Secret Life of Dorian Gray (1971) Commonwealth United/AIP: Harry Alan Towers. Helmut Berger, Richard Todd, Herbert Lom.

The Shining (1980) WB: Stanley Kubrick. Jack Nicholson, Shelley Duvall, Danny Lloyd.

Son of Dr. Jekyll (1951) Columbia: Seymour Friedman. Louis Hayward, Alexander Knox, Jody Lawrence.

A Study in Terror (1966) Columbia: James Hill. John Neville, Donald Houston, John Fraser.

Taxi Driver (1976) Columbia: Martin Scorsese. Robert DeNiro, Harvey Keitel, Jodie Foster.

Three Wax Men (1924) Viking: Paul Leni. Emil Jannings, Conrad Veidt, Werner Krauss.

Time After Time (1979) WB: Nicholas Meyer. Malcolm McDowell, Mary Steenburgen, David Warner.

The Two Faces of Dr. Jekyll (1960) Hammer/AIP: Terence Fisher. Paul Massie, Dawn Addams, Christopher Lee.

The Ugly Duckling (1959) Hammer: Lance Comfort. Bernard Bresslaw, Reginald Beckwith, Jon Pertwee.

Werewolf of London (1935) Universal: Stuart Walker. Henry Hull, Warner Oland, Valerie Hobson.

The Wolf Man (1941) Universal: George Waggner. Claude Rains, Lon Chaney, Jr., Bela Lugosi.

Chapter III

Abbott and Costello Go to Mars (1952) Universal: Charles Lamont. Bud Abbott, Lou Costello, Robert Paige.

The Amazing Colossal Man (1957) AIP: Bert I. Gordon. Glen Langan, Cathy Downs, William Hudson.

The Astounding She-Monster (1958) AIP: Ronnie Ashcroft. Robert Clarke, Kenne Duncan, Shirley Kilpatrick.

The Atomic Cafe (1982) The Archives Project: Kevin Rafferty, Jayne Loader, Pierce Rafferty. Documentary.

Attack of the 50-Foot Woman (1958) Allied Artists: Nathan Hertz (Juran). Allison Hayes, William Hudson, Yvette Vickers.

Attack of the Giant Leeches (1958) AIP: Bernard L. Kowalski. Ken Clarke, Yvette Vickers, Michael Emmet.

Attack of the Puppet People (1958) AIP: Bert I. Gordon. John Agar, June Kenney, John Hoyt.

The Awful Dr. Orloff (1961) Sigma III: Jesus Franco. Howard Vernon, Conrado San Martin, Perla Cristal.

The Beguiled (1971) Universal: Don Siegel. Clint Eastwood, Geraldine Page, Elizabeth Hartman.

The Black Cat (1934) Universal: Edgar Ulmer. Boris Karloff, Bela Lugosi, David Manners.

Blood of Dracula (1957) AIP: Herbert L. Strock. Sandra Harrison, Louise Lewis, Thomas B. Henry.

Cat Women of the Moon (1953) Astor: Arthur Hilton. Sonny Tufts, Marie Windsor, Victor Jory.

Un Chien Andalou (1928) Experimental film: Luis Buñuel & Salvador Dalí. Simone Mareuil, Pierre Batcheff, Luis Buñuel.

The Day After (1983) ABC-TV: Nicholas Meyer. JoBeth Williams, Jason Robards, John Lithgow.

The Day the World Ended (1956) American Releasing Corporation (AIP): Roger Corman. Richard Denning, Lori Nelson, Paul Birch.

Devil Doll (1936) MGM: Tod Browning. Lionel Barrymore, Maureen O'Sullivan, Lucy Beaumont.

The Diabolical Dr. Z (1966) U.S. Films: Jesus Franco. Mabel Karr, Fernando Montes, Estella Blaine.

Les Diaboliques (1955) Filmsonor: Henri-Georges Clouzet. Simone Signoret, Vera Clouzet, Paul Meurisse.

The Disembodied (1957) Allied Artists: Walter Grauman. Paul Burke, Allison Hayes, Joseph E. Wengraf.

Dr. Cyclops (1940) Paramount: Ernest B. Schoedsack. Albert Dekker, Janice Logan, Thomas Coley.

Dr. Strangelove (1964) Columbia: Stanley Kubrick. Peter Sellers, George C. Scott, Sterling Hayden.

Eyes Without a Face aka **The Horror Chamber of Dr. Faustus** (1959) Lopert: Georges Franju. Pierre Brasseur, Alida Valli, Edith Scob.

Fail-Safe (1964) Columbia: Sidney Lumet. Henry Fonda, Dan O'Herlihy, Walter Matthau.

Five (1951) Columbia: Arch Oboler. Susan Douglas, William Phipps, James Anderson.

Forbidden Planet (1956) MGM: Fred McLeod Wilcox. Leslie Nielsen, Anne Francis, Walter Pidgeon.

The 4-D Man (1959) Universal: Irvin S. Yeaworth, Jr. Robert Lansing, Lee Meriwether, James Congdon.

Freaks (1932) MGM: Tod Browning. Olga Baclanova, Leila Hyams, Wallace Ford.

Ghost Story (1981) Universal: John Irvin. Fred Astaire, Melvyn Douglas, John Houseman, Alice Krige.

The Haunting (1963) MGM: Robert Wise. Claire Bloom, Julie Harris, Richard Johnson.

Homicidal (1961) Columbia: William Castle. Jean Arless, Patricia Breslin, Glenn Corbett.

Horror Hotel aka **City of the Dead** (1960) Trans-Lux: John Llewellyn Moxey. Patricia Jessell, Betta St. John, Christopher Lee.

Horrors of the Black Museum (1959) AIP: Arthur Crabtree. Michael Gough, June Cunningham, Graham Curnow.

House on Haunted Hill (1958) Allied Artists: William Castle. Vincent Price, Carol Ohmart, Richard Long.

The Hypnotic Eye (1960) Allied Artists: George Blair. Jacques Bergerac, Allison Hayes, Merry Anders.

The Incredible Shrinking Man (1957) Universal: Jack Arnold. Grant Williams, Randy Stuart, April Kent.

The Innocents (1961) 20th Century-Fox: Jack Clayton. Deborah Kerr, Martin Stephens, Pamela Franklin.

Invasion of the Body Snatchers (1956) Allied Artists: Don Siegel. Kevin McCarthy, Dana Wynter, King Donovan.

Invasion of the Body Snatchers (1978) UA: Philip Kaufman. Donald Sutherland, Brooke Adams, Veronica Cartwright.

Journey to the 7th Planet (1962) AIP: Sidney Pink. John Agar, Greta Thyssen, Ann Smyrner.

The Leech Woman (1960) Universal: Edward Dein. Coleen Gray, Gloria Talbott, Grant Williams.

Lock Up Your Daughters (1956) New Realm: Sam Katzman (producer). Bela Lugosi.

The Mask aka **Eyes of Hell** (1961) Roffman-Taylor & Beaver-Champion Attractions/WB: Julian Roffman. Paul Stevens, Claudette Nevins, Bill Walker.

Mesa of Lost Women (1953) Howco: Herbert Tevos & Ron Ormond. Jackie Coogan, Allan Nixon, Richard Travis.

Meshes of the Afternoon (1943) Experimental film: Maya Deren. Maya Deren, Alexander Hammid.

Murders in the Zoo (1933) Paramount: Edward Sutherland. Lionel Atwill, Kathleen Burke, Charlie Ruggles.

The Nightcomers (1972) Avco Embassy: Michael Winner. Marlon Brando, Stephanie Beacham, Thora Hird.

1984 (1956) Holiday Film Productions/Columbia: Michael Anderson. Edmond O'Brien, Jan Sterling, Michael Redgrave.

1984 (1984) Atlantic Releasing Corp.: Michael Radford. John Hurt, Suzanna Hamilton, Richard Burton.

Outer Space Jitters (1957) Columbia: Jules White. Moe Howard, Larry Fine, Joe Besser.

Panic in Year Zero (1962) AIP: Ray Milland. Ray Milland, Jean Hagen, Frankie Avalon.

Queen of Blood (1966) AIP: Curtis Harrington. Florence Marly, John Saxon, Basil Rathbone.

Queen of Outer Space (1958) Allied Artists: Edward L. Bernds. Eric Fleming, Zsa Zsa Gabor, Laurie Mitchell.

Repusion (1965) Royal Films: Roman Polanski. Catherine Deneuve, Ian Hendry, John Fraser.

Rocketship X-M (1950) Lippert: Kurt Neumann. Lloyd Bridges, Osa Massen, John Emery.

Rosemary's Baby (1968) Paramount: Roman Polanski. Mia Farrow, John Cassavetes, Ruth Gordon.

The She-Creature (1956) AIP: Edward L. Cahn. Chester Morris, Marla English, Tom Conway.

Space Ship Sappy (1957) Columbia: Jules White. Moe Howard, Larry Fine, Joe Besser.

The Stepford Wives (1975) Columbia: Bryan Forbes. Katharine Ross, Paula Prentiss, Patrick O'Neal.

Strait-Jacket (1964) Columbia: William Castle. Joan Crawford, Diane Baker, Leif Erickson.

The Tenant (1976) Paramount: Roman Polanski. Roman Polanski, Isabelle Adjani, Melvyn Douglas.

The Terror from the Year 5000 (1958) AIP: Robert Gurney, Jr. Ward Costello, Joyce Holden, Salome Jens.

The Tingler (1959) Columbia: William Castle. Vincent Price, Judith Evelyn, Darryl Hickman.

Unknown World (1951) Lippert: Terry Morse. Bruce Kellogg, Marilyn Nash, Victor Kilian.

Voodoo Woman (1957) AIP: Edward L. Cahn. Marla English, Tom Conway, Touch (Mike) Connors.

The War Game (1966) Pathe Contemporary: Peter Watkins. Michael Aspel, Dick Graham (narrators).

White Zombie (1932) UA: Victor Halperin. Bela Lugosi, Madge Bellamy, John Harron.

The Wicker Man (1973) WB: Robin Hardy. Edward Woodward, Christopher Lee, Britt Ekland.

The World, the Flesh, and the Devil (1959) MGM: Ranald MacDougall. Mel Ferrer, Inger Stevens, Harry Belafonte.

Chapter IV

Abbott and Costello Meet the Mummy (1955) Universal: Charles Lamont. Bud Abbott, Lou Costello, Marie Windsor.

A*P*E (1976) Worldwide: Paul Leder. Rod Arrants, Joanna DeVarona, Alex Nicol.

The Ape Man (1943) Monogram: William Beaudine. Bela Lugosi, Wallace Ford, Louise Currie.

Attack of the Mushroom People aka **Matango** (1964) Toho/AIP-TV: Inoshiro Honda & Eiji Tsuburaya. Akiro Kubo, Yoshio Tsuchiya, Hiroshi Koizuma.

The Awakening (1980) Orion: Mike Newell. Charlton Heston, Susannah York, Jill Townsend.

The Bat Whispers (1931) UA: Roland West. Chester Morris, Una Merkel, Chance Wood.

Beast of Borneo (1935) DuWorld Pictures, Inc.: Harry Garson. John Preston, Mae Stuart, Eugene Sigaloff.

Beauty and the Beast aka **La Belle et la Bête** (1946) Discina/Lopert: Jean Cocteau. Jean Marais, Josette Day, Marcel Andre.

Blood from the Mummy's Tomb (1971) Hammer/AIP: Seth Holt & Michael Carreras. Andrew Keir, Valerie Leon, James Villiers.

A Boy and his Dog (1976) Marvin: L.Q. Jones. Don Johnson, Susanne Benton, Jason Robards.

The Brain that Wouldn't Die (1959) AIP: Joseph Green. Herb (Jason) Evers, Virginia Leith, Adele Lamont.

The Bride and the Beast aka **Queen of the Gorillas** (1958) Allied Artists: Adrian Weiss. Charlotte Austin, Lance Fuller, Johnny Roth.

Bride of the Gorilla (1952) Realart: Curt Siodmak. Lon Chaney, Jr., Barbara Payton, Raymond Burr.

The Cabinet of Dr. Caligari (1919) Decla/Goldwyn: Robert Wiene. Conrad Veidt, Werner Krauss, Lil Dagover.

The Cat and the Canary (1928) Universal: Paul Leni. Laura LaPlante, Creighton Hale, Lucien Littlefield.

The Creature from the Black Lagoon (1954) Universal: Jack Arnold. Richard Carlson, Richard Denning, Julie Adams.

The Creature Walks Among Us (1956) Universal: John Sherwood. Jeff Morrow, Rex Reason, Leigh Snowden.

The Curse of the Mummy's Tomb (1964) Hammer & Swallow/Columbia: Michael Carreras. Terence Morgan, Fred Clark, Ronald Howard.

The Entity (1983) 20th Century–Fox: Sidney Furie. Barbara Hershey, Ron Silver, Jacqueline Brooks.

The Face Behind the Mask (1941) Columbia: Robert Florey. Peter Lorre, Evelyn Keyes, Don Beddoe.

Flesh Gordon (1972) Graffiti Productions: Mike Light. Jason Williams, Suzanne Fields, Joseph Hudgins.

The Fly (1958) 20th Century–Fox: Kurt Neumann. Al (David) Hedison, Vincent Price, Patricia Owens.

Forbidden Adventure in Angkor (1937) Roadshow: J.C. Cook.

Frankenstein Meets the Space Monster (1965) Allied Artists: Robert Gaffney. James Karen, Nancy Marshall, Robert Reilly.

From Hell It Came (1957) Allied Artists: Dan Milner. Tod Andrews, Tina Carver, Greg Palmer.

The Gorilla (1927) First National: Alfred Santell. Charlie Murray, Fred Kelsey, Alice Day.

The Gorilla (1930) WB: Bryan Foy. Joe Frisco, Harry Gribbon, Walter Pidgeon.

Gorilla at Large (1954) 20th Century–Fox: Harmon Jones. Cameron Mitchell, Anne Bancroft, Lee J. Cobb.

The House of Mystery (1934) Monogram: William Nigh. Ed Lowry, Verna Hillie, Mary Foy.

House of Wax (1953) WB: Andre de Toth. Vincent Price, Frank Lovejoy, Phyllis Kirk.

Humanoids from the Deep (1980) New World: Barbara Peeters. Doug McClure, Ann Turkel, Vic Morrow.

The Hunchback of Notre Dame (1924) Universal: Wallace Worsley. Lon Chaney, Ernest Torrence, Patsy Ruth Miller.

The Hunchback of Notre Dame (1939) RKO: William Dieterle. Charles Laughton, Maureen O'Hara, Edmond O'Brien.

The Hunchback of Notre Dame (1957) Allied Artists: Jean Delannoy. Anthony Quinn, Gina Lollobrigida, Alain Cuny.

The Hunchback of Notre Dame (1982) CBS-TV: Michael Tuchner. Anthony Hopkins, Lesley-Anne Down, Derek Jacobi.

The Incredible Two-Headed Transplant (1971) AIP: Anthony Lanza. Bruce Dern, Pat Priest, Casey Kasem.

Ingagi (1931) Congo Pictures: William Campbell. Sir Hubert Winstead, Daniel Swayne, Charles Gemora.

Island of Lost Souls (1933) Paramount: Earle C. Kenton. Charles Laughton, Leila Hyams, Richard Arlen.

Jaws (1975) Universal: Steven Spielberg. Robert Shaw, Roy Scheider, Richard Dreyfuss.

Kentucky Fried Movie (1977) United Film Distribution: John Landis. Marilyn Joi, Saul Kahan, Marcy Goldman.

King Kong (1933) RKO: Merian C. Cooper & Ernest Schoedsack. Fay Wray, Robert Armstrong, Bruce Cabot.

King Kong (1976) Paramount: John Guillermin. Rick Baker, Jeff Bridges, Jessica Lange.

Konga (1961) AIP: John Lemont. Michael Gough, Margo Johns, Jess Conrad.

The Lost World (1960) 20th Century–Fox: Irwin Allen. Claude Rains, Michael Rennie, Jill St. John.

Love Life of a Gorilla (1937) Jewel Productions.

Mars Needs Women (1966) AIP-TV: Larry Buchanan. Tommy Kirk, Yvonne Craig, Byron Lord.

Mighty Joe Young (1949) RKO: Ernest B. Schoedsack. Robert Armstrong, Terry Moore, Ben Johnson.

The Monster and the Girl (1941) Paramount: Stuart Heisler. Ellen Drew, Robert Paige, Paul Lukas.

The Monster of Piedras Blancas (1959) Filmservice Distributors: Irvin Berwick. Les Tremayne, Don Sullivan, Jeanne Carmen.

The Monster Walks (1932) Mayfair Pictures: Frank Strayer. Rex Lease, Vera Reynolds, Mischa Auer.

The Mummy (1932) Universal: Karl Freund. Boris Karloff, Zita Johann, Edward Van Sloan.

The Mummy (1959) Hammer/Universal: Terence Fisher. Peter Cushing, Christopher Lee, Yvonne Furneaux.

The Mummy's Curse (1945) Universal: Leslie Goodwins. Lon Chaney, Jr., Virginia Christine, Peter Coe.

The Mummy's Ghost (1944) Universal: Reginald LeBorg. Lon Chaney, Jr., John Carradine, Ramsay Ames.

The Mummy's Hand (1940) Universal: Christy Cabanne. Dick Foran, Peggy Moran, Tom Tyler.

The Mummy's Shroud (1967) Hammer & 7 Arts/20th Century–Fox: John Gilling. Andre Morell, John Phillips, David Buck.

The Mummy's Tomb (1942) Universal: Harold Young. Lon Chaney, Jr., Turhan Bey, Wallace Ford.

Murders in the Rue Morgue (1932) Universal: Robert Florey. Bela Lugosi, Sidney Fox, Leon Waycroff (Ames).

Mystery of the Wax Museum (1933) WB: Michael Curtiz. Lionel Atwill, Fay Wray, Glenda Farrell.

The Navy vs. the Night Monsters (1966) Realart: Michael Hoey. Mamie Van Doren, Anthony Eisley, Bobby Van.

The Phantom of the Opera (1925) Universal: Rupert Julian. Lon Chaney, Mary Philbin, Norman Kerry.

The Phantom of the Opera (1943) Universal: Arthur Lubin. Claude Rains, Nelson Eddy, Suzanna Foster.

The Phantom of the Opera (1962) Hammer/Universal: Terence Fisher. Herbert Lom, Heather Sears, Thorley Walters.

Return of the Fly (1959) 20th Century–Fox: Edward L. Bernds. Vincent Price, Brett Halsey, David Frankham.

Revenge of the Creature (1955) Universal: Jack Arnold. John Agar, Lori Nelson, John Bromfield.

Savage Girl (1932) Commonwealth Pictures: Harry S. Fraser. Rochelle Hudson, Walter Byron, Harry F. Myers.

Schlock! (1973) Jack H. Harris: John Landis. Saul Kahan, Joseph Piantadosi, Eliza Garrett.

Seven Footprints to Satan (1929) First National: Benjamin Christensen. Thelma Todd, Creighton Hale, Sheldon Lewis.

Son of Kong (1933) RKO: Ernest B. Schoedsack. Robert Armstrong, Helen Mack, Frank Reicher.

Swamp Thing (1982) Embassy: Wes Craven. Louis Jourdan, Adrienne Barbeau, Ray Wise.

Svengali (1931) WB: Archie Mayo. John Barrymore, Marian Marsh, Bramwell Fletcher.

Tanya's Island (1980) International Film Exchange: Aldred Sole. D.D. Winters (Vanity), Richard Sargent, Don McCloud.

Target Earth! (1954) Allied Artists: Sherman Rose. Richard Denning, Virginia Gray, Kathleen Crowley.

The Terror (1928) WB: Roy Del Ruth. May McAvoy, Louise Fazenda, Edward Everett Horton.

The Thing with Two Heads (1972) AIP: Lee Frost. Ray Milland, Roosevelt Grier, Don Marshall.

The Time Machine (1960) MGM: George Pal. Rod Taylor, Yvette Mimieux, Alan Young.

The War of the Worlds (1953) Paramount: Byron Haskin. Gene Barry, Ann Robinson, Les Tremayne.

Wham, Bam, Thank You Spaceman (ca. 1974) Boxoffice International: Harry Novak (producer). Jay Rasumny, Dyanne Thorne.

White Pongo (1945) PRC: Sam Newfield. Richard Fraser, Maris Wrixon, Lionel Royce.

The Wizard (1927) Fox: Richard Rosson. Edmund Lowe, Leila Hyams, Gustav von Seyffertitz.

Womaneater (1959) Fortress: Charles Saunders. George Coulouris, Vera Day, Peter Wayn.

Zamba the Gorilla (1949) Eagle-Lion: William Berke. Jon Hall, June Vincent, George Cooper.

Chapter V

Beauty and the Robot aka **Sex Kittens Go to College** aka **Teacher Was a Sexpot** (1962) Allied Artists: Albert Zugsmith. Mamie Van Doren, Tuesday Weld, Mijanou Bardot.

The Blob (1958) Paramount: Irvin S. Yeaworth, Jr. Steve McQueen, Aneta Corseaut, Olin Howlin.

A Clockwork Orange (1971) WB: Stanley Kubrick. Malcolm McDowell, Patrick Magee, Warren Clarke.

Eegah! (1962) Favorite Films: Nicholas Merriwether (Arch W. Hall, Sr.). Arch Hall, Jr., Marilyn Manning, Richard Kiel.

The Eye Creatures (1968) AIP-TV: Larry Buchanan. John Ashley, Cynthia Hull, Warren Hammack.

The Giant Gila Monster (1959) McLendon Radio Pictures: Ray Kellogg. Don Sullivan, Lisa Simone, Shug Fisher.

Horror of Party Beach (1964) 20th Century–Fox: Del Tenney. John Scott, Alice Lyon, Allen Laurel.

How to Make a Monster (1958) AIP: Herbert L. Strock. Robert H. Harris, Gary Conway, Paul Brinegar.

I Was a Teenage Frankenstein (1957) AIP: Herbert L. Strock. Whit Bissell, Gary Conway, Phyllis Coates.

I Was a Teenage Werewolf (1957) AIP: Gene Fowler, Jr. Michael Landon, Whit Bissell, Yvonne Lime.

The Incredibly Strange Creatures Who Stopped Living and Became Mixed-Up Zombies aka **Teenage Psycho Meets Bloody Mary** (1963) Fairway International: Ray Dennis Steckler. Cash Flagg (R.D. Steckler), Carolyn Brandt, Toni Camel.

Invasion of the Saucermen (1957) AIP: Edward L. Cahn. Steve Terrell, Gloria Castillo, Frank Gorshin.

Night of the Comet (1984) Atlantic Releasing: Thom Eberhardt. Catherine Mary Stewart, Kelli Maroney, Robert Beltran.

Pretty Poison (1968) 20th Century–Fox: Noel Black. Anthony Perkins, Tuesday Weld, Beverly Garland.

Privilege (1967) Universal: Peter Watkins. Paul Jones, Jean Shrimpton, Mark London.

Teenage Zombies (1960) Governor Films: Jerry Warren. Don Sullivan, Katherine Victor, Steve Conte.

Wild in the Streets (1968) AIP: Barry Shear. Christopher Jones, Shelley Winters, Diane Varsi.

Chapter VI

Abbott and Costello Meet Frankenstein (1948) Universal: Charles T. Barton. Bud Abbott, Lou Costello, Bela Lugosi.

Blacula (1972) AIP: William Crane. William Marshall, Denise Nicholas, Vonetta McGee.

Blood and Roses (1961) Paramount: Roger Vadim. Mel Ferrer, Elsa Martinelli, Annette Vadim.

Blood Bath (1966) AIP: Jack Hill and Stephanie Rothman. William Campbell, Marissa Mathes, Lori Saunders.

The Blood Beast Terror (1969) Tigon/Pacemaker: Vernon Sewell. Peter Cushing, Robert Flemyng, Wanda Ventham.

Blood for Dracula aka **Andy Warhol's Dracula** (1974) Bryanston: Paul Morissey. Udo Kier, Joe Dallesandro, Arno Juerging.

Brides of Dracula (1960) Hammer/Universal: Terence Fisher. David Peel, Peter Cushing, Martita Hunt.

Captain Kronos, Vampire Hunter (1973) Hammer/Paramount: Brian Clemens. Horst Janson, John Carson, Shane Briant.

Count Dracula aka **El Conde Dracula** (1970) Towers of London: Jesus Franco. Christopher Lee, Herbert Lom, Klaus Kinski.

Count Yorga, Vampire (1970) AIP: Bob Kelljan. Robert Quarry, Roger Perry, Michael Murphy.

Countess Dracula (1971) Hammer/20th Century–Fox: Peter Sasdy. Ingrid Pitt, Nigel Green, Sandor Elés.

Daughters of Darkness (1970) Gemini & Maron: Harry Kümel. Delphine Seyrig, Daniele Ouimet, John Karlen.

The Devil Bat (1941) PRC: Jean Yarbrough. Bela Lugosi, Dave O'Brien, Suzanne Kaaren.

The Devil's Mistress (1966) Holiday: Orville Wanzer. Arthur Resley, Joan Stapleton, Forrest Westmoreland.

Does Dracula Really Suck? aka **Dracula and the Boys** (1969).

Dracula (1931) Universal: Tod Browning. Bela Lugosi, David Manners, Edward Van Sloan.

Dracula (1973) ABC-TV: Dan Curtis. Jack Palance, Simon Ward, Nigel Davenport.

Dracula (1979) Universal: John Badham. Frank Langella, Laurence Olivier, Donald Pleasence.

Dracula A.D. 1972 (1972) Hammer/WB: Alan Gibson. Christopher Lee, Peter Cushing, Stephanie Beacham.

Dracula Has Risen from the Grave (1968) Hammer/WB-7 Arts: Freddie Francis. Christopher Lee, Rupert Davies, Veronica Carlson.

Dracula Meets the Outer Space Chicks (1968).

Dracula, Prince of Darkness (1966) Hammer/7 Arts: Terence Fisher. Christopher Lee, Barbara Shelley, Andrew Keir.

Dracula, the Dirty Old Man (1969) Whit Boyd Productions: William Edwards. Vince Kelly, Ann Hollis, Bunny Boyd.

Le Frisson des Vampires (1970) ABC/Films Modernes: Jean Rollin. Sandra Julien, Jean-Marie Durand, Dominique.

Horror of Dracula (1958) Hammer/Universal: Terence Fisher. Peter Cushing, Christopher Lee, Michael Gough.

House on Bare Mountain (1962) Olympic International: R.L. Frost. Bob Cresse, Laura Eden, Angela Webster.

Kiss of the Vampire (1963) Hammer/Universal: Don Sharp. Clifford Evans, Noel Willman, Edward De Souza.

Kuroneko aka **The Black Cat** (1968) Toho: Kaneto Shindo. Kichiemon Nakamura, Nobuko Otowa, Kiwako Taichi.

London After Midnight (1927) MGM: Tod Browning. Lon Chaney, Marceline Day, Edna Tichenor.

Love at First Bite (1979) AIP: Stan Dragoti. George Hamilton, Susan Saint James, Richard Benjamin.

Lust for a Vampire (1971) Hammer/Levitt-Pickman: Jimmy Sangster. Ralph Bates, Yutte Stensgaard, Barbara Jefford.

Mark of the Vampire (1935) MGM: Tod Browning. Bela Lugosi, Carroll Borland, Lionel Barrymore.

The Night Stalker (1972) ABC-TV: John Llewellyn Moxey. Darren McGavin, Carol Lynley, Barry Atwater.

La Noche de Walpurgis aka **Werewolf vs. the Vampire Woman** (1974) Universal Entertainment Corp./Ellman: Leon Klimovsky. Paul Naschy, Gaby Fuchs, Barbara Capell.

Nosferatu (1980) 20th Century–Fox: Werner Herzog. Klaus Kinski, Isabelle Adjani, Bruno Ganz.

Nosferatu, the Vampire (1922) Film Arts Guild: F.W. Murnau. Max Schreck, Alexander Granach, Gustav von Wangenheim.

The Return of Count Yorga (1971) AIP: Bob Kelljan. Robert Quarry, Mariette Hartley, Roger Perry.

Return of Dracula (1958) UA: Paul Landres. Francis Lederer, Norma Eberhardt, Ray Stricklyn.

Return of the Vampire (1944) Columbia: Lew Landers. Bela Lugosi, Nina Foch, Frieda Inescort.

Salem's Lot (1979) CBS-TV: Tobe Hooper. James Mason, David Soul, Reggie Nalder.

The Satanic Rites of Dracula (1973) Hammer/WB: Alan Gibson. Christopher Lee, Peter Cushing, Michael Coles.

Scars of Dracula (1970) Hammer/Levitt-Pickman: Roy Ward Baker. Christopher Lee, Dennis Waterman, Jenny Hanley.

Son of Dracula (1943) Universal: Robert Siodmak. Lon Chaney, Jr., J. Edward Bromberg, Louise Allbritton.

The Spider Woman Strikes Back (1946) Universal: Arthur Lubin. Brenda Joyce, Gale Sondergaard, Kirby Grant.

Taste the Blood of Dracula (1970) Hammer/WB: Peter Sasdy. Christopher Lee, Geoffrey Keen, Linda Hayden.

Twins of Evil (1971) Hammer/Universal: John Hough. Peter Cushing, Mary Collinson, Madeleine Collinson.

L'Ultima Preda del Vampiro aka **Playgirls and the Vampire** (1960) Gordon Films, Inc.: Piero Regnoli. Lyla Rocco, Walter Brandi, Mario Giovannini.

The Vampire (1957) UA: Paul Landres. John Beal, Coleen Gray, Kenneth Tobey.

The Vampire Lovers (1971) Hammer/AIP: Roy Ward Baker. Ingrid Pitt, Pippa Steel, Madeleine Smith.

La Vampire Nue (1969) ABC: Jean Rollin. Olivier Martin, Maurice Lemaitre, Caroline Cartier.

Vampire Playgirls (1974) Hemisphere: Jean Brismee. Erika Blanc, Jean Servais, Daniel Emilfork.

Vampyres (1974) Cambist: Joseph Larraz. Marianne Morris, Anulka, Murray Brown.

The Velvet Vampire (1971) New World: Stephanie Rothman. Celeste Yarnall, Michael Blodgett, Sherry Miles.

Vierges et Vampires aka **Virgins and Vampires** aka **Crazed Vampire** aka **Caged Virgins** (1971) Boxoffice International: Jean Rollin. Marie Pierre Castel, Mirielle D'Argent, Philippe Gaste.

Le Viol du Vampire (1967) ABC-Selsky: Jean Rollin. Solange Pradel, Ursulle Pauly, Nicole Romain.

Chapter VII

An Angel for Satan (1966) Discobolo Cinematografica: Camillo Mastrocinque. Barbara Steele, Antonio De Teffe, Claudio Gora.

Black Sunday aka **La Maschera Del Demonio** aka **Revenge of the Vampire** (1960) Galatea & Jolly/AIP: Mario Bava. Barbara Steele, John Richardson, Andrea Checchi.

Blood and Black Lace (1964) Woolner: Mario Bava. Eva Bartok, Cameron Mitchell, Thomas Reiner.

Castle of Blood aka **La Danza Macabre** (1964) Woolner: Antonio Margheriti. Barbara Steele, George Riviere, Margrete Robsahm.

The Crimson Cult aka **Curse of the Crimson Altar** (1968) Tigon/AIP: Vernon Sewell. Boris Karloff, Barbara Steele, Christopher Lee.

8½ (1962) Cineriz/Embassy: Federico Fellini. Marcello Mastroianni, Claudia Cardinale, Anouk Aimee.

The Ghost aka **The Spectre** (1962) Magna: Riccardo Freda. Barbara Steele, Peter Baldwin, Elio Jotta.

The Horrible Dr. Hichcock (1962) Sigma III: Riccardo Freda. Barbara Steele, Robert Flemyng, Harriet White.

I Lunghi Capelli della Morte aka **the Long Hair of Death** (1964) Cinegai: Antonio Margheriti. Barbara Steele, Giorgio Ardisson, Halina Zalewska.

Nightmare Castle (1965) Emmi Ci/Allied Artists: Mario Caiano (credited as Alan Grunewald). Barbara Steele, Paul Muller, Helga Line.

Piranha (1978) New World: Joe Dante. Bradford Dillman, Heather Menzies, Barbara Steele.

The Pit and the Pendulum (1961) AIP: Roger Corman. Vincent Price, Barbara Steele, John Kerr.

Revenge of the Blood Beast aka **She-Beast** aka **Sister of Satan** (1966) Europix-Consolidated: Michael Reeves. Barbara Steele, Ian Ogilvy, John Karlsen.

Silent Scream (1980) American Cinema: Denny Harris. Rebecca Balding, Cameron Mitchell, Barbara Steele.

Terror Creatures from the Grave (1965) MBS Cinemat & G.I.A./International Entertainment Corp: Massimo Pupillo. Barbara Steele, Riccardo Garrone, Walter Brandi.

They Came from Within aka **Shivers** aka **The Parasite Murders** (1976) Trans-America: David Cronenberg. Paul Hampton, Joe Silver, Barbara Steele.

Chapter VIII

The Birds (1963) Universal: Alfred Hitchcock. Rod Taylor, Tippi Hedren, Jessica Tandy.

Frenzy (1972) Universal: Alfred Hitchcock. Jon Finch, Barry Foster, Alec McCowen.

Psycho (1960) Paramount: Alfred Hitchcock. Anthony Perkins, Janet Leigh, Vera Miles.

Psycho II (1983) Universal: Richard Franklin. Anthony Perkins, Vera Miles, Meg Tilly.

Rear Window (1954) Paramount: Alfred Hitchcock. James Stewart, Grace Kelly, Raymond Burr.

Rebecca (1940) Selznick: Alfred Hitchcock. Joan Fontaine, Laurence Olivier, Judith Anderson.

Shadow of a Doubt (1943) Universal: Alfred Hitchcock. Joseph Cotten, Teresa Wright, Macdonald Carey.

Vertigo (1958) Paramount: Alfred Hitchcock. James Stewart, Kim Novak, Barbara Bel Geddes.

Chapter IX

Attack of the Crab Monsters (1957) Allied Artists: Roger Corman. Richard Garland, Pamela Duncan, Russell Johnson.

A Bucket of Blood (1959) AIP: Roger Corman. Dick Miller, Barboura Morris, Anthony Carbone.

House of Usher (1960) AIP: Roger Corman. Vincent Price, Mark Damon, Myrna Fahey.

It Conquered the World (1956) AIP: Roger Corman. Peter Graves, Beverly Garland, Lee Van Cleef.

The Last Woman on Earth (1960) Filmgroup: Roger Corman. Betsy Jones-Moreland, Anthony Carbone, Edward Wain (Robert Towne).

The Little Shop of Horrors (1960) Filmgroup: Roger Corman. Jonathan Haze, Jackie Joseph, Mel Welles.

Masque of the Red Death (1964) AIP: Roger Corman. Vincent Price, Hazel Court, Jane Asher.

Not of This Earth (1957) Allied Artists: Roger Corman. Paul Birch, Beverly Garland, Morgan Jones.

The Pit and the Pendulum (1961) AIP: Roger Corman. Vincent Price, Barbara Steele, John Kerr.

The Premature Burial (1962) AIP: Roger Corman. Ray Milland, Hazel Court, Richard Ney.

Tales of Terror (1962) AIP: Roger Corman. Vincent Price, Peter Lorre, Basil Rathbone.

Tomb of Ligeia (1965) AIP: Roger Corman. Vincent Price, Elizabeth Shepherd, John Westbrook.

The Undead (1957) AIP: Roger Corman. Pamela Duncan, Richard Garland, Allison Hayes.

The Viking Women and the Sea Serpent aka **The Saga of the Viking Women and Their Voyage to the Waters of the Great Sea Serpent** (1957) AIP: Roger Corman. Abby Dalton, Susan Cabot, Betsy Jones-Moreland.

Wasp Woman (1959) Allied Artists: Roger Corman. Susan Cabot, Fred (Anthony Eisley), Barboura Morris.

X — The Man with the X-Ray Eyes (1963) AIP: Roger Corman. Ray Milland, Diana Van Der Vlis, John Hoyt.

Chapter X

The Bride and the Beast aka Queen of the Gorillas (1958) Allied Artists: Adrian Weiss. Charlotte Austin, Lance Fuller, Johnny Roth.

Bride of the Monster aka Bride of the Atom aka Monster of the Marshes (1956) Banner-DCA: Edward D. Wood, Jr. Bela Lugosi, Tor Johnson, Tony McCoy.

Glen or Glenda? aka The Transvestite aka I Changed My Sex aka I Led Two Lives aka He or She? aka Glen or Glenda, Which Is It? (1953) Screen Classic Production/Weiss: Edward D. Wood, Jr. Bela Lugosi, Daniel Davis (Edward D. Wood, Jr.), Dolores Fuller.

Necromania (1972) Swedish Erotica/Noel Bloom: Edward D. Wood, Jr. With Edward D. Wood, Jr.

Night of the Ghouls aka Revenge of the Dead (1959) Edward D. Wood Productions & Atomic Productions: Edward D. Wood, Jr. Criswell (Jeron Charles Criswell King), Kenne Duncan, Tor Johnson.

Orgy of the Dead aka Orgy of the Vampires (1966) Astra: A.C. Stephen. Criswell (Jeron Charles Criswell King), Pat Barringer, Fawn Silver.

Plan 9 from Outer Space aka Graverobbers from Outer Space (1956) DCA: Edward D. Wood, Jr. Bela Lugosi, Vampira (Maila Nurmi), Tor Johnson.

Chapter XI

Andy Warhol's Frankenstein (1974) Bryanston: Paul Morrissey. Udo Kier, Joe Dallesandro, Monique Van Vooren.

Blood Feast (1963) Box Office Spectaculars: Herschell Gordon Lewis. Connie Mason, Thomas Wood, Mal Arnold.

The Bloodthirsty Butchers (1970) Mishkin & Constitution: Andy Milligan. John Miranda, Annabella Wood, Berwick Kaler.

The Body Beneath (1971) Nova International: Andy Milligan. Gavin Reed, Jackie Skarrellis, Richmond Ross.

Color Me Blood Red (1965) Box Office Spectaculars: Herschell Gordon Lewis. Don Joseph, Candi Conder, Scott H. Hall.

Creepshow (1982) WB: George Romero. Hal Holbrook, E.G. Marshall, Adrienne Barbeau.

Dawn of the Dead (1979) United Film Distribution: George Romero. David Emge, Ken Foree, Gaylen Ross.

Deranged (1974) AIP: Jeff Gillen. Roberts Blossom, Cosette Lee, Robert Warner.

Don't Answer the Phone (1981) Crown International: Robert Hammer. James Westmoreland, Flo Gerrish, Ben Frank.

Don't Go in the House (1981) Film Ventures International: Joseph Ellison. Dan Grimaldi, Robert Osth, Ruth Dardick.

Don't Go in the Woods Alone (1982) Seymour Borde: James Bryan. Nick McClelland, James P. Hayden, Mary Gail Artz.

Don't Look in the Basement (1974) Hallmark: S.F. Brownrigg. Rosie Holotik, Ann McAdams, William Bill McGhee.

Don't Open the Window (1976) Newport: Jorge Grau. Ray Lovelock, Christina Galbo, Arthur Kennedy.

Eaten Alive (1975) Virgo International: Tobe Hooper. Neville Brand, Mel Ferrer, Carolyn Jones.

The Flesh Eaters (1964) Cinema: Jack Curtis. Martin Kosleck, Rita Morley, Byron Sanders.

Friday the 13th (1980) Paramount: Sean Cunningham. Betsy Palmer, Adrienne King, Harry Crosby.

Friday the 13th Part II (1981) Paramount: Steve Miner. Amy Steele, John Furey, Adrienne King.

Friday the 13th 3-D (1982) Paramount: Steve Miner. Dana Kimmell, Paul Kratka, Tracie Savage.

The Funhouse (1981) Universal: Tobe Hooper. Elizabeth Berridge, Shawn Carson, Jeanne Austin.

The Gore-Gore Girls (1972) Lewis Motion Picture Enterprises: Herschell Gordon Lewis. Frank Kress, Amy Farrell, Hedda Lubin.

The Gruesome Twosome (1967) Mayflower: Herschell Gordon Lewis. Elizabeth Davis, Chris Martel, Gretchen Welles.

Halloween (1978) Compass International: John Carpenter. Jamie Lee Curtis, P.J. Soles, Donald Pleasence.

Halloween II (1981) Universal: Rick Rosenthal. Jamie Lee Curtis, Donald Pleasence, Charles Cyphers.

The Hills Have Eyes (1977) Vanguard: Wes Craven. Dee Wallace, Susan Lanier, Robert Houston.

I Spit on Your Grave (1979) Cinemagic: Meir Zarchi. Camille Keaton, Eron Tabor, Richard Pace.

Last House on the Left (1972) Hallmark: Wes Craven. David Hess, Lucy Grantham, Sandra Cassel.

Maniac (1980) Films Around the World: William Lustig. Joe Spinell, Caroline Munro, Gail Lawrence.

Martin (1979) Libra: George Romero. John Amplas, Lincoln Maazel, Christine Forrest.

Motel Hell (1980) UA: Kevin Connor. Rory Calhoun, Paul Linke, Nancy Parsons.

Mother's Day (1980) UFD: Charles Kaufman.. Nancy Hendrickson, Deborah Luce, Tiana Pierce.

My Bloody Valentine (1981) Paramount: George Mihalka. Paul Kelman, Lori Hallier, Neil Affleck.

New Year's Evil (1981) Cannon: Emmett Alston. Roz Kelly, Kip Niven, Chris Wallace.

Night of the Living Dead (1968) Walter Reade-Continental: George Romero. Duane Jones, Judith O'Dea, Russell Streiner.

Prom Night (1980) Avco Embassy: Paul Lynch. Leslie Nielsen, Jamie Lee Curtis, Casey Stevens.

She-Devils on Wheels (1968) Mayflower: Herschell Gordon Lewis. Betty Connell, Pat Poston, Nancy Lee Noble.

Snuff (1976) Monarch Releasing Corp.: Alan Shackleton (U.S. distributor).

Something Weird (1968) Mayflower: Herschell Gordon Lewis. Tony McCabe, Elizabeth Lee, William Brooker.

A Taste of Blood (1967) Creative Film Enterprises: Herschell Gordon Lewis. Bill Rogers, Elizabeth Wilkinson, Thomas Wood.

Terror Train (1980) 20th Century–Fox: Roger Spottiswoode. Ben Johnson, Jamie Lee Curtis, Hart Bochner.

The Texas Chain Saw Massacre (1974) Bryanston: Tobe Hooper. Marilyn Burns, Gunnar Hansen, Allen Danziger.

Tourist Trap (1979) Compass International: David Schmoeller. Chuck Connors, Jon Van Ness, Tanya Roberts.

2000 Maniacs aka **Two Thousand Maniacs** (1964) Friedman-Lewis Productions: Herschell Gordon Lewis. Connie Mason, Thomas Wood, Jeffrey Allen.

The Wizard of Gore (1971) Mayflower: Herschell Gordon Lewis. Ray Sager, Judy Cler, Wayne Ratay.

Chapter XII

Blow Out (1981) Filmways: Brian DePalma. John Travolta, Nancy Allen, John Lithgow.

Body Double (1984) Columbia: Brian DePalma. Craig Wasson, Melanie Griffith, Gregg Henry.

The Brood (1979) New World: David Cronenberg. Oliver Reed, Samantha Eggar, Art Hindle.

Café Flesh (1982) Mike Missile/Landmark: Rinse Dream. Pia Snow, Kevin Jaye, Ken Starbuck.

Carrie (1976) UA: Brian DePalma. Sissy Spacek, Piper Laurie, Amy Irving.

Crimes of the Future (1970) Emergent Films: David Cronenberg. Ronald Mlodzik, Jon Lidolt, Tania Zolty.

Desperate Living (1977) New Line: John Waters. Liz Renay, Mink Stole, Susan Lowe.

Dressed to Kill (1980) Filmways: Brian DePalma. Michael Caine, Angie Dickinson, Nancy Allen.

Eating Raoul (1982) 20th Century–Fox International Classics/Quartet Films: Paul Bartel. Paul Bartel, Mary Woronov, Robert Beltran.

Eraserhead (1977) Libra Films: David Lynch. John Nance, Charlotte Stewart, Jeanne Bates.

Female Trouble (1974) New Line: John Waters. Divine, David Lochary, Mary Vivian Pearce.

From the Drain (1967) Student film; director: David Cronenberg.

The Fury (1978) 20th Century–Fox: Brian DePalma. Kirk Douglas, John Cassavetes, Carrie Snodgress.

Multiple Maniacs (1970) New Line: John Waters. Divine, David Lochary, Mary Vivian Pearce.

Obsession (1976) Columbia: Brian DePalma. Cliff Robertson, Genevieve Bujold, John Lithgow.

Phantom of the Paradise (1974) 20th Century–Fox: Brian DePalma. Paul Williams, William Finley, Jessica Harper.

Pink Flamingos (1972) New Line: John Waters. Divine, Mink Stole, John Lochary.

Polyester (1981) New Line: John Waters. Divine, Tab Hunter, Edith Massey.

Private Parts (1972) MGM: Paul Bartel. Ayn Ruymen, Lucille Benson, John Ventantonio.

Rabid (1977) New World: David Cronenberg. Marilyn Chambers, Frank Moore, Joe Silver.

Scanners (1981) Avco Embassy: David Cronenberg. Stephen Lack, Patrick McGoohan, Jennifer O'Neill.

Sisters (1973) AIP: Brian DePalma. Margot Kidder, Jennifer Salt, Charles Durning.

Stereo (1969) Emergent Films: David Cronenberg. Ronald Mlodzik, Iain Ewing, Jack Messinger.

They Came from Within aka Shivers aka The Parasite Murders (1976) Trans-America: David Cronenberg. Paul Hampton, Joe Silver, Barbara Steele.

Vampire Hookers (1978) Capricorn Three: Cirio Santiago. John Carradine, Bruce Fairbairn, Trey Wilson.

Videodrome (1983) Universal: David Cronenberg. James Woods, Deborah Harry, Sonja Smits.

Bibliography

Books

Anobile, Richard. *The Film Classics Library: Dr. Jekyll and Mr. Hyde*. New York: Universe Books, 1975.
_____. *The Film Classics Library: Frankenstein*. New York: Universe Books, 1974.
_____. *The Film Classics Library: Psycho*. New York: Universe Books, 1974.
Baxter, John. *Science Fiction in the Cinema*. New York: Paperback Library, 1970.
Beck, Calvin Thomas. *Heroes of the Horrors*. New York: Collier, 1975.
_____. *Scream Queens*. New York: Collier, 1978.
Bogdanovich, Peter. *The Cinema of Alfred Hitchcock* (monograph). New York: Museum of Modern Art Library, 1963.
Bojarski, Richard. *The Films of Bela Lugosi*. Secaucus, N.J.: Citadel, 1980.
Bucher, Felix. *Screen Series: Germany*. London: Zwemmer/Barnes, 1970.
Butler, Ivan. *Horror in the Cinema*. New York: Paperback Library, 1971.
Castle, William. *Step Right Up! I'm Gonna Scare the Pants Off America*. New York: Putnam, 1976.
Clarens, Carlos. *An Illustrated History of the Horror Film*. New York: Putnam, 1967.
Cocteau. New York: Grossman, 1972.
Cremer, Robert. *Lugosi: The Man Behind the Cape*. Chicago: Regnery, 1976.
Derry, Charles. *Dark Dreams*. Cranbury, N.J.: A.S. Barnes, 1977.
di Franco, Philip. *The Movie World of Roger Corman*. New York: Chelsea House, 1979.
Douglas, Drake. *Horror!*. New York: Macmillan, 1966.
Everson, William K. *Classics of the Horror Film*. Secaucus, N.J.: Citadel, 1974.
Eyles, Allen, Robert Adkinson, and Nicholas Fry. *The House of Horror*. New York: The Third Press, 1973.
Gifford, Denis. *A Pictorial History of Horror Movies*. London: Hamlyn, 1973.
Haining, Peter, ed. *The Dracula Scrapbook*. New York: Bramhall House, 1976.
Halliwell, Leslie. *Halliwell's Filmgoer's Companion, 7th ed*. New York: Scribners, 1980.
_____. *Halliwell's Film Guide*. New York: Scribners, 1979.
Hardy, Phil, ed. *Science Fiction*. New York: Morrow, 1984.
Hogan, David J. *Who's Who of the Horrors and Other Fantasy Films*. San Diego: A.S. Barnes, 1980.
Hull, David Stewart. *Film in the Third Reich*. New York: Touchstone, 1973.
Keyes, Evelyn. *Scarlett O'Hara's Younger Sister*. Secaucus, N.J.: Lyle Stuart, 1977.
Kleno, Larry. *Kim Novak on Camera*. San Diego: A.S. Barnes, 1980.
Lee, Walt. *Reference Guide to Fantastic Films, Vol. 1–3*. Los Angeles: Chelsea-Lee Books, 1972–74.
Lennig, Arthur. *The Count*. New York: Putnam, 1974.
Lentz, Harris M. *Science Fiction, Horror & Fantasy Film and Television Credits*. Jefferson, N.C.: McFarland, 1983.

McCarthy, Todd, and Charles Flynn, eds. *Kings of the Bs*. New York: Dutton, 1975.
McCarty, John. *Splatter Movies*. Albany, N.Y.: FantaCo Enterprises, 1981.
McGee, Mark Thomas. *Fast and Furious: The Story of American International Pictures*. Jefferson, N.C.: McFarland, 1984.
Maltin, Leonard. *TV Movies, 1983–84 ed*. New York: Signet, 1982.
Mank, Gregory William. *It's Alive!*. San Diego: A.S. Barnes, 1981.
Manvell, Roger, ed.*Masterworks of the German Cinema*. New York: Harper & Row, 1973.
Meyers, Richard. *For One Week Only*. Piscataway, N.J.: New Century, 1983.
_____. *The World of Fantasy Films*. Cranbury, N.J.: A.S. Barnes, 1980.
Naha, Ed. *The Films of Roger Corman*. New York: Arco, 1982.
Nicholls, Peter, ed. *The Science Fiction Encyclopedia*. Garden City, N.Y.: Dolphin Books, 1979.
Parish, James Robert, and Michael R. Pitts. *The Great Science Fiction Pictures*. Metuchen, N.J.: Scarecrow Press, 1977.
Pattison, Barrie. *The Seal of Dracula*. New York: Bounty Books, 1975.
Peary, Danny, ed. *Close-Ups*. New York: Workman Publishing, 1978.
_____. *Cult Movies*. New York: Delta, 1981.
Pirie, David. *A Heritage of Horror*. New York: Avon, 1973.
_____. *The Vampire Cinema*. New York: Crescent Books, 1977.
Pitts, Michael R. *Horror Film Stars*. Jefferson, N.C.: McFarland, 1981.
Silver, Alain, and James Ursini. *The Vampire Film*. Cranbury, N.J.: A.S. Barnes, 1975.
Simon, Randy, and Harold Benjamin. *Edward D. Wood, Jr.: A Man and His Films*. Los Angeles: The Edward D. Wood, Jr. Film Appreciation Society, 1981.
Spiering, Frank. *Prince Jack*. New York: Jove Books, 1978.
Stanley, John. *Creature Features Movie Guide*. Pacifica, Ca.: Creatures at Large, 1981.
Steinbrunner, Chris, and Burt Goldblatt. *Cinema of the Fantastic*. New York: Galahad, 1972.
Taylor, John Russell. *Hitch*. New York: Pantheon, 1978.
Truffaut, François. *Hitchcock*. New York: Simon and Schuster, 1966.
Truitt, Evelyn Mack. *Who Was Who on Screen, 2nd ed*. New York: Bowker, 1977.
Turan, Kenneth, and Stephen F. Zito. *Sinema*. New York: Praeger, 1974.
Turner, George E., and Michael H. Price. *Forgotten Horrors*. Cranbury, N.J.: A.S. Barnes, 1979.
TV Feature Film Source Book, Vol. 19. New York: Broadcast Information Bureau, 1978.
Warren, Bill. *Keep Watching the Skies! American Science Fiction Movies of the Fifties*. Vol. 1, 1950–1957(1982), vol. 2, 1958–1962(1986). Jefferson, N.C.: McFarland.
Waters, John. *Shock Value*. New York: Dell, 1981.
Weldon, Michael. *The Psychotronic Encyclopedia of Film*. New York: Ballantine, 1983.
Wood, Edward D., Jr. *Orgy of the Dead*. San Diego: Greenleaf Classics, 1966.
Wood, Robin. *Hitchcock's Films*. New York: Paperback Library, 1970.

Periodical Articles

Ackerman, Forrest J. *Famous Monsters of Filmland, #3, April 1959*. "Monsters of Tomorrow."
Bartholomew, David. *Cinefantastique*, Vol. 4, #2, 1975. "Brian DePalma Interview."
Bartholomew, David. _____, Vol. 6, #3, 1977. "The Wicker Man."
Borst, Ronald V. *Photon*, #27, 1977. "Horror of Dracula."

Chase, Donald. *Los Angeles Times* (Calendar), March 14, 1982. "The New Star Producers."

Goodwin, Michael. *Penthouse*, February 1981. "Bad and Beautiful."

Sammon, Paul M. *Cinefantastique*, Vol. 10, #4, Spring 1981. "David Cronenberg."

Schreiner, David, *Weird Trips*, #2, 1978. "Ed Gein and the Left Hand of God."

Vale, V. and Andrea Juno, eds. *RE: Search* #10, 1986. "Incredibly Strange Films."

Vertlieb, Steve. *Cinemacabre*, #5, Fall 1982. "Dressed to Thrill: The Illusory Frenzy of Brian DePalma."

Winogura, Dale. *Cinefantastique*, Vol. 3, #4, 1974. "William Friedkin Interview."

Index

Numbers in **boldface** indicate photographs.

Rilla, Wolf 23–24
Ritter, Thelma 195
Riviere, Georges 171
RKO Radio Pictures 60, 98
Roach, Hal 122, 233
Roberts, Judith Anna 288
Robertson, Cliff 265, 268, 274
Robins, Oliver 26
Robinson, Ann 110
Robot Monster 26, 110, 294
Rock All Night 205
"Rock Around the Clock" 122
Rock 'n' Roll High School 285
Rocketship X-M 72, 298
The Rocky Horror Picture Show 8, 9, 294
Roeg, Nicolas 28, 29, 206, 216, 284
Roerick, William 208, 209
Roffman, Julian **61**
Roland, Jeanne 103
Rollin, Jean 157–59
Romero, George 178, 242, 243, 244, 245, 259, 261, 287
Room to Let 40, 296
Rooney, Mickey 122
Rope 193
Rosemary's Baby 19, 22, **79**–80, 294, 298
Rosemary's Baby (novel) 79
Rosenthal, Rick 252, 253
Ross, Gaylen 244
Ross, Katharine 80
Rothman, Stephanie 161
Rowland, Roy 26
Rubin, Benny 62
Rusoff, Lou 70, 207
Russell, Ray 215, 219
Russo, John 243
Ryshpan, Howard 277

S

Sabotage 190
Saboteur 190
Sager, Ray 240
Saint James, Susan 163
St. John, Jill 120
Salem's Lot 138, **162**, 249, 304
Salmanova, Lydia 2
Salt, Jennifer 262, 264
Sanders, George 23
Sangster, Jimmy 103, 156, 157

Sansom, John 149
Sapphire 165
Sarandon, Susan 10
Sargent, Joseph 12
Sasdy, Peter 22, 150, 153, 154, 155
The Satanic Rites of Dracula 152, 304
Savage Girl 96, 301
Savini, Tom 244, 245, 257
Sayles, John 44, 178
Scanners 279–81, 309
Scarface (1983) 273
Scars of Dracula 150, 304
Schaffner, Franklin 12
Scheer, Philip 125
Schickel, Richard 204
Schlock! 100, 301
Schoedsack, Ernest 98
Schrader, Paul 28, 54, 266
Schreck, Max 138
Schröder, Greta 2
Schüfftan, Eugen 66
Scob, Edith 66
Scorsese, Martin 52, 54, 205
Scott, George C. 69
Scott, Ridley 12, 117
Scott-Taylor, Jonathan 21
"Scream Your Bloody Head Off" 234
Scrimm, Angus 26
Sears, Heather **106**
The Secret Life of Dorian Gray 42, 296
Sellers, Peter 69
Seltzer, David 26
Seven Footprints to Satan 95, 301
Seven Footprints to Satan (novel) 95
The Seven Year Itch 74
Sewell, Vernon 177
Sex Kittens Go to College 130
Seyrig, Delphine 152–53
Shackleton, Allan 246
Shadow of a Doubt 191, **192**, 193, 306
Shaffer, Anthony 84, 203
Shakespeare, William 73
Shaner, John 222
Sharman, Jim 8
Sharp, Don 149
Shayne, Robert 12
She-Beast 176
The She-Creature 63, 298
She-Devils on Wheels 241, 308
Shear, Barry 133
Shearer, Moira 14
Shelley, Barbara 23, **25**, 148, 149

Urquhart, Robert 7
USC Film School 250

V

Vadim, Annette 155, **156**
Vadim, Roger 155
Vail, Myrtle 222
Vampira 229, 230, **232**, 233, 234
The Vampire 145, 305
Vampire Hookers 261, 309
The Vampire Lovers 155–56, 305
La Vampire Nue 159, 305
Vampire Playgirls 163, 305
"The Vampyre" (by Byron) 139
"The Vampyre" (by Polidori) 139
Vampyres 159, 305
Van Cleef, Lee 207, 208
Van Der Vlis, Diana **219**
Van Doren, Mamie 122, 130
Vanity 100
Van Ost, Valerie 152
Van Sloan, Edward 1, 2, 140
Vaughn, Robert 118
Veidt, Conrad 91, **94**, 140
The Velvet Vampire 161, 305
Ventham, Wanda 159
Vertigo 195, **196**, 197–98, 265, 266,
  273, 306
VeSota, Bruno 73, 210
Vickers, Yvette 65, 73, 110
Victor, Albert 39
Victor, Henry 58
Victor, Katharine 128
Victoria (Queen) 39
Videodrome 281, **282**, 283–84, 309
Vierges et Vampires 159, 305
"The Vij" 166
The Viking Women and the Sea Serpent 206, 306
Village of the Damned 23–24, **25**,
  116, 294
Le Viol du Vampire 158, 305
Vittes, Louis 116
Vogue (magazine) 131
Von Harbou, Thea 18
Von Stroheim, Erich 49
Von Sydow, Max 19
Voodoo Woman 63, 299

W

Wages of Sin 99, 226
Waggner, George 43, 44
Walker, Robert 193, 203
Wallachia (Rumania) 139
Walter, Jessica 38
Wanzer, Orville 160
The War Game 70, 199, 299
War of the Worlds 95, 110, 302
Ware, Irene 49
Warhol, Andy 160, 286
Warner, David 21, **41**
Warner Bros. 85, 122, 262
The Warriors 136
Wasp Woman 209, **210**, 211, 306
Wasson, Craig 273, 274
Waters, John 262, 286, 287, 288
Watkins, Peter 133
Waxman, Harry 84
Weaver, Fritz 117
Weaver, Sigourney 117
Wedekind, Frank 39
Wegener, Paul 2, **3**
Weird Fantasy (comic book) 109
Weird Science (comic book) 109
Weiss, George 226, 227
Weld, Tuesday **132**, 133, 135
Welles, Mel 222
Welles, Merri 223
Wells, H.G. 10, 120
Wells, Jacqueline 57
Werewolf of London 43, 296
*Werewolf vs. the Vampire
  Woman* 157
West, Nathanael 223
Westmore, Wally 32
Whale, James 1, 5, 261
Wham Bam, Thank You Spaceman
  118, 302
Whatever Happened to Baby Jane? 27,
  36, 294
The Whispering Ghost 140
White, Jules 62
White, Robb 75
White Pongo 98, 302
White Slaves of Chinatown 226
White Zombie 57, 299
Whitelaw, Billie 21
Whitlock, Albert 201
Whitmore, James 26
Who Slew Auntie Roo? 27, 294